Not For Sale

Finding Center in the Land of Crazy Horse

Written and Photographed by Kevin Hancock

THE IAN BOOK OF THE YEAR AWARDS

The Independent
AUTHOR NETWORK

**OUTSTANDING
NON-FICTION**

THE IAN BOOK OF THE YEAR AWARDS

"I finished your book at 3:30 this morning because I could not put it down. I was sorry there were no more pages to turn."

"Kevin, I just finished your book and need to tell you how much I was moved by it (and often to tears), on so many levels."

"Kevin, thank you for writing this book. Your story touched me, heart and soul."

"As I was reading, there were many times I actually had to put the book down to reflect on some of my own memories that were revived by your words."

"I laughed, I cried, and I was inspired by your passion."

"This book is personal and authentic, and written with great style."

"You are an amazing writer, speaking with your heart and spirit through your written words."

"It took me just one week to read your book. The words literally leaped off the pages at me."

"I am savoring your book, enjoying every word. I do not want it to end."

"I feel that I am more aware of my own inner self through your descriptive writing."

"We all need to be reminded of the truth of what actually happened, and continues to happen, to these Indian tribes, and then support any effort, small or large, to get beyond and correct the many lies of what has been written and taught to generations over so many years. Hopefully this book is a beginning of such an effort."

"I simply loved this book from start to finish."

Not For Sale: Finding Center in the Land of Crazy Horse by Kevin
Hancock was honored as the 2016 Annual National Indie
Excellence® Award winner in the category of Leadership.

Library of Congress Cataloging-in-Publication Data

Original printing: © 2015
Second printing: © 2016
Third printing: © 2017
ISBN 978-0-692-41099-8

Published by:
Seventh Power Press
4 Edes Falls Road
Casco, Maine 04015

AN INDIAN PRAYER

O GREAT SPIRIT, whose voice I hear in the winds, and whose breath gives life to all the world, hear me! I am small and weak; I need your strength and wisdom.

LET ME WALK IN BEAUTY, and make my eyes ever behold the red and purple sunset.

MAKE MY HANDS respect the things you have made and my ears sharp to hear your voice.

MAKE ME WISE so that I may understand the things you have taught my people.

LET ME LEARN the lessons you have hidden in every leaf and rock.

I SEEK STRENGTH, not to be greater than my brother, but to fight my greatest enemy–myself.

MAKE ME ALWAYS READY to come to you with clean hands and straight eyes.

SO WHEN LIFE FADES, as the fading sunset, my spirit may come to you without shame.

Special thanks to my best and most trusted friend, Alison. At every turn she insisted that I keep going back to Pine Ridge and that I keep writing. I would not have written this book, nor taken this full journey, without her encouragement, love, and understanding. I am blessed to be her husband.

Wopila Tanka!

Table of Contents

Acknowledgments

***INAJI!* (Halt)** First and foremost in my heart there is my family. My wife, Alison, and our daughters, Abby and Sydney, are the three most important people in my life. Each of them is a source of inspiration and joy for me. Their enthusiasm for this book and my personal journey to the Land of Crazy Horse is the essential ingredient that allowed the circle to become complete. My mom is also a vital factor in this book. Her spirituality helped release my own.

In the years leading up to this book, Deborah Dooley became a teacher, mentor, and friend who expanded my thinking and enabled my transformation from living with my head to living with my heart—from looking outward to looking inward. She also played an important role during the book-writing process itself. She always seemed to understand where I was going.

Ted Carter provided a local source of spiritual encouragement, while Dave Treadwell offered early editing support for what he felt this book could become.

All my friends and coworkers at Hancock Lumber are contributors to this book because they are so good at what they do. I am blessed to work at a company where everyone leads. Their interest in my travels to Pine Ridge helped reinforce my intuition to keep going back. Specifically, Erin Plummer and Kourtney McLean were instrumental with their editing feedback, graphic design work, and overall passion for this project. They saw it from the beginning as a natural extension of our shared business values and organizational mission.

Thank you to Dr. Phillip Song, Connie Pike, and Deborah Pelletier for helping me learn to embrace spasmodic dysphonia and to find my true voice.

Special thanks to my senior editor and friend, Deanne Stillman, whose skills and coaching helped transform a series of unpredictable adventures into a story that flowed. I learned a lot about writing from my time with Deanne, author of *Mustang: The Saga of the Wild Horse in the American West*, and other books. Thanks also goes to Melissa Hayes, who provided the technical edit which rounded this project into its completed form.

Finally, of course, there are my friends at Pine Ridge. Rosie Frier at the Singing Horse Trading Post gave me a place to call home and constantly supported me. Lester Lone Hill made the building of the Hancock House possible, and later made me his brother in a sweat lodge ceremony. Nick Tilsen showed me the good red road forward for the Oglala Sioux Tribe. Cecy Faster provided a peer relationship from away and a model for service at Pine Ridge. Bamm Brewer was the first to welcome me into his home, taught me about the buffalo ways, and showed me the Lakota spirit of self-reliance. Verola Spider shared her stories and taught me the "old ways," while Catherine Grey Day became a close friend and a dependable source of laughs and insight. Danny gave me the hug I will never forget and the bow I will always cherish. Finally, there is Pinky. Just typing her name makes me pause with appreciation. She was the one who answered my call, introduced me to Pine Ridge, and stood by me every step of the way. She is an amazing lady and close friend. There is no book without Pinky.

To all my friends who made this journey possible, I simply offer,

***Wopila Tanka!* (Big Thanks)**

Foreword by US Senator Angus King

If you had told me a couple of years ago that my friend, Kevin Hancock, would set off on a quest for enlightenment, sparked by a long-distance astrological reading which would lead him to a sweat lodge in a remote Indian reservation—well, let's just say that *skeptical* doesn't come close to covering it.

Kevin was (and is) what we used to call a "straight arrow." (Does anyone use that term anymore? Come to think of it, is there even such a thing anymore?) Small-town Republican, successful businessman, high school basketball coach, family man, conservative (in the best sense), civic-minded—this guy is not someone you would predict would undertake anything like the voyage of inner discovery chronicled in this extraordinary book.

But, he did.

I knew and worked with Kevin during a particularly tough period in his life, which preceded and largely foreshadowed the journey the book describes. If there was any business harder hit by the great recession of 2008 than residential construction, I don't know what it is. In fact, 2008—2012 wasn't a recession for that industry; it was a full-blown depression. Building permits for new homes in southern Maine fell by 66 percent in three years, and Hancock Lumber's sales fell right along with them. What made this especially hard for Kevin was the weight of history: Hancock Lumber is one of the oldest family-owned companies in the country (founded in 1848), and Kevin's dad had been one of the most successful and respected businessmen in Maine before his untimely death at the age of fifty-four. In those dark days, Kevin faced the very real prospect of losing it all and being the first Hancock in six generations to fail.

He didn't fail, however; through sheer hard work, a great team, some good decisions, a little luck, and his infectious optimism, the company made it through and is now stronger than ever. But, the road back took its toll and Kevin was physically and emotionally exhausted—to the point that he came to question the direction of his life and, not coincidentally, literally lost his voice.

What happened next is the amazing story Kevin tells here: Part history (and not very pleasant history at that), part spiritual journey, part moving portrait of some extraordinary people, and part leadership manual. This fascinating book will touch you and teach you on many levels. Most of us don't have the time (actually, don't *take* the time would be more accurate) to even think about the questions that Kevin raises, which is what makes this book so valuable. Through allowing us to share in his journey, and learn from his encounters, he is giving us a shot of condensed experience that can inform and guide our own path as we wrestle with life's recurring questions and challenges.

Like I said, I wouldn't have predicted that Kevin would write this book—but, I'm sure glad he did.

Angus S. King Jr.
United States Senator

Foreword by Ashoka Fellow and Oglala Sioux Tribe Member, Nick Tilsen

This book is an intriguing look into one man's journey to Indian Country. Kevin's experience has been organic and life-changing for him and the community of people around him. When first meeting Kevin, however, I must confess that my initial thought was, "Nice, here comes another donor."

You see, I run a nonprofit on the Pine Ridge Indian Reservation called the Thunder Valley Community Development Corporation (www.thundervalley.org), an organization that works to build sustainable communities that empower the people and protect the Earth. We are doing everything from sustainable housing and job creation to workforce development designed to help the Lakota people lift ourselves out of poverty. Naturally, we are always looking for resources. Yes, it might seem opportunistic that my first thought of a wealthy "white guy" coming to the Rez was resources. But, when you are running a nonprofit social enterprise in the poorest, most isolated community in America, it's an honest and truthful reaction.

The story, friendship, and journey shared in this book are filled with honesty, integrity, and transparency. That first conversation with Kevin intrigued me; I talked openly about the challenges we face and how my people don't need to be saved, but empowered. Kevin, in return, was willing to "take the gloves off" and engage in open dialogue about the history of broken treaties, the colonization of our lands, and ultimately how those things impact the Lakota people today.

In preparing for my meeting with Kevin, I looked on his website and read that he was the sixth-generation owner of Hancock Lumber Company, started in 1848. My first thought was, "Wow, we couldn't be more different. We are definitely not cut from the same cloth." When my ancestors were fighting off white settlers to protect our lands, culture, and way of life, his ancestors were building a lumber company on lands that were stolen from Maine Indians just a few hundred years earlier.

We finally met and shared our stories. I told him about our project and our organization; he shared his interest in learning about Pine Ridge and finding a way to help. The conversation lasted way longer than planned, as we jumped right into systems theory thinking and the root causes of poverty. Most importantly, after just one conversation, I realized that he really wanted to help, and that he understood what we were doing was a pathway to changing the Rez forever. I remember when Kevin left Thunder Valley that day I thought to myself that he is a good-hearted person who cares deeply about what has happened, and continues to happen, to my community and my people.

Every conversation we had from that time forward led to the next. Our personal relationship kept building. Our conversations were ones of learning, understanding, and exploring how we can change this world and make it a better place by coming together, versus staying apart.

What struck me with Kevin and his journey was that, although he comes from power and privilege, that didn't manifest itself in terms of how he communicates or treats people. It was clear that Kevin simply wanted to help because of a deep conviction he felt in his heart. Instead of taking it upon himself to send clothes or food to Indians here on Pine Ridge, he took the time to meet with different leaders, organizations, and people. He drew upon the work, knowledge, passion, and innovation that already existed here. His position was, "How can I be supportive of what you are already doing?" I greatly respected this approach, because there's a long history of charity, government policies, and decisions made by people outside of our reservation that have translated into perpetuating poverty in our communities.

Another important thing I noticed was that Kevin cared deeply about the challenges at Pine Ridge and was less focused on whether we were willing to share our culture. Many times the approach with outsiders is, "Teach me about your culture, your history and your ceremonial life ways, and then I'll see if I can find a way to support you." Why would I be willing to share these things first when our ancestors fought and died so that we would have them today? Kevin never pushed to experience ceremonies or gatherings. Our foundation was built on a brotherhood that transcends local tribes in favor of a collective desire to change the world and make it a better place. I believe that there are lessons in Kevin's journey for many people, including myself.

The bond Kevin and I have grown to share is based on the fact that the solutions rest in people coming together to solve social challenges through a collective and participatory process. We have to explore the true democratization of wealth, energy, food, water, and education. The power of solving these problems needs to get back into the hands of the people most negatively impacted by the status quo, but it does need to be in partnership with people from many different backgrounds, races, and tribes.

What I have learned through my relationship with Kevin is to remain open-minded, look at everybody as equals, and imagine the collective power we can create by coming together. In the beginning, I thought that Kevin and I couldn't be more different. But now, I realize that although our journeys started out differently, we are arriving at the same place. Like the Sacred Hoop of the Lakota medicine wheel, the beginning and the ending live in the same spot. Strength comes from the realization that the differences that once tore us apart might now be the opportunities that bring us together. I think this is something that is beginning to happen around the world.

Mitakuye Oyasin (we are all related),

Nick Tilsen
Oglala Lakota

Pine Ridge is simultaneously beautiful and stark, tragic and triumphant, discouraging and inspirational. All things are one thing here.

Our spirit was broken. Healing is necessary in order to move forward. We could stay where we're at and be bitter for a long time—and we would be in the right for doing so. But what message would we be sending to our children? What future would we be creating for ourselves?

—Nick Tilsen

Sunrise above the bluffs near the Singing Horse Trading Post, north of Manderson on the Pine Ridge Indian Reservation, in present-day South Dakota.

Author's Note

It was scary at times to write a book in which I was a central character.

It was so for two reasons: First, because I was not exposing some fictional creation. I was exposing myself, deliberately, and to the world.

Second, as this is a spiritual book, I was afraid I would give the impression that I consider myself uniquely spiritual, which is not how I feel. I do consider myself spiritual, but in the same way you are—in the same way all human beings innately are. Each soul is important, and we all should be special to ourselves. As Joseph Campbell once said, "We are the truth we seek to know."

In the end, this was a book that I needed to write, and the excitement of telling the story of how I found my voice in the Land of Crazy Horse always overcame the fear. My friend from Pine Ridge, Verola Spider, says, "If we don't share our stories, they die with us."

Bringing awareness to both the beauty and the challenges of the Pine Ridge Indian Reservation is a role I will never regret playing.

Kevin Hancock

Sitting Bull, like many other Indian chiefs of his time, faced a series of impossible choices as America rushed to meet its Manifest Destiny. Overreaching has consequences.

They made us many promises, more than I can remember, but they never kept but one; they promised to take our land, and they took it.

—Sitting Bull

This book is dedicated to the future of everyone with a past, and to all people searching for their own true voice . . .

PREFACE
What Brings You Here?

The burial grounds at Wounded Knee.

**The Old West is not a certain place in a certain time;
it's a state of mind. It's whatever you want it to be.**

—Tom Mix

"What brings you here?" the old woman asked me.

Moments ago I had watched her hustle out the front door of her modest home, climb into her car, and pull down the long dusty driveway. She turned onto the highway just long enough to drive right up beside me. She was rolling down the window before the wheels stopped turning.

"I have been visiting Pinky," was my reply.

"Oh, I know Pinky! She helped me get some insulation for my home last winter," she says.

"My name is Kevin," I say, extending my hand into the car.

We shake hands and smile. Then she quickly turns to business. From the empty passenger seat she grabs a small assortment of jewelry and holds it out toward me.

"I made all of these," she tells me.

She goes on to explain that during the summer she sells her jewelry from the wooden stand strategically located behind the historical marker that I have been reading.

"How much for that one?" I ask.

The necklace I am pointing to is wrapped around rawhide and contains an assortment of white, yellow, black, and red beads. In my short time here, I have already learned that these are the four colors of the Lakota medicine wheel. The medicine wheel itself symbolizes the Six Great Powers (West, North, East, South, Sky, and Earth). In addition, at the center of the wheel, some say a Seventh Power also lives. This is the power of the individual spirit, which is essential to a healthy Lakota society.

Between each string of colored beads is a long brown bead that looks like a seashell. At the bottom of the necklace hangs an eagle's-head pendant. The eagle is dark brown with streaks of white running from its beak to its neck. The eagle is celebrated in Lakota culture because it soars near the heavens.

"Well, I sell these all summer for thirty dollars. But, this is the off-season. Nobody travels through here this time of year. This time of year I sell them for twenty dollars," she explains.

"I really like it. I'll take it!" I reply.

We exchange a few passing thoughts, a twenty-dollar bill, and a necklace.

"Our people are poor in dollars, but rich in culture," is her last remark.

She pulls out of the dirt parking area and heads back up the winding driveway toward her humble home. A swirl of dust is pushed out in all directions behind her. Not another car has passed since the front door of her house first opened. I am alone again with the gray sky and shifting winds at the Wounded Knee Massacre Site, on the Pine Ridge Indian Reservation in the southwest corner of South Dakota. In more ways than one, I am a long way from home.

"Finally, some capitalism," I whisper to myself.

––––––––

What brings you here? I had been pondering that question in a much deeper way than the jewelry maker ever intended. It is the second to last day of October and I am two thousand miles away from home. Tomorrow is Halloween. My wife Alison says I always figure out how to not be home for Halloween. She says I will do practically anything to avoid this holiday. It is true that I struggle with Halloween. As a small boy my parents had to make me go trick-or-treating. Upon reflection, I think I disliked trick-or-treating partially because I didn't like to wear costumes, and also because I wasn't comfortable asking for things to be given to me. In any case, I never did enjoy Halloween, but I would like to think something deeper than that has brought me here. It is a long way to go just to avoid a holiday.

The historical marker at the massacre site at Wounded Knee.

A few paces in front of me stands a red wooden sign describing the events that transpired here. On the cold winter morning of December 29, 1890, the 7th Cavalry opened fire on the 356 remaining members of Chief Big Foot's band of Minneconjou Sioux who were camped here, having surrendered without incident the night before. The tribe

had fled Sitting Bull's camp to the north after he was killed in the panicked government response to the Ghost Dance ceremonies that had
swept across the Sioux reservations. They were trying to reach the Red
Cloud Agency at Pine Ridge where they believed they would be safe.
The group was largely unarmed and consisted mostly of women and
children. As the cavalry searched the site for weapons, a scuffle ensued.
A shot was inadvertently fired, and then hell broke loose. Four hundred
and seventy soldiers under the command of Colonel Forsythe had the
Sioux encampment surrounded. The Lakota men fought bravely, but
were outgunned. The killing was indiscriminate. There were few survivors. A storm came in that night as those still alive were transported to
Pine Ridge. There was no place for them to sleep in town, so the church
was opened and hay was spread across the wooden floorboards. Above
the altar a small sign read, "Peace on earth. Good will toward men."

Back at Wounded Knee, the dead lay frozen in the snow for days before the cavalry returned. The bodies were stacked in wagons and then
deposited in a mass grave on the hillside across the road from the sign
I am now reading.

> **Right near the flag of truce a mother was shot down
> with her infant; the child, not knowing that its mother
> was dead, was still nursing, and that was especially
> a very sad sight . . . Of course it would have been all
> right if only the men were killed; we would feel almost
> grateful for it. But, the fact of the killing of the women
> and more especially the killing of the young boys and
> girls who are to make up the future strength of the In
> dian people is the saddest part of the whole affair, and
> we feel it very sorely.**
>
> **—Oglala Chief American Horse,**
> **testifying to the Commission on Indian Affairs (1891)**

The massacre at Wounded Knee is the symbolic culmination of a chain
of events that began with the arrival of Columbus and the Spanish
conquistadors in 1492. In some ways it is the ending of the story of European conquest of the Americas and our nation's "Manifest Destiny"
to reach from sea to shining sea. It is a story of two worlds colliding and
one way of life dominating. Wounded Knee memorializes a saga that is
simultaneously unique yet timeless; man vs. man . . . tribe against tribe.

Over 120 years later, I have come to see what life is like on this reservation for the descendants of the people who were forcibly settled here so many years ago.

But *why*? What brings me here? No one suggested I come here. No one invited me. Pine Ridge has no direct connections to any of my roles back home. For me, these are fresh tracks.

Then again, the ocean's surf always produces unbroken sand.

––––––––––

This book found me. I did not set out to write it. In late October of 2012, I spent three days on the Pine Ridge Indian Reservation in South Dakota. In doing so, I was stepping far outside the boundaries of my own tribe.

Back home in Maine I was the CEO of a well-known local company. Hancock Lumber Company was established in 1848, and I am the sixth generation of my tribe to help lead it. In a state full of trees, our company is an important industry participant, and I had every right to feel fully occupied by my job.

I first traveled to Pine Ridge ostensibly to learn about the housing needs of the Oglala Sioux Tribe, and to see if Hancock Lumber might be able to help. But, honestly, that was a bit of an excuse. I was interested in the housing issues and I did want to help, but the answer to the question *What brings you here?* was deeper than that.

The truth is, I was worn out.

I had just finished helping our company through a series of challenges spanning nearly fifteen years. The hard work began after my dad died in 1997 at the age of fifty-four. Generational transitions can be complex for a family business, and ours was no exception. At the time I was sure I was ready for what lay ahead; that's how confident thirty-one-year-olds think, I suppose. It took almost a decade to reorganize the management, governance, and ownership of the company, and no sooner had that been done than the economy collapsed. Housing starts peaked in 2005, and by October 2007 they were in free fall. The deconstruction of the housing and mortgage markets was so severe that the entire national banking system was at risk. Every part of the country was affected. Maine was no exception. In 2005 there were 2,345 new single-family homes built in Southern Maine. In 2011 there were 790. The local market our company did business in had shrunk by 66 percent.

Hancock Lumber would overcome these challenges thanks to hard work, some luck, and a great network of committed employees and loyal customers. Today, by almost any measure, the company is very strong. But, the journey had taken its toll and I was tired—emotionally tired. In addition, and perhaps more importantly, I had begun to hear the voice of my own soul that was feeling incomplete. I had a growing sense that my job was not the totality of who I was. Increasingly, I wanted to express myself as a human being more broadly. I found this both confusing and exciting.

> **Every man contains within himself a ghost continent—a place to be circled as warily as Antarctica was 200 years ago by Capt. James Cook. . .he will see strange shapes amidst his interior ice floes and be fearful of exposing to the ridicule of his fellows what he has seen.**
>
> **—Loren Eiseley,** *The Ghost Continent*

The issue, I now realize, was not the external challenges that I had lived through. Many, many people had navigated much worse. On a global scale that transcends time, my experiences in fact were negligible; they were small. The real problem was not the circumstances, but rather my response. Within me lived a powerful impulse to take charge and protect my tribe whenever it came under duress. I felt a strong pull to save everyone, and I took on all the work that went with that instinct. Worse, I internalized this responsibility to the point where it consumed me in ways I could feel but not see. At the time I didn't understand the consequences of my behavior; I just worked. I fought through.

> **You must pay for everything in this world, one way or another. There is nothing free except the grace of God.**
>
> **—Mattie Ross,** *True Grit*

The price I paid for my approach was that I lost myself to both my role and my local circumstances. I had become consumed in protecting others. I had not yet learned that most everyone is capable of protecting themselves. I had not yet learned to share power. I had not yet learned to serve myself.

By modern American business standards one would not have noticed a problem. I was just doing my job, playing my assigned role, as most all of us have been taught to do.

My awareness of what was happening was ignited in the fall of 2008, at the peak of the economic crisis, when my mom innocently handed me two CDs.

"It's a gift," she simply told me.

The discs were a recording of an astrological reading by an evolutionary astrologer from the San Francisco Bay area. A woman who had never met me was reading my "natal chart" off nothing more than the date, time, and place of my birth.

From the moment I pressed "play," I was mesmerized by what I heard.

> *Hello, Kevin. My name is Deborah and your mother has hired me to be an astrological reader for you. That may be something you thought you would never have—an astrological reader.*

"You've got that right," was my instinctive response.

Evolutionary astrologists know that the body is a vessel and the soul is the being. Souls have multiple incarnations over time for the purpose of evolving. Life has the purpose of evolving. But, evolution is not a linear event. There are missteps. We all come into a life with a karmic pattern from our past. We enter each life to move beyond our past mistakes and to experience new growth, or so I was now being told.

As I sat alone and listened to my "gift," I was told that in my past life I had been the leader of a tribe in survival mode. In an effort to save my tribe I became dogmatic. Others did not feel heard by me. Even more damaging, I lost my sense of self in the role of protector. I grew to have no identity beyond my public responsibilities. Ultimately, I was not able to save my tribe (they perished), and that is the wound I carry with me into this lifetime.

Evolutionary astrology would likely be considered tomfoolery to most contemporary business leaders, but for me—well, it struck a deep chord. It made sense.

The biggest benefit of accepting my "gift" was that I began looking inward. The external world had become so demanding—so consuming—that it occupied me fully. Now, for the first time, I was looking inside myself for the source of truth.

I have since come to learn that this subtle shift in orientation can be life-altering. A small idea can be big.

Transformations take time, and I am no exception. In the beginning, the look inward lived on the outer edge of my consciousness. The outer world—the roles and responsibilities—they still were on center stage. But, the winds of change had started to blow and a new path was emerging—a path more focused on self and inner peace.

As the economic glacier continued its march, a new problem emerged. In the spring of 2010, I began to lose my voice. Subtle at first, the problem steadily grew until it became noticeable and painful. After a year of doctors, CAT scans, and other tests, I was finally diagnosed. I had spasmodic dysphonia (SD). A neurological disorder, SD is very rare but quite debilitating with regard to speech. When someone with SD speaks, the muscles around the voice box spasm and contract. For SD patients, speaking can become so difficult that you just avoid it, and this definitely applied to me. In a literal sense, I had lost the consistent and comfortable use of my voice. Talking was still possible, but often extremely challenging. When I would go to speak my voice was, at times, reduced to a barely audible whisper. Even worse, the pain of talking made doing so undesirable. Within a sentence or two I would frequently become so out of breath from forcing the words through my vocal folds that I became dizzy. Leading meetings all day, or even talking on the telephone for prolonged periods of time, was simply no longer possible.

At the time SD frustrated me to no end, but now I am actually thankful

I acquired the disorder. In fact, I now understand why it happened: It was my body's way of telling me I needed to change. Like the "gift" from my mother, it was another sign calling me inward, calling me home.

By 2012 our company was strong again. The economy had improved a bit; but more importantly, I had changed. I began to learn to let go of all the responsibility, to share the power. That year, our youngest daughter, Sydney, was a senior in high school, and our oldest daughter, Abby, a junior in college. I got the idea that I wanted to go do something just for me—a short trip, perhaps, outside my normal boundaries . . . a new experience. That summer my wife Alison and I were at an airport newsstand when I picked up the August edition of *National Geographic*. On the cover, a young Indian was galloping on a brown and white mustang across a grassy ridgeline. Both hands were extended on the reins and his ponytail blew in the wind. The title below read: "In the Spirit of Crazy Horse—Rebirth of a Sioux Nation."

I read the article on the plane with great interest as the past transgressions, modern poverty, and rebirth of Lakota spirituality were all described in both pictures and words.

"I think I want to go there," I said to Alison, leaning toward her as our flight barreled through the sky. "I want to see what life is like there now."

"You should do that," Alison replied, knowing my love of the American West and of history.

As my first job after college, I taught American history. As an adult, I had traveled to the West to hike or hunt many times. I just loved it there—the big spaces, the proximity to nature, the vastness of it all. In recent years, I had found myself reading book after book about the second half of the nineteenth century, when our nation's "Manifest Destiny" ran into the Plains Indians. That subject fascinated me. Over time, my reading got even more focused on the Great Sioux Nation of the northern plains and their experience with Western expansion. I read so much I became a bit of an informal expert.

For most white Americans living in the second half of the nineteenth century, the "winning of the West" symbolized all that was great about our country. The continent was ours to claim, conquer, and utilize. Its bounty seemed endless. For the Native Indian tribes of the American West, however, the story was very different. In the span of a single generation (1840—1880), their land would be taken and their culture demonized. Their nomadic way of life following the buffalo would be replaced with a sedentary existence of sequestration and deprivation. In 1840, the Lakota Sioux controlled a vast territory that stretched from the Missouri River to the Bighorn Mountains. Rolling grasslands, as far as the eye could see, were only broken by the sacred Black Hills of present-day South Dakota. The Lakota were the westernmost branch of the Sioux Nation, and the Oglala were one of the most powerful Lakota tribes. They moved as they pleased with the seasons and the massive herds of buffalo.

In June of 1876, the Lakota and several other tribes won their greatest military victory over the US Army at a battle on the Little Bighorn River. Soon thereafter, however, outnumbered and out of resources, they were forced to surrender. The reservation ("the Rez"), of which there were many, became home for virtually all Lakota peoples. One of the largest reservations, geographically and by population, was Pine Ridge. Land that had been promised to the Lakota forever ("as long as grass shall grow and water flow," Black Elk would later say) through the Treaty of Fort Laramie of 1868 was just taken. The Lakota were settled in a series of out-of-the-way places, scattered across the Dakotas. The federal government managed the reservations, the goal of which was first to segregate and then to "remake" the Indians as whites. The Oglala Sioux of Pine Ridge quickly became dependent upon the federal government for rations and survival. Public displays of their culture and traditions were forbidden. Children were removed from their homes and sent off to unforgiving Indian boarding schools to be converted. It is a chilling story that has, in large part, been forgotten.

Over many generations, we have taught ourselves to believe that Columbus "discovered" a new world; but, people already lived here, and I have come to meet the descendants of some of them.

Most Americans remember learning in school about the Battle of Little Bighorn. We remember it as "Custer's Last Stand." But, what happened after that? Where did the Indians of the northern plains go? What became of them? Where are they today? *Who* are they today?

For most Americans, the story stops at the Little Bighorn River in June of 1876. The Lakota Sioux and the other tribes who fought and won that battle are, from that moment forward, lost to history. It is as if they simply disappeared.

The grave markers at the Little Bighorn Battlefield National Monument stand as a reminder that the past and the present are never far apart.

Now, suddenly here I was, standing in the dirt turnoff at the massacre site at Wounded Knee, a Lakota eagle pendant hanging from my neck. On the surface this story is about the Oglala Sioux Tribe and how I came to know them. Below the surface, however, lives a tale of self-discovery that would connect me with notions and energies that transcend a single lifetime.

Over the course of six subsequent trips to the Pine Ridge Indian Reservation I would learn the following powerful lessons:

- The pull of the past is strong. This is due to the soul's prior journeys and the gravity of our own tribe's local conditions.

- Those who hold the power often overreach. They go too far.

- The path forward lies within. As Joseph Campbell said, "We are the truth we seek to know."

- Truth is personal, and you only find it by transcending "busyness" and "tribalism." You only find your truth by becoming self-aware, by individuating.

- When we serve ourselves we honor our tribe. In this way *selfish* is *selfless*. The Lakota once knew this, as it was the foundation of the "old ways." The vision quest . . . the sweat lodge . . . they were rituals designed to encourage individuals to be true to themselves, to be powerful and strong.

- It's all one tribe. The divisions and boundaries that separate us are artificial, inventions of tribalism, greed, and fear. *Mitakuye Oyasin* in Lakota means "We are all related . . . all things are one thing."

The Lakota were strong many moons ago when the individual was powerful. That personal power was deconstructed by a reservation system overflowing with dehumanizing and bureaucratic controls. But, what is lost can be found, of this the Oglala Holy Man, Black Elk, foretold.

Some who know the Lakota "old ways" say there is a Seventh Power which resides at the center of the Lakota medicine wheel. It symbolizes the strength of the individual spirit that lives within every soul, waiting to be tapped . . . whispering to us all. Despite the clamor of our external surroundings, we are the salvation we seek.

As I planned my first trip to Pine Ridge, however, I saw none of this. What I discovered there unfolded slowly; truth doesn't appear the moment you start seeking.

At Pine Ridge, the spirits are never far away.

Winds in the east, mist coming in. Like somethin' is brewin' and 'bout to begin. Can't put me finger on what lies in store, but I fear what's to happen all happened before.

—Bert, *Mary Poppins*

1
Breaking Rank
My First Trip to the Pine Ridge Indian Reservation
(October 28–31, 2012)

I love this picture. I took it on the first day of my first trip to Pine Ridge. It captures so many elements of the Pine Ridge experience. Nature overshadows the human footprint. The church itself is symbolic of the effort to "remake" the Lakota, yet the church lies abandoned. The church, the road, and the telephone poles are the only signs of human existence. From no vantage point can you see another building because it is a long way to the next one. When I took this picture, I just stopped my car in the road and got out. There was no traffic. Except for the wind, it was perfectly silent.

> **The Great Father sent his soldiers here to spill our blood . . . if the Great Father kept white men out of my country, peace would last forever; but if they disturb me, there will be no peace . . . the Great Spirit raised me in this land, and has raised you in another land. What I have said, I mean. I mean to keep this land.**
>
> —Red Cloud

> **The only good Indian is a dead Indian.**
>
> —General Sheridan, US Cavalry

Today is Sunday. The lone church bell in the old steeple back home in Casco Village has not yet rung. When it does ring, I will not hear it.

I am on a sunrise flight headed for Chicago, and then Rapid City, but my journey did not start this morning; it began a long time ago. It started as a whisper. I think all callings do.

It all began, I believe, with an attraction to the wilderness. I was introduced to the land beyond the roads by my high school science teacher, Eugene Whitney, and a geology field trip to the White Mountains just a short drive from the Lakes Region of Western Maine where I have lived my entire life. From the backyard of the house I grew up in I could see Mount Washington. Over the next few years, Mr. Whitney would take a small group of us hiking and camping several times. This, in turn, led to more hiking in the Presidential Range with a close family friend, Bill Holden. I quickly came to love hiking and camping on the northern portion of the Appalachian Trail.

The following year my family took a vacation to Yellowstone National Park and the Grand Tetons. This was my first visit to the American West, but it would not be my last. I was so captivated by what I experienced there that a few years later I decided to return on my own. It was now the summer after my sophomore year in college. I applied for and secured a summer job working at a hotel in Yellowstone. I did this without any outside influence or suggestions. Why? I don't really know. I just liked it there. It called out to me.

I flew to Bozeman, Montana, and spent the night in a motel room watching the Celtics and the Lakers in the 1986 NBA finals before boarding a company bus for the park the next morning. We traveled through Gardiner, Montana, on our way to Mammoth Hot Springs, which is the first hotel complex as you enter Yellowstone from the north. Upon arrival, we were trained for two days in the art of room cleaning. After successfully demonstrating the necessary skills, I "graduated" and was sent to work on the southern end of the park at a resort called Grant Village on Yellowstone Lake.

It was mid-June and our first assignment was to shovel the snow away from the first-floor windows so that the guests could see out of them when the hotel opened the following day. This is where I would spend the next ten weeks, working as a "room attendant" and hiking the Yellowstone backcountry.

I was so good at cleaning rooms that I was promoted just a few weeks after I started. They just called me into the office one morning and promoted me right there on the spot. They made me a "room inspector." I felt as if I had just been deputized. My parents always found this part of the story hard to believe. They had seen my room at home many times.

For the rest of the summer I was responsible for overseeing the cleaning of two hotel buildings at Grant Village. I now had room attendants that were assigned to me, and my job was to inspect the rooms upon completion and notify the front desk when they were ready to be occupied. We had a really good time, about as good a time as you can have cleaning rooms. As a result of this experience I always position new toilet-paper rolls so that they are pulled down from the front and folded into a point. But, my favorite new skill was how to "throw" a bedspread. I just loved to throw the bedspread, and to this day I can toss one with the best of them! I simply fluff the entire spread across my outstretched arms in a circular motion until it all comes to rest on my forearms. Then I toss it out into the air above the bed and, at just the right moment, snap the bedspread down. A perfect throw requires almost no adjustments and makes me smile with satisfaction. When our daughters Abby and Sydney were little, I used to show off this skill for them.

"Do it again, Daddy! Do it again!" I can still hear them saying this and jumping up and down with big smiles and wide eyes.

Virtually all the jobs in Yellowstone are seasonal, and Grant Village was no exception. We stayed in dorms and ate at the employee cafeteria. It was at Grant Village that I was first introduced to the more radical wing of the environmental movement. We arrived for lunch one day to find an "Earth First" member who had chained himself to the front door of the cafeteria, fully dressed in a bear costume. As the park rangers tried to talk to him he simply kept repeating, "Where will the bears go?" This went on until the rangers found bolt cutters and carted him off. I remember saying to my friends that perhaps he should be a little less worried about where the bears were going and a little more focused on where *he* was going. It's funny what small moments we all remember from a life full of them.

I made some good friends, the closest of whom became my hiking buddies. Cricket and Ed are two members of the gang that I remember. There were five of us in all on most trips. Each week we would look at the trail maps and then go to the ranger's station to register our next hike. Backcountry camping requires permits in Yellowstone National Park, and our hikes were always selected from an area marked "very strong bear warning." We didn't care. We were young. We just wanted to see grizzly bears!

We hiked nearly two hundred miles that summer, deep into the interior of Yellowstone and Grand Teton National Parks. The roads of Yellowstone are crowded in the summer. The backcountry is not. On most trips we would not see another person once we left the highway.

Hitchhiking was an essential part of our routine. None of us had cars, and just getting to trailheads involved traveling long distances. We each had our own handmade cardboard sign. Mine read, "Park Employee from Maine!" The sign worked great, as pretty much anyone from New England would stop and pick us up. That cardboard sign lasted the entire summer. Above the tree line, in the snowfields, we would sit on our signs and sled for what seemed like miles. I wish I still had that sign.

This is the only picture I have left of my summer working at Yellowstone. It was taken during our hike across the Alaska Basin in Grand Teton National Park. None of my clothing was waterproof, but it didn't really seem to matter; I was young!

My pack weighed over forty pounds. My equipment was definitely not professional grade, but it got me through. We covered a lot of ground and saw some exceptionally beautiful scenery. Typically we would arrive back at Grant Village after dark on the night before we were due to return to work. We never did see a grizzly bear! I did almost get run over by a black bear on a wooded mountain trail in a driving rainstorm one day, however. The bear and I both seemed equally wet, miserable, and surprised.

I loved the wildlife in Yellowstone, particularly the buffalo. Whenever I came across them, I was content to just sit and watch. I wouldn't want to leave. At the age of twenty, I could watch buffalo all day.

That summer experience in Yellowstone came and went. Nearly two years later, I graduated from Bowdoin College and got a job teaching history and coaching basketball at Bridgton Academy. "BA," as the school is known, is nestled on the side of Chadbourne Hill above the northwest end of Long Lake in Western Maine. It is the nation's only all-male, one-year, postgraduate prep school. Every spring the entire student body graduates. Every fall a complete new class arrives. My salary was $16,800 a year. I was twenty-two years old. My students were all eighteen or nineteen years old. I was happy to be there. It was a great first job.

My dorm was an old white three-story home called Edwards House. I lived on the first floor and the students lived above me. I remember being handed the keys to that house in July of 1988 and not believing it was mine. I found it all quite exciting! I couldn't actually believe that I had a job and a house . . . that someone was paying me . . . that I was living on my own.

I remember my interview with then headmaster Bob Walker. He was a relaxed and jolly gentleman in the last year of a distinguished career. He was a classic pipe-smoking, tweed-jacketed New England prep school headmaster. He looked the part. The interview went great until the final question, when he asked me if I could teach their Russian history class. I hesitated for just a moment, as I had never studied Russian history (but, then again, I had never taken an education class, either). None of that seemed like a problem to me at the time. I looked back across the desk and said, "Yes, sir. I can do that."

I guess it didn't seem like a problem to Mr. Walker either. He hired me.

It was, of course, an amazing time to be teaching Russian and Soviet history. The Berlin Wall was built in 1961 and it fell in 1989. Ronald Reagan was president, and the Cold War was still the organizational structure for the planet. Everyone knew about the Cold War. Today, just a generation later, many high school students I speak to do not know about the Cold War. In the 1980s, everyone knew. It is a bit stunning how rapidly history can be forgotten.

That which is forgotten is often repeated.

The summer after my first year at Bridgton Academy, Alison and I packed my red Volkswagen Jetta full of gear, picked up our friends Andrew and Jennifer (and all their gear . . . I don't really know how we fit), and headed west for a four-week summer vacation of hiking and camping. It was the kind of trip you could make when you were a young teacher with free summers and no real commitments. We tented out most nights. When we did stay in a hotel, all four of us shared a twenty-dollar room.

Alison and I had met at Bowdoin College where we belonged to the same coed fraternity. In fact, we first met when I (then a junior) was asked to call her out of a pledge lineup to see if she (then a freshman) had learned the names of all the house members. I am sure she didn't like me that night. In fact, she told me so not long thereafter! We recovered well from that unlikely start, however, to become drinking buddies, which soon evolved into close friends, then best friends, then a couple.

I had organized this trip, and therefore our primary destination was Yellowstone National Park. I was returning west. On the way to Yellowstone we drove across South Dakota, stopping in the Badlands National Park, as well as the Black Hills. Even though I did not recognize it at the time, this was my first visit to the Land of Crazy Horse.

Our big hike on that trip departed from a trailhead on Route 191 north of the town of West Yellowstone in Montana. We were in a very remote section of the park's upper northwest corner on a trail that took us just south of Electric Peak. I was once again in the heart of grizzly bear country and signs of their presence were everywhere, but we did not have an encounter. The trail ended on the main park road south of Mammoth Hot Springs, and we hitchhiked all the way back around to our car in a passing RV. My boots were so unkind to me on that hike that I cut them up with my knife, rubbed them in buffalo dung, and ran over them three times with my car on the way out.

From Yellowstone we traveled north to Glacier National Park. Andrew and Jennifer flew home from somewhere and Alison and I drove back across Canada. We saw our first bear of the trip in the dumpster at Dairy Queen on Route 302 in Glen, New Hampshire, forty-seven miles from home.

So there I am, twenty-three years old. Two trends have emerged in my life, neither of which I have recognized as being significant or connected. I am teaching history and I am drawn to the American West, especially to the backcountry. It all seems innocent enough.

A decade passes. Alison and I are married and we have two children. My dad had died in 1997, and I was now president of Hancock Lumber. The pull of my tribe had called me home.

One night I was out to dinner with a group of company managers. The wine was flowing at Bellini's Italian restaurant in North Conway, New Hampshire, when the conversation turned to hunting.

"Kevin, why don't you hunt?" someone teased me. (Everyone in the lumber industry in Maine hunts, it seems.)

Without thinking I sarcastically replied, "Because I am a big-game hunter."

Everyone laughed. No one realized at the time what had just been set in motion.

There is moose hunting in Maine, but it's not that difficult. You typically wait for one to cross a dirt logging road. I was talking big-game hunting in the American West, something hard to do where the odds were in the animal's favor.

About a year later, in the fall of 1999, twelve of us got off a plane in

Billings, Montana. We were going elk hunting!

Our weathered outfitter, Virgil Burns, picked us up in a well-worn extended-cab Ford truck hauling a horse trailer full of hay. Coors Lights were passed around and we departed for the ranch. The next morning we were on horses at daybreak headed deep into the Bob Marshall Wilderness, one of the most remote forests in America. It would be dark before we reached our tent camp that night, and four days before I'd see it in the daylight. We hunted for eight days and saw more grizzly bear than elk. The bears with the orange collars were the bad bears that had been tranquilized and removed from Yellowstone and Glacier National Parks. Our tent camp was ringed with an electric fence at night to keep the bears out. It was one of those places where you went to sleep knowing exactly where your rifle was. I put a loaded gun clip into my sleeping bag every night. Everyone on this trip was an experienced hunter, except for me. I had never been hunting. In fact, I was borrowing a rifle. I shot the only bull elk anyone saw on the entire trip on the seventh day, high in an alpine bowl just below the tree line. I will never forget that moment. I couldn't believe I'd actually hit him!

One of many bull elk I would go on to shoot at the Prairie Ranch in Fossil, Oregon.

That was my first elk hunting trip. I am now the trip organizer. I have since been elk hunting seven times, and the Prairie Ranch in Fossil, Oregon, is my favorite place to hunt, and like a second home to me. I love elk hunting. There is something primal about hunting elk in the American West. You are doing something man has done for thousands of years. I tell Alison I hear and see better when I return from a week in the West, chasing elk. She smiles and doesn't really believe me.

A few years later I am in Orlando at the International Builders' Show with three customers. We are walking through Downtown Disney enjoying the Florida night air when we enter a memorabilia store. We are aimlessly looking around. The American West is the last thing on my mind. I turn a corner in the store and come across a picture of Sitting Bull with his autograph written on a Buffalo Bill Cody Wild West show ticket. His weathered face, high cheekbones, large nose, and dark eyes look stoically out at me. His hair is parted down the middle into two ponytails that lay on the front of his chest. A single eagle feather stands up from the back of his head. The caption below the picture reads:

> **A Hunkpapa Lakota chief and medicine man under whom the Lakota tribes united in their struggle for survival on the northern plains. Sitting Bull remained defiant toward American military power and contemptuous of American promises to the end.**

At the bottom of the picture, just above the frame, there is a quote from Sitting Bull himself, who once asked:

> *What law have I broken? Is it wrong for me to love my own? Is it wicked for me because my skin is red? Because I am Lakota; because I was born where my father lived; because I would die for my people and my country?*

I can't resist. The picture is expensive, but I buy it. There is another picture right beside it of Geronimo with his autograph on a 1904 St. Louis Fair ticket. I buy that too. It cost twenty-five cents to go to the fair that year. Both pictures are large and must be shipped home where they hang on my office wall to this day.

Why couldn't I resist those pictures? I think to myself on the plane ride home.

How am I going to explain to Alison how much they cost? I also think.

It is at about this time in my life that I find myself reading more and more about the Plains Indians, America's Western expansion, and the two worlds that collided. A few years later I picked up that *National Geographic* in the airport with Alison, where the idea that became this trip was born—thirty years after Mr. Whitney first took me hiking.

This calling was soft, gradual. I could easily have missed it.

It has been a strange, slow route getting here, I think to myself as I pause from my thoughts to look out the window. It is now early afternoon on Sunday, October 28, 2012. I am sitting in seat 3A of a small passenger jet streaking west above a patchwork of farmland between Chicago and Rapid City. Later today I will meet Emma "Pinky" Clifford, who is the executive director of the Oglala Sioux Tribe (OST) Partnership for Housing. It is still hard to know the totality of what brings me here, and I am actually nervous. I have butterflies.

I sense that a search for something powerful is about to begin.

The opening ceremony at powwow is one of many places at Pine Ridge where the past and present meet.

Whose voice was first sounded on this land? It was the voice of the red people who had but bows and arrows. What has been done in my country I did not want, did not ask for it; white people going through my country. When the white man comes in my country he leaves a trail of blood behind him. I have two mountains in that country—the Black Hills and the Bighorn Mountains. I want the Great Father to make no roads through them. I have told them these things three times; now I have come here to tell them the fourth time.

—Red Cloud of the Oglala Sioux

It is easy to see why the Black Hills have their name. The pine forests and rocky mountain peaks rise out of a seemingly endless sea of grass and they just plain look black in a way that is a bit difficult to describe, until the moment you see them. *Paha Sapa*, as the Sioux refer to them, simply means "hills-black."

Pinky Clifford meets me at baggage claim with her friend Danny and his seventh-grade son Brayden, who have driven her to the airport so that she can ride back to the reservation with me. Danny, a Comanche from Oklahoma, is tall, strong, and quiet with dark black hair falling down his back. The airport is small, but not crowded. I quickly spot Pinky as she does me. I just know it is she even though we have never met. Pinky has thin dark hair with a touch of gray. I can sense her warmth as she walks toward me. I already feel good about this lady who agreed to host me.

In arranging this trip I sent a number of e-mail inquiries, searching for an initial contact person on the reservation. In each message I explained that I wanted to learn about the housing needs at Pine Ridge to see if I could help. Pinky was the only person who responded, and this is why we are now together. We both were taking a risk.

We grab my bags and my rental car and go to lunch. By the time we reach the restaurant I can already tell Pinky is a woman of purpose, someone who keeps busy. In addition to her housing responsibilities she also owns a convenience store on the reservation in her hometown of Manderson.

Over lunch Pinky tells me about the big high school basketball tournament held annually in Rapid City during the Christmas holiday in which many of the reservation schools come to play each other. She says they have non-reservation teams as well. The event is a big deal in these parts. Through our e-mail communications Pinky knows of my connections to basketball and my love for coaching. As a hobby I have been coaching middle school girls' basketball at Lake Region (our local public school) for nearly fifteen years.

"You should bring your school team and play in the tournament," Pinky says.

Although she is not formally involved in organizing the tournament, I can tell she could make it happen if I were to just say "yes."

Pinky is a mentor. That is the simplest way to describe her. She uses the term many times during our first afternoon together. She is likely in her early sixties, and constantly in storytelling mode. Her mind is always moving to the next topic and new ideas.

I bet everyone on the reservation knows Pinky Clifford, I think to myself.

As we eat, Brayden wants to know who my favorite NBA team is. He is disappointed when I tell him. He is not a Boston Celtics fan. His team is the Dallas Mavericks. He is convinced they won the NBA title last year. I try to tell him they lost to the Miami Heat, but he won't hear it.

After lunch Danny and his son leave us. Pinky joins me in my rental car and we drive south toward the reservation where the tour begins. Pine Ridge lies southeast of the Black Hills, and we travel in that direction through the small town of Hermosa. Entering the reservation we pass over Red Shirt and Cuny Tables before crossing into the southern unit of the Badlands National Park, which lies within the reservation. We see cattle, pronghorn antelope, dozens of deer, and a big old badger. We stop the car and get out because Pinky is very excited about the badger.

"It is the biggest one I have ever seen," she tells me.

"Me too," I reply.

On my first visit I was struck by the remoteness of Pine Ridge. Time, it felt, moved differently here.

Time is an illusion.

—Albert Einstein

It is late in the day and the sun is descending through overcast skies. The reservation seems endless to me. Traveling south, then east, then south again, we drive through barren land, arriving every twenty minutes or so at a small village that often is not more than a cluster of houses and a school. There are no stores, stop signs, or gas stations in most of these villages. Many of the houses are trailers. There are no big houses. There are no fancy houses. Every house is in pretty much the same condition. They all look like they were built at the same time. There are no businesses either. The primary source of employment appears to be the neighborhood school. Someone drives the bus. Someone teaches. Someone cleans the halls. I have never seen so little commerce in a place where people actually live. What I don't see is as much on my mind as what I do.

"The unemployment rate is over eighty percent here," Pinky tells me. "It is hard to find a job."

I am soaking up everything I see and every thought she shares.

As nightfall approaches we arrive at Pinky's hometown of Manderson, which, like most communities here, is small. On the way into town, with the sun nearly set, we see a teenage boy running on the road as several friends gallop on their horses through the high grass beside him. None of them are using saddles.

"He is training for the New York marathon," Pinky tells me.

"I ran the New York marathon," I reply.

Upon learning this Pinky wants me to turn around so she can stop the young runner and introduce me. I convince her to let him keep running.

Pinky, I have already realized, is all about making connections.

I have come to love this sign north of Manderson that tells me I am getting close to Pinky's Store. A hand-painted sign on a sheet of plywood symbolizes the essence of the intimacy that is Pine Ridge.

As the sun falls into the western horizon we pull into Pinky's Store. It is the only business I have seen all afternoon. It is a modest cement structure with a single door and window on the south side facing the parking lot. The small convenience store also contains a Laundromat in the back corner. Pinky tells me that youth gangs are a challenge for many communities here. There are young people in the dusty streets with bikes and ponies as the sun's last light fades.

Inside the store I am introduced to the two teenage girls who are working that evening, as well as a retired policeman who is the guard for cash-up and closing. Pinky buys me dinner off the shelf. I pick out a packaged sandwich, orange juice, and a chocolate chip cookie. I will eat this later at the Singing Horse Trading Post a few miles back up the road, where Pinky recommended I stay.

As we stand near the back of the store, I ask Pinky what she is most optimistic about with respect to the future of Pine Ridge.

"Our schools," she replies, "particularly our college."

"More than half the population here is under the age of twenty-five. Education is very important to us here. The young people are our future," Pinky explains.

"They [the federal government] thought we would just disappear and assimilate," she continues. "But we have remained strong. We have kept our culture alive. Our language is still spoken, our traditions are still followed, and our values are still cherished."

An old man standing near us joins the conversation and questions whether the government likes this.

"Every time we rub two nickels together they get nervous," he interjects.

We all smile and laugh. I can already feel an independent and feisty spirit here that I really like.

This tribe is not done yet, I think to myself, and remember a quote from that 2012 *National Geographic* article where I first sensed the thread of defiance that still endures at Pine Ridge:

When the lights go out for good, my people will still be here. We have our ancient ways. We will remain.

—**Angel Martinez**

Eventually we leave the store and drive to the Singing Horse Trading Post. The Lakota moon is full and sits low in the sky, just above the green gate at the end of the long driveway. It is the same moon that rose over these grasslands in the nineteenth century when the Lakota roamed freely and made camp where they pleased. I untie the gate and we drive up the dirt road.

The green gates of the Singing Horse Trading Post north of Manderson. Little did I know I would open and close these gates dozens of times in the years ahead.

From the gate you cannot see the Singing Horse Trading Post. It is hidden behind a rolling grassy hill, as many things here are. We arrive at the small compound and park the car. To my right the outline of the corral can be seen under the light of the moon. A rustic gray cabin sits beside an even smaller brown one. To my left a mobile home has permanently staked its claim. A portable basketball hoop and a swing set sit below the main building, which is the trading post itself, a split-level home with brown wood siding and a large daylight basement. Dogs and cats come to attention as we cross the gravel and enter the store on the home's lower level.

Rosie the owner, who happens to be German, is there waiting for us.

No sooner have we met than I am curious about her story.

"Meet me at the store at seven-thirty in the morning," Pinky instructs me on the way out.

"Okay. Thank you Pinky," I reply.

I can tell we are going to be busy tomorrow.

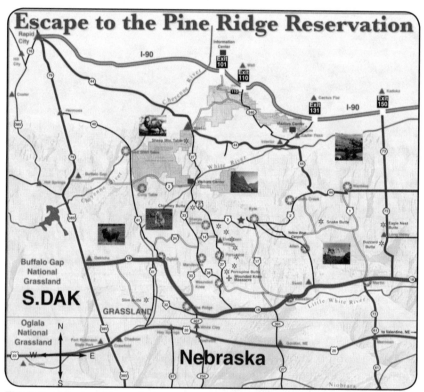

This is the map I used to navigate my way around the reservation on my first trip to Pine Ridge. At the time I didn't know where I was going, nor what had brought me here.

It is now late at night and I am lying in bed in one of two small guest rooms just off the living area above the trading post. I am exhausted, but my mind is scrambling to sort through what I saw today.

A single lamp on the small bedside table offers just enough light to examine the map of Pine Ridge that Pinky gave me. "Escape to the Pine Ridge Reservation," its heading reads.

That's what I'm doing, I think to myself.

I have found a place where, at this point, just four people know me. It is a place beyond the boundaries of my roles and responsibilities. A businessman in the prime of his work career is not supposed to be wandering around and exploring in this way. A businessman is supposed to be working, reading charts, holding meetings, and making decisions. As far as those stereotypes go, I have broken rank.

So did Pinky. She too "broke rank" and walked past the boundaries of her own tribe and roles in making time to host me.

We all get stereotyped in different ways, I suppose, yet we all want to define ourselves more broadly than we are seen.

What a big and isolated place this is, I think to myself as I look over the map and retrace today's path.

The Pine Ridge Indian Reservation is located in a remote corner of a remote state. It is hard to describe how isolated it is unless you have been there. If you have been, then you know.

At 2.2 million acres in size (3,472 square miles), Pine Ridge is one of the largest reservations in America. Most of the scattered communities you come across are small housing clusters with a school and possibly a convenience store. The two largest towns are Kyle (near the center) and Pine Ridge (on the southern edge). Within the reservation of Pine Ridge there is also a town named Pine Ridge. The town of Pine Ridge, just a couple of miles from the Nebraska state line, is the seat of the tribal government and the Bureau of Indian Affairs.

The 2000 census lists the population on the Rez at 15,521, but most local estimates place it at around 40,000 people. Pine Ridge is one of those funky places where people are difficult to count. The population is fluid. Some people stay right there, while others come and go.

Pine Ridge is officially home to the Oglala Sioux Tribe, and many people who live here are, in fact, Oglala. However, many are not Oglala. They may be Lakota, but part of another band, or they may be Dakota and not Lakota at all. In some cases they may not even be Sioux, but rather from some other tribe altogether. There is also a small population of non-Native people who live here.

In addition, through years of "mixed" marriages and births, many people here have ancestral blood from multiple tribes and races. As a result, there is no one tribal name that describes all the people who live here. Everyone, after all, has their own story. Even Pine Ridge is a melting pot.

So, what to call the people who live here? In this book I am going to use the words Oglala, Lakota, and Sioux, while acknowledging that this is not always the case.

After just one day I can tell that history is strong in the hearts and minds of the Oglala Sioux. In many respects the past is the present at Pine Ridge. In fact, being at Pine Ridge makes me reconsider the very meaning of time itself.

What is the past? Is it really gone?

What is the present? Is it really here?

What is the future? Is it actually now?

Is time itself even linear at all as we suppose it to be?

When the Lakota were placed once and for all on their reservations in the years surrounding the Battle of Little Bighorn, the proposition from the federal government was a simple one. If you (Indians) agree to come here (to the reservation), we (the federal government) will provide for you. We will feed you, clothe you, and build houses for you. We will educate your children and supply you with the basic tools of agriculture. We will teach you to be Christians and to someday live peacefully and prosperously among the whites. That was the deal. I have come to call this deal the "final offer" as it wasn't optional.

I was struck today by the degree to which that final offer is still alive for the people of Pine Ridge, even though its origins date back to the 1870s. The federal government, in the eyes of the tribe, is still very much "on the hook" for the original commitments it made so long ago.

The lack of commerce at Pine Ridge is as striking to me as the natural beauty of the landscape and the generous hearts of the people who live here. There are very few businesses at Pine Ridge. Since there are very few businesses, there are very few jobs. Many of the jobs that do exist are government jobs.

"Where are the businesses?" I said to Pinky. "Where does everybody work? Where does everybody shop?"

I didn't understand what I was looking at. I was confused.

The economy at Pine Ridge revolves around the government and its responsibility to provide for its residents. That is how the reservation was set up, and that is how it still works today. Everybody knows it. Nobody tries to hide it.

The statistical results, however, are staggering. Pine Ridge is one of the poorest places in America. It is not just poor by American standards; it is poor by reservation standards. Unemployment exceeds 80 percent. Only a small minority of people has a formal job.

Pine Ridge is economically dependent upon its government. This dependence is rooted in the belief that the federal government must continue to honor the terms of its final offer. A deal is a deal no matter how old or dysfunctional.

> *I have advised my people this way: When you find something good on the white man's road, pick it up; but when you find something bad, or it turns out bad, drop it and leave it alone.*
>
> **—Sitting Bull**

The economic and social challenges at Pine Ridge are literally written on the walls of the buildings themselves.

The economic rules at Pine Ridge are very different from the ones I grew up with in Maine. In Maine, most everyone works. Earning your own living through work is a value that is woven into the ethos of the state. Government is rarely discussed in terms of personal economic solutions. Those are things you earn for yourself. From the time you are a teenager in Maine you work. That's just what everybody does. You don't even really think about it, you just work.

Aroostook County, at the tip of northern Maine, for example, is approximately twice the size of the Pine Ridge Reservation. Well north of Montreal, this isolated county has a population density of eleven people per square mile, similar to Pine Ridge. Though remote and relatively poor by New England standards, it is a place where most everyone works. Unemployment is 7 percent, and over 70 percent of families own their own home.

Interestingly enough, *Aroostook* is an Indian word meaning "beautiful river," as the early inhabitants of this region were Micmacs, Abnakis, and Malecites. Mohawks and Iroquois also frequented this land. The white men were first attracted to the area in the early 1800s in pursuit of the massive pine trees that grew here, which made excellent masts for sailing ships.

Even in Maine, Columbus had not discovered a "new world"; people already lived here.

If you travel to the northernmost part of Maine today you will marvel at the neatness of the homes and front yards that you drive by. Individual pride in property ownership stands out here. Adults and their families sometimes move south, leaving Aroostook County for job opportunities. At Hancock Lumber we have a number of employees who grew up there. They almost always are among the hardest-working and most dependable people you can find. It is noteworthy how isolated communities develop their own cultural traditions about values connected to work and property. The past influences the present, as values are transferred from one generation to the next.

Author Dan Sullivan defines the French word *entrepreneur* as "someone who takes a risk to create something new." Sullivan explains that there is a connection between the presence of entrepreneurs and the overall economic health of a community:

> *There is a direct correlation between the number of entrepreneurs in a country [a society] and the standard of living that everyone enjoys. Conversely, countries with few entrepreneurs are often more impoverished.*

Sullivan also points out that entrepreneurs place a high value on self-sufficiency while rejecting the notion of entitlement:

> *The attitude of entitlement says I am owed something—by society, by government, by the company, by my family. This attitude imprisons the individual in a lifetime of unfulfilled expectations, grievances and self-pity.*

My favorite Dan Sullivan quote is one of his shortest:

> *The price for growth is to give up your grievances.*

I think about that statement as I turn off the light for my first night's sleep at Pine Ridge.

The sign in front of this housing cluster at Wounded Knee symbolizes the long-standing ineffectiveness of government at Pine Ridge.

It's hard being left behind.
It's hard to be the one who stays.

—The Time Traveler's Wife

The following morning what I saw (and didn't see) yesterday is still very much on my mind. Specifically, my attention is focused on the dramatic housing crisis Pinky described, and which I saw with my own two eyes. The housing catastrophe at Pine Ridge begins with the fact that there are very few jobs, so most people are unemployed. Think about that; *most* people are unemployed. In addition, there are no banks (although the following year, the Lakota Credit Union did open its first branch in Kyle). To further complicate the situation, much of the property is "trust land" in which both the individual landowner and the federal government share ownership rights. To this day the federal government retains a trustee responsibility over lots of land at Pine Ridge, theoretically for the benefit of the Oglala Sioux Tribe.

Land ownership rights are both limited and complicated at Pine Ridge. In addition, access to credit is scarce. As a result, home ownership is rare.

Many people here rent public housing units. There is, however, a significant shortage of rental homes and apartments, so many people apply and wait. People often end up living with family members, even sleeping in basements. The homes that are available are generally in poor condition, with little insulation, worn-out floors, and leaking ceilings. There are still many homes here without indoor plumbing. Lots of people can't afford to pay their electric bill and go without power and/or heat for periods of time throughout the year. Many people live in trailers. When the Federal Emergency Management Agency (FEMA) is ready to retire a temporary disaster-relief housing trailer, it often gets sent here, where it becomes someone's permanent home. There is a housing crisis at Pine Ridge. There has been one for a long time. The issues just keep piling up.

This morning Rosie cooks me a huge breakfast of eggs, bacon, hash browns, and toast. She serves me tea. Breakfast is hearty and well received. This is our first real chance to get to know each other. I tell Rosie I was struck yesterday by how little commerce I saw.

"It is hard to run a business here," Rosie explains. "As a result, very few people do. Most people who live here get the majority of their income from the government. Their checks arrive every two weeks. Within two to three days of those checks arriving, ninety percent of the money will have been spent off the reservation because there is nothing to buy here. This is one of our greatest problems. Money is slow to arrive and quick to leave."

Rosie has dark hair and speaks with a German accent. She is very fit, but not tall. She is wearing blue jeans, work boots, and a flannel shirt. You can tell she works hard with her horses, her small ranch, and her business. Rosie takes care of herself in a place where it's not easy to do so. She is proud and thoughtful, yet cautious around newcomers. I can tell she hasn't completely figured me out yet.

That's ok, I think to myself. *Neither have I.*

The town of Whiteclay, Nebraska, is one example of how money leaves Pine Ridge. By tribal ordinance it is illegal to sell, possess, or consume alcohol within the boundaries of the reservation. Just south of the town of Pine Ridge is the Nebraska state line. Just two hundred feet across that line is the unincorporated town of Whiteclay, which has twelve residents and four liquor stores. Those four stores sell the equivalent of 4,500,000 cans of beer annually or 12,500 cans per day. It is 2.1 miles from Pine Ridge to Whiteclay. It takes four minutes to drive there and perhaps thirty minutes to walk. Whiteclay is the saddest little "town" in America. A contingent of vagrants lives in a shanty village near the liquor stores. It is not a place to get out and walk around.

"Not for sale." That's what this picture says to me, and its connotations reach beyond just alcohol.

One does not sell the earth upon which the people walk.

—Crazy Horse

Alcoholism is a major challenge at Pine Ridge, affecting nearly all families in some way. This problem is not new. As far back as 1882, President Arthur created a fifty-square-mile buffer around the reservation within which whiskey sales were prohibited.

Alcohol is one of many paradoxes here, but for me the biggest paradox is the relationship between the people who live here and their government. On one hand, the Lakota of Pine Ridge are steadfast in their belief that the federal government must continue to honor its commitments dating back to the founding days of the reservation. On the other hand, living off those commitments has produced dramatic poverty and widespread dependence.

"The past is never far away here," I say to Rosie.

She thinks about this for a few moments and then replies, "In Germany, eventually we had to face our past [referring to the Nazi era] and say it's time to move on."

The room is quiet as we both reflect. I have been here less than twenty-four hours, but I already have a sense of how deep-seated and complex the issues are. A new public housing unit built here will likely be in disrepair within just a few years. There is a storm beneath the surface that still rages. I can feel it. The people of Pine Ridge have unfinished spiritual business that reaches back generations and across time. There is healing that still needs to occur.

Everything seems exceedingly complicated here, and I get the sense that not much changes. Few people seem to expect anything meaningful to get done. The past inspires modest expectations here.

Some time passes.

Eventually Rosie speaks, "You know there was an essay on a college placement exam in which the students were asked to describe an escalator. Most kids here have never seen or been on one. How would you expect them to describe it?"

More silence.

"If no one ever showed you a trumpet, why would you want to play one?" Rosie continues.

I will never forget that question. The circumstances of our local conditions pull hard on us all.

The late-fall hay shines in the morning sun on the hills above the Singing Horse Trading Post.

My head is riddled with thoughts as I thank Rosie for breakfast and walk to my car. The morning sky is dramatic, however, and the late-season grass glitters like gold (how ironic) behind the Singing Horse Trading Post. I stand still for a moment and just look out across the landscape. The black clouds appear to touch the earth as they are chased off by the rising sun. The sky is bright in one area and dark in another. The same sky offers different views depending on where I look.

As directed, I arrive at Pinky's Store at 7:30 a.m. The village of Manderson consists of several clusters of small homes with lots of well-traveled vehicles and spare parts in most every driveway. There is plenty of trash around and dogs are everywhere. I have never seen more dogs in one place than at Pine Ridge. Some dogs belong to people and others don't. They just kind of live independently as residents of the village.

After visiting for a while with Pinky at the white plastic table in the back of the store, we leave and drive south toward Wounded Knee. Pinky has a funeral to attend at 9:00 a.m. for a young man who recently committed suicide, so she has arranged for her friend and colleague, Lester Lone Hill, to show me around. Pinky specifically wants me to see the Red Cloud School just north of town. Education is always at the forefront of her mind.

Lester and I are supposed to have a tour of the school, but no one in the office is really expecting us or available, so we just walk around. This is fine with me because what I really want to do is walk up the hillside to the burial site of Chief Red Cloud. We chat comfortably as we walk, as if we have known each other for some time. Lester is a war veteran who walks with a slight limp. We move along at a slow but steady pace. Lester is wearing cowboy boots and blue jeans. He wears tinted glasses and his long gray hair is wrapped in a ponytail that extends out from under his hat and falls down the back of his Western-style shirt. I can already tell that he is a good man. His calm presence and friendly mannerisms invite friendship and trust.

Chief Red Cloud is buried in the cemetery above the Red Cloud School. The cemetery is intriguing in the stories it reveals and conceals. Like my own voice disorder, it speaks in a whisper.

Later on, Lester shows me some housing and describes the work they are doing at the OST Partnership for Housing. Both Lester and Pinky have a habit of pointing out the "ownership" homes as we drive by them. I am not sure what this means, so I ask. These are simply homes that people actually own. They are so rare that they get pointed out.

After meeting Pinky for lunch at the Lakota Café, Lester and I visit tribal headquarters where I meet both the president and the vice president of the tribe. Quite a few times today I have figuratively "pinched myself" to make sure I am really here. This makes me think even further about why this place, that so few people ever come to or even contemplate, is so deeply enchanting to me.

Lester and I next drive north and then east toward the town of Kyle to visit the cultural center at Oglala Lakota College. Once inside, I listen to a recorded audio presentation of the Sioux Nation's history, where life before the coming of the white man (the Wasichu) is described, as are the treaties, the broken promises, the battles, and the injustices. As the narrator speaks and tribal music plays, the viewer is escorted around the room from left to right to a series of numbered pictures, maps, and artifacts that line the walls. The Battle of Little Bighorn occurred on June 25, 1876. The ghost dances of 1890 precede the murder of Sitting Bull on December 15. Finally, on December 28, Bigfoot and his tired band are massacred by the 7th Cavalry at Wounded Knee. The narrator describes the event as a "crime against humanity" for which seventeen Congressional Medals of Honor would later be issued. Those medals have never been retracted and the government has never formally apologized for what transpired that day, the narrator explains.

Later that evening I meet Pinky, Danny, and Brayden for dinner at Bette's Kitchen on Black Elk Road just south of Manderson. Her house sits pretty much where Black Elk sat over eighty years ago when he told the story of his life that would later become the basis for the famous book, *Black Elk Speaks*. In fact, Betty is a descendant of Black Elk, the most famous Oglala Holy Man of the twentieth century.

Dinner is a memorable event and a bit hard to describe. Bette's Kitchen is, literally, what it says. You go to her house and you get your food in her kitchen. You just take a plastic plate and load up. The dining room itself is the first room you enter when you walk inside. It consists of five or six tables where guests can sit. A fireplace anchors the northwest corner. Family pictures dating back generations line the walls. During dinner Betty's granddaughter comes running into the room in full costume. She is going to be Catwoman for Halloween and she is all excited.

During a quiet moment, I ponder why Betty with a "y" calls her restaurant Bette's with an "e," but quickly conclude it doesn't matter. I'm just happy to be here.

After dinner I convince Brayden to take our picture. It is the only picture I have of Pinky, Danny, and me together from my first visit to Pine Ridge.

I was glad I convinced Danny's son to take this picture of Pinky, Danny, me—and the back half of Betty's dog—after dinner at Bette's Kitchen.

The following morning Rosie is making me another breakfast of champions as we renew our conversation about life at Pine Ridge and how best to help. Making a lasting difference feels complicated here.

The conversation turns to horses. Rosie tells me that there are many wild horses at Pine Ridge living within people's fence lines. Barbed wire rules the West, even at Pine Ridge. For some reason, this surprises me. In nature's eye, it is not long ago when the entire West was fence-less, and all the inhabitants, whether they had two legs or four, roamed freely. Today all the animals, wild and tamed, live with the barbed wire.

"The grass here is a miracle in itself. It is among the richest in the world. It's eighteen percent protein," Rosie continues.

"Wow," I reply. "I wonder what caused the grass here to be so nutritious?"

Quiet fills the room as Rosie considers this question.

"I believe in God," Rosie answers.

More silence.

"If nobody in your family ever had a job, how would you know how to value work?" Rosie asks, breaking the thoughtfulness of a quiet moment that seems to accompany many conversations here. Silence is welcomed at Pine Ridge as an important participant in any meaningful exchange of ideas. This makes me think of the partial loss of my own voice to spasmodic dysphonia, and how that forced me to learn to embrace silence myself.

A short time passes as my mind wanders back to what Rosie said yesterday:

> *If nobody ever showed you a trumpet,*
> *why would you want to play one?*

"Even after-school jobs are difficult for young people to get," Rosie explains.

The role of government is stronger here than the role of the individual when it comes to economic problem solving, but that was not always so.

Before the coming of the white man the Great Spirit (a term in Lakota spirituality that is largely synonymous with nature itself) provided opportunities for the Lakota people; but, you still had to earn your way. You had to go find the buffalo, then kill the buffalo, then skin the buffalo, then dry the meat, then make your clothing and tools from the remains. Small communities cared for themselves and each other. The society was communal, but everyone who could work did work. Everyone had a role.

The reservations changed everything. Suddenly there were no roles. Survival used to mean living in partnership with the Great Spirit. Now, survival meant living in dependence upon the Great Father. Much is written about the corrupt and inefficient systems that existed for delivering rations in the early decades of the reservation. Food and necessary supplies were often late to arrive and of poor quality. The best beef was sold into white markets. The poorest beef, often spoiled on arrival, went to the reservations. This was the new world of the Lakota. They were dependent upon poorly administered rations for survival. Promises were regularly broken. Corruption was common. In this way, from the very beginning, people learned that government was not effective and could not be trusted. The government that promised to take care of people instead ignored and exploited them. Many here believe it has continued that way to the present day.

Distrust of government runs deep at Pine Ridge, and it is easy to understand why. Even though the government system was poorly administered, mismanagement was not the greatest injustice. The greatest injustice was the system itself, which created dependency and left the people with nothing much to do. The notion that "government should take care of me" is strong in the culture of the reservation. If I am hungry, I go see my government. If my home is in need of repair, I go see my government. Solutions are government-centric at Pine Ridge, and they don't produce good results.

"There is a lot of government here," I say to Rosie.

"Whatever you are born into becomes your specialty," Rosie replies.

This makes me think of my own life experiences within the tribe I was born into. Growing up I never thought about working in the family business, but in hindsight, I am sure others around me expected that I would.

"We all come from a tribe," I say to Rosie.

I have already grown fond of Rosie. I pack my bags and give her a hug. She was not expecting this; but, she lets me hug her all the same. I leave behind two Hancock Lumber coffee mugs that read "I Love the Smell of Sawdust in the Morning" and a promise to return. My next stop is Pinky's Store.

"You can leave the gate open behind you," is the last thing Rosie says to me.

"Will do," I reply. "Thank you."

There is nothing quite like a full moon in the morning over the Land of Crazy Horse. The land is sacred to the Lakota. Something that belongs to everyone cannot be "sold."

"I want you to go and tell the Great Father that I do not want to sell any land to the government . . . [He picked up a pinch of dust and added] not even so much as this."

—Sitting Bull

The Lakota moon is setting to the west as I open the gate. A short drive later I am at Pinky's, where on this morning, there are more dogs than people in the dirt parking lot.

"You can never help a child too much," Pinky tells me from the white plastic table at the back of her store a few minutes later. These words just sit in the air.

I already love Pinky. Pinky has a spirit and presence about her that draw me in. The power of her words often commands reflection and contemplation.

"Think about what's next," she instructs me.

What a great statement: *think about what's next*. We can always look to the past, but ultimately we need to move forward.

Pinky and I would go on to sit together many times at the white plastic table in the back of her store. Time was never rushed here. In fact, it slowed down.

During the last three days, Pinky and I have discussed the housing needs at Pine Ridge and brainstormed ways in which Hancock Lumber might help. I thank Pinky for her hospitality and tell her what a special person I think she is. Pinky gives me some local jam, some buffalo lotion, and some hand-painted cards for Alison as gifts. In return, I give Pinky something I have brought with me. It is a check for $2,500 made payable to the OST Partnership for Housing. Pinky was not expecting this. It was not something I had mentioned or offered to do. It is a surprise. I had made the check out before leaving. I decided to bring it with me and just see if the cause felt right. In hindsight, Pinky and I were both taking a risk in our first meeting. We both were investing time and trust in each other before we truly knew if that trust was warranted. Sometimes you just have to take that leap.

Pinky holds the check for a moment in silence and then tears come to her eyes. She begins to cry, but stands strong and proud at the same time.

"You won't believe what this will do for our organization," she says looking right at me. We hug four times (before I knew four was the sacred Lakota number). She is all smiles even though tears are flowing.

"Love you, Pinky," I say just after I turn to leave.

Wow, I think to myself as I navigate the sleeping dogs in the parking lot like Captain Hook through alligators. *We just met two days ago.*

After leaving the store, I drive south because I want to go back to Wounded Knee. I drive slowly up the dirt road leading to the cemetery, as it is filled with deep ruts. I park the car and get out. Colored ribbons attached to fence posts flutter in the fall wind. There is a lot of spiritual power here. Of course the history is important, but the spiritual energy is what brings me here. I have already come to understand this. I couldn't wait to come here this morning—to stand here, alone, with the sacred energy of the grass, the wind, and the burial grounds.

> **As you dare to recognize your ancient past your creative self will leap with renewed energy.**
>
> **—Anslie Roberts, *Beyond the Dreamtime***

The Lakota call what happened here a massacre. The cavalry called it a battle. What you see depends upon where you stand.

I reach inside my shirt and pull out my eagle pendant necklace. I hold it in my right hand and then let it fall upon my chest on the outside of my shirt. I know I am about to leave, but I don't really want to. There is a silent power to this place that holds me. We all know those moments in our lives when it is time to go, but we are not quite ready.

I can feel a transformation brewing inside me. At the beginning of this trip I was primarily focused on matters of the head.

"What's wrong with the economy?" "How do we fix things?"

But, my head is not what brought me here. If I were following my head I would be at my desk back in Maine right now.

The cemetery at Wounded Knee is filled with wooden crosses, prayer flags, overgrown plots, and spiritual power.

Scars have the strange power to remind us that our past is real.

—All the Pretty Horses

Increasingly, I find myself occupied with matters of the heart, deep-seated matters stirring within my soul. I was starting to understand that the partial loss of my voice was symbolic of a deeper wound that was seeking release. I couldn't yet connect all the dots, but I knew I was searching for answers. In looking at Pine Ridge's past, I was somehow accessing the source of my own demons.

> **We all got secrets. I got them same as everybody else – things we feel bad about and wish hadn't ever happened. Hurtful things. Long ago things. We're all scared and lonesome; most of the time we keep it hid.**
>
> **—Frederick Buechner, theologian**

Eventually I sit down near the stone wall at the entrance to the cemetery, where my mind wanders back to my bookshelf in Casco, which is filled with stories about Lakota history.

Why do I have this deep personal fascination with their story? I think to myself.

The intimacy I feel is palpable for me. As I sit there looking out over the mass grave, what I have learned about Lakota history flashes before me . . .

"GOLD!"

"The Land of Promise—Stirring News from the Black Hills."

"The Glittering Treasure Found at Last—A Belt of Gold Territory Thirty Miles Wide."

"It Can Be Reached in Six Days—Expeditions Forming All Along the Frontier."

Thus read the headlines of the *Chicago Inter-Ocean* newspaper on the morning of August 27, 1874. General Custer, the one the Lakota called *Pahuska* or *Long Hair*, had discovered gold on Sioux tribal lands.

Prospectors flooded the Black Hills in the spring of 1875. Their encroachment onto Lakota treaty lands would receive only token resistance from the US government, who, after all, made the initial discovery and then marketed the announcement. The trail Custer and the 7th Cavalry cut across the grasslands of the Dakotas would forevermore be known to the Lakota as "The Thieves' Road."

All that was to follow violated the Treaty of Fort Laramie of 1868 that guaranteed the Lakota their land and peace with the whites for all time:

From this day forward all war between the parties to this agreement shall forever cease. The government of the United Sates desires peace, and its honor is hereby pledged to keep it.

—Article I

The United States hereby agrees and stipulates that the country north of the North Platte River and east of the summits of the Bighorn Mountains shall be held and considered to be unceded Indian territory, and also stipulates and agrees that no white person or persons shall be permitted to settle upon or occupy any portion of the same; or without the consent of the Indians first had and obtained, to pass through the same.

—Article XVI

The hard-fought war over the Bozeman Trail was thought to have created a lasting peace between the United States and the Sioux, but all that changed when Custer's expedition "discovered" gold in the Black Hills just a few years later.

You have driven away our game and our means of livelihood out of the country, until now we have nothing left that is valuable except the hills that you ask us to give up . . . The earth is full of minerals of all kinds, and on the earth the ground is covered with forests of heavy pine, and when we give these up to the Great Father we know that we give up the last thing that is valuable either to us or the white people.

—Wanigi-Ska (White Ghost)

The Black Hills is my land and I love it . . . and whoever interferes will hear this gun.

—Sioux Chant

In 1980 the Supreme Court ruled that the United States government violated the Fifth Amendment rights of the Lakota by taking their property without just compensation. The Lakota were awarded millions of dollars in financial damages, but refused the money (which still sits in trust to the present day).

"Our land is not for sale," was their reply.

———

Since my college summer working in Yellowstone, I have been fascinated with wild buffalo. I can sit and watch them all day.

By now I have left Wounded Knee. In fact, I have driven off the reservation and onto the Buffalo Gap National Grasslands, where the majesty of the landscape captivates me.

Buffalo Gap . . . what a great name, I say to myself out loud in a spasmodic dysphonia—free voice. I have always found it fascinating that my voice is normal and unconstrained when I am alone, speaking to myself.

The grasslands are beautiful. As I scan them, I can easily imagine the massive herds of buffalo stretching to the horizon in the days before the barbed wire, before the railroad, and before the coming of the Wasichu. It is hard to fully appreciate how plentiful the buffalo once were here. In the early decades of the nineteenth century, it is estimated that over thirty million buffalo lived on the Great Plains alone. In his book *American Buffalo,* author Steven Rinella describes a scene in which the German Prince Maximillian traveled onto the Great Plains in the 1830s and saw buffalo in overwhelming abundance:

> *He wrote of how "whole herds were often drowned in the Missouri" and described places where eighteen hundred or more dead buffalo were collected in some of the sloughs of the river. Along the Red River, another traveler noted that "drowned buffalo continue to drift by in whole herds throughout the month, and toward the end for two days and nights their dead bodies formed one continuous line in the current." He watched thousands come to rest against the banks. It smelled so bad that he refused to eat his dinner, and he wondered if he was witnessing a rare tragedy. When he put the question to his Indian guides, they told him that every spring was "about the same."*

The Union Pacific Railroad, breakthroughs in tanning technologies, and greed would ultimately combine to seal the fate of the American buffalo. By the early 1870s, great commercial hunts were being organized.

It was a sordid bunch that led the buffalo-hunting rampage on the Great Plains. So indiscriminate was the killing that the boom lasted only a decade or so before the buffalo ran out. The first massive hunts took place outside of Dodge City. The buffalo were dropped in their tracks and skinned only for their hides, with the rest of the carcass left where it fell. These killing fields would have been a dramatic scene to view and certainly incomprehensible to the Plains Indians. Residents of Dodge City complained of the intolerable odors that drifted across the plains with the blowing wind. In the winter of 1871—1872 alone, five hundred thousand buffalo hides were shipped out of Dodge. The post–Civil War West had become a wild place in the American sense of the word, but it was becoming increasingly less natural in the eyes of the Lakota people. By the end of the nineteenth century, there would be less than one thousand buffalo in the United States, most of which were confined to zoos and ranches. The end of yet another era had come.

As my drive continues, I think about the day in front of me. I have a hotel reservation for the night at the State Game Lodge in Custer State Park. I have not felt good about this reservation since I made it. To be completely honest, I had a strong feeling from the beginning that this hotel was haunted, and I just don't want to deal with a new set of ghosts tonight. I am already carrying a car full of them with me from Pine Ridge.

From the moment I pull in, I know I am right. It is off-season in the Black Hills and the entire resort is eerily empty. Overall, this makes for an amazing time to visit. The roads are vacant and the wildlife is abundant. The animals move undisturbed and feed with urgency. Winter is coming.

Many hotels in the park are already closed for the season. This one closes in a week. I enter and check in. Even though I am regretting my actions, I keep moving forward. Payment in advance is required, so I have already bought the night. One woman, dressed the part for Disney's Haunted Mansion, is at the bell desk. Yes, a bell desk. I want to ring the bell, but she is standing right in front of me.

I am assigned to a room on the second floor where President Franklin Roosevelt once slept. The woman at the bell desk is proud of this factoid, but it only makes me feel worse, as if the ghost spirit of this dead president is up there waiting for me. I go up the creaking stairs to the second floor where every door is open. Every room looks creepy, including mine. Every room is empty, including mine. I really think I am the only person staying here tonight. I go into my room and sit on the bed which squeaks and shifts in response. For what seems like the longest time I just stare at myself in the old mirror on the wooden bureau.

Eventually, I put on my hiking gear, look around, and say to myself, "No way". I think I actually said it out loud.

I leave the room and walk back past all the open doors and down the creaky stairs. At the landing, I gaze into the cavernous dining hall. One staff person is serving one guest. That makes four of us here. The lady at the bell desk looks at me quizzically as I reenter the lobby. I feel like I am back in elementary school and my teacher knows I have done something wrong.

"I am going hiking," I say, feeling the need to explain myself. "I'll be back tonight."

I know I am not coming back tonight. I feel like she knows as well. I am carrying all my stuff with me. I wonder if she will someday read this and remember me?

Crazy Horse under construction in the Black Hills, not far from Mount Rushmore. Who has the biggest monument changes nothing, however.

> ***The white men have crowded the Indians back year by year until we are forced to live in a small country . . . and now our last hunting ground, the home of the People, is to be taken from us. Our women and children will starve, but for my part I prefer to die fighting rather than by starvation.***
>
> **—Red Cloud**

In the deserted town of Custer, I stop for lunch at a diner before driving north to see the Crazy Horse Memorial and then Mount Rushmore. The view of both is compromised for me. After my experience at Pine Ridge, looking at Mount Rushmore is not quite the same. I know how this land was acquired and what that did to the people who lived here. I am not comfortable at the Crazy Horse Memorial either. It's a tourist destination, and I just don't feel the spiritual energy. It seems more about one-upmanship. It's almost like, "If the presidents are carved into a rock here, then an Indian chief should be, too."

The battle continues.

I wonder if Crazy Horse would have approved? He disliked public attention. He was never photographed and always averse to self-promotion. He didn't want to adopt the white man's ways. He just wanted his people to be left alone.

The memorial is quite commercialized, with tollbooths, transportation buses, ticket counters, Plexiglas, and pavement—lots of pavement. Fresh from the rustic authenticity of Pine Ridge, I was hoping for something more simplistic and reflective: a nature trail through a pine forest, to a quiet viewing area, perhaps. I understand why the carving is here, however; given all that has transpired, its presence is important. Most people vacationing in the Black Hills might not remember the Lakota at all otherwise.

I, for one, prefer standing alone in the dirt at Wounded Knee. Others may well feel differently and that's okay too. Either way, ironies abound here. The Black Hills have become a major tourist destination built on a single theme—patriotism.

***I think you had better put the Indians on wheels so
you can run them about whenever you wish.***

—Red Dog

Patriotism is the marketing theme of the Black Hills.

Later that day, I stand alone at Mount Rushmore. The carvings are impressive. The scene is beautiful. The same emotions stay with me, however. I already know too much about how this land was acquired.

I leave Mount Rushmore around 4:00 p.m. and drive into Custer State Park to travel the Wildlife Loop trail. I am on safari. It is a perfect time of day and year to look for wildlife. I am pretty much alone, passing two cars in three hours. There are more buffalo here than people.

I come upon a herd of well over a hundred buffalo grazing across a field below the road. I pull over and get out with my binoculars to watch. Time has lost some meaning for me on this trip. I have nowhere to go, nowhere to be. I am learning to leave busyness, tasks, and projects behind. I am learning to just *be*.

The buffalo are grazing in my direction. In fact, they come right onto the road in front of me and linger. I am so close that I can hear their sandpaper-like tongues licking salt off the pavement. Off to the side, two large males are butting heads in a duel for supremacy. One calf is hobbling after his mother on three legs; his fourth leg appears broken at the ankle. Buffalo are not more than twenty feet away. I stand behind my car at times and halfway in it at others, depending on the attention I am receiving. This scene plays out for more than an hour. I took an amazing video with my iPhone of my car weaving slowly through the herd, as I tried to depart. The buffalo moved out of my path only when it pleased them to do so.

Around the next bend, I stop and watch a herd of wild burros. A short while later, as the sun sets, I come upon a large group of pronghorn antelope crossing the road. The antelope are well known for not letting people get too close, so this is a unique experience. I "park"—in the middle of the road, of course—and just get out.

The sun is setting into the pine forest at the far edge of the grasslands, creating an ever-deepening mixture of red colors in the scattered clouds. I get back into my car and drive in the direction of the setting sun. Mule deer cross the road in front of me.

I soon leave Custer State Park and enter Wind Cave National Park; only the sign lets me know I have done this.

The road winds its way across the meadow and I follow it slowly. Over the next several miles, I encounter fifteen bull elk, no more than two at a time. All of them are mature with six-by-six antlers or more, and some are among the largest I have ever seen. I feel like I am the only person in the wilderness, and I don't leave the meadow until it has become totally dark. The elk are my totem animal and I never get tired of watching them. It was hunting them that brought me back to the West as an adult, in a final chapter drawing me even closer to Pine Ridge.

There is no separation between the natural and the supernatural.

—Ainslie Roberts, *Beyond the Dreamtime*

It is dark as I drive uphill and emerge onto the expansive upper grasslands of Wind Cave National Park. Suddenly, a massive herd of elk rushes to the edge of the road in front of me and then pauses. Once again, I put the car in park and get out. Elk are stamping their feet, chirping and grunting as they organize their group decision. Should we cross? They pause and then launch, crossing right in front of me. All of my senses are called into play. I can barely see their outlines as they rush the road and climb the ridge to my left. I can hear the thundering of their hooves on the pavement and the grunting and chirping of their calls. I can smell their classic, unforgettable scent. My eyes can barely make out an occasional set of antlers above the brown mass of bodies as they move. I would guess there are more than two hundred elk in this herd. Some cross quickly, while others don't dare. Eventually they all make it and head out onto the open plains. By the moonlight I can see the big dark mass that is the herd moving in unison as they jog away.

As I resume my drive, I make the next turn and rather suddenly need to break for a very large lone bull buffalo that appears out of nowhere, just off the right corner of my car. We stare each other down. It has the feeling of an actual exchange. I look at him. He looks at me. I switch to low beams which he seems to appreciate. Slowly, as if to reinforce who is dictating the action, he crosses in front of me and calmly disappears into the darkness on the other side.

The large lone buffalo that emerged from and returned into the darkness, near the end of my first day in the Black Hills.

I am smiling as I descend back into the town of Hot Springs. I still don't know where I am staying tonight, but I don't really care. If anything, I like the feeling. At the age of forty-six, how many nights do I have in which I don't know where I am staying? It's beautiful, actually.

In town, I stop for gas and water. I am drinking lots of water and the reason is beyond thirst. The water is cleansing and it unites me in some way with that which created it.

I ask the young guy at the other pump how far it is to Denver.

"About six hours, I think," he replies. "I'm not really sure, though, because I never go there. I like it right here. I just wish there were some jobs. There are no jobs. There is no opportunity here," he tells me.

Well, you should see Pine Ridge, I think to myself.

Toward the end of town I see a Best Western. I park and walk inside. This hotel has a registration desk. There is no bell desk at the Best Western. I book a room for one night for $38 and then enjoy a satisfying dinner across the street at Pizza Hut. As I eat, I pore through the small red binder that is my journal. I still have no idea that my journal will become the foundation for a book I am soon to start writing. Right now, it is just a collection of personal notes that require constant unscrambling. I have not watched TV or read a paper in three days. I have no interest right now. I like that feeling. I am sure the world's headlines will be fine without me for a short while. These thoughts remind me of what my friend and evolutionary astrologer, Deborah Dooley, told me as I sat on the couch in her small second-floor office near Stanford University's campus: "The tribe is okay, Kevin."

This was Deborah's way of telling me I could start paying more attention to myself. I remember crying when she said this.

> **This interior region of our being is often disinclined to stay hidden. In spite of our guarding, our hidden otherness wills to play a commanding role in the making of who we are.**
>
> **—Merle Steva, First Parish Church, Saco, Maine**

Today has been a day of contrasts. It began in the place the Oglala Sioux were moved to and it ended in the place they were moved from. I already understand why the open pine forests, grassy meadows, rocky peaks, and abundant wildlife made the Black Hills so sacred and valuable to the Lakota people. Today, many of them can't even afford to drive here. As I climb into bed, I can almost see the conflicting emotions on the faces of the presidents themselves.

When you know the true history of how the Black Hills were taken from the Sioux, it seems like such an awkward place for the great presidents to be memorialized; this conflict can almost be detected on their faces. "Uneasy lies the head that wears a crown."

> **Your young men have devastated the country and killed my animals . . . they do not kill them to eat them; they leave them to rot where they fall. If I went into your country to kill your animals, what would you say? Should I not be wrong and would you not make war on me?**
>
> **—Bear Tooth of the Crow Indians**

"Boo!" That was the text I sent Abby and Sydney this morning—one a junior in college, and the other a senior in high school. I can still say "Boo!" and "Happy Halloween!" to both of them, even though they are young adults and this is a holiday that I am once again avoiding.

Who knows what mysterious activity occurred at the nearly-abandoned State Game Lodge that I high-tailed out of last night . . .

Yesterday was special in the simplest of ways. I didn't know where I was going. I stopped and ate when I was hungry, and slept when I was tired. I had no schedule. There were no appointments or deadlines. When you are by yourself, you don't care what you look like. I find this refreshing as well. We are the same on the inside no matter how we look on the outside. I would like to put more of these days in my life!

Today I am headed for Denver and tomorrow I am flying home. I leave the Best Western at 5:30 a.m. and drive under a full Lakota moon down and out of the Black Hills and back onto the Buffalo Gap National Grasslands. Around 7:00 a.m. I roll into the ranch town of Lusk, Wyoming, one of those wonderful prairie towns where the elevation (5,015 feet) exceeds the population (1,447). Dawn is breaking as I arrive and the morning light is amazing.

Prior to the railroad, Lusk was the last stage stop coming up from Cheyenne on the way to the Black Hills. The "Stage & Express Line" that ran through here shuttled passengers back and forth to the Black Hills from a point south of town known as Rawhide Buttes. The buttes were a natural landmark, rising out of the grasslands for trappers, traders, and Indians alike. The stage line lasted only eleven years, before the small horse-drawn boxes on wooden wheels were replaced by the iron horses of the railroad. There is a great little historic marker on the right -hand side of the highway heading south from Lusk that describes the history and folklore of this place:

RAWHIDE BUTTES

Rawhide Buttes once served as a favorite camping spot for Indians and fur trappers. Several different tales explain the origin of the name. One account holds that this locale served as a departure point from which trappers sent fur pelts, or "rawhides," east to St. Louis. Another story tells of a reckless young man who killed an Indian woman while journeying to California during the 1849 gold rush. Attempting to avoid trouble, his fellow travelers surrendered the man for punishment and then watched in horror as the Indians skinned him alive at the base of the Buttes—thus, the name "Rawhide Buttes." In 1874, a military expedition led by Lieutenant Colonel George A. Custer

discovered gold in the Black Hills of Dakota Territory. Hoping to capitalize on the ensuing rush of prospectors, the entrepreneurial team of John Gilmer, Monroe Salisbury, and Mathewson Patrick organized the Cheyenne and Black Hills Stage and Express Line in 1876. The arrival of the Chicago and North Western Railroad led to the demise of stage coaching. The last Black Hills-bound stage departed from Cheyenne's Inter-Ocean Hotel on February 19, 1887. The end of an era had arrived.

As I read this, I can't help but think that Pine Ridge has little more than a grocery store today. Then again, that's more than Rawhide Buttes has anymore.

For me, there is nothing like witnessing the sun's first light on the northern plains.

I have heard that you intend to settle us on a reservation near the mountains. I don't want to settle. I love to roam over the prairies. There I feel free and happy, but when we settle down we grow pale and die.

—Santana, Chief of the Kiowa

When the sunlight is just right everything has a magical look to it. When you are outside for an entire day, you really notice the short time periods of extraordinary light. This morning happens to be one of those times. The changing sun reminds me that we never travel the same road twice.

Lakota is pronounced "La-COE-ta." I write this in my journal as I sit beside the Rawhide Buttes historical marker. My head swirls with ideas.

I stop a lot to take pictures. I back up a lot to get pictures of something I drove by, or to look again at the same site from a different angle. In this country you can back up in your lane for as long as you want and as fast as the car will go. The engine is definitely meant to go forward, however, as it makes a high-pitched whining noise each time I back up with gusto. I stop at every historical marker. I see that as part of my mission on this trip. I am doing field research. I think about how frustrated anyone riding with me would be. This has to be a solo mission; no one else could put up with my starting, stopping, standing, watching, writing, water-drinking, bathroom breaks, and picture-taking. I have changed the batteries in my camera six times in four days.

As I drive, I find myself thinking about my own religion and the small white church in the village I grew up attending. It is a Protestant church and therefore part of the Christian faith. The church played a delicate role at Pine Ridge, as it has done in other colonized corners of the world. Lakota spiritual ceremonies were banned for decades following the Battle of Little Bighorn. Back in the day, becoming American meant becoming a Christian, and the Lakota were forced onto that train. I am struck by how much fighting has occurred to force one's religion on others, struck by how many tribes across time have seen "their" god as the best god.

We do not want any churches because they will teach us to quarrel about God.

—Chief Joseph

There is one God looking down on us all.

—Geronimo

The concrete remains of historic Fort Laramie cast shadows to the present day.

**I will kill any white man who crosses
the North Platte.**

—Red Cloud

The last stop of my trip comes at historic Fort Laramie near the North Platte River. I almost drive by it, thinking twice about taking the detour. The urge to hurry on to the next event is never far beneath the surface for me. It is a change I am seeking to make within myself, and this time I am successful.

I am glad I chose to go to Fort Laramie, as it is such an important part of the story. The historical marker at the entrance to the fort calls it the "single most important location in America's expansion west." Opened as a trading post in 1839, Fort Laramie served as a frontier military outpost from 1849 to 1890. It was a center for the fur trade, a stopping point along the Oregon Trail, and a relay station for the Pony Express. The Pony Express was a short-lived but incredible enterprise lasting from April 1860 until October 1861, and Fort Laramie was a critical relay point. The mail was carried by horse and rider from St. Joseph, Missouri, through Fort Kearny, Nebraska, just south of Pine Ridge.

From there, the route went through Fort Laramie to Salt Lake City and ultimately on to its final destination in Sacramento, California. A group of 120 different riders traveled 650,000 miles during the life of the route. Only a single mail bag was ever lost, and only one rider was ever killed by Indians. The telegraph line arrived at Fort Laramie on August 5, 1861. Technology from the East was never far behind the settlers heading West.

This old, open door at Fort Laramie was symbolic of my entire journey to Pine Ridge. Something yet unknown had invited me into this new world, invited me to step away from the busyness of my own tribe, to clear my mind and to reach my soul.

Civilization has been thrust upon me, and it has not added one whit to my love for truth, honesty and generosity.

—Chief Luther Standing Bear of the Oglala Sioux

After leaving Fort Laramie, I drive for quite some time before stopping for gas in Cheyenne, Wyoming. It is here that the grasslands surrender to the "progress" of humanity. From here, it is 101 miles to Denver. I am not ready to leave the wilderness just yet, however. So, after a little more driving, I spend the rest of the day hiking in Rocky Mountain National Park, jumping yet another herd of elk along the way.

Early that evening, I drive down into Denver. I reach the airport hotel just as the sun's last light paints the sky a collage of red, yellow, and orange. I feel like it is just for me. The Lakota sun is saying good-bye for now. Tomorrow, I am going home.

The Lakota sun followed me all the way to Denver before saying good-bye over the Rocky Mountains.

This war did not spring up here in our land; this war was brought upon us by the children of the Great Father who came to take land from us without price, and who, in our land, do a great many evil things.

—Spotted Tail of the Brule Sioux

2
Transcendence

The dirt road that travels over Cuny Table from Pine Ridge to Hot Springs invites soul-searching and self-reflection.

> *I must first know myself, as the Delphian inscription says; to be curious about that which is not my concern, while I am still in ignorance of my own self would be ridiculous.*
>
> **—Plato**

It is 19 degrees as I back out of my driveway in Casco. Christmas is eight days away.

It is less than four miles from my house to my office, but my mind still wanders as I drive. Today, I am thinking about how my first trip to Pine Ridge, two months ago, has helped to accelerate changes I want to make within myself. By now, the national economy has stabilized some, and this has definitely helped our business. At the same time, the most important changes, I feel, have come from within.

Early in my career, I used to spend lots of time thinking about what other people needed to do differently or better. That's the traditional nature of the CEO's role, I suppose. Increasingly, however, I have become much more focused on what *I* need to do. Last week, in fact, I put Gandhi's famous quote on our conference-room wall:

We must be the change we wish to see in the world.

Since I began focusing more energy internally, things have gotten easier for me, smoother. I am spending less time trying to change other people and more time trying to change myself. My spasmodic dysphonia has definitely promoted this path, but that, too, came from within.

This morning I am going over final preparations for our upcoming board of directors meeting. As a family business, Hancock Lumber could choose to govern itself without an independent board of directors; but, in our view, outside directors play an important role in supporting and checking management's work. The board is a valuable ingredient in the recipe for shared leadership.

After final board meeting preparations, I work with our human resources director on "Performance Gold" plans for the coming year. *Performance Gold* is the term we use for our bonus system in which every employee participates.

After lunch, I drive to our lumberyard in Windham where our store managers and logistics team leaders are conducting an "OTIF" process improvement strategy session. "OTIF" stands for "On Time and In Full" delivery. Meeting shipping deadlines is one of our customers' top priorities. "Time" on the job has a very different meaning for me than "time" at Pine Ridge.

After this meeting, I stop at Walmart and load a shopping cart full of gloves, mittens, and hats that I am going to package and ship to Pinky at Pine Ridge tomorrow. I know she will make sure they get to people who need them.

My last stop of the day is Lake Region Middle School, where I coach our eighth-grade girls' basketball team in their victory over Cape Elizabeth. Later tonight our daughter, Abby, comes home for a short Christmas break. She is the point guard on the basketball team at Trinity College in Hartford, Connecticut; she will not be home long. Tomorrow night, Sydney's high school team has a game. It is Christmas in Casco, which means it is also basketball season.

High school sports are big in Maine. They are also big at Pine Ridge. I have come to believe we are not so different after all. Local conditions can vary dramatically, but people are people.

"This has been a pretty typical day with my own tribe," I think to myself, as frost overtakes the windows in my home office later that night. I actually say those words out loud, and my voice sounds fine. Just a short while ago, I had to huddle my players in close for them to even hear me speak. My voice is at its worst whenever there is background noise, so a gymnasium full of squeaking sneakers and cheering fans is quite difficult for me. Coaching with a restricted voice is an interesting challenge that has actually made me better at it. I interrupt the flow of the game less, and let the players lead more; in this way, they learn on their own, making the lessons more powerful. Coaches spend a lot of time trying to prevent individual mistakes, but that is where the growth occurs.

You can learn a lot by losing your voice.

As I lean into my chair, my mind wanders back in time to my earliest images of the American West.

When I was a boy, I would play for hours at my grandparents' house with the set of plastic cowboys and Indians that we kept there. I would set them up on the brick floor in front of the fireplace, because they wouldn't stay upright on the carpet. I would lose myself in time, arranging them for great battles. That's what plastic cowboys and Indians were for. I wish I could remember who I chose to win.

Tonto, the Lone Ranger, John Wayne, Clint Eastwood, Grizzly Adams, *Gunsmoke*, *Bonanza*, and many other fictional characters and stories colored the televisions and movie screens of my childhood. It was hard to distinguish them from Sitting Bull, Geronimo, Chief Joseph, and General Custer. Real characters with fictional twists met fictional characters with elements of truth added to them. What part of the Wyatt Earp or Jesse James story was real? What part was imagined and invented?

A glorified version of the American West, the white men who tamed it, and the Indians who defied them had been embedded into the American psyche. Distinguishing fact from fiction was not a primary concern. The Hollywood version of the story worked just fine.

Film and television built an entire genre around a romanticized interpretation of "winning" the West.

Back at my desk the next morning, I think again about the change that I can feel unfolding within me. An inner awakening is slowly occurring, and I have become conscious of it. Confusing at times, invisible at others, something inside me is stirring, and Pine Ridge is enabling that process of self-discovery and personal exploration. Losing consistent access to my voice forced me to slow down and think. In the quiet that followed, I began to hear the whispers of my soul.

What brings you here? the jewelry maker innocently asked me, as I stood for the first time at the Wounded Knee Massacre site.

"That's a great question," I replied.

The answer was unclear.

No one invited me to Pine Ridge; I invited myself, and my official purpose there was quite limited. I was just interested, really interested, in this land, these people, and their story. It all felt so intimate, almost like I had been there before. There was a palpable energy at Pine Ridge for me, but the source of its origins was a mystery. I couldn't tell if it was Pine Ridge's energy, my own personal energy, or the union of the two. Nonetheless, it was real and powerful.

Being at Pine Ridge was, after all, very different for me. At Pine Ridge, only a few people even knew who I was, and my days there were void of firm commitments or obligations. In Maine, I was a lot about my roles and responsibilities. I had many of them, and they had every right to occupy me.

The history of Hancock Lumber and the history of my hometown are somewhat intertwined. The town was incorporated in 1841 and the company was established in 1848. The "office," as most everyone in town calls it (even those who don't work there often refer to it that way), is located in the village's north end, just across the street from Pleasant Lake. The population of Casco is around four thousand people, and that number more than triples in the summer as campers, vacationers, and cottage owners return to the Western Maine lakes. Casco is approximately forty-five minutes west of Portland and two and a half hours north of Boston. It is less than an hour to the ocean traveling east and an hour to the White Mountains going west. In my way of thinking, it's a pretty perfect place to be from.

The office itself is an old red building that stretches west, away from the lake along the Edes Falls Road. It is hard to distinguish between the Edes Falls Road and the Hancock Lumber parking lot, as the road runs through the center of it. When I was Little League age, this site was pretty much the entire company. My brother, my father, my grandfather, my great-grandfather, and even my great-grandfather's grandfather all worked here. I, too, come from a tribe.

Today, Hancock Lumber has three sawmills, ten stores, and twelve thousand acres of timberland. Once coveted and marked as "King's Pine" by the Crown of England for its use as sailing ship masts, the most valuable tree species growing on our land is the majestic eastern white pine. If you are going to grow eastern white pine trees for a living, you had better take a long view, as it takes eighty years or more to grow one. It really is a crazy business, because in the six-generation history of our company, we've had the equivalent of just two crop cycles. Whenever I think of this, I am always jealous of my friends who grow pumpkins, potatoes, or corn!

Our sawmills produce boards and related pine products that are sold throughout North America and the world. Across southern Maine and the White Mountains of New Hampshire, our stores supply building materials and construction services to professional contractors. Our company has 425 employees, many of whom have worked here for a long time; I am one of them, having started working here twenty-three years ago.

In addition to the job of running the company, I had taken on other leadership roles in our community and industry. I served as the chairman of the Northeast Retail Lumber Association. A few years later, I became the youngest chairman ever of the National Lumber Dealers' Association in Washington, D.C. At home, I led committees to save community centers and reorganize school districts. I served as president of the board of trustees at Bridgton Academy, co-chaired the local town fair known as "Casco Days," and even coached the eighth-grade girls' basketball team at Lake Region Middle School. I was a husband, a father, and a busy man. I enjoyed every part of it; I was just busy. I had a lot of roles and they all involved some form of leading and caretaking. People even asked me if I might run for governor or some other public office someday; that seemed, even to me, like a natural progression of the path I was on.

It is only recently, however, that I became aware of the degree to which my internal identity (my personal sense of self) and my external roles had become intertwined. I joined the company in 1991; the same summer, my dad was diagnosed with cancer. Chemotherapy pushed back his lymphoma, and for a number of years he was healthy again, until it returned in 1996. He died early in 1997, at the age of fifty-four. My dad, like all of us, was a bit complex. He was very loving and universally well-respected, but he could also be quite dominating. When he entered a room, everyone knew he was there. As his son, my relationship with him was wonderful, but also somewhat complicated, I now realize. Naturally, he had lots of expectations for me, and I was definitely influenced by them, in both overt and unseen ways. Don't get me wrong; he was an amazing person, mentor, friend, and father. I feel proud and blessed to be his son. I just can see now, from a distance, that the expectations he had pulled on me.

After he died, my mother, brother, and I were responsible for the business, and we found it more challenging than we might have imagined, organizing a plan for its future. In hindsight, I am sure my strong-willed tendencies didn't always help the situation. Nonetheless, in 1998, I became president of Hancock Lumber.

So, there I was, thirty-two years old and not really ready for the job or fully aware of what lay ahead. I was confident I was ready, however. I had lots of leadership energy and competitive spirit that served me both well and poorly, depending upon the circumstance.

The company grew with the housing boom through 2005, and then our sales declined when the banking and housing markets collapsed in 2007. It was an economic storm that challenged even the strongest companies in our industry. The task of reorganizing the company's leadership systems after my dad's death, combined with the stress of the economic collapse, took its toll on me. At the time, I couldn't really see that. I just kept working. I remember lots of mornings during this period being at my office at 6:00 a.m., Saturdays and Sundays included.

My awakening began to take shape shortly thereafter when my mom, a deeply intuitive and spiritual person, introduced me to Deborah Dooley, the evolutionary astrologist.

In the fall of 2008, at the peak of the housing crisis, my mom handed me two discs as a gift.

"I think you will be interested in these," she told me with a thoughtful smile.

A few days later in my home office, I sat alone, listening. Wood paneling and the quiet ping of truth surrounded me. At first, I was numb with disbelief as to how this woman I had never met could know me so well (in some ways, better than I knew myself). With no more information than the date, time, and place of my birth, Deborah was revealing the essence of my being to me. Her soothing voice and thoughtful words stirred my soul.

Upon reflection, I have come to see that moment as the beginning of my personal transformation, so let me share with you what Deborah told me:

> *Evolutionary astrology is rooted in two beliefs: the first is that all of life is interconnected; the second is that we each have a soul that takes us from one lifetime to the next, with the purpose of evolving across incarnations. Individually, and collectively as a species, we all have the intention of evolving across lifetimes.*

A chart accompanied the two audio discs. On the chart there was a circle divided into twelve sections. Astrological symbols were spread across the diagram, and lay scattered in the various sections. Some sections of the circle were empty, and some were full. Lines connected certain aspects of the chart to other areas. It made no sense to me, but Deborah knew this and she patiently began explaining it to me. I was looking at my own natal chart, showing me how the heavens were organized at the place and time of my birth. In addition, it provided a glimpse into the nature of my most recent past life, and the direction my soul wished to take in this one.

> *Your natal chart is your blueprint, Kevin. It provides insight into the origins of your past lives and it shows your destiny in this lifetime. The chart reveals the lessons that you came here to learn. We come into each life with a set of energies, but those energies have a high end and a low end; therefore, there are many possible destinies for you.*

Holy shit! That's some chart, I thought to myself, upon hearing it all explained.

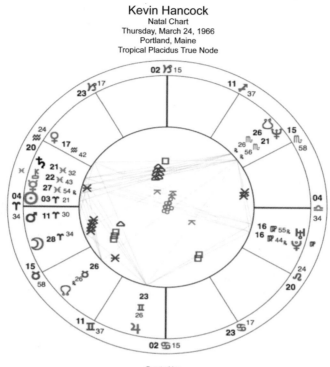

Kevin Hancock
Natal Chart
Thursday, March 24, 1966
Portland, Maine
Tropical Placidus True Node

Created by
Deborah Dooley

Deborah proceeded to tell me that I had a lot of Aries energy (so much so, that it is rare), with my moon, my sun, and my rising sign all residing in my Aries house. Aries loves adventure and exploration. It has the intention of developing courage within oneself, but, playing the role of leader, as Aries often do, masks fear. As I listened, I could definitely see myself in that context.

> *Doing the same thing all the time will give you a sense of restlessness, Kevin. You have a tremendous amount of power. You are an extremely powerful character. With this much Aries power, you are sure to like your freedom and independence. The low end of Aries energy is aggression, dominance, and impatience. The downside of Aries energy is fear, but Aries don't have much permission to be in contact with their own fear.*

Deborah explains that my Aries energy is balanced, however, because my Aries sun sits in my Pisces house. "And, you can't get more different than that!" Deborah says, with playful emphasis.

You have a lot going on in your Pisces house, the house of the personal unconscious. It is the spiritual house, the window into the past. You have lots of karmic residue from your past life that wants to play itself out in this lifetime. You like having a tribe. This is something you have done before. Pisces energy likes to take care of others—it has lots of heart—it is quite the opposite of Aries energy. In this way, you are balanced.

Next, Deborah tells me about the place that I came into this life from, represented by my south node. For me, this originates in the house of Scorpio.

There is lots of transformation that wants to happen in your unconscious this lifetime. In the old days, Scorpio was known as the house of sex, death, and money, thought to be ruled by the underworld. Today we know Scorpio to be the house of the Shaman. The Shaman is the spiritual leader—the priest, pastor, or tribal medicine man that people look to for guidance, wisdom, and security. That's the background of your past life.

The house of sex, death and money, I think to myself. *How fun!*

Deborah continues by describing my past life experience in more detail.

In your past life, you were a person of status, wisdom, and control. In fact, you had so much power—you were looked up to so much—that you lost yourself in the role of leader. This happens quite often to leaders. Movie stars are a good example. Elvis, for instance, was dying inside. He kept getting larger in the external world, but we could see something was not right on the inside. Michael Jackson would likely be another example. Finally, they just do themselves in, because they become so lost in their role that they don't know how to be a person any longer. You had a great sense of obligation, duty, and caretaking for the tribe in your past life. Your life was very public. You didn't have any personal life. That is what is familiar to you.

I press pause on the recording. A feeling of numbness surrounds me. The truth of Deborah's words has frozen me in place. Some time passes. Eventually, I reach back out to my laptop and click "play."

In every lifetime we are here to accomplish different things, Kevin. What has been accomplished in one lifetime holds no spiritual value to be repeated in the next. Getting to the top is celebrated in our society, but for someone who has already done that (like yourself)—to repeat that—is to miss the opportunity to grow. Repeating this is not your path in this lifetime.

As Deborah continues, the connections strike deeper.

In your past life you were born into a position where power was naturally given to you, like a king to a prince. You were very capable as a leader, but your position was given to you. A part of you knew this, that you never really accomplished it on your own, and it left you with a sense that something was missing.

That story line fits this life, as well, I think to myself. Perhaps, in this way, my lessons are being repeated.

Deborah continues by explaining that Jupiter sits in my third house, the house of Gemini. A host of small squares sits beside it, denoting the non-harmonious aspects of my past life experience.

There were some serious missteps in your past life, personal evolution, as a result of your leadership role. You had a problem with communication. You were very challenged to see outside of your own reality. You had little tolerance for different perspectives and other realities. You had lots of compassion for humanity, but more in a global way. People easily felt overpowered by you.

With a bit of humor, Deborah adds that with all that Gemini energy, she is pretty sure that I like to talk a lot! She then continues, speaking about the difference between my purpose in this life and the last one.

Where you are coming from is complex, Kevin. You come into this life with lots of survival energy (Aries) and lots of caretaking energy (Pisces). Where you are headed is simpler—Taurus energy itself is simple—it's the ability to just be. It's about taking in what you have acquired and manifested so deeply, that you have the sense of complete contentment and fulfillment. That's not something that comes easy for you. Think of a lion, basking in the African sun; that's Taurus energy. That's where your soul wants to go. It wants this life to be about enjoyment more so than achievement.

In a calm and patient voice, Deborah tells me that getting there will not be easy.

You have a powerful soul and it needs to do some real internal work in this lifetime. Anything you do for yourself, that deepens your sense of self, is right for you. Anything that gives you a sense of your soul being fulfilled . . . still . . . peaceful . . . calm . . . content . . . deep inside you . . . that creates a space for a deeper connection with yourself; those things are good for you. This will not come easy for you, Kevin. It will feel easier to keep returning to the public leadership roles, to governing. But, this isn't your destiny in this lifetime, despite the skill and the pull. This life is about calming down the power you carry inside you. This life is about seeing your own personal truth outside your role as leader.

As the first disc ends, I eject it and put in the second one. I feel alone in the truth of what this woman, whom I have neither met nor spoken to, is describing.

You will continue to be a leader, but HOW you lead wants to be transformed in this lifetime. If you miss this . . . if you go backwards . . . there will be some learning lessons, some of which will likely come to you through your health.

Deborah tells me "we" know this because Pluto sits in my sixth house, the house of health.

Deborah then teaches me about the "transits of Pluto" and how they point to certain periods in my life, past and present, where the winds of change shall blow.

The tenth house is your career house. That house is empty for you (meaning there are no symbols present in that house). That means your career is not the most important thing for you in this lifetime. You will, of course, continue to have a career, but just understand that career building is not your core purpose in this lifetime. Next year (2009), Pluto will begin a long transit through your career house, lasting until the year 2020. During this period, you are going to desire a lot of changes in relationship to the role you've been playing in your work. These changes are normal and good. It is important for you to understand them as the source of your restlessness. This is a time not to make hasty changes. The role you felt obligated and duty-bound to . . . the role you became over-identified with . . . you are going to want to change your relationship with that role. It is important to understand that change for you, Kevin, is going to be more internal than external. You could very well keep doing the same thing and be completely rewired on the inside. Then, your work would hold a different space inside of you, and others, in turn, would likely begin to experience your leadership differently. Don't move prematurely. I know you feel restless, Kevin.

Deborah concludes with a final message.

Men in our culture don't tend to open themselves to their unconscious struggles. That is why, in part, you see so much anger and frustration in the world today. You will need support as you make this journey, Kevin. Pay special attention to the people who you feel connected to, who invite more inquiry within you. Also, look for a community where you can have no responsibility as caretaker. Look for a place where you can allow yourself to be served. Big changes are coming, Kevin. You are becoming aware of the patterns you wish to change. Many blessings to you.

––––––––––

Winter came and went, as it has always done. A circle ended, and then started again from its place of origin.

Work, basketball, voice therapy complemented by Botox injections, and correspondence with my new friends at Pine Ridge occupied my Maine winter. As always, there was plenty to do.

––––––––––

The sound familiar to all airline travelers chimes through the cabin, informing passengers that the use of approved electronic devices is now permitted on JetBlue flight #493, with nonstop service from Boston to Denver. By now, it is early spring and six months have passed since Pinky first met me at the Rapid City baggage claim. I am headed back to Pine Ridge where something there is calling me in, calling me home.

Out the small airplane window, I can see that the landscape has changed. The eastern woodlands have given way to the great rivers and farm fields of the Midwest. I sit in silence as my attention drifts back to the two comments Deborah made at the conclusion of my natal chart reading—before we ever met, before I ever contemplated traveling to Pine Ridge, and before I lost the full use of my voice:

> *Look for a community where you can have no responsibility as care-taker. Look for a place where you can allow yourself to be served.*

> *If you go backwards, there will likely be learnings that materialize through your health.*

As my flight barreled west, snacks were served. When the stewardess indicated my turn had arrived, I chose animal crackers, which I love. I began eating away, but then paused when I came to a horse-shaped cracker. The horse has new meaning for me now. As much as the Lakota of the nineteenth century were the "buffalo people," they were also the "horse people." The Lakota, the buffalo, the plains, and the horse formed a magical quadrangle that resulted in unprecedented freedom, mobility, and self-sufficiency into the farthest reaches of the northern plains. Ironically, the horses they rode were descendants of the small herds the Spanish conquistadors brought. The very people that began the continent's colonization brought the horse with them, which symbolized nineteenth-century Lakota independence. We think of the horse as one of many icons of the American West, yet at the time of Spanish arrival, there weren't any here. There were no pigs, no cows, no sheep, no apples, and no potatoes, either. The Europeans, who in God's name conquered the continent, brought the tools, seeds, and live-stock that formed the basis for their view of proper land use. America before the Europeans was a very different place than we might imagine.

Who else looks at a horse-shaped animal cracker and has such thoughts? I ask myself.

Then, I eat the horse.

As my plane continues west, I have voices on my mind. Historically, the people of Pine Ridge have been marginalized by the society that conquered them. They must feel as if, in some ways, their voice has been stolen. For different reasons, I can relate. I know what it feels like to lose a voice.

In the spring of 2010, approximately eighteen months after I had my natal chart read, I began to have trouble speaking. The process was gradual, and for some time I didn't notice the trends that were developing. For a while, I thought I had a sore throat or a cold that simply would not go away. I found myself straining to speak. I could get all the words out, but it just felt uncomfortable. In response, I unknowingly began dipping my chin into my chest while speaking, in an effort to compensate. Other bad habits followed, and soon people were asking me what was wrong. This was all quite ironic because if I was well known for anything, it was probably public speaking. Kevin, the public speaker, was losing his voice.

The symptoms got steadily worse, so I went to my primary-care physician in Portland. I was then referred to a specialist across town. The specialist put me through a series of tests, my least favorite of which was the black camera tube that got inserted through my nose and down into my throat. The doctor failed to put forth a specific diagnosis and suggested some therapy, but my condition continued to deteriorate. Later that year, while having Thanksgiving dinner at my brother's house, a fellow dinner guest from the medical profession listened to me speak for less than two minutes and said confidently, "I know what you have. You have spasmodic dysphonia [SD]."

That night, I searched the term on the Internet; the description seemed to fit, so I went back to see my specialist. He was less than impressed by the Thanksgiving diagnosis, but he did refer me this time to another specialist. A few weeks later, I was sitting in front of Dr. Song at the Massachusetts Eye and Ear Infirmary in Boston. After another series of voice tests, a CAT scan, and more black camera tubes through my nose, I was diagnosed. The Thanksgiving dinner guest was right: I had SD.

On February 10, 2011, I had my first treatment. There is no known cure for SD, but its symptoms can be managed, partially. The treatment involves periodic injections of botulinum toxin (Botox) into the voice box. So, once every three months or so, I drive to Boston for an early morning appointment. In the tiny procedure room on the eleventh floor, high above the Charles River, Dr. Song and I visit before he gives me an injection. The actual procedure takes about four minutes, and then I go. The process is not an exact science, as each patient reacts differently and requires a unique dose. Sometimes the procedure has a positive effect, and other times it doesn't work at all. During the best result periods, I have no tightness or pain in my throat when I speak. Slowly, however, the Botox, which serves as a muscle relaxant, wears off and the difficultly speaking returns again. The drug does not cure the underlying disorder; it simply masks the symptoms for a time.

Many people who aquire the disorder end up with a "choppy" voice which breaks in and out like the satellite radio in my car on a Maine country road. I, however, experience the disorder differently. My voice does break off at times, but the biggest problem for me is the pain, tightness, and loss of air that accompanies speech. At its worst, SD can leave me gasping for air after a single sentence. I often feel as if it takes a major athletic surge of force to even talk at all. My strained voice dips deep down into my throat as all the muscles in the region spasm, contract, and fight each other in a chaotic and panicked scramble to force out just a few words.

From a medical perspective, the exact cause of SD is unknown. It is believed that SD issues begin at the base of the brain in the basal ganglia, which regulates involuntary muscle movement. The disease is rare. The National Spasmodic Dysphonia Association estimates 50,000 people in North America have the disorder, which puts the odds of me acquiring it at 0.009 percent. SD commonly begins without explanation, often with people in their forties.

While medical science says there is no known cause (or cure) for the disorder, deep inside I know why I got SD. It was my body's way of warning me that I needed to change. My SD came on during the peak of my stress in relation to my leadership roles within my own tribe. As the housing market collapsed, my protective leadership inclinations intensified. Without consciously knowing it, I had internalized all the responsibility for my tribe's security. Under duress, I had reverted back to the familiar karmic patterns Deborah had described, from my past life experiences. In response to my prolonged instinctive reaction, my body struck back.

Today, despite the "pain in the neck" that SD can be, I tell people it was a blessing that I received it. It was the push I needed to see who I wanted to become, and to really, truly commit to changing and letting go. My SD was a sign and I could see it. It was a blessing.

I didn't necessarily need to change my roles (for example, change jobs); I just needed to change my relationship to those roles. The change that needed to occur was internal, not external. It all suddenly seemed so clear. I began the process of talking less, trusting more, spending time on me, empowering others, mentoring others and inviting more people to lead. I ended up inviting everyone to lead—every manager, every employee, and every customer. I transformed my view of our company from something I led, to something they led. I stopped viewing myself as the leader, and began to see myself as the facilitator, as the person who could give away power. I learned to ask questions. I learned to listen. I learned to be patient at crucial moments, where previously I would have responded with decisive action.

I truly believe SD saved my life, uplifted our company, and opened the door for me at Pine Ridge. Pine Ridge is that place Deborah referred to as being just for me, that place where I have no responsibility and I can just allow my soul to be served.

These were my thoughts as I sat in seat 3F, while flight #493 began its final descent into Denver.

It does not require many words to speak the truth.

—Chief Joseph of the Nez Perce

I could feel a new sun rising for me in the Land of Crazy Horse, and I was excited to return.

Even though I am increasingly living with my heart, not my head, I still know that data is valuable. In my time between trips to Pine Ridge, I found myself doing lots of research, trying to make sense of what I had seen. I needed to put some data and context to the stark economic conditions and social challenges I encountered there.

Every five years or so, the Bureau of Indian Affairs (BIA) issues a document titled, "The American Indian Population and Labor Force Report." Local leaders from the 561 federally recognized tribes certify that the data is accurate.

As of the 2005 report, the total tribal enrollment across America was 1,978,099. As a percentage of the available workforce across the entire tribal population, unemployment was 49 percent. In August 2005, unemployment across America stood at 4.8 percent. The disparity of economic opportunity between Indian and non-Indian in modern-day America is statistically stunning; when you look more closely at Pine Ridge, the numbers get even worse.

Of the 115,513 tribally enrolled Indians in South Dakota in 2005, 43,146 of them lived or accessed services at Pine Ridge—the largest enrollment of any reservation in the Great Plains region. In 2005, 32 percent of Pine Ridge's population was "not available for work," due to age, disability or health conditions. Of those eligible to work, 89 percent were unemployed. As a result, only 7 percent of the total population at Pine Ridge was employed in 2005 according to the BIA.

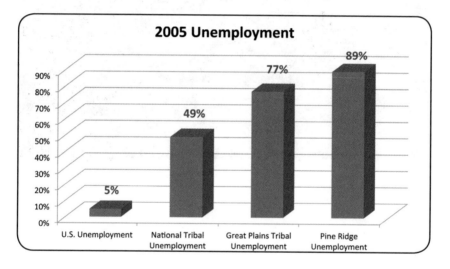

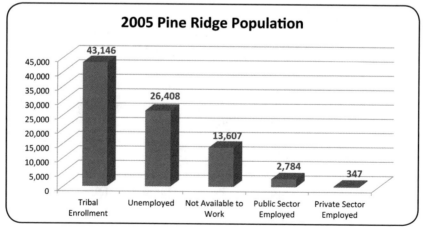

Every time I look at these statistics, it causes me to just stop. Hancock Lumber has more private-sector jobs than the entire Pine Ridge Reservation. I sit motionless and stare into my laptop screen. The data is so dramatic that I checked it with multiple sources. Consider, for example, the following statistics from the American Indian Humanitarian Foundation (www.4aihf.org) as of January 31, 2013:

- 97 percent of the Pine Ridge population lives below the federal poverty line.

- Heart disease is twice the national average.

- The infant mortality rate is the highest in North America (300 percent above the national average).

- Annual median income is $2,600 to $3,500.

- Nearly two-thirds of all homes are considered "severely substandard" (without water, electricity, insulation, or septic).

- Average life expectancy is 45 to 48 for men and 52 for women, surpassed in the Western Hemisphere only by Haiti.

- The teen suicide rate is 150 percent higher than the national average.

- The diabetes rate is 800 percent higher than the national average.

- The school dropout rate is over 70 percent, and teacher turnover is 800 percent higher than the national average.

- Alcoholism affects eight out of ten families on the reservation, and the death rate from alcohol-related problems is 300 percent higher than the national average.

The statistics are overwhelming. They reinforce what I saw with my own eyes during my first visit—no commerce, no jobs.

Maybe nothing ever happens once and is finished.

—William Faulkner

As statistics and images of oppression, idleness, and dependency dance in my head, the flight attendant asks us all to make final preparations for landing. A few moments later, I am back on the ground in the American West.

My flight lands shortly after 11:20 a.m. to crystal blue skies above the snowcapped Rockies. A warm breeze blows from the northwest. It is already 71 degrees. I ride the shuttle bus to the Enterprise Rent-A-Car lot where a cadre of sharply dressed young men and women greets me. Nicholas assists me at the counter, and then accompanies me outside to select a car.

"Which one would you like?" he asks, as we cross the pavement.

"Anything that is not white," I reply, knowing full well this time where I am going and how much mud, dust, and dirt is in my future.

At 1:00 p.m., I pull into the small town of Kersey, situated northeast of Denver. Pickup trucks are everywhere; I have the only car I can see. I love towns like this, and I find myself lingering as I keep taking pictures of this authentic piece of the American West. Periodically, some of the locals stare at me, as if they can't imagine what I am photographing.

I have committed to avoiding the use of GPS technology this week. It seems counter to my solo journey, and the mission of disengaging. I have my maps instead. I am confident in my ability to self-navigate.

Sure enough, it doesn't take long before I am lost—really lost.

When was the last time you were truly lost? I mean lost, as in you didn't know what state you were in?

I can't really tell you anything about this picture, because I was totally lost when I took it!

The roads have all turned to dirt. I know I am either in Colorado, Wyoming, or Nebraska, but I am not sure which. There are no houses. No towns. Just fields and pastures, as far as the eye can see. I am happily lost, however, in a desolate but beautiful place where silence rules and old buildings stand as long as they can, before piling upon themselves. Nothing is torn down here. Mother Nature must do that work herself.

It seemed appropriate that I was lost. Since my first visit six months ago, I had been pondering many questions about myself and my attraction to Pine Ridge, with few clear answers. I was definitely still searching.

In the months between visits, Pine Ridge was often with me. My heart was strong for the problems and challenges faced by the people who lived there, but I also had a growing understanding that it was their journey to make. Scores of people have come here to "fix" them, to change them. But you can't fix other people; you can only love them and support them. We all must fix ourselves as we see fit. We all must make our own journey. My contribution to Pine Ridge was just being interested. Awareness, in and of itself, is a powerful act.

I am really lost on this dirt road. Not only do I not know where I am, chances are you don't know anyone who has ever been where I am. At one point, I pulled into a nuclear missile silo installation (not kidding; you know the ones that we put in place back in the day, ready to depart for the Soviet Union). I can't help but wonder who this one is aimed at today, and why? I park the car and stand in front of the gate. I can see for miles in all directions. There is not another person in sight, yet I know I am being watched (or, at least recorded). It feels eerie. Studies have shown that you don't need to actually see the presence that is watching you to know that eyes are upon you. How fascinating. How do we know?

I want to take a picture of the missile silo, but instead I stand frozen in place, not daring to do so. Will they arrest me if I photograph this place? Is that illegal?

Finally, I take a breath, gain some courage, and start photographing.

This is the first place I have ever been in the American West where the use of deadly force is pre-authorized. The message on the fence is not complicated. I get the point, get back in the car, and slowly pull away.

In the nineteenth century, it was understood that "deadly force" was authorized in the American West. Today, signs are posted. My, how we've progressed!

But, I am still lost.

Back on the dirt county road, tumbleweeds roll past me. Finally, I come across a rancher on a tractor grading his stretch of road. I then do something my wife says men rarely do; I get out, and ask for directions. In return, he gets off the tractor and provides them.

"At the next intersection turn right on 6. Go straight until you come to 9, then turn left on 9 to 8. Take 8 to 17, then turn left on 17, which will bring you to the interstate," he informs me.

I have nothing to write with, and my short-term memory for such things is notoriously poor.

"Could you repeat that one more time?" I ask. He is kind enough to do so.

"By the way," I ask, "what state are we in?"

"Nebraska," he replies. "We're in Nebraska."

I jog back to my car, repeating the numbers in my head.

As it turns out, I was driving near the precise corner where Colorado, Wyoming, and Nebraska all meet. If you look on a map, you can see it—south of Bushnell, in the area known as Panorama Point (the highest point in Nebraska at 5,424 feet).

"In this life you don't always end up where you think you're going" I say aloud as my car rumbles down the county road.

Eventually I find I-80, but I am now several hours "behind schedule." I worry for a moment about making it to Fort Robinson before dark. In hindsight, being lost in the Nebraska panhandle was one of the highlights of my trip; the worries soon faded. I was just going where my journey wanted to take me.

I join Route 71 north to and through Scottsbluff, Nebraska. The North Platte River runs through Scottsbluff, and as I cross it, I repeat aloud what Red Cloud once said:

I will kill any white man who crosses the North Platte.

In town, I stop for gas and a chocolate shake.

"How many people live in Scottsbluff?" I asked the woman behind the counter.

"Too damn many. Especially in the Walmart parking lot," she responds.

I can tell she has given this answer before and isn't joking. Her grandchildren are playing with blocks at the far end of the counter.

"Here you go, hon," she says with a smile, handing me my shake.

"Thank you," I reply.

As I continue north, I am once again alone on the highway. This land is just so vast. I can feel the isolation, the smallness of man. It's hard to believe there wasn't enough room for everyone, Indians and whites. It is also hard to believe that the army could even find the Indians, let alone catch them.

By now, I have listened to all possible radio stations; country music, talk radio, pop culture, and evangelical channels have all had their say. Sometimes a single push of the button makes it all the way around to the station I was on initially. This time, the dial stops on National Public Radio. NPR is doing a segment on gun control legislation in the American West. The reporter is describing a controversial billboard in Greeley, Colorado (that I might have seen myself today, had I not gotten lost). The billboard has a picture of three traditionally dressed Native Americans with a reminder that surrendering their weapons in exchange for a lifetime of government support did not work out so well for them. The billboard reinforces the innate understanding most Americans have that our nation's promises to care for Native people were a dramatic failure.

The billboard I missed in Greeley, Colorado, because I was lost speaks to our national understanding that we have let Native peoples down. Most Americans intuitively know it is a wrong that has not yet been made right. The circle is broken, unfinished.

It is late in the day as I arrive at Fort Robinson State Park. I am excited to be here. There is always a nervous energy about me at the forts and battlefields, where the Lakota story unfolded. I get butterflies in my stomach, like before playing in a big game. I feel as if I am entering a new zone of proximity to the actual events themselves. Literally, I can *feel* the energy of the events that transpired flowing into me. These sensations are heightened by the fact that I am usually the only person there.

The sign above the main building reads:

Through these portals passed the world's finest horsemen.

I get the impression the sign is referring to the cavalrymen who lived here (not the Lakota warriors they chased), so I am not sure it's accurate. The Nebraska State Historical Society marker nearby tells the fort's story:

FORT ROBINSON

In March, 1874, the US Government authorized the establishment of a military camp at the Red Cloud Indian Agency on the White River. Home of some 13,000 Indians, many of whom were hostile, the Agency was one of the most troublesome spots on the Plains.

Fort Robinson played an important role in the Indian wars from 1876—1890. Crazy Horse surrendered here on May 6, 1877, and was mortally wounded that September while resisting imprisonment. In January 1879, the Fort was the scene of a major battle as the result of the Cheyenne Outbreak led by Chief Dull Knife.

The military is all about straight lines, while the Lakota are all about circles.

Across the street, on the south side of Route 20, a small marker briefly memorializes the events that became known as the Cheyenne Outbreak:

> **One hundred and forty-nine Northern Cheyenne Indians led by Dull Knife were taken into custody by troops from Fort Robinson on October 23, 1878. Imprisoned in the log cavalry barracks, they escaped on January 9, 1879. Fort Robinson soldiers pursued the Cheyenne until the last ones were killed or captured on January 23, 1879.**

There is a lot of history here.

I stand for a long time at the site where Crazy Horse was killed . . . a long time.

Crazy Horse was one of the last Lakota leaders to surrender, and this made many of the reservation's chiefs jealous. Having already transitioned to the reservation system, some saw him as a threat to their status and power. But, this new world of the whites did not interest Crazy Horse. On the night he died, he refused a white man's bed, insisting instead on being placed on the floor. When he died, his friend Touch-the-Clouds pointed to his body and said, "This is the lodge of Crazy Horse." For me, this sentence exemplifies the Lakota understanding that our sacred power lies within.

Disinterested in the ways of the Wasichu to the end, Crazy Horse was never photographed, and his burial site remains a mystery.

I lay my original Wounded Knee necklace on the marker, and consider leaving it there. Ultimately, however, I decide to keep it with me. The necklace is a symbolic reminder of the mysterious quest I am on. It is a reminder that I am searching—searching for what brings me here.

The Fort Robinson historical marker commemorating the spot where Crazy Horse was fatally wounded. My eagle pendant necklace hangs on the right side of the engraved words.

Everything is silent, except the wind blowing through the bare trees and the leaves rustling across the lawn. I feel no urgency to move. I just linger.

Eventually, I do pack up and move on. Nightfall is approaching, and I still have about two hours of driving left in order to get to the Singing Horse Trading Post. I leave Fort Robinson in a reflective silence. The radio is off as I drive through Crawford (population 1,107), wondering to myself how often they change that sign.

As the sun sets on what feels like me and only me, I stop the car at the final historical marker of the day.

BUTTE COUNTRY

Perhaps no spot in Nebraska is so surrounded by historical and geographical landmarks as this one. Numerous landmarks of the period of the Indian Wars are visible from here. The site of a legendary battle between the Sioux and Crow Indians, Crow Butte, lies directly to the south. It was also a pioneer landmark for Indians, soldiers, and cattlemen.

> *Approximately half a mile northwest of this point is the site of the Treaty Tree. There, in September 1875, while thousands of members of the Sioux Indian Nation looked on, the Allison Commission made an unsuccessful attempt to buy the Black Hills area from the Indians. It was not until after the bloody campaigns of 1876 that the Sioux Commission, headed by George Manypenny, succeeded in purchasing the area.*

I look around, turning 360 degrees. I am able to picture the scenes that the historical marker describes. History lives here; at least, it does for me. I think about how much the world has changed in a short period of time. The very concept of navigation by landmarks is all but gone from our planet today. When was the last time you used a natural landmark to identify where you were and in what direction you needed to travel?

Indians fought Indians here. Indians fought whites here. This land was controlled by whoever was the strongest. In fact, it still is.

I stand on this site until the sun is no longer visible, before returning to my car and moving on.

The last town before Pine Ridge is the unincorporated, alcohol-dispensing town of White Clay, Nebraska.

At 8:30 p.m. I pass carefully through White Clay, my least favorite town in Nebraska. I don't want to hit anybody wandering across the road, and it is actually something I look out for. A couple dozen people are lingering in small, scattered groups in this town that only exists to sell alcohol to Indians.

Later on, deep inside the reservation, "Devil Woman" by Cliff Richard plays on the radio as I drive through the abandoned streets of Manderson, under the watchful eyes of high street lamps.

> *I drank that potion she offered me*
> *I found myself on the floor*
> *Then I looked into those big green eyes*
> *And I wondered what I'd come here for*

I pass Pinky's Store and say "Hi, Pinky" out loud. A few people are outside, but they are well outnumbered by the stray dogs.

Still heading north, I pass the intersection for BIA 14, and soon thereafter turn right onto the private dirt road that winds its way up to the Singing Horse Trading Post. It is 9:08 p.m. when I put the car in "park" and get out and open the gate. Gordon Lightfoot's "Sundown" is playing on the radio.

> *Sometimes I think it's a sin*
> *When I feel like I'm winnin' when I'm losin' again.*

The same warm breeze that greeted me in Denver welcomes me back to Pine Ridge.

———

The next morning I find myself alone at the kitchen table after an inconsistent night's rest. I never seem to require much sleep in the Land of Crazy Horse.

A single log rises from the floor to the ceiling in the center of the room. My back is to "my" bedroom. To my right, I look out the casement windows to the west. It is sometime before 7:00 a.m. Rosie has early business in Rapid City and has already left.

It was great to see Rosie last night. We hugged and sat on her blue sectional couch, catching up. My voice was weak, but we sat close enough together in the quiet room to converse successfully. It has only been six months since we first met, but we talk now like friends.

Rosie asks about my drive from Denver and I laugh, perplexing her with my description of the route I took to get here. I then begin talking about Fort Robinson, which prompts Rosie to tell me about the Crazy Horse ride her friend Bamm Brewer leads each year. The four-day horseback ride begins at Fort Robinson and ends at Pine Ridge. Hundreds of young Lakota make the trip, camping along the way and telling stories about their history, culture, and traditions.

I want to go on the Crazy Horse ride! This is my immediate reaction. I wonder if I could make it and keep up? *Not sure about that*, I think to myself.

I need to leave shortly, as I am scheduled to meet Lester Lone Hill at the Oglala Sioux Tribe Partnership for Housing office at 8:00 a.m. My first trip to Pine Ridge revealed a housing crisis that impacts most families on the reservation. The housing problems, like other issues at Pine Ridge, are so dramatic that they seem overwhelming and unfixable. I reflected upon the housing issues in the weeks after I returned home from my first visit, and, while it was clear I could not "fix" the problem, I certainly could do something to help. So, I worked with Pinky and Lester to design a simple home that would fit on a vacant lot just a short drive from their office. Mark Hopkins, the manager of our store back in Bridgton, Maine, helped me produce a list of materials that would be needed to build it. Our purchasing office invited our vendors to participate by donating materials, and a few, like Andersen Windows, stepped forward to help, donating all the windows for the home. The majority of the materials were simply taken out of our own stock inventory, donated by us, and loaded into a container. We then hired a trucking company to transport the container across the country to the vacant lot in a neighborhood just south of town, known as Fraggle Rock. Today is the day the container arrives, and I am going to help unload it.

Monica Evans, from our sawmill shipping office, told me last week that the container would be at the building site by 8:00 a.m., and that we would only have three hours to unload it, as part of the shipping price.

I smiled when I heard this, but said nothing.

Those deadlines are such an East Coast thing, I thought to myself. *They don't mean much here on the reservation.*

I leave Rosie's house at 7:30 a.m. The air is crisp, but not cold. All the animals turn to greet me. Tails start wagging as the screen door closes behind me. The cats pause to consider me. All the pets live outside here. It sounds silly to even say that, actually; of course they do. The houses at Pine Ridge barely have enough room for all the people, and the dog's place in Lakota society has always been outside. In Maine, dogs and cats are house pets, but that's not how it goes at Pine Ridge (which the animals here seem to be completely fine with).

Rosie's dogs (Rowdy, Melo, and Buffalo) act like they know me. They don't get up at first. Instead, they just wag their tails in the dirt. Eventually, they rise and meet me at the car. I sit in the driver's seat as they take turns putting their front paws on my lap. I talk them back out of my car and say good-bye, promising to return.

American flags snap toward the south in the stiff morning breeze, and there is a lot of trash blowing around as I drive through Wounded Knee. I am always drawn to the American flags at Pine Ridge. Like military service itself, they are common here. Occasionally, I pass a flag flying upside down. Other flags I have seen have a mounted Lakota warrior inposed upon them. The Lakota have such a paradoxical and complex relationship with their government.

Tell them at Washington if they have one man who speaks the truth to send him to me, and I will listen to what he has to say.

—Sitting Bull, 1867

To many at Pine Ridge, it feels as if the distress calls have gone unanswered.

The flag should never be displayed with the union down, except as a signal of dire distress in instances of extreme danger to life or property.

—Section 176(a), US Flag Code

Mornings are quiet here. As I drive south toward the town of Pine Ridge, I pass only a few cars and see even fewer people. I arrive at the small office of the OST Partnership for Housing shortly before 8:00 a.m. Rosemarie Dillingham is the only person there. Rosemarie is the office manager, and she sits at the lone desk in the tiny reception area. Rosemarie has gray hair and a constant supply of enthusiasm. Like many people I have met at Pine Ridge, Rosemarie is smart, thoughtful, and highly intuitive. She is happy to see me; we hug and visit. Lester has not arrived yet.

After a while, I decide to drive down to the construction site by myself and see if anyone is there to start unloading. Upon arrival, I talk for a few minutes with the truck driver. He has no idea who I am. He doesn't know I have donated all these materials and then flown out here to help unload them. A few minutes later, a forklift comes into view driving up the side of the road. The man operating the forklift works for the housing authority. I tell him I was scheduled to meet a group here at 8:00 a.m. to unload the trailer.

"Well, that's Indian time. It starts when you get there," he laughs.

Another guy from the housing authority shows up a few minutes later. Seeing the Colorado license plate on my car he says, "Bring some of that legal marijuana up with you next time."

We all laugh.

We soon realize a forklift won't help, and that everything will need to be unloaded by hand. Shortly after this realization, the two guys from the housing authority leave. I am by myself again.

Lester arrives eventually and we greet each other happily.

No one has given too much thought as to where the workers will come from to unload this trailer. Lester decides the prison would be a good source of assistance, and leaves to go get some inmates. He returns frustrated by how much paperwork is now required. He says he needs to go back to the office and type a letter to the judge. Again, it is just me there. It is now well after 9:00 a.m., and we haven't even unlatched the trailer door.

Then, Pinky arrives! We are happy to see each other. Pinky is always full of energy, ideas, and next moves. She never stops thinking and planning. Today, for example, she wants me join the National Low Income Housing Coalition.

Pinky is excited about this home, and I start to get the sense that even one small house is a big deal for this community. Pinky tells me that it will "give a good family who has fallen through the cracks a chance to live in a decent home." Pinky goes on to speak about the four Lakota values: bravery, generosity, fortitude, and wisdom.

"Wisdom doesn't come until you are old," she tells me.

A friend of Pinky's arrives wearing a Washington Nationals baseball cap. I am surprised to see that cap, so I ask him about it.

"Oh, I have a good friend with season tickets there," he replies, and then it hits me.

It does make sense. Washington, D.C., is very important here. In fact, Washington, D.C., matters as much here as it does anywhere in America. D.C. is where the money comes from. The BIA, HUD, the Department of Health and Human Services, welfare checks, social security checks, food subsidies, used FEMA trailers for housing—all of it comes from D.C.

Irony is one of my favorite words to describe Pine Ridge. The place that perhaps likes Washington the least is also the place most dependent upon it.

Maybe that isn't so ironic, after all. Being dependent upon your colonizer for well over a century can't possibly foster goodwill and appreciation.

As we wait for prisoners to be released (it's close to 10:00 a.m. by now), the East Coast blood in me keeps looking at the trailer and thinking, *Well, let's just get started anyway.* No one else seems to be in a hurry. The driver, having traveled through the night to get here, has gone to sleep for the day in the bed in his cab, without seeming to care about the unloading time.

As we continue to wait, Pinky's friend begins talking about the "old-time Indians."

"They were tougher than hell," he explains. "Most people don't realize that life on the plains was feast or famine for them."

This was also true for the early settlers in the region.

"It was the isolation that really got to the early white homesteaders," he continues. "If you read the letters they wrote back home, that is what they speak of, the isolation and deprivation. It was a tough existence."

The view of the neighborhood from the vacant lot where the new house, with the materials Hancock Lumber has donated, will be built.

I am sitting on the back of the tractor-trailer just kicking my feet.

At least now the door is open, I think to myself.

As I look north across the field, the big blue water tower that reads PINE RIDGE in white letters stands out in the distance. All the products are still inside the enclosed container on the truck, waiting to be unloaded. I realize I don't care. I am just happy to be here and excited about what I am doing. I can move at this pace. It's refreshing.

The neighborhood itself is a collection of small ranch-style homes. There are no garages. There are no second floors. Each home looks pretty much like the next one. There is quite a bit of trash and stuff lying around.

The workers from the prison never materialize, but Lester and Pinky do round up five young guys somehow, and we spend the next four and a half hours together unloading the lumber and building materials that will become the new home. All the products in the trailer must be taken out by hand, one piece at a time, and reloaded in a gray storage container. Pinky has organized volunteer work groups to help build the home over the summer, with a completion goal of early August.

This is the foundation for the "Hancock House," as Pinky calls it, and the group of local volunteers Pinky and Lester rounded up to unload the trailer.

In preparing for this trip, I had envisioned arranging a series of somewhat formal interviews with a list of set questions I wanted to ask. I was soon reminded, however, that the best opportunities for learning are often informal, this one included.

The five of us go to work unloading the trailer piece by piece, talking as we go. It is hard work. By the time we finish, our shirts are wet with sweat. Most of the guys are very interested in sports. In turn, I am very interested in them. One of the young men is wearing a New England Patriots T-shirt, representing Maine's favorite NFL team. The Pats are his favorite as well.

"So, where's Maine?" he wants to know.

I am happy about the time I spend unloading the trailer. I don't think all the guys realize exactly who I am. I know for a fact a couple of them think I am the truck driver. They were all confused when I told them I flew to Denver. As far as I was concerned, this was perfect. I don't want to be a chief or a public figure here. I love the anonymity of it all, and I can see the good in each of them by the time we are done.

In the middle of the unloading process, Pinky grabs me for a brief lunch at the Pine Ridge Retreat Center. I didn't want to go at the time.

I didn't want to leave the crew and the work of unloading, but Pinky insisted. The quick break for lunch turned out to be great.

At the Retreat Center, I meet the pastor, Karen Rupp. Karen is a small but peacefully energetic woman with bright eyes and a knowing smile. Along with a few other people who are already there, we share sandwiches, pasta salad, and fruit punch. Over lunch, Karen describes the work of the center that includes providing meals for those who stop by (which happens regularly while I am there). Anyone who wants a lunch knocks on the door and one of the local Lakota volunteers brings a sandwich down the half flight of stairs leading to the main entrance. Knocks sound on the door every thirty to forty-five seconds during the course of my visit. Boxes of clothing are scattered outside, and a few people come by and go through them.

Boxes of donated clothing are scattered across the picnic tables outside the Pine Ridge Retreat Center.

As lunch time ends, a local Lakota pastor walks in with his wife. The pair is accompanied by an elderly woman with a significant walking handicap. She moves slowly up the stairs, working her way to a seat at one of the white plastic tables that fills the kitchen. By now, there are eight to ten people in the room. Everyone becomes involved in the conversation. People are eager to tell me more about Pine Ridge. Everyone seems quite willing to describe the challenges facing their community:

"People lose hope here."

"The life expectancy is forty-five for males."

"Two to four families share most homes.
Multiple generations live in almost every home."

"Over 85 percent of the people who live here are
unemployed."

"New possessions are questioned here. Everybody worries that everybody
else is on the take."

"People often sell their food stamps two for one [$20.00 of food stamps
for $10.00 of cash]. People have non-food needs too."

Throughout the entire conversation, people knock on the door regularly as they come by for food. It is lunchtime at Pine Ridge.

After lunch, Karen shows me some of the local jewelry and artwork she helps people sell. In the process, I ask Karen the same question I have been pondering myself for the past six months.

"Karen, what brings you here?"

"It's a calling," she humbly replies.

The rest of the trailer still needs to be unloaded, so Karen and I share a hug as I prepare to leave. I don't need to know someone very long before I will hug them.

As I start down the stairs to leave the Retreat Center, the woman with the crutches calls out to me, "Do you know what my last name is?"

I try to never hurry a conversation here, so I stop, turn, lean on the thin metal rail by the stairs, and give her my full attention.

"No," I reply with interest. "What is your last name?"

"Short Bull. My last name is Short Bull."

Smiles fill the room, as everyone seems to know what is coming next.

"*Short* describes my temper, and *Bull* describes my toughness," she tells me proudly.

The entire room has a good laugh. Big smiles are everywhere. I wave good-bye and head back down the stairs. As I open the door, I can see that a storm is coming. The temperature is falling.

Everyone I have ever met at Pine Ridge has been friendly and kind to me. People here have big hearts. As I walk across the gravel parking lot, I can't help but think that Pine Ridge is a place that gives you a piece of its heart and takes a piece of yours in return.

———

Everyone was all smiles as we shook hands and went our separate ways at the end of the day. Go Patriots!

It's well after 2:30 p.m. when the trailer is finally unloaded. Afterward, I hang out at the OST Partnership for Housing office where I buy two dream catchers from a young couple that needs gas money to get home. People here live that close to the edge. Subsistence, for many, is day to day.

By the time I begin the drive back to Singing Horse, it is late afternoon. I turn the dial to KILI Radio. On this afternoon, the Tribal Council happens to be meeting, and KILI is covering it live.

"Every time one of our elders passes, our language goes with them," one speaker states.

The conversation turns to housing. Apparently there is an initiative under-way to obtain one thousand used FEMA trailers. It is not clear when the trailers will be available. The discussion becomes animated when the subject turns to *who* will get the trailers once they arrive. One woman steps to the microphone and asks, "When am I going to get my trailer?"

Another woman comes forward with a similar inquiry.

"Who is going to get them? How are you going to allocate these trailers?" she asks.

This brief discussion highlights one of the unique aspects of the Pine Ridge economy. Most resources come from the government, and there is never enough for everyone. So, how do these scarce resources get allocated? By what system are they divided up? This is the political side of Pine Ridge, and it is full of controversy, distrust, and waiting; most of all, there is waiting.

Pine Ridge may be the most government-centric community in America. This is understandable and puzzling at the same time. It is understandable because the reservation was founded upon the premise of government care; and, clearly, that care is still required for survival at Pine Ridge today.

Someone at Pine Ridge once said to me, "The government said we would not be capable of taking care of ourselves; therefore, they needed to be our guardians, our caretakers. Okay, well, let's look at the job they have done. Let's look at how that has gone."

This is the baffling, political side of Pine Ridge, as government has had over 130 years to dispense resources, empower residents, and create economic opportunity. By any statistical measurement, that process has produced an economic disaster; yet, people here continue to look to the government for solutions. If the definition of insanity is doing the same thing and expecting different results, could the modern-day government-centric culture of Pine Ridge be viewed as crazy? I am curious to know if people who live here think that another 20, 40, or 100 years of government-led solutions will produce something different, or more of the same?

Most residents here believe that since the government made promises in the second half of the nineteenth century, they should be held accountable for keeping them. Even if those promises are the very thing standing in the way of Pine Ridge evolving, should the people who live here still fight to make sure they are kept?

In an abstract sense, it is like fighting to retain the very system that holds you down. I can't say I know what is right, and the decisions are not mine to make, but these are the thoughts that come to my mind as I drive back to Rosie's. I have been told that there are over eight hundred government programs which direct funds and resources to Pine Ridge. If this is true, that is approximately one government program for every forty-five people who live here. It is hard to see momentum for a stronger and more independent Lakota future coming from this direction. In Lakota spirituality, the direction one faces is considered to be important.

————————

As afternoon turns to early evening, I am sitting in the grass, leaning on a wooden fence post looking down over the Singing Horse Trading Post. I have been walking the fields and just sitting with the horses for nearly two hours, doing nothing, one might say. Silence surrounds me as a light wind blows. The air is always moving here in the Land of Crazy Horse.

My favorite fence lines in the world are in the hills above the Singing Horse Trading Post. They tell a story if you sit there quietly and listen.

At the dinner table at Singing Horse later that night, I find myself in the company of four women who are all friends of Rosie's. It is my lucky night, they tell me! Rosie has prepared turkey, peas, salad, and bread. The room is cozy and the conversation is warm and open.

Other than Rosie, Catherine Grey Day is the only person at dinner I have met before. Catherine lives in one side of the small trailer beside Rosie's house and helps out around the Trading Post from time to time. Catherine is a resilient woman. The weathered lines on her beautifully worn face tell the story of a lifetime of reservation living on the northern plains. Her gray hair is pulled back in a ponytail, and glasses rest upon her nose above her near-permanent smile. When Catherine smiles, the whole world seems to get a bit brighter.

"What has changed through the years?" I ask the group.

"Clusters," is the first reply.

The term is used to describe the reservation's housing communities. In earlier times, people lived more remotely, spread apart from each other. In recent decades people have moved, or been moved, down into small villages along the highway.

"When I was a kid, we had no electricity. Kerosene lamps lit our evenings. We were outside all day. We read a lot at night. There was no running water. We had outdoor toilets. We got around when we needed to with horses and a wagon," someone else explains.

I am constantly reminded that history is young here.

I ask about the difficulties and challenges of life on the reservation.

"Well, we kind of have to laugh it off. There is not much we can do about it. Go with the flow, you know. We need that Lakota sense of humor to survive here," someone comments.

The sentence *There is not much we can do about it* reminds me of what I was told about my own voice when I was first diagnosed. My situation was described as incurable. Drugs were the only way to soften the hard edges of the disorder.

"Be careful with whom you align," one of the women confides.

This is a consistent theme across the reservation, and I have been told this before. Everything is political here.

"I am a recovering alcoholic. I am also a recovering Catholic," Catherine says with her now-familiar smile.

Everyone has a big laugh at this.

"Boarding school, that's where I lost my language," Catherine continues. "So many atrocities have been committed for many generations."

"Why is alcoholism so problematic here?" I ask.

"We are lacking an enzyme, so we can't really handle alcohol," is one reply.

"It's a form of medication," someone else answers.

"Why do people stay here?" I ask.

"If you live off the Rez, you get nothing . . . only the crumbs."

"We are a very oppressed people," someone interjects.

The word *colonization* comes up frequently at Pine Ridge, and this reality had never occurred to me before I visited. The Lakota were colonized. Our history books don't write the story this way, but that's what happened. A foreign civilization came to the land of the Lakota and claimed it for their own. Their land was taken, their means of subsistence (the buffalo) was destroyed, and they were sequestered away from the conquering society. Along the way, many promises were made and then broken, or unfulfilled. Distrust runs deep.

"Christianity is one of the biggest oppressors. We had our own way of life; it wasn't a religion in the traditional sense, but it all worked and flowed together. It was beautiful and in sync. Christians came and told us it was all devil's worship," Catherine explains.

"I am thankful for the American Indian Movement [AIM]. They opened up the eyes of a lot of us to come out of our denial. They increased awareness of our own belief systems and our own way of life. They helped us all regain our pride in our heritage again," she continues.

It is hard to understand what this feels like from the Lakota perspective. Imagine being colonized.

"That was 1965. Now, I am working to decolonize myself. I am walking away from Christian traditions, such as Christmas. I am angry that I can't speak my own language. I am angry that my boarding school experience took that part of who I am away." By now, Catherine is in full form and I am content to just sit and listen to her share her experiences.

I am so thankful for this dinner. Time stood still for me as we ate, laughed, and shared perspectives. I was humbled and honored by the way the group opened themselves up to me, by the way they trusted me. I am not interested in passing judgment on what anyone has to say here. I am just interested in understanding their perspective, their reality. Awareness is the goal. Awareness without judgment is where my own soul wants to go, and, coincidentally, what the Lakota of Pine Ridge need.

Slowly the dinner conversation winds down. One by one, the group breaks up, until it is just Catherine and me. I call her "Grandma," and she likes this.

"*Unchi*. That's the Lakota word for 'grandma,' " Catherine tells me.

"Okay, Unchi," I reply.

Catherine has taken a special interest in me and I in her.

"Your heart is in a good place," she says with confidence.

Intentions matter here, I think to myself.

Back home in Maine people ask me what I do at Pine Ridge.

"Not much, really; I mostly just hang out there," I typically reply.

For me, Pine Ridge is that place Deborah Dooley foretold, where life slows down and I don't have responsibilities.

"Escape to the Pine Ridge Indian Reservation," the map on the front seat of my car reads.

Catherine knows I am going to meet Nick Tilsen, the young executive director of the nonprofit organization, Thunder Valley, in the morning. Nick is her nephew, or great-nephew, or cousin, or something like that. Anyway, she is glad I am going to see him. She assures me I will like him and that he will like me.

"I am sure you are right about this, Unchi," I reply.

She takes out a notepad and writes something for me to give to Nick tomorrow. The note simply reads:

Hello, Toska—just a note to let you know I think you are an
AWESOME person.

Make this a good day! I met and I am getting to know Kevin too.
He has a good heart.

Underneath her words Catherine draws a happy face.

The daylight basement at the Singing Horse Trading Post is one of my favorite places at Pine Ridge, especially at night after the store is closed.

As this day draws to a close, I find myself alone in the Trading Post, situated in the daylight basement of Rosie's home. The store is closed for the night and a magical energy fills the space between the dream catchers, drums, jewelry, and art. It is a great place to be alone and reflect. As I watch the dream catchers swing gently to the soft breeze from an open window, I have a growing sense that I am beginning to transcend my own local condition and roles. Furthermore, I am beginning to understand that the "expectations" I felt to act a certain way were actually self-imposed. The past was pulling on me; but, as Deborah Dooley pointed out, the source of my constraints was internal.

We have everything we need to heal ourselves within ourselves.

—Thunder Hawk Martinez, Oglala Sioux Tribe

The more I release my own sense of self, the stronger I feel. I can already see that becoming more self-aware doesn't limit your contribution to your own tribe; it actually enhances it. The old traditions of Lakota spirituality embodied this. In traditional Lakota society, the central government was small, difficult to even find. The individual was the source of power.

Seeking your personal truth, living *your* path was the Lakota way that made the individual strong and, in turn, enhanced the power of the whole tribe.

If I had learned this lesson earlier in my life, I might not have lost my voice. Then again, if I had not lost my voice, I might not have learned this lesson at all.

We cannot redirect the circumstances into which we were born. In this way, the past pulls on us all. However, we do have the power to transcend and progress. In fact, we carry it with us everywhere we go; the power to transcend lies within.

The Lakota have known about the power of the individual spirit for a long time. In fact, some people at Pine Ridge who think deeply about the "old ways" refer to it as the Seventh Power—the one that lives in the center of the Sacred Medicine Wheel.

The external circumstances we are born into pull on us all to act a certain way. In the end, however, we each came here to individuate, transcend, and evolve. You are on the journey your soul signed up to make.

"I wish it need not have happened in my time,"
[said Frodo].

"So do I," said Gandalf, "and so do all who live to see such times. But that is not for them to decide. All we have to decide is what to do with the time that is given us."

—J. R. R. Tolkien, *The Fellowship of the Ring*

3
One Day, Four Heroes

I will never forget this one day at Pine Ridge, spent with four amazing people who are rising above and expanding their circles.

They made it okay to be Lakota again.

—Nick Tilsen

There is something magical about the early morning at Pine Ridge. Each one is so peaceful and quiet. Alone with the rising sun, rolling clouds, and blowing grass, it is as if all the transgressions and failed promises of the past are somehow gone, like they were never actually real to begin with. Nature cares not about wars and treaties, it seems.

It is 34 degrees as I unlatch the chain and watch gravity do the rest; the green metal gate that I closed last night swings open. Moments later,

I turn left onto BIA 14 and drive over the hills above Rosie's horse pasture. I look to my left at the fence line I sat against last evening. It is right where I left it.

I drive in silence for miles without seeing another car. Eventually, I start pushing buttons until the digital dial on the center console reaches 90.1 FM, the home of KILI Radio. I turn up the volume, then partially open both front windows. Pounding drums and high-pitched chants fill the air; I can feel the car's subtle vibration in response. With my right hand, I extend my iPhone out in front of me toward the windshield and press "record." I film the road falling beneath me as the car travels forward to the rhythmic beat. My head is nodding front to back in cadence. I am completely immersed in both the landscape and the music. I have come to call this my "morning commute" at Pine Ridge.

When the music ends, my adrenaline rush slowly fades because it is now time for politics on KILI Radio. On this morning, a district chair has the next hour of airtime. He begins by asking permission to speak in front of the tribe's elders, and then offers condolences to the families of those who have recently passed. After that, the district chair turns to business. His mood also changes; it tightens. Where there is government at Pine Ridge, tension and distrust are typically close behind.

"We don't know what's going on," states the district representative.

"We aren't getting reports back from the Tribal Council. What is happening at the tribal level? We don't know."

Statements such as this are common at Pine Ridge. When I first came here, I was expecting distrust and skepticism toward Washington, D.C., but I was surprised by the high degree of political conflict within the tribe itself. The political system seems to be in a constant state of confusion. Rumors and gossip are commonplace. Conflict is the norm. The population of the reservation is relatively small, but getting everyone on the same page is a struggle. It feels like the American-imposed political system doesn't fit. It only endures. It's like a glove that's too small. You wear it because you are cold, in spite of the fact that it limits your dexterity.

Then again, infighting on the reservations can be traced all the way back to the time of Crazy Horse. Old habits live on and are passed down until they are eventually transcended. This is the essence of evolutionary astrology, and I can see it at Pine Ridge. Lessons are repeated until they are learned. I know this on a personal level, as transcending my own karmic habits is what brought me here. We are all just trying to move forward, I suppose.

The next topic for discussion is the $1 million community development grant the representative's district is soon to receive.

"Please come to the meeting at the district school tonight to learn more about this grant and tell us how you think it should be used," he comments.

After a brief pause, the results of the recent election for district treasurer are discussed. The election committee has reviewed the outcome and determined that a revote needs to take place, as one candidate was inadvertently left off the ballot. Listeners are reminded that all candidates for public office must first pass a hair-follicle drug test and a personal background check.

There is a lot of government per person at Pine Ridge, and one would be hard-pressed to say that this has served the people well.

Government at Pine Ridge is founded on two diametrically opposed principles. The first is tribal sovereignty and the second is federal care. As one of 561 federally recognized tribes, the Oglala Sioux view themselves as having a unique nation-to-nation relationship with the United States government. This status of "sovereignty" suggests a high degree of freedom and self-determination, which has been historically offset by the second founding principle, federal care. The combination of these two incongruent concepts is difficult to unravel. On the one hand, the Lakota assert their right to political autonomy from the federal government while, on the other hand, expecting extra financial support and care in return.

Political divisions and infighting have plagued the reservation since the time of Crazy Horse and Red Cloud.

Everything political seems complicated here, and the government's reach is long, extending into almost every aspect of life, including land ownership. The federal government's original land plan was to assign individual plots to adult males through a process known as "allotment." The size of the parcel would depend upon the size of the family. In all cases, however, the federal government recognized that the concept of private land ownership was foreign to the Lakota. As such, the government was concerned that left to their own devices, individual tribal members might be swindled out of the land's future value. To guard against this threat, the government retained trustee guardianship rights over the land it allotted. In this way, both the Native landowner and the federal government shared title. I find it surprising that a land ownership structure born in the 1880s still endures at Pine Ridge today.

The Dawes Act, which created the allotment system in 1887, unfortunately did great harm to Native American land holdings across the Great Plains. Indian lands were surveyed and each adult male was given the opportunity to select a parcel. Once that process was completed, much of the land that remained was declared to be "surplus" and sold to white Americans. From 1887 until 1934, it is estimated that two-thirds of the total remaining Indian land base in America (90 million acres) was taken out of Indian control.

The demise of Indian territory was seen as a great economic opportunity, and newspaper headlines in the late 1880s spread the word far and wide:

GRAND RUSH FOR THE INDIAN TERRITORY

NOW IS THE CHANCE TO PROCURE A HOME IN THE BEAUTIFUL COUNTRY

OVER 15 MILLION ACRES OF LAND NOW OPEN FOR SETTLEMENT!

Loss and gain often share the same circle; Pine Ridge is an enduring example.

The district report nears its conclusion as I pull the car over in the dirt parking area beside the Sharps Corner Baptist Church. I am perplexed and a bit depressed. I turn the radio off and try to let the silence return, but my mind wanders back to the political system. It just doesn't seem to fit the people here. The current political structure is very different from how the Lakota governed themselves before the coming of the Wasichu. Central government in traditional Lakota society was virtually nonexistent. Today, government at Pine Ridge is practically omnipresent. There is no doubt that government programs and services are essential to the people of Pine Ridge, but I can't help but think there is a point at which more government becomes counterproductive. Government programs have come up short here; there is no denying that. The power of the individual needs to be made strong again in order for balance to be restored. Too much central control dulls the senses of any organization's members.

In 2013, Malcolm Gladwell published the book, *David and Goliath: Underdogs, Misfits, and the Art of Battling Giants.* I read the book late that year and sent a copy to all my friends at Pine Ridge for Christmas. In his book Gladwell wrote that,

Power has an important limitation.
It has to be seen as legitimate, or else its use has the
opposite of its intended effect.

When I read this, I immediately thought of government at Pine Ridge.

In that same book, Gladwell describes the concept of an "inverted-U curve":

> *A classic inverted-U curve can be seen in the relationship between alcohol consumption and health. If you go from not drinking at all to drinking one glass of wine a week, you'll live longer. And if you drink two glasses a week, you'll live a little bit longer, and three glasses a little bit longer still—all the way up to about seven glasses a week. That's the upslope: the more the merrier. Then there's the stretch from, say seven to fourteen glasses of wine a week. You're not helping yourself by drinking more in that range. But you're not particularly hurting yourself either. That's the middle part of the curve. Finally, there's the right side of the curve: the downslope. That's when you get past fourteen glasses of wine a week and drinking more starts to leave you with a SHORTER life. Alcohol is not inherently good or bad or neutral. It starts out good, becomes neutral, and ends up bad.*

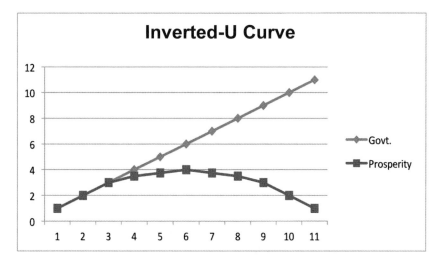

This is a theoretical example of an inverted-U curve, showing a relationship between more government control and individual prosperity.

The inverted-U curve can be applied to many things, including the relationship between government control and individual prosperity at

Pine Ridge. In the early stages of the curve, government programs and financial support improve lives. In the middle stages, the results become muted. The return begins to diminish. Ultimately, on the right side of the curve, the correlation actually becomes inverted. At this stage of the cycle, increasing government responsibility inversely impacts individual prosperity. Taken to the extreme, this is easy to understand. If government is given the responsibility of doing everything, then individuals are relegated to the role of spectators.

Back at Hancock Lumber, I have been thinking a lot about the proper role of central leadership. In order to create a company where everybody leads, I believe the top bosses have to show restraint. Of course, there are times when the senior managers need to be decisive, but more often, patience is required.

In the last couple of years, we have been working at Hancock Lumber to put more of the decision-making activity in the hands of the front-line people who actually do the work. We have accomplished this by increasing the quantity and quality of real-time information everyone receives, and by creating more "huddles" and "focus groups" where team members meet to review results and discuss action steps.

In this regard, I have tried to lead by example. I used to be the center point of most meetings I attended, controlling the agenda and doing a lot of the talking. Today, if you were to sit in on a team meeting I am participating in, you would most likely find me in the second row or off to the side. My favorite meeting agenda has actually become a blank piece of paper. I prefer to see, whenever possible, what topics surface if I hold back from selecting them. Losing my voice to spasmodic dysphonia brought this on, and in short order I could see the power of listening more, talking less, and sharing leadership more broadly across an entire organization.

Through the partial loss of my voice, I have come to see the obvious: The front-line employees who do the work of making our products and servicing our customers *know* where the opportunities to improve reside. They are eager to identify those opportunities and take responsibility for them if management will show the trust to let them do so. There is a lot of power in the knowledge of the whole. An organization where everyone leads will, I feel, almost always outperform an organization led by just a chosen few. Everyone has a voice that wants to be heard more authentically. Losing mine helped me learn this.

Eventually, I rouse myself and shake off the malaise I acquired during the district report. Nick's office is just up the road, and it is time for me to meet him.

———————

Nick's organization has a great mission. Thunder Valley (www.thunder-valley.org), is a community development corporation that advocates for a revival in traditional Lakota values and culture, as a means of creating greater self-reliance and autonomy for the people of Pine Ridge. Its signature initiative is the creation of a new housing community. Home ownership is rare on the reservation, and that makes this project unique.

Nick's office stands out here for its tidiness. It is clear this is a place of well organized activity. As I enter the small single-story building, I see a series of inspirational quotes that line the walls. The individual offices are modern and well kept.

Nick is not here yet, so I am shown into the conference room where the word "regeneration" is posted on the wall followed by a definition:

REGENERATION:
Renewal or restoration of a body after injury.

Regeneration. That's it. That's what brings me here, I think to myself, with regard to my own lost voice.

Finding my voice has a dual meaning for me. On the literal level, I am seeking to regain a consistent and comfortable speaking voice, lost to spasmodic dysphonia. On a more abstract level, my journeys to Pine Ridge are about removing myself from my public roles for the purpose of reengaging the voice that lives within me, the true inner voice of my own soul. Pine Ridge is that place Deborah Dooley foretold where my inner being could be served. In this, the unlikeliest of ways, I feel that the Lakota of Pine Ridge and I are on a shared journey. We are both searching to regain a once-powerful voice.

Moments later, Nick arrives. As he enters the room, I can tell I am in the presence of someone special. Nick is young and strong. His dark black hair falls behind him in a single ponytail. A large porcupine quill necklace with the Thunder Valley emblem rests on the outside of a gray Under Armour athletic shirt. Nick brings an air of maturity, confidence, and understanding with him into the room, and I have the immediate sense that we are going to be friends. We give each other a smile and shake hands. For the next two hours, we are lost in conversation.

Nick Tilsen and I stand together at the Thunder Valley offices on the day we first met.

"There has got to be a better way to do things; what we have been doing hasn't worked very well," Nick states.

Nick believes all of that can change. Furthermore, I can quickly tell that he doesn't believe the full solution lies with government. Nick believes that reengaging traditional Lakota values is the path for his people. In this way, looking back is moving forward.

At the center of Nick's vision is the new housing community he plans to create. The community is going to sit on thirty-four acres of grassland that slowly rolls up the gentle hills behind his office. The key to this project is that it sits on "fee land," which means it is owned outright by the Thunder Valley Development Corporation, without the complexity of federal government trustee oversight.

Nick goes on to tell me that many people at Pine Ridge live without running water or year-round heat and electricity. Homes without furnaces are common here. In creating the reservation system, many Lakota believe that the federal government took responsibility for providing housing to the people of Pine Ridge and has since grossly underdelivered on that commitment. Nevertheless, people continue to look to the government for housing solutions.

This calls forward one of the great unanswered political questions for the future Pine Ridge:

How long should the original government promises
(that created the reservation) last?

Regardless of legal obligations, how long do the residents of Pine Ridge want to rely upon the federal government for their own economic security? Even if we reaffirm the federal government's responsibility to nineteenth-century promises, do the people who live here want to continue to rely upon them? What are the chances that another century of government care will produce different results?

"This community we are going to build is designed to support the healing and regeneration of our people," Nick tells me.

"Our spirit was broken. Healing is necessary in order to move forward. We could stay where we're at and be bitter for a long time; and, we would be in the right for doing so. But what message would we be sending to our children? What future would we be creating for ourselves?" Nick asks rhetorically.

"This community [Thunder Valley] is not just about buildings," Nick continues. "It's about creating a revival in our social structure. Our traditional social structure has been broken and we need to rebuild it. People need control of their own communities. We need to transition from renting to owning, and Thunder Valley can serve as a prototype for doing so."

A picture is worth a thousand words regarding the housing conditions at Pine Ridge.

I already understand Nick's vision. Home ownership is rare, and utility costs here are among the highest in the nation. Renters can pay as much as $400 per month in utility bills alone. Many cannot afford this expense and go without utilities altogether, or at least periodically throughout the year. People live week to week at Pine Ridge, and home occupancy costs represent a disproportionately high percentage of their income. This is where Nick's next idea comes in.

Thunder Valley is going to be a "net zero" green community that generates its own energy by combining solar, wind, and geothermal power on-site with efficient building techniques. In this respect, the community will be tapping back into nature to provide the resources necessary for self-sufficiency. The money saved on utility bills will be enough to pay the mortgage costs associated with home ownership. This one small idea is powerful. It is an example of returning to the Lakota connection with the Earth, as a means of self-reliance in the future. It is the past showing the way forward.

As I look out the conference-room windows and across the grasslands, the completion of this new community seems far away. But, it also occurs to me that the very idea of Thunder Valley is important. All things are invented twice, first in the mind. A revolution is an idea before it is an action.

"This reservation is very big and very isolated, so we need to regenerate our ability to take care of ourselves. No one is coming to save us," Nick reflects.

Nick's comments make me think of my own travels in the Land of Crazy Horse and how remote and isolated it is. There is definitely a lot of land here, and often nobody in sight. At 2.2 million acres in size, with an approximate population of 40,000 people, there are 55 acres of land for every person at Pine Ridge. In the towns of Pine Ridge and Kyle, you will always see people; but, across the entire reservation, large tracts of land are unoccupied. In most places on the reservation you can just stop your car right in the middle of the road and get out if you see something that interests you. Despite the availability of space and the government's promises of care, there is a dramatic housing shortage here.

"The shortage is approximately five thousand homes," Nick tells me.

The government is responsible for housing, and there isn't any. I find myself constantly returning to this irony.

> **Whenever the head of a family shall, in good faith, select an allotment of said land upon such reservations and engage in the cultivation thereof, the Government shall, with his aid, erect a comfortable house on such allotment.**
>
> **—Congressional Act of 1877**

Shortly after returning home from this trip, I found myself sitting at my desk in Casco estimating the cost of solving the housing shortage at Pine Ridge. If the average cost of constructing a home at Pine Ridge were $140,000, that would put the total cost of building 5,000 homes at $700 million ($700,000,000), a nine-digit number. That's a big number and a small number, at the same time. For the local community of Pine Ridge, that is a very big number. For our national government, it's a small number. For example, as of March 2013, the cost of the US war in Iraq was estimated at $1.7 trillion ($1,700,000,000,000). That's a thirteen-digit number.

I still keep a big old Royal 4000 calculator on my office desk. Why? I don't know (it was there when I got there, is one interesting answer). It is one of those archaic calculators that makes a sound every time you push a button, as if to tell you it is paying attention. It only extends calculations to twelve digits, though, so I open up a fresh Excel file on my laptop and begin typing in data. Unlike my Royal 4000, Excel doesn't care how many digits are involved.

I punch in the data and then pause, staring at my screen. The cost of addressing the housing shortage at Pine Ridge is 0.04 percent of the cost of the Iraq War (less than one half of one-tenth of a percent). This blows my mind. I sit and don't move for quite some time, before deciding to search for another example. I quickly find one in our government's response to a recent natural disaster.

Early on the morning of October 29, 2012, Superstorm Sandy moved ashore, centered on New Jersey and Long Island. It was an extremely destructive storm. By far the worst of the hurricane season that year and the second-costliest hurricane in US history, its estimated damages exceeded $68 billion (eleven digits). Government agencies at all levels rushed to respond, and Congress moved swiftly to support the local efforts. The Congressional Disaster Relief Appropriations Act of 2013 allocated $829.2 million through the Department of the Interior to aid the rebuilding and recovery efforts. The funding was later reduced to $786.7 million, after sequestration.

A single storm on the East Coast had triggered a rush of federal financial aid greater than the total cost of the century-old housing shortage at Pine Ridge. Ironically, the funds for the Hurricane Sandy relief effort were dispersed through the Department of the Interior, the same department that oversees the Bureau of Indian Affairs.

Examples like these are easy to find; if you live at Pine Ridge, you must notice.

———

This sign always makes me think about the choices we have in the path we travel; the journey is full of bullet holes, marking lessons learned. Long after the bullets are gone, the dents remain.

"Big organizations make terrible decisions sometimes," Nick observes.

This statement brings my mind back to the conference table where Nick's passionate and convincing perspectives keep coming.

"Our poverty here is not an accident," he continues.

There is a pause in the conversation and silence fills the room.

"We must be willing to ask ourselves the hard questions," Nick reflects. "We never really adjusted to living a non-nomadic lifestyle. We were not farmers. Some Indian tribes were farmers, but not us, not here."

"Look what they did. Look what their management of our future turned into," Nick says to me.

"A government system that doesn't fit or match our culture was imposed upon us," Nick continues. "The current system has led to lots of disenfranchisement. There is a lot of nonparticipation here. It's a system that many people don't trust."

Nick tells me that the tribal housing authority is preparing to build more rental units this year, twenty-six in all. At that rate, it would take 192 years to build the 5,000 homes that are needed. Each year, at this pace, twenty-six families would be selected and the rest would remain on waiting lists.

"We got screwed," Nick summarizes, "but, at the end of the day, it's like, okay, now what?"

More silence fills the room.

"When you have nothing, what do you turn to?" Nick asks me. "You turn back to your spiritual faith."

The places we come from influence all of us, and Nick is no exception. Nick's mom is Oglala and his dad is the son of a Russian immigrant who came to America through Ellis Island. Despite different backgrounds, both sides of Nick's family were deeply involved in what Nick calls "the struggle to hold on to our traditional ways." Nick's grandfather, Ken Tilsen, was a nationally recognized civil rights attorney from St. Paul who defended many of the nation's leading American Indian Movement (AIM) activists, and was on the reservation during the famous 1973 siege at Wounded Knee.

In October of 1972, three caravans of Native activists departed from Los Angeles, San Francisco, and Seattle. The groups met in Minneapolis before continuing on to our nation's capital, arriving the week before the presidential election. In a cross-country journey that would become known as the "Trail of Broken Treaties," AIM illegally occupied the Bureau of Indian Affairs headquarters. After barricading themselves inside the building and destroying much of the property, they presented a list of demands to President Nixon and Congress, known as the "Twenty Points." Their demands included:

- Restoration of treaty making and the establishment of a treaty commission to make new treaties with the sovereign Native Nations.

- A review of past treaty commitments and violations.

- Restoration of 110 million acres of land taken from Native Nations by the United States.

- Abolishment of the Bureau of Indian Affairs.

AIM's demands read as if they hoped to wipe the slate clean and start over, to literally turn back the hands of time. But, you can't start over. You can look backwards for context, but when you move . . . well, you have to move forward.

There is an important distinction to be made between the American civil rights movement and the AIM. Desegregation (integration) was the goal of the civil rights movement. The restoration of sovereignty (segregation) was the goal of the AIM. The paradox of the American Indian Movement is visible in the "Twenty Points" that simultaneously called for more federal government financial support, yet less federal government intrusion.

On February 23 of the following year, national members of the AIM joined approximately two hundred local residents and seized the town of Wounded Knee in protest of tribal president, Dick Wilson, and of the United States government's failure to honor past treaty obligations. A seventy-one-day standoff with federal marshals and the FBI ensued. The siege made national headlines, and the damage to Wounded Knee was so substantial that the town was not fully reopened until the 1990s. Both Russell Means and his fellow AIM leader, Dennis Banks, received federal indictments, but their case was dismissed in 1974 for prosecutorial misconduct. Over eighty-years after the original massacre at Wounded Knee, war was still being waged at Pine Ridge.

While the federal government was definitely an object of attention during the 1973 siege, much anger also lay within the Indian community itself. AIM followers and many Pine Ridge residents were fed up with what they saw as the corruption, inefficiency, and intimidation in

Dick Wilson's tenure as tribal president. Wilson was accused of organizing "Goon Squads" (Guardians of the Oglala Nation) who blocked roads across the reservation and terrorized opponents, often employing violence. The Lakota community, both inside and outside Pine Ridge, was divided.

These were dangerous times at Pine Ridge, but that did not stop Nick's grandfather from bringing his son, Mark, with him to the reservation. It was there, during the height of the conflict, that Nick's mom and dad met.

Nick was born in 1982, as he says, "out of revolution and activism."

We are all a product of our tribe.

Nick's parents would go on to help build the KILI Radio station, and Nick lived at Pine Ridge until he was five years old. When his parents divorced, Nick's dad moved back to Minnesota, while his mother stayed at Pine Ridge. From that point on, Nick went to school in Minnesota, but spent holidays and summers with his mom in Porcupine, going to ceremonies and being a part of his Lakota community.

"I walked in two worlds," Nick tells me. "It was hard and emotional, but I have a distinct worldview because of it."

When Nick says this, I can't help but think of the two worlds I am walking in and the way in which this path is helping me seek my own distinct voice and view.

"They made it okay to be Lakota again," Nick reflects, speaking of the AIM activists of the 1970s. "They encouraged us to be proud, to embrace who we are."

Nick is not alone in coming home.

"The population of South Dakota is declining, but the population of the reservation is growing," Nick explains. "Why is this? Well, it's not jobs and opportunity that brings people here. It's reconnecting with your cultural identity, with the essence of who you are; that's the power of Pine Ridge. If you are Oglala, you can travel anywhere in the world and not find what you find here, what you find here as an Indian."

Thunder Valley began as a spiritual circle of young people who shared sun dance and sweat lodge experiences.

"Our spiritual circle reconnected many young people to their culture, as well as to their responsibility to serve their people," Nick continues.

"There is a need here," Nick tells me. "Where there is a need, there is a responsibility."

"Let's build economic independence *through* our culture, instead of around it," Nick continues.

Nick's own vision for his future came to him during a sweat lodge experience in which his ancestors appeared to him and asked him a series of questions.

How long are we going to let other people make decisions
for us and our children?

Are you not a warrior for your people?

As warriors long ago, we rode into battle. We did so not knowing the out-
come of the battle; what we did know was that battle was a necessity, so we
rode on despite not knowing what the future held.

"The message for me in that vision was to act positively and to not operate from a position of fear or negativity," Nick explains.

As I listen to Nick, I am moved by his openness.

"We need to get back to the structural issues of why there is so much poverty," Nick calmly states.

Outsiders might feel that the poverty here is a result of the tribe's unwillingness to abandon their culture and spirituality in favor of "modern" American thinking. Nick believes otherwise. He will say that his people have lost their way because they were forced into a governmental and cultural structure that does not coalesce with their true spirituality. They have struggled, in large part, because of this disconnect. Reenergizing this community, therefore, lies in reconnecting, not disconnecting with the past.

"Remember who you are."

—Mufasa to Simba in *The Lion King*

Nick's perspective is one that I share. As a global community, it would be a "game changer" if we all could learn to celebrate cultural diversity as much as we do biodiversity. Much attention is appropriately given to animal species at risk of extinction, but what about cultural extinction? How much attention does that get? How much effort goes into preserving at-risk cultures versus eradicating them? For nearly a century, our government's goal was to "remake" the Lakota as whites. Even if this was well-intentioned, the notion is filled with hubris: "The only way you can prosper is to adopt our culture and customs." In my view, there is much about Lakota culture that our country and planet needs: respect for all living things, oneness with nature, tribal generosity, vision quests in search of personal power, and more. At the same time, traditional American culture has attributes that would be valuable at Pine Ridge.

The goal should not be the eradication or abandonment of one culture in favor of another, but rather the connectivity of cultures. The best of mankind is distributed like a puzzle throughout all the peoples of the world who, in the end, are not so different after all.

"It's all about bringing economic activity onto the Rez," says Nick back at the conference table. "It's about putting the power back into the hands of the people."

"Every day at four-thirty p.m. I see the cars headed north traveling back to Rapid City. Those cars are filled with people who work here at our schools and agencies, but live off the reservation because there is no housing," Nick concludes.

My new friend, Nick Tilsen, has plans to change that.

It's 11:30 a.m. I've totally lost track of time. As our conversation ends, I am feeling spirited and thankful for this unique opportunity. I am convinced that Nick and I were meant to meet. In order for this connection to materialize, however, we each had to take steps toward the other. If we both had kept to our own small circles, our paths most certainly would not have crossed. Expanding circles and connecting tribes is an exercise I already believe in.

We clasp hands and share a hug. We both seem to know that a valued relationship has just begun.

Back in the car, I first drive east to the main campus of the Oglala Lakota College, where I park and look out over the landscape. I then retrace my route before turning south onto BIA 27 toward Porcupine. The radio is off, the windows are open, and truth is in the air. A new wind is blowing for me at Pine Ridge.

Just a few miles west of Wounded Knee is the site where Chief Big Foot first surrendered. The sign is covered in graffiti and the small turnout is littered with debris, which always confuses and troubles me.

After visiting the spot where Chief Big Foot surrendered, I stop at the Wounded Knee Massacre site. A documentary film crew is there. They are consumed with their work and don't notice me, so we don't talk. In just two visits to Pine Ridge, I have read this red plywood sign with white letters so many times that I have it partially memorized. "The last armed conflict between the Sioux Indians and the United States Army" occurred right here on the cold morning of December 29, 1890, sparked by a scuffle for a single rifle.

The energy of that moment still lives here. I can feel it. "*Mitakuye Oya-sin*," I eventually whisper. This Lakota phrase translated simply means, "We are all related," or "We are all brothers."

I buy two more necklaces from a young couple that approaches me near the Wounded Knee sign. They need gas money, they tell me. We talk for a few minutes about people we know in common. I am both proud and excited that I am able to do this. I ask them where they buy their art supplies. They tell me they buy them from Rosie at Singing Horse.

I feel at home here, I think to myself.

When the trading is done, I get back into my car. I am off to my second appointment of the day: to meet Alberta Eagle at the Red Cloud School.

Alberta Eagle stands in front of the Red Cloud School's Holy Rosary chapel on the day we met.

Alberta is the community relations director for the Jesuit-led Red Cloud School, located just north of the town of Pine Ridge. A modern church of brick and stone sits prominently in front of the school on the central lawn.

I walk into the office and ask for Alberta. A few moments later, she appears.

We shake hands, exchange smiles and walk outside.

"I find your interest in us so interesting," Alberta says to me as we cross the school grounds.

Alberta is not what I had envisioned. She is young and filled with enthusiasm. She has dark black hair and is wearing jeans and a gray North Face polar fleece jacket. For some reason, I was expecting the community relations director to be more of the classic librarian type, the longtime keeper of historical records.

We are immediately deep in conversation as we slowly walk across the grounds. She tells me about the school. Its story is an amazing one. In 1887, Chief Red Cloud petitioned the US government to allow the local Jesuit missionaries known as "Black Robes" to build a school. The petition succeeded and, in the years that followed, local Lakota men and women helped the Jesuits construct the original school from clay bricks made from a nearby creek. The school has endured and grown from those humble beginnings to the present day. Today, Red Cloud School serves approximately six hundred Lakota students through its Montessori program, two elementary schools, and a college preparatory high school.

We enter the Holy Rosary chapel and sit about halfway down the center aisle. The wooden pew creaks and adjusts itself as we settle. Alberta has so much she is ready to tell me. This is the second time this has happened to me today. Both Nick and Alberta have opened their hearts to a stranger, and I believe this is reflective of both their storytelling culture and their pride in this community. Furthermore, I sense they both see that more connectivity is needed. Isolation is not a requirement of cultural preservation, and cultures aren't static; they evolve.

Alberta is extremely articulate. Community relations director is the perfect job for her.

"I grew up on the reservation," Alberta whispers. She is whispering because we are in the chapel, but it gives the impression she is telling me a secret story.

"I was raised by my grandmother, and lots of family members and relatives came and went there. My family had problems with alcohol and my dad wasn't around very much. My mom gave birth to me at a very young age. She was not ready to take care of a child, so she gave me to my grandmother."

The silence of the Rosary is noteworthy as I listen to her story. The big wooden doors behind us open occasionally, letting in the light of day as someone else enters.

"Teen pregnancy was common when I was growing up," Alberta continues. "In fact, it was popular; but, my grandmother told me that was not my path. I owe a lot to my grandmother. It was a strong home to be raised in. I was blessed in this way."

Alberta remembers her great-grandmother, as well. "She was born in 1901 and was part of the first boarding school system. She died in 1996," Alberta explains. "It wasn't that long ago," she continues, referring to the time when the government's policy was to remake Indian children as whites. Her great-grandmother, like many of her generation, distrusted outsiders generally and government agents, specifically.

"Food was scarce on the reservation during the time of my grandmother and my great-grandmother," Alberta tells me. "Food was rationed. Entering the boarding school system was the safest, surest way to eat and have clothing. That's why her parents sent her there. It was about having food, clothing, and a safe place to sleep."

Alberta's grandmother learned a trade at boarding school, and later in life was a proponent of boarding school for Alberta. This led Alberta away from Pine Ridge to the Marty Indian School in southeastern South Dakota, where she graduated in 1995. After graduation, she attended Western Dakota Technical Institute in Rapid City.

By 1997, Alberta was back on the reservation, working for a construction company in the town of Pine Ridge. "Their work ran out and I was laid off," she explains.

She was in need of a job and found one at the Red Cloud School, where she worked as the assistant to the superintendent for nearly a decade.

"I loved that job," Alberta tells me.

I feel honored to listen as she retells her tale. Alberta is an amazing storyteller, in the best tradition of her people.

Time passed and the school superintendent encouraged Alberta to go back to school and pursue a college degree. "He told me I had hit a pay ceiling in my current job, and that I had potential beyond what the role I played for him could offer me."

By this time, Alberta was a single mother balancing the responsibilities of working and raising her family.

"The identity has been taken away from many young men in our community," Alberta says reflectively.

"It is a cultural identity crisis of sorts, created by the lack of opportunity to provide. All the things men traditionally did in our society to provide for their people have been lost," she continues.

> *I know why a lot of young people try to kill themselves on the Rez. We're all in constant danger of losing ourselves, losing our identities. It's a daily struggle for each and every one of us to be fully Lakota. And sometimes we lose the struggle, and then the men take out their feelings of worthlessness on the women, the women take out their feelings of worthlessness on themselves, and everyone takes out their feelings of worthlessness on the children.*
>
> **—Thunder Hawk Martinez**

This picture came from the end of the day after we unloaded the donated building materials. I really enjoyed spending time with those guys. I could easily see the good in each of them by the time they drove away. A shortage of talent is not Pine Ridge's problem. The people who live here are smart, fun, kind, creative, and thoughtful. This is partly why the challenges facing their community are so perplexing.

After Alberta left her job working for the superintendent at Red Cloud School, she moved to Albuquerque, New Mexico, and stayed there for five years. Life was challenging off the reservation.

"It was hard," Alberta explains. "I didn't know anybody, and I was afraid of losing my connection to my people back home. I was afraid of this both for my children and myself. I did not want to lose the part of me that was Lakota. During those periods of my life when I have left the reservation, I have been reminded that racism still exists. Away from the reservation being Lakota means being different, and being different was hard for my kids in New Mexico. On top of all that, we just missed it here. This place [Pine Ridge] has a powerful hold on you."

While in New Mexico, Alberta attended the Southwest Indian Polytechnic Institute. She was still a single parent, so she also worked. She found a job as an administrative assistant at a law firm in Albuquerque that specialized in mortgage foreclosures.

"It was painful to watch," Alberta tells me. "People would show up trying to make payments and the foreclosure firm's reply was most usually, 'No, we are taking your house.' "

Alberta worked there during the peak of the mortgage market collapse. When the mortgage foreclosure activity eventually slowed down, Alberta was laid off. As it turns out, Alberta and I were both wrestling in different ways with the challenges of the housing and mortgage market collapse. The world is smaller than we think.

"At that point, I had no job and no money for rent, so I decided it would probably be best if we just went home," Alberta goes on to explain.

Alberta's grandmother had died shortly after Alberta departed for New Mexico.

"My grandmother's vision of what I should have been was for me to leave Pine Ridge," Alberta continues.

Alberta moved back home to Pine Ridge, but with her grandmother gone she didn't have a home. Alberta and her children lived with several different families while she looked for work. She kept checking back with the Red Cloud School for job openings, and finally one materialized. The Red Cloud School was searching for a community relations director. Alberta applied and was hired.

"There is just nothing to rent here [at Pine Ridge]," Alberta tells me.

"There is no housing. We may have to move to Rapid City just to find a place to live. I am not sure what that will mean for my job. If we have to move to Rapid, that would mean a two-hour drive each way to get back to the Red Cloud School for work. As a mother of four, and with the cost of gasoline being what it is, that would be really difficult."

"The lack of day-care centers is another challenge here," she continues.

"I went to New Mexico to go to school, because I want to be a business owner someday. I want to be self-employed. I want to own a retail store that sells clothing right here on the reservation," Alberta tells me. "Most of the money people do have here gets spent off the reservation. It's such a shame."

Alberta begins to cry. She doesn't break down. She is not weak, remorseful, or resentful. It is simply the act of sharing this story, her story, that has brought tears to her eyes.

She wipes them away and continues.

"Sometimes other students would ask me silly questions that were full of stereotypes," Alberta explains, thinking back to her own boarding school days. " 'Do you still ride horses?' 'Do you still hunt for your food?' 'Do you still live in a tepee?' "

We sit quietly for a few moments before Alberta looks down at her watch. An hour has gone by in the blink of an eye. Alberta has a meeting back at her office that she is now late for, so we leave the chapel and walk back across the quiet campus together.

After saying good-bye, I walk back to the car, reflecting upon Alberta's openness. It was like she had been waiting for someone to come and listen. She wanted to share her story, and I feel blessed that she chose to share it with me. Alberta is a great representative for the Red Cloud School and for her people. I am happy to have met her.

As I turn the car on, I think back upon the very first statement she made as we walked to the Rosary:

Your interest in us is so interesting to me.

Once again, I am driving away in silence, lost in thought. I have been honored today to meet two resilient people, Nick and Alberta. Both are young, talented, and passionate. Even more striking to me, however, was their openness. I feel I have been led into the big heart of the Lakota people.

———

As I near the Singing Horse Trading Post, my mind transitions to what is next.

Rosie is taking me horseback riding this afternoon, and I am quite excited. The horse is such an integral part of the Lakota story, and I have been looking forward to the opportunity to ride one across the rolling grasslands at Pine Ridge.

As I pull up the winding dirt driveway, Rosie is readying two horses by the saddle barn. I jump out of the car, say hi, and run up to the house and change. When I return just a few minutes later, Rosie asks me to extend my hand to the handsome brown quarter horse in front of me named Partner. Rosie wants to see if the horse thinks we are a good match. The horse takes a few sniffs of me. We look each other in the eye.

"He likes you," Rosie says in her distinct, German accent. So, I climb on.

For the next two hours, Rosie and I, along with two horses and three dogs, ride the hills above the trading post. The dogs are all a mix of Lab and malamute. They know exactly where we are going. They wander off to the edge of a draw or the top of a hill to see what they can see, smell, and uncover. The entire time they are hunting. They are exceptionally tuned into nature and their surroundings. They disappear, but always return to check on us. Occasionally our path follows a small trail, and at other times, there is no trail at all. We are just kind of wandering around.

My horse, Partner, and I in the hills above the trading post. I am excited to ride a horse at Pine Ridge!

Partner is the most amazing horse I have ever ridden. He is a retired roping horse who was a champion in his day. I don't have to do much of anything as we ride. It is easy to get his attention—stop, turn, back up, speed up, or slow down. Rosie encourages me to rub his neck and talk to him every once in a while when he does a good job.

"He likes that," Rosie tells me.

The air at Pine Ridge is incredibly crisp! So crisp, in fact, that it has a distinct presence of its own. The traditional characteristics of air, invisible and unnoticeable, do not apply here. Each breath is an event, noteworthy and tangible.

The ride is perfect. From most vantage points, we can look to the northwest at the chalky white cliffs of the Badlands. Beyond the Badlands, perhaps fifty miles away, we can clearly see the Black Hills.

Like Nick and Alberta, Rosie is an amazing person. Born and raised in Germany, Rosie visited America as a young adult. With a backpack and no final destination, she traveled across the United States, stopping where she wanted to or needed to, in order to find work and earn some money before continuing on. That journey led her here. Pine Ridge had called her in.

Today, Rosie runs one of the few private businesses on the entire reservation. Running a business is not easy anywhere, and it is especially not easy here. The Pine Ridge Area Chamber of Commerce lists approximately sixty businesses as members. Perhaps forty of them are located on the reservation itself, and all of them are small. Private businesses at Pine Ridge are few and far between, and Rosie, through her perseverance and acumen, owns one of them. In this way, Rosie is an important role model and community leader. She is someone making her way independently, surviving without the government in a place where doing so is not common. Rosie is tough, kind, and resourceful; it takes all three to survive here.

There is no getting rich in Rosie's business at Pine Ridge. You just try to make enough money to sustain yourself and help those you can along the way. Financially, you live season to season here. You get by.

As our ride draws to a close, our horses move side by side down through the final pasture back to the trading post. It feels amazing to be on a horse in the windswept grass, looking out to the Black Hills, as the Lakota did centuries before me.

Rosie on her horse as we descend back down to the Singing Horse Trading Post, which you can see just over Rosie's right shoulder.

Always in the backdrop of my Pine Ridge experience there is Pinky. Pinky was the only person to respond to my initial search for a friend here. She is the one who hitched a ride to the Rapid City airport to meet me at baggage claim on the first day of my first visit. From that moment forward, she has always looked out for me here, and is constantly connecting me to new people. Tonight, Pinky has insisted that I come back into Pine Ridge (the town) to meet her longtime friend, Cecy Faster. When Pinky invites me to meet someone, I know there will be value, so I have quickly learned to just say "yes." After horseback riding and a quick shower, I am back in my car headed south to Karen Rupp's Retreat Center.

This hand-painted sign at the small white church on the road from Manderson to Wounded Knee asks simply for restraint.

The drive from the Singing Horse Trading Post to the town of Pine Ridge takes thirty to forty minutes, I would guess. I have never actually measured it, though, as that would be out of alignment with what brings me here. I leave my watch at home on top of my white wooden dresser every time I go to Pine Ridge. (I have since learned to leave my watch at home all the time.) Symbolically, this is a rebellion against the disciplined requirements of the modern world. I don't want to know what time it is at Pine Ridge. The sun rises, crosses the sky, and sets. The moon follows. The cycle repeats itself. A watch only hinders my understanding of time.

I do love the drive from Singing Horse to Pine Ridge. I can picture the entire route with my eyes closed. I leave Rosie's gate and turn left onto pavement. In about a mile, I pass the intersection of BIA 14, where I go left when I am heading over to see Nick at Thunder Valley. The way to Pine Ridge is straight ahead, however. On the right, I soon pass the old wooden sign for Pinky's Store. Just before entering the small village of Manderson, I pass one of my favorite cemeteries on the hillside to my right. On the left, there is a small white church, marking the beginning of town. Dogs lay in the dirt at Pinky's Store, and a few people are outside mingling around. The Wounded Knee District School is on the left, near the water tower that bears the district's name. Another church on the right marks the end of town. From there, I pass by Bette's Kitchen, scattered houses, grazing horses, a few American flags, and another cemetery before arriving in the actual town of Wounded Knee, which is smaller than Manderson and has neither a convenience store, nor a single place of business.

On the hill to the left sits the church at the famous Wounded Knee gravesite. Below the gravesite, just across BIA 27, is the red historical marker where I was first asked what brought me here, prior to purchasing the eagle pendant that currently hangs on the outside of my blue-checkered shirt. The route to the town of Pine Ridge does not actually go by the red historical marker, but you can see it from the intersection as you turn right. The road becomes more highway-like as it climbs away from Wounded Knee Creek, and the open views are spectacular on this spring evening. There is nothing like the color splash of the rising and setting sun at Pine Ridge—nothing. It is as if twice each day the sun and Mother Earth are one. Every shade of yellow and orange is visible across the cornfields and grasslands, as the road descends back down in a long, straight line until it intersects with US Highway 18, the Oyate Trail. From there, I turn right and it is just a short drive into town.

The late-afternoon sunlight upon the landscape is mesmerizing as I drive south to Karen Rupp's Retreat Center. Driving alone in the Land of Crazy Horse at sunrise or sunset does wonders for the soul.

We cannot acquire wisdom without consciousness, and yet we have to sacrifice our identification with ego consciousness before we can approach a loving and devoted relationship to the spirit within us called the Self. Wisdom does not live in the ego; it lives in the soul, in the heart rather than the mind.

—Alice O. Howell, *The Dove in the Stone*

From the moment you meet Cecy, you know you are with a great spirit. Cecy and her friends have been driving to Pine Ridge from Minneapolis twice a year for over twenty years. Together, they form a sewing circle. Each year, they bring sewing machines, cloth, and supplies to Pine Ridge and help the women who live here make household items such as quilts, pillows, and decorative wall hangings.

This is the first time I met Cecy. We have since become friends.

The group is mingling in the utilitarian kitchen of the Retreat Center when I let myself in and walk up the half flight of stairs. Baked beans are simmering in a large Crock-Pot and hot dogs are waiting beside them. I meet everyone and then we all sit comfortably around the white plastic tables in the center of the room. They are interested in me. I am interested in them. They tell me their story. I tell them mine. No one is in a hurry. We share smiles, laughs, and experiences. This is how it goes for me at Pine Ridge. When I meet people here, I immediately feel as if I have known them for a long time. The connections are soulful and spiritual. They are connections of the heart. It's like all the people who come here are drawn here in the same way. I think it is also partly because I am never in a hurry when I am at Pine Ridge. The environment here inspires complete focus and attention on the person in front of you.

"We are a Band-Aid organization," Cecy tells me. "We don't come here to solve the reservation's complex problems. We just provide a change of pace for ourselves and the people we work with here. Twice a year, for a few days at a time, we help a few local women. We provide some temporary relief from the complex problems in their lives that we often see and hear about. We have some laughs, share some stories, and sew a few items. We bring some fun to their lives, but we get way more out of it than we give. Coming here has changed us all on the inside. It has changed how we look at people. These women have lives here that are vastly different from our own. We have become close friends with many of them. In fact, today we often work with the children and grandchildren of the original women that we first met."

Cecy is calm in her demeanor. She has peace in her soul and that energy radiates from her. I can see it and feel it as we sit and talk.

"It's not about making any big changes," Cecy continues. "It's not about fixing things. Our visits to Pine Ridge are just about bringing some variety, fun, and friendship from the outside world into people's lives. That's what brings us here."

"What has changed here in the last twenty years?" I ask her.

"It hasn't changed a lot from what I can see," Cecy replies. "There always seem to be new programs and projects springing up, but within a few years they aren't here anymore. Even the little things seem to not last long. For example, you might donate some toys or books to a preschool. Then, you walk through a year or two later and they are gone. You learn that the best thing you can share here is your time and attention."

Back home, Cecy actively works on many of the same issues that challenge the reservation at Pine Ridge. Minneapolis—St. Paul is home to the largest urban Indian population per capita in the country. Many Native peoples were resettled there as part of the official government relocation efforts designed to urbanize and assimilate them. The same challenges often plague urban Indians; alcohol abuse, unemployment, high dropout rates, and violence are commonplace.

Cecy and I talk about alcohol abuse at Pine Ridge.

"Alcohol is illegal, but that hasn't stopped anyone from drinking," Cecy observes.

We both share our impressions about the lack of jobs and industry. Is there something about this culture that discourages economic activity, we wonder?

"Pizza Hut and Subway are the only two new businesses I remember seeing open here in the last twenty years," Cecy comments.

Cecy seems at peace with Pine Ridge. She and her friends clearly love coming here.

"There is something about this place that hooks you in and calls you back," Cecy says.

"I know exactly what you mean," I reply.

The conversation turns playful and we all just visit and enjoy the moment. I depart before dinner. I love beans and franks, but not as much as a Pine Ridge sunset. I shake hands with everyone a final time and then Cecy and I hug. We share a common spirit with respect to Pine Ridge. I am so pleased to have met Cecy and her sewing circle of friends.

———————

Cecy and her friends complete a transformative day for me in my solo journey at Pine Ridge. In this single day, I have met a visionary developer born from the spirit of revolution who is determined to restore independence through traditional Lakota values; I met a resourceful and eloquent young mother whose journey symbolizes the modern experience of her people and whose openness touched my heart; I went horseback riding with a tough but caring woman of German descent who came here with nothing more than a backpack and proceeded to stay and build one of the few independent businesses at Pine Ridge; finally, I sat at the Retreat Center while baked beans simmered in the presence of a graceful woman from Minneapolis, whose sewing circle has been working with Lakota women for over twenty years. I have spent the day in the presence of four amazing people—Nick, Alberta, Rosie, and Cecy—who are all functioning in meaningful ways within this community, beyond the world of government.

I began this day still feeling a bit dazed and confused about the future of Pine Ridge, as I listened to the district report on KILI Radio. My soul needed a wider variety of personal Pine Ridge connections, beyond the realm of government; I needed more human perspectives. Nick, Alberta, Rosie, and Cecy provided just that.

Media sources can depress and divide, I think to myself, reflecting upon the negative energy I took from the radio broadcast this morning.

Pine Ridge in person, however, has only been inspiring, my thoughts continue.

Then again, my blessing has always been that I see the good in people. When I stand face to face with people, I typically see their beauty, not their blemishes. Today, that was really easy.

One day. Four heroes. No judgment. Everyone was loved today, just the way they are, myself included.

I gave up beans and franks with Cecy's sewing circle to watch this sunset alone, on a dirt road east of Pine Ridge.

Great Spirit, Great Spirit, my Grandfather, all over the Earth the faces of living things are all alike.

—Black Elk, Oglala Holy Man

4
The Apology

**America has always turned a blind eye to what
we done to our own.**

—Cecil Gaines, *The Butler*

I know why Rosie's dogs lay in the dirt and sleep most of the day; they
are exhausted from the night's activities. The dogs spend the entire
night on guard, barking at predators, prey, and shadows, both real and
imagined. They protect their encampment on the plains, just like their
ancestors before them.

I wake up under brown flannel sheets in my room at the Singing Horse
Trading Post. On the opposite wall hangs a painting of a mounted warrior, alone atop a butte under a full Lakota moon. Two of the walls are
painted white, while the others are covered in pine paneling (just like
the kind we make at Hancock Lumber). Two small quilts are hanging

on the wall beside my bed. In the opposite corner there is a desk. My blue jeans hang from a metal hook below an elk caricature. The room is carpeted and the two casement windows face west toward the land of the setting sun. Even though it is early morning, everything I look at is full of color and rich in detail. I see things more clearly when I come to the Land of Crazy Horse. As I lay in bed, I give thought to why this is so.

First, I know when I come here, I am escaping the busyness of everyday life. At Pine Ridge, I have no roles or responsibilities. My Microsoft Outlook calendar is empty. My phone is off, and I avoid television and the Internet. At home, on a typical day, I can watch ESPN and MS-NBC while exercising in my basement. Over breakfast, I can scan the electronic messages that came in since I last fell asleep. Even my alarm clock is actually designed to be an iPhone terminal. In this way, I can literally fall asleep with my global connectivity. Infrastructure has gone to great lengths to make sure Americans are constantly linked to the information grid. Bypassing that communication superhighway is a part of what brings me here.

Second, there is no escaping nature at Pine Ridge. The northern plains make a single human being feel simultaneously small and all-powerful. The sun, wind, and clouds interact with the endless rolling grasslands in a way that causes one to pause and be silent.

Finally, there is Lakota spirituality. The Lakota see all living things as being connected, related, and interdependent. Life, in any form, comes from and returns to the same source. When I am here, I can actually feel this connectivity.

To discover me within you can be deafening.

—Anslie Roberts, *Beyond the Dreamtime*

Pine Ridge is a great destination for anyone who is searching for deeper meaning and understanding at the soul's level. This is what brings me here and keeps me coming back. I lost the consistent use of my voice due to my internal response to external circumstances, but I know my true voice still lives within me. I believe I can regain it by looking inward. Pine Ridge strengthens my ability to do this.

I always find it curious that I have come to regain my balance in a place where so many others have lost theirs.

These thoughts make me think of the challenges that come with sharing this story and the reasons why my very presence here might be questioned or even dismissed.

First, as a business leader, I am supposed to be "on the job" all the time, pushing for more. I am not supposed to be sitting on fence lines, feeling my connectivity with the energy of all living things. The loss of my voice made me revisit this assumption; then, I learned the power of making room for others to lead. This led to a new goal of making the role of the traditional leader smaller, so that everyone's voice could become stronger.

Second, as a white man, I am not necessarily supposed to be writing about Native American issues. There is a feeling among some that "only Indians can speak for Indians." But, that notion is tribal, and it doesn't fit the Lakota belief that we are all related. Additionally, I am not speaking for anyone other than myself. Ultimately, you can see Pine Ridge as a Lakota problem, or, you can see it as a human problem. It all depends upon where you want to draw your lines. I have chosen to see big circles, not small ones.

Third, as a male, I have been programmed a bit to suppress my inner feelings, fears, and doubts. Men are expected to stand tall and keep our soul-searching private. Better yet, we are supposed to repress our callings in favor of sacrificing for our tribe. But, this notion doesn't fit me either. I actually gain strength from confronting my vulnerabilities. Opening up to what scares me makes me stronger.

Finally, daring to talk about connecting with nature and "seeing more clearly" risks the perception that I am describing my spirituality as unique. But, I'm not. I believe the power to see the oneness of all things exists within us all. In Lakota society, before the coming of the Wasichu, all individuals could receive visions, take messages from animals, and find the energy source that connects all living things. If this is rare today, it is only because people have stopped searching. To the extent that I feel unique, it is in the same way I believe we all are.

These are my thoughts as I rise from my bed, starting a new day. We all want to transcend some of the expectations and social norms we were born into.

––––––––––

The food is amazing, but the conversation is even better. Rosie and I sit for well over an hour having breakfast together. How can I be here at Pine Ridge with my business responsibilities back home, she wants to know?

I tell Rosie that I work with a group of people who are given, and have accepted, lots of responsibility. When I was younger, I used to try to be involved in every aspect of the business to prove that I was capable and in control. This is a big part of what wore me down and cost me my voice. Now, I am more interested in sharing power than collecting it, more interested in letting go than holding on. During that personal evolutionary process of learning to share more responsibility, something interesting happened. The performance of the business improved. My own performance improved. Engagement, as defined by the people who worked at Hancock Lumber, strengthened, and profitability increased. Pretty much everything got better, easier.

I have learned that the best way to make an organization grow and improve is to share responsibility. I no longer believe in organizations where a small group of people corners the market on leadership. That's actually what has happened at Pine Ridge. I believe in organizations where everyone leads. When the Lakota lived this way, before the reservation era, they were powerful.

For me, the two most valuable business lessons I have learned are listening and restraint. Listening is more powerful than speaking. Furthermore, for me, the purpose of listening has evolved. I often used to listen in preparation to correct people or change their thinking. Now, I listen just to listen. I listen just to know how they feel. The key to getting people to share how they truly feel is not to judge their statements. Awareness is the only goal. As for restraint, well, that's a simple concept. Restraint is to have the power, but not use it. Restraint is patience, and it may be the ultimate leadership skill.

"The boss gets first dibs on all the work," I say to Rosie.

By this, I mean that that top leaders of any tribe can either hoard responsibility or share it. Today, thanks to spasmodic dysphonia, I constantly think about how I can make my role in the organization smaller by making everyone else's bigger. I don't want a smaller role because I am less committed. I love my job and the tribe that I belong to. I want a smaller role because I want to push the power and decision making out to the people who actually do the work of making our products and servicing our customers.

I tell Rosie that we put a lot of energy and resources into efficiency and process-improvement training. The purpose of that activity is to strengthen the work environment by eliminating waste and increasing our focus on the customer. Increasing efficiency is not just about making more money. It is definitely important for the business to be highly profitable, but "lean" operating practices have a higher calling for me. Efficiency is about improving the quality of people's lives, so that the work doesn't drain all their time and emotional energy. Instead, I want the work to flow smoothly and harmoniously. In a healthy company, people should have lots of time and energy for their passions outside of work. Work should complement a life, not consume it.

To this end, one of the initiatives we have recently launched at Hancock Lumber is to target a forty-hour work week for our hourly employees and fifty hours for sellers and managers. Prior to this initiative, the hourly work week averaged forty-seven hours, and many managers and sellers were working sixty or more hours. If you add an assumption about drive time to and from work, this just makes for too long a work week. I am looking to restore balance for everyone, not just myself.

The second component of this initiative is to create a compensation structure where people can make the same or more money, all while reducing work hours. This is what I refer to as the "higher calling of lean" (the human purpose of becoming more efficient and accurate). Across our company, we put bonus plans in place that we call "Performance Gold." The plans were designed to allow every member of the team to earn more money for increases in accuracy, efficiency, and safety.

Our initiative has been successful. The work week has shortened, while income levels have risen. This, in turn, puts a bit more balance back into people's lives.

Rosie finds this all quite interesting, and goes on to tell me about her business and the joys and challenges of making it work. I am inspired by what she does, as I have always felt that small sole proprietorships can be very demanding on the individual owner. One challenge Rosie and I both agree on is that being responsible for a business twenty-four/seven can consume you if you let it. At peak performance, the operation of a well-run company can look easy, but that is deceiving.

This is a picture of the Hancock Lumber sawmill in Casco, with a region of our timberland in the background known locally as "Jugtown." As Pine Ridge is the land of grass, Maine is the land of trees.

"Success looks easy to those who weren't around to watch it being made," I say to Rosie.

Breakfast is finished, our conversation winds down, and it is time for me to leave. I know I am Rosie's customer, but we have also become friends. I also know that our conversation is valuable, as Rosie doesn't have access to many other business owners. What she does here is quite rare.

We share a hug, and then I turn and walk toward my car where the dogs are waiting for me.

"You can't get in the car this time," I tell them both as I rub their thick, rugged hair (they both love to put their front paws in my lap when I first get into the car without closing the door).

"I'll be back someday soon," I promise.

Rosie's dogs know just how to position themselves to make sure I give them some attention before leaving the property.

My red Subaru with Colorado plates is loaded up with jewelry, blankets, drums, and positive energy. As I am about to get in, Catherine Grey Day comes out of her trailer to say goodbye.

"You don't mind if I e-mail you, do you?" Catherine asks me.

"I would love that!" I reply.

"Remember, in Lakota there is no word for good-bye," Catherine says.

"In Lakota we always say, 'See you later.' "

I know the phrase for see you later in Lakota so I use it.

"*Toksa Ake*, Catherine," I say.

"*Toksa Ake*, Kevin," she counters.

Replacing the word *Good-bye* with the phrase *See you later* is one of my favorite Lakota concepts. For me, it means in this life or the next. The Lakota know that only the thinnest of veils separates the two worlds.

Just as I am about to climb into my car and head for Pinky's Store, Rosie comes back outside. I have forgotten the drumstick for my new drum.

"Thanks for what you are doing here on the reservation" is the last thing Rosie says to me.

I wave good-bye and get into the car.

As I pull down Rosie's winding gravel drive, the radio is tuned to 94.7 KCNB out of Chadron, Nebraska, where Phillip Phillips's hit song "Home" begins to play . . .

> *Settle down, it'll all be clear*
> *Don't pay no mind to the demons*
> *They fill you with fear*
> *The trouble, it might drag you down*
> *If you get lost, you can always be found*
> *Just know you're not alone*
> *'Cause I'm going to make this place your home.*

I love spending time in the white plastic chairs that bear Pinky's name.

Even I am on "Indian time" now. I told Pinky I would come by the store at 8:00 a.m., but I don't arrive until 8:40 a.m.

The sky is bright and crisp this morning. Five exhausted dogs are spread out on the concrete in front of the store, warming themselves. They don't even lift their heads as I walk by. It was a big night for them, I can tell.

Pinky is sitting at the white plastic table with the chairs that bear her name. She always greets me with her warm, knowing smile, like she has been expecting me all her life. People are important to Pinky, and she treats them as such.

As usual, Pinky has a gift for me. She hands me a clear plastic bag filled with a chalky white vegetable I have never seen before. "It is timpsila," she explains. "Wild turnip strings." Timpsila can be dug by hand in the spring on the South Dakota prairies. These roots are commonly used in soups and stews, or simply for decorations.

We talk for a while about Pinky's friend, Cecy Faster, and her sewing circle, before Pinky turns the conversation to what she calls the "Hancock Home."

"We have a housing crisis in our community," Pinky says. "By the time you come back in August, this house will be built. One more 'ownership' home at Pine Ridge is a big deal here."

Our conversation wanders from one topic to the next. Neither of us has an agenda or a timeline. We are just visiting. It feels liberating.

"There is too much oppression in this world," Pinky says.

She tells me the story of an Afghan woman whom she hosted during a visit to the United States many years ago.

"She was not allowed to touch or be touched by men in any way. If she was touched, even accidentally, she could be punished back home," Pinky explains.

"We are all just a person away from that kind of life," Pinky observes.

Despite the oppression that has influenced Pine Ridge, Pinky can see that others around the globe are even more restricted and constrained.

We sit in silence and reflect upon what Pinky has just said, as her customers come and go at the front of the store. Four people are working this morning and each customer is well serviced.

"The Age of Aquarius is dawning, Pinky," I tell her.

Pinky says she also knows this to be true.

My friend and evolutionary astrologist, Deborah Dooley, knows that mankind is currently "in the doorway" between the Piscean and Aquarian Ages. An astrological age lasts for over two thousand years, so the transition from one age to the next is both lengthy and rare. Many astrologers refer to the transitional period as "the cusp," which is a time when one age begins to initiate its influence as the energy of the receding age wanes. The Piscean Age was defined by tribes banding together for survival. The Aquarian Age is to be a period where tribal identities disintegrate in favor of a single global humanity (of which the Oglala Holy Man, Black Elk, foretold).

Between visits, I tell Deborah about my experiences at Pine Ridge, and she is worried for the Lakota people. "The Lakota have become accustomed to their status as victims, I'm afraid," Deborah confides. "This is a Piscean trait that encourages people to close ranks. The Lakota are not alone in this. Tribes all over the world that have banded together tightly, and see themselves in survival mode, are experiencing great difficulty. Look at the Middle East, for example. Many cultures are addicted to their tribal mode, and letting go of their survival instincts will be extremely hard for them."

Aquarian energy is fast and matter-less. It symbolizes a time in which people will want to transcend their existing tribal structures and historical boundaries in favor of a single global community. Some will find this all quite threatening; when you look closely at what is happening around the world you can actually see the fear of the new age revealed in the eyes of some. Under duress, we often cling to the past, to what is familiar.

The Age of Aquarius was first made popular in American culture in the 1960s and '70s, and it soon came to define the period's counterculture revolution. War, racism, segregation, government power, corporate greed, dogmatic churches, and rigid educational systems were all exposed in the eyes of the revolutionaries. Peace, love, brotherhood, unity, and individual freedom became the new values of choice. In October 1967, the musical *Hair* debuted off-Broadway with "Aquarius" as the opening song:

> *When the moon is in the Seventh House*
> *And Jupiter aligns with Mars*
> *Then peace will guide the planets*
> *And love will steer the stars*
> *This is the dawning of the Age of Aquarius.*

When it comes time to leave, Pinky walks me outside. It is always a heartfelt good-bye when we part. In the car, I open the small white envelope Pinky gave me with the timpsila. Inside is a card. On the cover is a picture of a dog and a deer, coming nose to nose in friendship. The caption reads:

> *You never know when you are going to make a friend,*
> *but you always know when*
> *you have found a good one.*

The card is signed, "Pila Maya, Pinky. See you in August."

Pinky's store is the unofficial community center of the small town of Manderson, located deep within the boundaries of the reservation.

Today, I am leaving Pine Ridge, but not the Lakota story. I plan to spend the next several days traveling back in time through the land the Lakota used to own. I am going north to the Black Hills and then west to the great buffalo hunting grounds along the tributaries of the Yellowstone River. Along the way I will visit sacred sites and battlegrounds. I will rewind the story. Both Pine Ridge and evolutionary astrology have made me realize that time itself is not as simple as it appears. Time, I now believe, is circular, not linear. The past, present, and future all share the same small room.

The Lakota were swept up in the rush of America's "Manifest Destiny," and their world has not yet settled back into rhythm. I can see and feel this imbalance at Pine Ridge, and it makes me sad. Balance is everything in Lakota spirituality. Interestingly enough, I too am seeking to regain my own balance, my own sense of personal well-being. Perhaps balance is restored one person at a time.

A short while after leaving Pinky, dust is swirling everywhere. The best decision I made on this trip so far was to rent a car that was not white. I cross the White River under a clear blue sky and gain elevation to a stretch of land known as Cuny Table, located in the northwest corner of the reservation. From this plateau, I can stop my car anytime I want in the middle of the dirt road and look out over vast stretches of territory. The road feels as if it was abandoned long ago and I alone have rediscovered it. For all I can see at this moment, I am the last person on Earth.

As I leave Pine Ridge, I see a great deal of irony in the fact that the land we had to take from the Lakota is so sparsely populated today. People do live here and businesses, primarily ranches, are run here. However, the most common scene involves no cars, no houses, and no people. As far as the eye can see, there is just fenced grazing land; often, you cannot even see any cattle. The fences themselves look guilty to me at times, like they don't really belong and they know it. It is not uncommon here to see a cow on the wrong side of a fence, standing longingly beside it, trying to figure out how to get back in. I find this so interesting. It is as if being outside the fence makes even the cows uneasy. Should a boundary, like a reservation, last for all time just because those who went before us created it?

The view from Cuny Table, looking back over the reservation. There is a great quiet here that stirs the soul.

Boundaries have momentum, so it is healthy and necessary to revisit their very premise. Just four generations ago in Lakota lineage, there were no fence lines here, and every living thing roamed freely, as this was the intention of the Great Spirit. Sometimes going backwards is moving forward.

As I drive, I think about what I have already learned of the old Lakota traditions.

Hanbleceya (han-blay-CHE-ya) is a Lakota word that means "to cry for a vision." Young Lakota men coming of age would embark on a Hanbleceya (vision quest) as a rite of passage from childhood to adulthood. Alone in the wilderness, wandering, fasting, and praying, an individual would seek spiritual guidance, direction, and purpose. Participants would often experience a great vision or powerful dream that provided insight into their true path. Deliberately seeking a deeper truth, vision questers separated themselves from their community to find their calling, and, in doing so, strengthened their tribe. The Lakota knew there was power in solo journeys into the wilderness.

I am on such a journey.

A lone warrior cries for and receives a vision. Seeking is the biggest step in the vision-quest process.

**The religion of the Indian is the last thing about him
that the man of another race ever understands.**

—Charles Eastman

It is 11:00 a.m. when I cross the Cheyenne River and enter Custer County. I nearly didn't make it this far, however. A few miles back, I was close to being without a car. I had gotten out to take a picture and, as usual, I had left my car running in the middle of the road. This time, however, I'd also left the car in gear! As I moved away from my car, it too began to move away from me. By the time I noticed, the car was twenty yards away and rolling forward. I quickly pivoted and sprinted after it. Fortunately, I had left the driver's-side door open. I ran and jumped back into the moving vehicle, just a moment before it would have rolled down into a ditch that I would not have been able to drive back out of. Who knows when the next car would have come by to rescue me? This was a close call indeed, but I had a big laugh to myself all the same.

The dirt road I am driving on empties onto Route 79, south of Rapid City, where I turn left and head for the town of Hot Springs, just a few miles away. Hot Springs is a small vacation town on the southern edge of the Black Hills, just below Wind Cave National Park. In the summer, it bustles with activity. Most of the year, as is the case today, it is a sleepy and quiet place. I love this town in the off-season for its empty streets and lonely storefronts.

I am staying at the Best Western, just past Dairy Queen on the southern side of town. It is around noon when I go there to check in. No one is at the front desk, so I push the button that says "press here," and a bell chimes. A few moments later, a man comes out of the office and asks how he can help me. I say hi and tell him I have a reservation for the night and am just looking to check in and drop off my bags.

"No rooms are released until two p.m.," he replies. "They are still being cleaned."

There aren't five cars in the parking lot, including his and mine. The hotel must have at least sixty rooms. Although I am living in my peaceful vision-quest frame of mind, I can't resist saying, "Well, how about the rooms that weren't occupied last night?"

He doesn't think this is funny. "I'm sorry. No rooms are released until two p.m. That's our policy," he stoically replies.

I pause for a moment to regroup before responding, "No problem. I'll come back later after all the rooms have been cleaned. Thank you."

The outside temperature reading in my car says 44 degrees as I enter Wind Cave National Park. It feels colder than that, however, as snowflakes swirl across the sky. Exiting the car, the wind makes my eyes water and I feel there is symbolism in this. Whenever I cross into Wind Cave National Park, I envision a different sign that reads, "Entering Lakota tribal lands reserved permanently for the Sioux Nation by the Treaty of Fort Laramie of 1868." I always wonder who knows the true story of how this "public" land was acquired.

The buffalo, as usual, are everywhere, and the history and politics of these grasslands and pine forests doesn't seem to interest them. Spring has only just arrived in the Black Hills, and grazing is the order of the day. The wind strengthens and the snowflakes grow larger. I put on my wool hat and head out for a walk. I am going to spend the afternoon with the buffalo.

The trail crosses a small brook and then follows the edge of the open forest. Straight ahead and to my right are miles of grasslands. I can smell the elk and I see some deer. It is just me, the wind, and a valley full of buffalo. My plan is to hike for a while and then find a tree and just sit under it with my binoculars, looking out across the vast buffalo flats that dominate the upper portion of the park.

In Lakota spirituality, the buffalo and the people are brothers.

"You don't always have to be busy," my friend Deborah Dooley is fond of reminding me.

There comes a time when the world gets quiet and the only thing left is your own heart. So you'd better learn the sounds of it. Otherwise, you'll never understand what it's saying.

—Sarah Dessen, *Just Listen*

The tree I sit under is a tough old pine. It sits alone on a hilltop, surrounded by golden grass. There are other trees nearby, but the grasses rule here. Each tree is its own island.

There are no humans in sight. The only sounds belong to nature. It is mid-afternoon and most of the buffalo are resting away from the broken timber, well out onto the open plains. If you are a buffalo, this is smart, and learned over time by generations of buffalo before you. The elk are likely bedded down in some thick patch of timber. If you are an elk, this too is smart and also learned over time by generations of elk before you. Everyone, myself included, has his or her space on this day. I am listening to the silence when a woodpecker interrupts from a nearby tree. Silence, too, is a noise that can be heard.

Eventually, I return to walking. I am not sure what makes me decide to sit or walk. Where there is neither time frame nor destination, it is interesting to see what one decides to do. Back home, lots of people go for "power walks" that are designed to go as fast as possible, with maximum physical exertion. In Lakota lands, I prefer to go for "spirit walks" where the goal is just the opposite. I feel thankful for the opportunity to be here as I drift along.

"Oh boy!" I exclaim, as I step in a fresh pile of buffalo dung. I feel my misstep before I see it.

"So much for my good fortune," I say out loud, with a shrug of my shoulders.

The tree I sat under in Wind Cave National Park.

I take one last look at the tree I sat under before leaving the grasslands behind and descending into the forest below. I wonder if anyone else has ever sat under that tree, leaning against the jagged bark among the scattered cones and needles.

The trail down into the forest is hard to follow. Humans may not have used it since last fall, and this year's grass remembers not who passed this way last year. I wind down the steep embankment where the narrow path reveals itself and follows a babbling creek. Nearby, a hot spring bubbles and steams. The smell of sulfur is in the air. The trail passes through a series of small canyons, where I can imagine Lakota hunters springing out and descending upon a small but unsuspecting buffalo herd. The trail continues beside the creek before making a big loop back to its place of origin, where my car is parked. By now, it is late in the afternoon.

I return to the Best Western where the same man checks me in, as if we have never met. I shower and then organize my notes. I am always afraid of losing them. As a newcomer to field research, losing my journal or my camera are my two great fears.

I am not at the Best Western long, as I want to return to the park for sunset. It is feeding time for the buffalo, elk, deer, and antelope, and with them is where I want to be.

The sun is low in the sky as I reenter the park. The scene is beautiful and the wildlife is everywhere. Wind Cave is one of America's best-kept national park secrets. In fact, it is actually a double secret. The first secret is what an amazing place it is to watch wildlife (rivaled only by Yellowstone). The second secret, of course, is the story of how this land was acquired. Patriotism is the Black Hills's marketing theme, built upon Custer's first expedition to the region, the brave settlers that followed, and the tribute to the presidents at Mount Rushmore.

I watch the buffalo until the last light fades. It is easy to blame the people of Pine Ridge for their current plight. It is easier on ourselves to blame them. If we blame them, we can avoid coming to terms with how they got here. There is momentum and simplicity in the notion that Columbus discovered a new world.

———————

I am not sleeping on this trip. However, I am neither frustrated nor fatigued by this. There is a powerful energy flowing through me this week that is palpable and different. I sleep for a few hours and then just wake up feeling fresh and alert. It is 28 degrees at 6:15 a.m. when I leave the hotel the next morning and load my bags back into my car. Although it is early May, I turn the car on to defrost the windows. I am energized by the crispness of the air and excited about the day in front of me.

Today, I am continuing my journey through the sacred lands and hunting grounds that the Lakota used to own. I feel the Lakota spirit here, as much as I do at Pine Ridge. The spirit world is not governed by artificial boundaries; reservations can't hold them.

This day will take me north through the Black Hills and on to other small towns such as Pringle, Custer City, Deadwood, and Belle Fourche. From there, I will travel west into Wyoming on my way to Devils Tower, one of the great spiritual sites of the Lakota world. Then, I will go west again toward the Bighorn Mountains. It is a vast territory, and it amazes me that the Lakota covered it on horseback and on foot.

The morning light summons silence and awe as I reenter Wind Cave National Park. The Black Hills are marked by dramatic rock formations, open pine forests, and rolling grasslands. As I drive, I marvel at the natural beauty of the landscape. My mind wanders and I find myself thinking about something Nick Tilsen told me just two days ago back at Pine Ridge. He said, to his knowledge, the US Government has never officially apologized for breaking the Treaty of 1868, or for the cultural and economic oppression that followed. Suddenly, an idea comes to me and I pull the car over hastily, into a small gravel turnout. Lakota society was communal and no one spoke for everyone. All voices were important. Government was informal and the power went to the people. It is from this spirit that my idea flows.

Why can't I write an apology? I ask myself.

I turn off the car, grab my journal, take out my pen, and eagerly begin to write. The words flow from my pen:

THE APOLOGY

To the Lakota people and all the First Nation tribes of the northern plains:

My name is Kevin Hancock and I would like to apologize. I have learned the history of your people and I am aware of the devastating impact America's western expansion had upon you.

I apologize that we put our needs above yours.

I apologize that we slaughtered the buffalo with which you coexisted.

I apologize that we broke our treaties.

I apologize that we took your land under the guise of our own industriousness, and as if we had God's blessing.

I apologize that we saw your race and culture as inferior and treated you as such.

I have also learned about the neglect and federal mismanagement of your reservations in the twentieth century, and for this, too, I would like to apologize.

I apologize that we restricted your constitutional rights to free speech and religion.

I apologize that we restricted your rights to gather and to bear arms.

I apologize that we sold off your property without your consent or just compensation.

I apologize that we sent your children off to unforgiving boarding schools to be "remade."

Finally, I have seen modern-day life at Pine Ridge, and I would like to apologize for the conditions a century of oppression and mistreatment helped create.

I wish we could go back and rewrite history. I wish we could start over and do it differently. I wish we could have seen that there was room for everyone. I wish we had not overreached.

I hope you will accept this apology and that we can now join together in the Lakota tradition that says all people are one people. An apology from one person may seem small. It changes nothing in many ways. At the same time, this is how I feel, and I do not believe I am alone. I believe there are hundreds of millions of people across America who are also sorry.

I hope this apology contributes to the process of healing, letting go, and moving on.

Having met your people, I believe in your future.

Sincerely,

Kevin Hancock

I quietly put my pen away in the silver binder rings of my journal and get out of the car. The crisp Black Hills air engulfs me as I walk reflectively in a slow circle. People who have been marginalized need understanding and respect in order to heal. Perhaps an apology from the people can be even more powerful than an institutional apology from a bureaucratic government. Perhaps the last thing the Lakota need is another official proclamation.

I stop circling and take a deep breath. The air flows in through my nose and descends into my body. The power of the air spreads through me. I close my eyes and extend my arms in prayer to the Great Spirit.

"I apologize," I say out loud.

I say this once, but keep my eyes closed and arms extended for quite some time, just breathing. I don't know if any cars pass me as I do this. I am deep within my own thoughts.

The Age of Aquarius is dawning, I think as I open my eyes. Everything in my sight is rich with color and detail. I feel very alive. I feel free. I feel light.

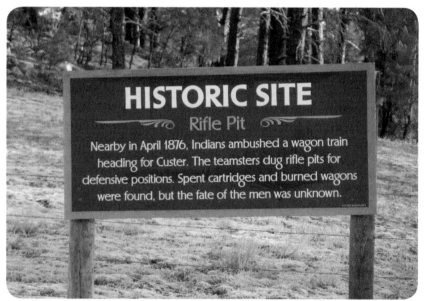

One hundred years after America broke free from British rule, our nation was still conquering and colonizing in the American West.

If we ever owned this land we own it still, for we never sold it. In the treaty councils the commissioners have claimed that our country has been sold to the government. Suppose a white man should come to me and say, "Joseph, I like your horses, and I want to buy them." I say to him, "No, my horses suit me, I will not sell them." Then he goes to my neighbor, and says to him, "Joseph has some good horses. I want to buy them but he refuses to sell." My neighbor answers, "Pay me the money, and I will sell you Joseph's horses." The white man returns to me and says, "Joseph, I have bought your horses and you must let me have them." If we sold our lands to the government, this is the way in which they were bought.

—Chief Joseph of the Nez Perce

I stop farther down the road at a historic marker that describes the remnants of the early mining town of Sheridan, a town that now lies below the lake, under thirty feet of water. The morning light glides through the timber and across the meadows. I almost never listen to classical music, but on this morning the radio dial stops there and soon I find myself listening intently. I can feel my own energy uniting with the other energy sources around me. My eyes tear up and I actually begin to cry.

The German composer, Johann Pachelbel, wrote *Canon in D* in the late 1600s. Some speculate that it was composed for the wedding of Johann Sebastian Bach's oldest brother, who was a student of Pachelbel's. Interestingly enough, the *Canon* was largely lost to history until it was rediscovered in the twentieth century, and now stands as one of the most popular compositions of all time.

Imagine that, I think to myself. *A story of great beauty is forgotten and lost to history before being rediscovered and unearthed.*

Scattered snow lingers in the corners of the meadows as I continue north, then west toward Devils Tower. Sometime later, having returned to contemporary music, Pink's hit song "Just Give Me a Reason" begins to play:

It's in the stars
It's been written in the scars on our hearts
That we're not broken, just bent
And we can learn to love again

Pachelbel to Pink, I think to myself. *That's almost as dramatic a change as Casco to Pine Ridge.*

South of the Belle Fourche River, I pass through the town of Aladdin, Wyoming (population 15). Fifteen people now live in Aladdin, more than 135 years after the Battle of Little Bighorn was fought because there wasn't enough room for everyone.

As I near Devils Tower, my anxiety builds.

I can actually relate to Richard Dreyfuss's character in Steven Spielberg's 1977 blockbuster film, *Close Encounters of the Third Kind.* Playing the role of Roy Neary, Dreyfuss has a UFO encounter while surveying a power outage in rural Indiana. His wife Ronnie, played by Teri Garr, is adamant that Roy should move on as if it never happened, but Roy is unable to do so and instead the encounter becomes an obsession. Roy soon finds himself building tower objects he does not understand. As the television plays in the background, Roy sees the news report of a train crash involving toxic chemicals near Devils Tower in Wyoming, and he instantly knows that is where he is being called.

My dad loved this movie, and I remember going to see it with my whole family. I can close my eyes and picture the original movie poster with the lights of the giant alien spacecraft turning the night sky red above Devils Tower.

My favorite scene from the movie is the final one. As the famous five tones play in rapid succession, the mother ship appears from deep space and lands. The door slowly opens, light appears, and missing people from the past emerge, followed by the glowing extraterrestrials themselves. These beings clearly have vastly superior technology, but instead of using it selfishly, they showed restraint.

The parallels between the movie and my story are not lost on me. Roy Neary feels as if he has been called to this specific spot on the northern plains, but, he does not know why. He feels pressure to reject the calling, but ultimately finds himself unable to resist, and pushes on into the unknown.

The divergence between the movie and the actual historical events are equally striking. The Lakota were living off this same land when a distant and overwhelming force arrived from the East. In this story, however, the superior power (America) does not show restraint; instead, they take the land and subjugate the Native peoples. In *Close Encounters*, the aliens from another world chose a different path. Although they possess the capabilities to conquer, they do not do so. To have the power to dominate and not use it is the essence of Aquarian energy, and the great final message of the movie.

It's all about where you are going,
no matter where you've been . . .

This verse of a pop song is playing on the radio as I near the next small town on my route.

I have butterflies as I drive through Alva, Wyoming (population 50), just like I used to in prelude to a big game. I know at any moment I am going to round a corner and glimpse Devils Tower again for the first time. I can sense it before I can see it. When the sensation reaches its peak, I round a curve and there it is, calling me home.

How did I know that my first view of Devils Tower would come at that precise bend in the road? Why was I filled with such anticipation and nervous energy? I can't explain it, but I sure could feel it. It is a feeling I have never had before in anticipation of a geographic landmark. All I can say is, at that moment, what I saw was stunning. I am sure lots of people drive around that corner and say something like, "Oh, look! There it is!" But, for me, the emotion and connection to the moment was tied to energies deep within my soul. At that moment, I totally understood the Lakota sense of spiritual connection to this place. The tower stands alone, surrounded by grasslands and pine trees as it torques out of the earth into a twisted, spiraling formation. It simultaneously looks as if it has just arrived and as if it has stood there since the dawn of time. It is hard for me to take my eyes off it. I am transfixed.

The tower leaves my sight for a while as the road winds through Hulett (population 383). I take a close look at the Deer Creek Taxidermy storefront as I drive through town. The spirituality of hunting in these forests and grasslands is very appealing to me at this moment.

On the edge of town, I cross the Belle Fourche River held down by red rock walls. The meaning, use, and significance of rivers cannot be overstated when reflecting on the traditional Lakota way of life. Today, water is brought to us. We hardly even realize this happens, or that it's been possible only in the most recent moments of human history. For most of Lakota history, the people went to the water. So, too, did all the other animals and living creatures. Without water, there was no life. Travel routes, hunting patterns, and camp locations all depended upon water. Today, it is just taken care of. The water is brought to us and we don't give it a second thought.

In the time of Crazy Horse, both the two-leggeds and the four-leggeds went to the water.

As I drive closer and closer to Devils Tower, my clarity is unbelievable. I am completely lost in the moment—just this moment, just this place, just right now—totally immersed in my surroundings, everything as one thing. And, my heart is pounding.

My first view of Devils Tower occurred just west of Alva, Wyoming. I could feel the tower's presence before I could see it.

A dark mist lay over the Black Hills, and the land was like iron. At the top of the ridge, I caught sight of Devils Tower upthrust against the gray sky as if in the birth of time the core of the Earth had broken through its crust and the motion of the world was begun. There are things in nature that engender an awful quiet in the heart of man; Devils Tower is one of them.

—N. Scott Momaday

5
Finding Center

I first told the story of my spiritual encounter at Devils Tower to my friend, Nick Tilsen, several weeks after I got back home. At the time, I was worried that people wouldn't understand what I experienced there. Nick paused over the phone and then replied, "Don't worry, Kevin; that vision was just for you. It wasn't meant for anybody else."

You know how everyone's always saying seize the moment? I don't know, I'm kind of thinking it's the other way around, like the moment seizes us.

—Nicole, *Boyhood*

I park my car shortly after noon. It is 72 degrees. In the mostly empty parking lot, I change into shorts and walk onto the Tower Trail. Even though the path is only 1.3 miles long, it will be well after 2:30 p.m. before I reemerge.

The tower rises 1,276 feet above the Belle Fourche River Valley. President Roosevelt proclaimed it the nation's first national monument in 1906. The tower narrows as it twists and ascends. It is approximately 1,000 feet in diameter at the bottom and 275 feet at the top. "Devils Tower" is the American name given to this site by Colonel Richard Dodge, following an 1873 military expedition. The Lakota referred to it, however, as *Mato Tipila*, or the "Bear's Lodge." One Lakota story tells of two boys who strayed far from their village where they encountered Mato, the great bear. Mato was a massive beast with paws as big as a tepee, and he wanted to eat the boys, so he chased after them. As he was just about to pounce, the boys prayed to Wakan Tanka, the Creator of all things, for help. Suddenly, the ground shook underneath them and a huge rock thrust up from the earth, lifting them high into the sky. This made Mato very angry. He tried everything to climb the rock tower and reach them, leaving huge scratch marks on all sides of the rock formation before sauntering off in frustration. Soon thereafter, a great eagle descended from the sky, lifted a boy in each talon, and gently lowered them to the ground. This is the Lakota story of how Mato Tipila was created. From the beginning of time to the present day, the site has held great spiritual meaning for all the northern plains tribes.

For me, Devils Tower is the most spiritual place I have ever been. I am struck by how personal and intense my connection to the tower feels. I stand motionless, alone on the trail. I am totally immersed in my surroundings, just looking up through the scattered pines at the massive spiraling rock formation. The warm sunlight flows into me as the wind rustles softly. When I do walk, I feel as if I am floating along the path and through the pines. I know I am walking, but it feels as if I am floating.

Occasionally, a few other visitors walk by me in the opposite direction. I am slowly moving clockwise around the Tower. As people pass, I am interested in what they see. My heightened state of awareness allows me to gauge the emotions of those who pass me. A few see and sense what I am experiencing, but most are too busy inside for that. They are hustling through and keeping to a schedule, talking as they go about affairs and events far away from this sacred place. The physical body and the spiritual core are not always in unison. When the two become one, a great sense of truth and power emerge. This is a place for solitude, quiet, and reflection. I have all my energy on the Tower, but I did not consciously set out to do this. It is as if my spiritual energy took me by the hand and started running when we exited the car. I am following, not leading.

As I float along the dirt path, a tree filled with dead leaves stops me in my tracks as I pass under it. The tree is speaking to me and nodding in affirmation. It is telling me that I am home. I stop and stand in peaceful union with this tree, its rattling leaves, and the wind that stirs them. In the moment, it all feels perfectly true and natural. This is the first time a tree has ever spoken to me. Perhaps, better said, this is the first time I have heard one.

When the tree is done speaking, it simply stops. The tree becomes completely still. One moment every leaf is rustling and the next moment every leaf is motionless. This makes me smile. "Toksa Ake," I say to the tree, as all the leaves move again one final time, as if to say "see you later" in return.

As I walk, I have flashes of rational thoughts that ask, *Is this really happening?* I drift out for a moment to the sounds of a plane passing overhead. As quickly as I recognize this sound, I let it go and the noise ceases, even though the plane has not yet passed. I am walking between two worlds.

I did not need this sign to know I was in a sacred place. My body knew where it was on its own.

In the old days, experiences such as this were common for the Lakota. Today, many people might read this passage and find it comical, or perhaps even think I have lost my mind. In a sense, that is close to correct. I haven't actually lost my mind, though. I have just learned to let it take a back seat. I am learning to live with my heart and to connect with the single energy that makes up all living things.

I pass by prayer flag after prayer flag as I move along the trail. My hands are extended and I feel the texture of the trees as I walk. Hardwoods, softwoods, needles, and bark; I feel the differences in each aspect of each tree. No two trees are the same. That's amazing when you think about it.

I come to a big rock that invites me to stop and lay down. My legs dangle over the edge as the warmth of the sun stored by the rock seeps into my body. I drift away into a meditative state. As people pass by, I can feel what kind of souls are passing me—open, free, busy, nervous, calm, or distracted.

I feel as if I can see, but I am certain my eyes are closed. I have the sensation that my eyelids are drifting up and letting in a clean and peaceful light. This sensation goes on for some time. I am in no hurry to rush it away. Instead, I turn myself over to whatever is happening and let it take me. My whole body feels warm. After some time, the light that my closed eyes see gives way to a figure. The figure increasingly becomes the object of my attention, although I can't initially make out what it is. At first, it is simply part of the light, but slowly it becomes something independent, distinct from the light itself. In time, I can see that the figure is walking away from me. It is walking through rich, tall grass that is being blown gently by the wind. I look closer (without opening my eyes). Soon thereafter, I can distinguish the figure. It is a lone buffalo. As soon as I come to see that it is a buffalo, it stops and looks directly back at me. The buffalo and I make eye contact. For an instant we both are frozen in time. No sooner does this happen, however, than the buffalo turns completely white and flashes into a bright light and then vanishes.

A few minutes later, I come back into the present and slowly open my eyes.

My breathing is heavy. I know what has just happened to me and immediately understand it to be significant. I just got totally lost outside of (or inside of) my physical surroundings. I was not consciously looking for a vision experience; visions don't work that way. You don't call them up on command; rather, you meet them halfway. When you put your soul and spirit first, you open the door for things of the other world to come calling. My heart is pounding as I walk because I know the importance the White Buffalo Calf Woman story holds in Lakota lore, and I just saw her.

The Story of the White Buffalo Calf Woman
(As described in Stonee's *Lore, Legends and Teachings*)

One summer many, many moons ago the Seven Sacred Council Fires of the Lakota Nation came together and camped near the Black Hills. Food was scarce, and the chiefs sent two of their best men out to search for game. This was before the coming of the horses and so the braves were on foot. They searched everywhere, but could find no signs of game, so they decided to climb to the top of a high hill where they could overlook the whole country. Halfway up the hill they saw a figure coming toward them, but this figure was not walking in the traditional sense. It was floating. From this they knew that the being was holy.

As the figure came closer, the hunters could tell that it was a human form. As the figure drew even nearer they could see it was a woman of great beauty. She wore a white buckskin robe and had a red dot painted on each cheek. One of the men had impure thoughts of lust and went to touch the woman. As he embraced her there was a great flash of light and his body was instantly reduced to ashes and bones. The buffalo woman then spoke to the lone man that remained:

"Good things I am bringing, something holy to your nation. A message I carry for your people from the buffalo nation. Go back to the camp and tell the people to prepare for my arrival. Tell your chief to put up a medicine lodge with twenty-four poles. Let it be made holy for my coming."

The young man did as he was told and the camp was prepared. After four days, the White Buffalo Woman appeared carrying a bundle in both arms. She entered the medicine lodge and circled the people, stopping before the chief where she opened the bundle to reveal a sacred pipe and a wooden bowl. She filled the pipe with willow-bark tobacco and showed the people how to use it correctly. Then she circled the lodge four times in representation of the circle without end that is the road of life.

"The pipe is alive; it is a red being showing you a red life and a red road. And this is the first ceremony for which you will use this pipe. You will use it to celebrate Wakan Tanka, the Great Mystery Spirit. The day a human dies is always a sacred day. The day when the soul is released to the Great Spirit is another. Remember: This pipe is very sacred. Respect it and it will take you to the end of the road. The four ages of creation are in me; I am the four ages. I will come to see you in every generation cycle. I shall come back to you. Toksha ake wacinyanktin ktelo, I shall see you again."

With this the White Buffalo Woman left the medicine lodge, walking away in the same direction from which she had come toward the setting sun. As she began to disappear into the red ball on the horizon, she stopped and rolled over four times. The first time she turned into a black buffalo, the second time into a brown buffalo, the third time into a red buffalo, and finally, the fourth time, into a white female buffalo calf. Finally, she disappeared in a flash of light.

Soon thereafter the buffalo appeared on the plains in great numbers, allowing some of their own to be killed so that their two-legged brothers might live. From that day forward the buffalo provided everything the Lakota needed for survival, from meat to clothing to shelter and tools. In this way the buffalo and the Lakota lived together in harmony.

To this day, a white buffalo is the most sacred living being one could encounter.

Nothing like this has ever happened to me before. I was not consciously searching for a vision when I got out of my car and started walking down the Tower Trail. The sensations came to me and took me. They began moments before I rounded the bend in my car and saw the Tower "again for the first time." That phrase keeps coming into my head and it makes me think of Deborah Dooley and the concept of past life experiences. *Perhaps I have been here before, just not in this lifetime,* I think to myself without judgment. The sensations intensified when I parked and started down the trail on foot. The floating sensation was dramatic. By the time the lone hardwood tree filled with dead leaves stopped me, I knew something magical had come over me, and I completely let myself go to where I was being called.

"For me, this is the center," I say to myself. "I have found my center."

I keep lingering and lingering on the Tower Trail. I have never been in less of a hurry to move in my life. I don't want this circular walk around the great Tower to end, but I know that this is the nature of all circles; they end, yet they continue. Tomorrow I have forts and battlegrounds to experience but for today, this spot holds me, so I just keep lingering. I watch the climbers climb as the prayer flags dance in the breeze. For me, at this moment, time has no meaning.

Eventually, I find myself back in the parking lot at both the end and the beginning of my journey. I put the few belongings I have with me back in the car and slowly walk into the restroom, located diagonally across the parking lot. On the wall inside is a green chalkboard, upon which nothing is written. The slate has been wiped clean, like my own soul, offering a fresh start. I go to the board, pick up the white chalk, and leave my mark.

I left this message on the bathroom wall at Devil's Tower. Paha Sapa *is the Lakota word for Black Hills, KH, my initials, and OST stands for* Oglala Sioux Tribe.

I miss my family! This is such an important point for me to communicate. I am content here on the Lakota trail *and* I miss my home and my family, as well. Both are truths for me. You don't have to leave one community to join another. Love is not finite; our circles can be bigger than we think.

Later that afternoon, as I drive west out of Gillette, Wyoming, the Bighorn Mountains come into view for the first time.

Awhile later, I cross the Powder River. I have read so much about this river and know its significance to the Lakota. It is flowing swiftly, north by northeast, from the Bighorn Mountains to where it will meet the Yellowstone River. The water that flows past me will end up in the Gulf of Mexico. I want to dip my hands into it, but the bank that I stand on is much too steep. You can't cross, or even access, these rivers just anywhere.

The vastness of Lakota territory amazes me. It takes two days driving at Western speed limits in modern cars to cross the 1868 Treaty lands. There was room for everybody here physically; the limitations were mental. That idea comes back to me time and time again. There was room for everybody. It didn't have to be this way, but it was this way, and now we all, both the conquerors and the conquered, must pay. There is no victory in colonizing others and leaving them behind.

The same warm northwest wind that I felt at Pine Ridge is still blowing in my face.

I don't know where I am staying tonight, and I love that feeling. I find it exciting and liberating!

At exactly 5:00 p.m., I make my hundredth journal entry of the day in Fort Phil Kearny's lonely gravel parking lot. The fort is situated on the edge of the Bighorn Mountains, in the heart of the hunting grounds the Sioux fought the Crow to take, and then the Wasichu to keep.

The stockade walls of Fort Phil Kearny protected the Bozeman Trail along the eastern edge of the Bighorn Mountains.

The gate creaks in the wind as I enter the confines of the fort. I am the only person here. It is perfect. Whatever story Fort Phil Kearny has to tell on this cool spring evening, it will tell to me alone.

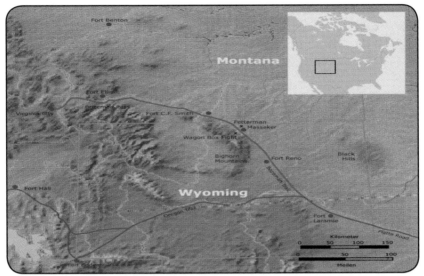

The Bozeman Trail cut through the last great buffalo hunting grounds on the northern plains. It was a faster route to the Montana gold fields.

Fort Phil Kearny was one of three forts constructed by the US Army along the Bozeman Trail in 1866. There was a time when staying inside these gates was necessary for survival. In what would later become known as Red Cloud's War, the Lakota united with the Northern Cheyenne and Arapaho to disrupt travelers and fight the US Army sent to protect them. The largest battle of that war took place just a few miles from where I am standing. On the clear but cold morning of December 21, 1866, a woodcutting detachment was sent from the fort. Little did this small group know that as many as a thousand mounted warriors hid nearby and were ready for a fight.

Soon, the woodcutters were under attack, and reinforcements from the 18th Infantry and the 2nd Cavalry were hastily dispatched to provide relief. Captain William J. Fetterman lobbied to lead the rescue effort and was chosen to do so. He was sent out with orders not to get drawn into a major engagement. The Sioux by now, however, had become tactical masters at luring the military into ambushes, and this was to be one such day. A small band of warriors, led by Crazy Horse himself, coaxed the rescue party farther and farther forward into a grassy box canyon where the unseen mass of the Indian force waited. By the time Fetterman and his men knew what was coming, it was too late to change the course of events. Fighting bravely, Fettermen's troops battled their way to the top of what is now known as "Massacre Hill," where he and eighty-two others lost their lives. In the end, the fighting was hand-to-hand; Indian accounts of the battle spoke of the bravery and courage with which the white men fought.

Ironically, Captain Fetterman had once boasted that with no more than eighty men he could "ride through the entire Sioux Nation." Like Lieutenant Colonel Custer would do a decade later, Fetterman had overplayed his hand.

Red Cloud's War led to what the Lakota believed would be a lasting peace. The US Government agreed to close the Bozeman Trail and abandon the forts that guarded it. This land would be guaranteed to the Indian tribes of the northern plains forever through the Treaty of Fort Laramie of 1868. Shortly after Fort Phil Kearny was abandoned, the Sioux burned it to the ground.

I can feel the anticipation as my car pulls to a halt in the gravel parking area, just a few miles from the fort where Fetterman and his men made their final stand. The silence is vibrant as I stand motionless, reading the inscription at the stone monument out loud to the spirits and the wind.

I am completely lost in history and nature for the second time today. I walk out along the ridge as far as the trail will take me. Upon returning to the monument, I pause and read it out loud, yet another time. No one else is here and on this day, no one else is coming. As was the case at Devils Tower, I feel like I am rediscovering an old place for the first time.

Long after the blood dries and the battle cries fade, the grass still grows and the wind still blows across what remains of the Bozeman Trail.

I couldn't stop reading this inscription at the Fetterman Massacre Site. I was mesmerized by the story and the scene, as if I knew it personally somehow.

This is big country. I have been on the Lakota trail for thirteen hours today when I arrive in Sheridan, Wyoming (population 17,698), near the Montana border. I check into the Days Inn just off exit 25, drop my bag on my bed in room 203, and walk back out. I gas up the car, wash the windshield, and grab more water for tomorrow. I drive through the old part of town as day turns to night, before having a great Mexican dinner at a local joint called Los Agaves.

On this night, I barely sleep; the energy churning within me is just too powerful. Sleep is not something my body seems to need right now. A spiritual awakening is occurring and the energy that is being unleashed is not interested in bedtime. My soul feels free, reborn. The vastness of nature, my proximity to this specific story, and the simple act of serving myself have, over time, combined to release a new state of being. I can now actually put my consciousness on my spirit—a warm bubble I can specifically locate and feel within my chest, near my heart. My head is not the source of my being, and this is new learning for me. This small piece of understanding is a game changer.

Downtown Sheridan, Wyoming.

The next morning I leave the Days Inn as the sun crests the nearest hill to the east. It is 6:15 a.m. Paul Simon sings on the radio as I cross the state line into Montana:

> *When I think back on all the crap I learned in high school,*
> *it's a wonder I can think at all.*

I am excited about the new day as I cross the legendary Tongue River. I exit the highway and drive down a dirt road to the river's edge. Once again, however, I can't reach the water, as the bank is just too steep.

The hills here look Jurassic in nature to me. They are just so big, the biggest hills I have ever seen. In one spot, I can see seemingly forever, yet moments later I can only see the face of a single grassy ridge on either side of me. A massive Union Pacific train surges powerfully along in the same direction I am traveling. There is not a tree in sight as I drive under low rolling clouds through a heavy mist. Moments later a sign welcomes me to "Crow Country."

Crow Country is big country.

On the northern plains, the Sioux and the Crow had long been enemies in the battle for horses and hunting grounds. In fact, the Fort Laramie Treaty of 1851 had been almost as much about creating peace between the plains tribes as it was about peace with the Wasichu. As the Lakota and Northern Cheyenne tribes grew stronger, they continued pushing west and north into what traditionally had been Crow territory. By conquest they took over the eastern hunting grounds of the Crow, including the Tongue and Power River valleys. The Crow, whose population was smaller, were pushed northwest and upriver along the Yellowstone. By the early 1860s, the Lakota had claimed all the former Crow lands from the Black Hills to the Bighorn Mountains as their own; politically, they insisted the federal government deal with them regarding this territory. The notion that the Lakota acquired much of their Western territory in the same way it was later taken from them always causes me to pause. Long before the whites arrived, Indian fought Indian here.

> *I hear the white men say there will be no more war. But this cannot be true. There will be other wars. Men have not changed, and whenever they quarrel they will fight, as they have always done.*
>
> **—Chief Plenty Coups**

The Crow would later guide for and fight with the US Army in their campaign against the Sioux, in an effort to retain rights to their ancestral homeland. Chief Plenty Coups, who would become the great leader of the Crow Nation in the last decades of the nineteenth century, went on a vision quest when he was eleven years old. He fasted in the mountains for several days before his vision came to him. In his vision, he saw buffalo too numerous to count emerging from a hole in the ground. The buffalo were of different colors, had strange tails, and made unnatural sounds. After coming out of the hole, they ran off into the distance and disappeared. Then, Plenty Coups saw himself as an old man. At this time, in his vision, a strong wind began to blow. It blew down all the trees in the forest until only one was left standing.

Upon returning home, he told his story to the tribal elders, who interpreted his vision to mean that the white men would take over all the Indian lands, destroy the buffalo, and change their way of life. All Indian cultures would be decimated except for one, represented by the single tree left standing. This lone tree represented the Crow people.

Chief Plenty Coups further interpreted his vision to mean that his people could survive only by learning to work with the white man; this belief would guide his actions as the chief of his people. By the early twentieth century, Plenty Coups would become one of the best-known head chiefs in America, well regarded for his thoughtful words.

> *Education is your most powerful weapon. With education, you are the white man's equal; without education, you are his victim, and so shall remain all your lives.*

> **—Chief Plenty Coups**

At 2.3 million acres, the Crow Reservation is approximately the same size as Pine Ridge. Today, the tribe has an estimated 11,000 members, 70 percent of whom live on the reservation. The grasslands stretch endlessly here, and I can picture the buffalo grazing freely, in great numbers, in the days before the coming of the Wasichu. As I drive through the reservation, the modern-day realities of poverty, unemployment, and reservation life come into view. Pine Ridge and the Crow Reservation are not so different in this regard. They fought on different sides, but ended up in similar places.

***When the buffalo went away, the hearts of my people
fell to the ground, and they could not lift them up
again. After this nothing happened. There was little
singing anywhere.***

—Chief Plenty Coups

It is 7:30 a.m. when I cross the Little Bighorn River. Shortly thereafter,
I find myself driving by the entrance to the Little Bighorn Battlefield
National Monument. This is the famous battlefield; as such, the gate
is locked. There is no standing at this battlefield unsupervised. Visitors
must wait until the employees arrive and the park is open. That's okay
with me, because it is not my first stop, anyway. Eight days before the
Battle of Little Bighorn in June of 1876, a lesser-known but equally
fierce battle took place about an hour's drive to the southeast on the
grassy knolls and scattered timber surrounding Rosebud Creek. That is
my next destination.

My car winds through a lush valley that narrows as I drive south. The
road follows a small creek with scattered stands of timber on the ridges
of both sides. Soon I arrive at a red dirt road on my right that turns
off for the Rosebud Battlefield. It is still early morning and I find inner
peace in returning to yet another historic site where virtually no one
goes. A modest stone marker identifies the point of battle with a simple
inscription:

GENERAL CROOK'S TROOPS HALTED HERE. INDIANS ATTACKED FROM THE NORTH AT DAWN. FIGHT BEGAN HERE 8:30 AM, JUNE 17TH, 1876.

To the Lakota, the Battle of the Rosebud is known as the fight "where
the girl saved her brother." During the battle, a Cheyenne warrior by
the name of "Comes-In-Sight" had his horse shot out from under him
and found himself stranded in the open grass, under heavy rifle fire.
Seeing the situation unfold, his sister, "Buffalo Calf Road Woman,"
mounted her own horse and raced through a fury of bullets to rescue
her brother. One young girl's single act of bravery gave birth to the
historic fight's name.

General Crook had become a famous frontier fighter by "using Indians to catch Indians"; 1,250 men traveled under his command, accompanied by a large contingent of Shoshoni and Crow. Their mission was the same as Custer's: to round up and bring in all the remaining non-reservation Indians, dead or alive. The fact that these Indians were living peacefully on lands guaranteed to them forever by the Treaty of 1868 mattered little now. Gold had been discovered in the Black Hills.

An Indian force of nearly a thousand mounted warriors, led by Crazy Horse, left Sitting Bull's great camp and rode all night to meet the troops at dawn of the following day. Sitting Bull had not wanted them to go, as his vision told him they must wait for the army that attacks from the east (General Custer).

A dramatic daylong battle ensued across three miles of terrain. The battle was fought to a standstill, with Crook believing he had held off a force of men that vastly outnumbered his own (the actual count of men on both sides was essentially the same). The following day, Crook would retreat and retrace his path all the way back to his camp on Goose Creek (near Sheridan), where he would remain for seven weeks regrouping and awaiting reinforcements.

The view from atop the knoll that Crook's forces defended on June 17, 1876.

When the grass was tall and the horses strong, we broke camp and started across the country to the mouth of the Tongue River. Then Sitting Bull and Crazy Horse and all went up to Rosebud. There we had a big fight with General Crook and whipped him.

—Two Moons

It is 45 degrees and wet as I walk alone through the battlefield where the girl saved her brother. The familiar northwest wind has turned cold, but the songbirds continue to sing as they have done all week. Once again, I am in a place where I do not want to leave. This quiet place with a big story is calling me.

At the conclusion of my walk, I read the sign near the picnic tables beside the empty gravel parking lot:

THE LAND SPEAKS

Be silent, close your eyes, and listen to the breeze as it rustles through the prairie grasses. To many, the whispering sounds make this a spiritual place.

———

The Little Bighorn Battlefield National Monument on the Crow Indian Reservation in Montana is a much different place than the Rosebud Battlefield State Park. One has to search for the Rosebud Battlefield, in part by driving through someone's front yard down a narrow dirt path. The Little Bighorn Battlefield is a much more significant site; it is located just east of I-90, where it crosses the winding path of the Little Bighorn River. The Burlington Northern Santa Fe Railway runs parallel to the interstate on the west side, and the battlefield is located in the first wave of hills above the river to the east.

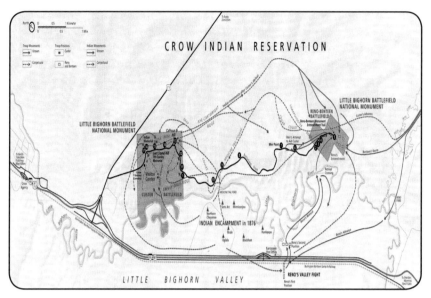

This is the map I used to study the battlefield, courtesy of the National Park Service.

What a sight it would have been to see the Indian encampment on the morning of June 25, 1876. It was a hot, hot day. Children were playing in the cool waters known to the Indians as the Greasy Grass River. A herd of ponies too large to count (likely 20,000 to 30,000) grazed in the valley, west of the river, where an estimated 7,000 Lakota, Cheyenne, and Arapaho had come together to make their camp. Those gathered shared a common bond in their rejection of reservation life and their desire to continue to live nomadically as their ancestors had done, following the buffalo on the northern plains.

In mid-May, General Custer and the 7th Cavalry had marched west from Fort Abraham Lincoln in the Dakota Territory with 1,200 men, under General Terry's command. By June 23, they were following the travois trail of what they would refer to as Sitting Bull's camp. By the size of the path the traveling village left behind, Custer could clearly tell they were closing in on a massive group of Indians.

> **We scouts thought there were too many Indians for Custer to fight . . . It was the biggest Indian camp I had ever seen.**
>
> **—White Man Runs Him, Crow scout**

From Last Stand Hill where Custer's small black grave marker stands in the blowing grass, you can look west down into the ravines where intense fighting occurred, and then out across the Little Bighorn River to the grassy plain where the Indian encampment sat. Each tribe had its own circle of tepees within the greater encampment. Starting to the north and moving south were the Northern Cheyenne; below them, near the river, were the Sans Arc and Minniconjou camps; to the west, away from the river, were the Brule; farther west, Crazy Horse and the Oglala held camp; south of the Brule and Oglala camps were the Blackfeet, and farthest south of them all lay the large camp of Sitting Bull and the Hunkpapa.

On June 24, aided by his Crow and Arikara scouts, Custer had located the general whereabouts of the Indian encampment. Custer, who had been in a hurry the entire trip, now moved even faster. His greatest fear was not that the Indians would attack, but rather that they would flee. Custer wanted a battle and he wanted it quickly; any size would do. Both the Democratic National Convention in St. Louis and the Centennial Exhibition in Philadelphia were only days away; Custer needed a victory now, so that word of his military triumph might make it back to these important public events.

Knowing that his troops had been spotted, Custer hastily ordered a battalion, led by Major Marcus Reno, to attack the southern end of the Indian camp. To prevent a possible southern escape, he then ordered Captain Frederick Benteen to lead three companies to a line of bluffs, two miles south. When these orders were given, Custer had still not seen the Indian village personally and did not know the full extent of its massive size.

> **"Hadn't we better keep the regiment together, General? If this is as big a camp as they say, we'll need every man we have."**
>
> **—Benteen to Custer**

> **"You have your orders."**
>
> **—Custer to Benteen**

Custer's grave marker is the only one in black. As I stand there I can picture the horrific final moments as the small group is finally overrun. Overreaching has consequences.

As the attack was launched, the Lakota, Cheyenne, and Arapaho scrambled to respond. Barely clad warriors rushed to find their weapons and horses, while women and children ran from the oncoming cavalry charge. As Reno attacked to the south, General Custer took over two hundred soldiers to the north, with plans to attack the upper portion of the great village.

Reno's battalion did cross the Little Bighorn River, but the Indians quickly blunted the charge, forcing Reno and his men to dismount and form a battle line. The battle line was soon overrun and chaos ensued. Reno and his troops retreated back across the river into a thicket of hardwood timber. Under intense fire, Reno's men eventually broke from the timber and fought their way up a treacherous embankment to an exposed hilltop above the river; here, they would unite with Benteen and remain surrounded, under intense pressure, until late the following day. Only half of Reno's soldiers would make it up the bluff. Those that did, watched helplessly as their fellow soldiers were stripped and mutilated below. It was not a scene for the faint of heart. Reno and Benteen were pinned down and fighting for survival. Meanwhile, Custer and his men were isolated several ridges to the north, without any hope of reinforcements.

To this day, it is not exactly clear what happened to Custer and his men, as there were no military survivors. In 1890, the army erected 249 headstone markers across the battlefield to show where Custer and each of his men had fallen. Forty-one of those headstones are clustered together on the river's side of what is now referred to as "Last Stand Hill." General Custer, his brother Tom, and Lieutenant William Cooke are among them. In a last-effort defense they had shot their horses to create a breastwork from the Indian onslaught.

> *My every thought was ambition—not to be wealthy, not to be learned, but to be great. I desired to link my name with acts and men and in such a manner as to be a mark of honor, not only to the present but to future generations.*
>
> —Custer (years earlier),
> in a letter to his wife, Libbie

Some say that Custer was found with a smile on his face. Others say he was found with his genitals cut off and stuffed in his mouth. From the Lakota perspective, the Great Spirit had watched over them on this triumphant day. The Hunkpapa war chief, Gall, would later claim that the Great Spirit presided over the battlefield, riding a dark black war pony, encouraging the warriors to be brave and push hard.

The Lakota, Cheyenne, and Arapaho celebrated their victory and then broke camp, scattering into smaller bands in all directions. The United States government responded by intensifying its campaign. Sitting Bull and his Hunkpapa band would flee to "Grandmother's Country" (Canada), where they spent several uneasy years in the cold grasslands to the north, before returning to the United States to surrender. Crazy Horse and his Oglala band would continue to outrun the US Army as long as possible. But, the winter of 1877 was particularly cold, the buffalo scarce, and the pursuit relentless. In the spring of that year, Crazy Horse rode into Fort Robinson and surrendered, having concluded that his dwindling force of warriors could no longer protect the women, children, and elderly under his care. That fall he was bayoneted while being arrested on false charges and died of his wounds later that night. Jealousy among reservation Oglala flamed the rumors that led to his arrest and death.

Crazy Horse's birth name was Cha-O-Ha, which means "in the wilderness." He lived this name, often spending time alone and avoiding the campfire fame sought by other warriors. To this day, there are no known photographs of Crazy Horse, but sketches have been drawn as his image continues to capture the imagination.

This sketch of Crazy Horse, drawn by Stan Hamilton, hangs on the wall in my office at home. Each time I look at this rendering of the elusive warrior, I am drawn deep into his eyes.

Crazy Horse was the bravest man I ever saw. All the soldiers were shooting at him, but he was never hit.

—Arapaho warrior

Years later, numerous Indians who were camped with Sitting Bull told army officers that if Custer had asked for a council, he could have led them all in without a fight. Sitting Bull himself echoed these sentiments in subsequent interviews. We will never know if this was possible.

The soldiers do not possess ears.

—Nineteenth-century Lakota saying

As night falls, I am standing beneath the Roosevelt Arch at the northern gateway to Yellowstone National Park, having decided to make this the final destination of my trip. The park was created by an act of Congress on March 1, 1872. Crazy Horse and Sitting Bull were still roaming freely that year. This is where my journey to Pine Ridge first began. Over twenty-five years ago, I passed through this arch as a college junior, riding on a TW Services bus (TW Services managed all the hotels and concessions in the park) on my way to housekeeping training. Fifteen years later, I would stand under that same arch with Alison, Abby, and Sydney on a Western family vacation. I had no idea the first time I passed through this arch that I was on my way to Pine Ridge. Callings are funny that way; they begin as a whisper long before we're even listening.

Sydney and I under the Roosevelt Arch on family vacation, July 30, 2001.

How did it get so late so soon?

—Dr. Seuss

Alison and Abby on the Snake River during that same trip "out West."

The night before my flight home, I wake up suddenly in the middle of the night. *Snap . . . snap . . .* I bolt upright in bed. *Wow!* I have never sprung upright in bed from a dream before or since. I am breathing heavily and sweating, completely startled. As I regain my composure, the dream that just woke me is fresh in my mind:

> *I am driving a Hancock Lumber pickup truck over Leach Hill in Casco, headed for the village. We have just driven past my childhood home. My friend, Bill Chalmers, is sitting in the front passenger seat. This is odd, because I don't believe I have ever been in a car with Bill. Bill is in the insurance business and his company insures Hancock Lumber. A third person is sitting in the back, but I can't see who it is. I just know someone else is there. The ride is calm and peaceful. Everyone is smiling and it is a summer day as we descend the hill. Suddenly, the brakes stop working and summer turns to winter as ice appears on the road.*
>
> *The truck accelerates to a very high speed like the Rock 'n' Roller Coaster at Disney World. The truck slides left and right on the ice. I have no control. We are moving very fast toward a large telephone pole. I am sure we are going to crash and die. At the last instant, we regain control, only seconds before impact. The truck decelerates smoothly, as if the Disney ride has ended, and all is well once again in the world. The vehicle steers itself peacefully to the side of the road and stops. We all have a big laugh. The third person in the backseat then disappears. I never do see who it was. "Well, at least you can file this accident report yourself," I say to Bill with a smile, but as I turn to look at him, he has my dad's face. My dad is smiling back at me.*

The following morning I am wearing my eagle pendant necklace on the outside of my shirt as I carry my red Pine Ridge drum (that I purchased from Rosie) into the terminal. The drum receives lots of attention and questions from fellow travelers.

"What do you do there at Pine Ridge?" a young woman asks me as we wait to pass through security at the Bozeman airport.

"Not very much," I reply. "I am just interested in the people who live there," I tell her. "I have friends there and I think they have an important story."

As I gather my belongings and leave security, my mind wanders back to last night's startling dream. The image of losing control, nearing disaster, and then having it end safely reminds me of the journey I have been on within my own tribe since my father died. That is the same journey that cost me the comfortable use of my voice.

Evolutionary astrology believes that souls carry "karmic wounds" that are not limited to a single lifetime. The Hindus call this *samsara*—imprints left on the subconscious mind by dramatic experiences in this life or previous lives. In addition, souls can have relationships with each other across multiple incarnations, where patterns play out again and again until they are resolved and transcended.

So, how might the "karmic dots" of evolutionary astrology be connected in my case? Or, to say it differently, how might the story my natal chart reveals answer the original jewelry maker's question,

What brings you here?

Well, in evolutionary astrology terms, that story might go something like this:

> **I had a past life experience connected somehow to the history of the Lakota people, possibly even Pine Ridge.**

> **In that past life experience, I was a shaman or spiritual leader of some type, responsible for the well-being of the tribe.**

This may have been a role I was born into, part of a family tradition within the tribe.

The tribe I belonged to came into a life-or-death situation. I became consumed in my role, losing my sense of self in the process.

In the struggle for survival, my Triple Aries energy took over and I became quite dogmatic, doing all I could to help save my tribe.

In the end, however, my tribe perished.

This is the wound I carried forward into this lifetime, unresolved and to be continued . . .

In this current lifetime, I intentionally incarnated into a similar situation inheriting leadership of yet another tribe. I did this because I had unfinished business; I needed to try again.

My new tribe, from this lifetime, also went through a period of struggle.

Even though time and place had changed, my soul could not differentiate between this life and the last, because it was the same energy field, the same template.

So, it reacted instinctively and I reverted to dogmatic and protective tendencies, imprinted deep within me, and that transcend a single lifetime.

Internally, a battle occurred as I attempted to repress the images of my past tribe's decimation and to change the outcome for this one. This inner conflict manifests in my throat, which is the body's spiritual site for repressing emotions.

As a result, I lost my voice. This was a warning from my soul regarding the path I was on, which triggered me to stop and reassess.

At which point, a lifetime of soft whispers called me back to Pine Ridge.

I heard and answered that call.

At Pine Ridge, I embarked on a soul's journey that released my past wounds, perhaps at the actual place of their origin.

My dad shared similar wounds and was somehow connected.

In a past lifetime, our roles may also have been intertwined, even reversed.

In this way, my moving forward released him somehow, as we likely belong to the same tribal morphic field.

If evolutionary astrology is involved in my story, this is what the path might look like. I understand that many people may dismiss and judge this perspective. But, this doesn't really change anything. Personally, I don't find evolutionary astrology to be any less believable than the ancient stories of the world's leading religions. In addition, I actually can't come up with a better explanation for what brings me here.

No worries. Regardless of how you think I developed such a magnetic attraction to Pine Ridge, it's all okay. I'm here, and it's therapeutic for me. That's what really matters right now. Anyway, we aren't meant to know it all while we are here. That would only serve to dull the experience and slow the learning.

I am staring out the big windows at the runway, watching my plane take on fuel. As I move around the airport, I feel as if I am floating, even though I know I am walking. It is the same sensation I experienced at Devils Tower. My arms and legs are covered with tiny bug bites from standing alongside the banks of the Powder River. The river that was guaranteed to the Lakota people "as long as grass shall grow and water flow." I still have the sensation that I am moving back and forth between two worlds, but I can also sense that these two circles are beginning to unite as one. I am excited to go home.

"Toksa Ake," I whisper out loud, as my ticket is scanned and I board the plane.

In the movie Close Encounters, *the overwhelmingly powerful culture from far away made contact and then left; the alien culture resisted the temptation to plant their flag and claim the land as their own. Leave it to science fiction to come up with an implausible ending . . .*

The Earth is the Mother of all people, and all people should have equal rights upon it. You might as well expect the river to run backward as that any man who was born a free man should be contented when penned up and denied liberty to go where he pleases.

—Chief Joseph, Nez Perce

6
Let the Wind Blow through You

The wind always seems to blow at the burial ground at Wounded Knee.

**The opportunities for grasping the substance
of life have faded as the pace of modern activity
has increased.**

—Vine Deloria Jr.

In his book *The Lakota Way,* storyteller Joseph Marshall describes a memory from elementary school. It was recess and Joseph was on the playground. Two white classmates were teasing him because he was an Indian. They called him many bad names that day. Back home that night, Joseph told his grandfather what happened. His grandfather listened patiently. When Joseph had finished, the old man paused and then replied with a question:

"Words can hurt, Joseph, but only if you let them. They called you bad names. Were you changed into the things they called you?"

"No," Joseph answered.

"You cannot forget what they said any more than you cannot feel the wind when it blows. But if you learn to let the wind blow through you, you will take away its power to blow you down. If you let the words pass through you, without letting them catch on your anger or pride, you will not feel them."

I think about this story as I prepare to leave Casco and make yet another trip to Pine Ridge. I can feel the winds of change blowing into my own life, and I am eager to see where they take me. The dream I will never forget appears to have been a tipping point, as a much deeper sense of calm and peace has come home with me from Pine Ridge. This, in turn, has changed how I manage and help lead my tribe. I am more patient, trusting, and deliberate in my actions. Even more to the point, the business doesn't hold me in the same way anymore. I love Hancock Lumber and am passionate about both its mission and the people who work there. But, I no longer feel a burden to make it all work by myself. I also no longer see the company as the source of my identity. I feel as free and light as the day I "floated" through the Bozeman airport, even though nearly four months have passed.

Even being told that my SD is incurable no longer holds the same meaning for me. I have stopped seeing my voice disorder simply as a medical condition; I now also see it as a spiritual one. As the soul becomes less constrained, perhaps the throat will follow. It's all connected, after all.

It is the last day of July and I am looking at squares.

The Great Plains east of the Rocky Mountains did not look like this in the nineteenth century. Today, however, squares are what I see as JetBlue flight #493 makes its approach into Denver. The farmland below is divided into boxy boundary lines, separated by barbed wire and dirt roads. It all looks so organized from above. Very little naturally takes the shape of a square, however. An egg, a tree trunk, a raindrop, the seasons, migration patterns, the Earth, the moon, the sun, and even life itself all form or flow in a circle, a Sacred Hoop.

Furthermore, everything that lives within the Sacred Hoop is related, sharing the same matter and energy. Through this philosophy, it is possible to understand why the Lakota would regularly communicate with their four-legged brothers, the birds in the sky, and other living creatures. When one sees all living things as part of your own family, the paradigm changes and a new set of possibilities emerges.

I find this all quite symbolic, as I have come to believe that by traveling to Pine Ridge, I am somehow returning to the place of origin with respect to my own discomfort. By revisiting the past, I am learning to release it. Like the track at our local high school, the starting point is also the finish line. Circles, it seems, are more dynamic than they first appear.

The essence of the Lakota medicine wheel is the shape of a circle and the number four.

Joseph Marshall's book, *The Lakota Way*, also recounts numerous stories he heard as a child on the Rosebud Indian Reservation in South Dakota. Lakota stories are a way to preserve history and, more importantly, to teach values. The four great Lakota values are GENEROSITY (it is better to give a lot than to have a lot), COURAGE (to learn to face danger without running away), RESPECT (to show reverence for all living things) and WISDOM (the ability to see things as they really are). There are other Lakota values, as well. In fact, my favorite story in the book is about the power of humility, or *unsúciyapi* (pronounced un-shee-ee-cee-HAH-pee) and it goes something like this:

Long ago, before the coming of horses, a Lakota woman named No Moccasins and her husband Three Horns lived on the northern plains. Three Horns had been a great warrior "far past the time when most men lost the strength." Even as an old man he appeared strikingly handsome and strong; he was considered wise until the last days of his life. In many ways, No Moccasins lived humbly in the supporting shadow of her husband's camp.

Years went by and eventually it was time for the great warrior to pass on to the next world that lives beside this one. Just days before his death, Three Horns invited all the elders to gather in his lodge, for he had a final story he wanted to tell:

> **"I am thankful to the Great Mystery for bringing me into this world as a Lakota. I have lived a good life and I am ready for the next. Before I leave, I have a story to tell, and I ask that after the sun comes up tomorrow you tell this same story to all the people gathered here."**

As a young warrior, many moons ago, Three Horns was captured by the enemy and held as a slave.

> **"I was led around naked; everyone laughed. I was made to work. I pulled drag poles like a dog until my hands and knees were bleeding. They teased me; they threw dirt in my face. Women pulled up their dresses in front of me and laughed, showing me that I was no longer a man. They gave me no food, so I had to fight with the dogs for scraps. At night they bound me hand and foot and stretched me between two stout poles. There was no way to escape."**

Much time passed and Three Horns felt that all was lost. Then, one night while the village of his captors slept, his wife appeared before him dressed in a man's clothes. She had left her village alone to rescue her husband. Armed with a knife, she set Three Horns free and they escaped into the night. Before arriving home, No Moccasins insisted that Three Horns not tell the story of how he escaped. She did not want any credit for her husband's rescue and did not want to disgrace him as a warrior. And, so it was for many years. But, in the last days of his life, Three Horns was determined that the true story should be told.

> *"I have asked you old ones to our lodge to witness for me. It is time to repay the great debt I owe my wife. Throughout my life I was fortunate as a warrior and somehow I was able to win some honors and gain a reputation. Yet all those honors are not mine, because I could not have achieved them if my wife had not risked her life . . . because of her deed, I took to the warpath each time with one thought in mind: to be worthy of my wife."*

Three Horns went on to tell the elders in his tepee of the bravery she displayed in rescuing him, but mostly he spoke of her humility.

> *"I have known good people in my life. Many were wise, honorable, generous, and brave. But none, except this old woman who sits beside me as always, had the one strength that gives true meaning to all others—humility. Thus, I have spoken."*

This story brings lightness to my heart and tears to my eyes each time I read it, including today, shortly before landing in Denver. I think I love this story because it represents the loss of ego I am seeking. It also represents the power of storytelling for those who tell them. In sharing his most secret story, Three Horns was not just honoring those he loved; he was also releasing himself.

———

I love this sign every time I see it. It tells me I have crossed the boundary and reentered the "Old West."

As I think again about No Moccasins and the power of humility, I am driving north through Cheyenne, Wyoming, and I am not feeling good about something I just did. Back in Denver, I had a weak moment in line at the Budget rental counter. The process of getting a car had been slow. From the time I collected my bags until the time I received car keys, over ninety minutes had expired. The shuttle bus took forever and the line was even longer. The staff at the counter appeared oblivious to the pace, giving me the impression that this was the normal speed. As I stood and stood in line, I grew frustrated.

My turn finally arrived and I was motioned to the counter. When the sales agent offered me an upgrade for just $8 per day from the midsize car I had rented, I took it. As an extra act of service, he then gave me what amounted to a double upgrade. I thought nothing of it at the time, as I was distracted by my impatience. I just wanted to get out of line and get going. I was anxious to get back to Pine Ridge.

But now, an hour later, I am uncomfortable. The Ford Explorer Limited I am driving feels too fancy for me and my solo journey to Pine Ridge. The vehicle is big, black, leathery, and, suddenly, uncomfortable in its luxury. It really bothers me, to the point where I give serious thought to turning around and returning it. I even call the Budget 1-800 line to ask how I might trade back down! I told the representative on the phone that I knew this was an unusual request. A few miles back in Fort Collins, Colorado, I actually exited I-25 to drive twenty minutes away from the highway to the local Budget location to see if a voluntary downgrade was possible. None of this worked. I was saddened by my decision and lack of humility at the counter back in Denver. This vehicle was mine for the week.

I eventually got used to the car; once at Pine Ridge, it didn't really stand out in the way I had worried that it might. The SUV was dusty and dirty by then. In addition, as I looked around, I was reminded that I was in ranch country, which is the land of big trucks and oversized SUVs. It all worked out just fine. I often worry when worrying is not necessary. I will never forget, however, how much it bothered me at the time, and, in hindsight, I am glad that it did. This is often the way for me. My fears are almost always worse in my head than the actual events themselves. Fear, for me, is pretty much always an inside job.

———

Hail piles up on the sides of the road as I travel through southeastern Wyoming. The temperature falls from 72 to 60 degrees in less than ten minutes. I can't say that I have ever experienced a temperature change quite like it. My black Ford Explorer and I turn onto Route 151, just east of Lagrange. Shortly thereafter, I cross into Banner County in the Nebraska panhandle. The pavement here turns red, and this makes me think of the great Oglala holy man, Black Elk, who often spoke of the "good red road" as the proper path for his people to follow.

Black Elk, or Hehaka Sapa, is the most famous Oglala holy man of the twentieth century, having received a powerful vision when he was only a child. He was born free in December of 1863 (possibly 1862), near the Little Powder River (in present-day Wyoming), before the breaking of treaties. As a young boy, he had never seen a Wasichu. He was a second cousin to Crazy Horse and was camped with him along the Greasy Grass River the day Custer and the 7th Cavalry attacked. Years later, in December of 1890, he rescued survivors of Big Foot's Minneconjou band at Wounded Knee Creek. Black Elk would later go on to travel the world as a character in Buffalo Bill Cody's Wild West Show. After returning home, he would live out the remainder of his life in a small log cabin just south of Manderson, not far from Pinky's Store.

In 1930, historian John Neihardt met the Oglala holy man for the first time; he returned to Pine Ridge the following year to sit in the prairie grass and record Black Elk as he shared the stories of his life. The resulting book, *Black Elk Speaks*, is considered to be one of the most authentic interpretations of Lakota spirituality ever published. Black Elk felt a connection to Neihardt and saw good in his heart. He also felt a calling to pass on and preserve the history and spirituality of his people. He, too, was releasing himself and perhaps his entire tribe through storytelling.

Black Elk, likely at Pine Ridge, late in his life (c. 1930s).

As I sit here, I can feel in this man beside me a strong desire to know the things of the Other World. He has been sent here to learn what I know, and I will teach him.

—Black Elk to John Neihardt

My spiritual assimilation into the natural landscape takes root easily as I drive through the northwest corner of Nebraska and settle into my journey. When I am here on the northern plains, my senses are reversed and it is the man-made creations that stand out as intrusive. For me, as was true for the Lakota in the second half of the nineteenth century, the icon of deconstruction is the railroad; each time a powerful train churns past, I can feel the tension between that which was and that which is.

The train I watched pass through the Nebraska panhandle, south of Pine Ridge, on my third trip to the reservation.

I let the sights, sounds, and vibrations of the train leave my spirit before the caboose passes. I return my attention to nature. For me, the power of this landscape is inescapable. The vastness of the plains brings with it a sense of individual smallness. I can see for miles in all directions. The soil is rich here and the thick grasses sway and dance in the wind as I lean against the hood of my SUV and let the energy of the plains consume me.

Back in the vehicle, the radio is on when the emergency broadcast signal interrupts my thoughts. It is that sound we all have been trained to know, but are challenged to mimic. The distinctly mechanical and disruptive noise is always followed by what seems to be the same person's voice no matter where you are in America. How does this one person provide all the emergency announcements?

After a series of pulsating beeps, I learn there is a "severe thunderstorm warning, including quarter-size hail and sixty-mile-per-hour winds" in the area. Listeners are encouraged to "move to an interior room on the lowest floor of the building."

The storm is moving east at forty miles per hour, just north of Scotts-bluff, and I can see it ahead of me as I cross the North Platte. On the hilltop to my left, a herd of horses appears well aware of what is happening and has bunched together in a tight circle. They stand close together with their ears up, necks extended, and tails moving constantly. They, too, are on high alert.

Nobody needs to tell the "four-leggeds" when a storm is brewing on the northern plains.

When the Lakota lived on the grasslands in buffalo-hide tepees, they also knew when a storm was brewing. Most of us today, however, have lost this natural and intuitive connection to nature. We have come to rely on the artificial and repetitive sirens of the emergency broadcast system to alert us.

I pull over to watch the storm travel just a few miles north of me. As I get out, raindrops gently fall. I tilt my head back, close my eyes, extend my arms, and let the rain fall upon me and the wind blow through me. That phrase, "Let the wind blow through you," has stuck with me since I first read it. Until coming to Pine Ridge and connecting with Lakota spirituality, I had spent my entire life experiencing the wind as hitting me. The wind and I collided. Now, I take a different approach. When I am outside with nature and a wind is blowing, I release myself to meet it; I close my eyes and join it. I quickly descend into a relaxed state and picture the wind blowing right through me, as if the wind and I are one thing, not two. You might say this is an imagined experience, but who is to say the wind is not blowing through me when I let it? You might try it sometime and see what you think.

I stop in Scottsbluff for dinner and to let the angry clouds pass. Ironically, this pause makes my encounter with the storm even closer, as I travel east and then north through Sheridan County on the way to Rushville, which is the last small town before the final drive into Pine Ridge. For the longest time after dinner, the storm and I seem to be on a collision course until the very end, when I just slip past the angry clouds before they consume the long empty road behind me. Thunder rolls across the sky and shakes the earth. Lightning illuminates the top of the billowing cloud mass as bolts break out and dive into the earth below. As I pass by the leading edge of the great storm, I pause and look back over my left shoulder. The view is breathtaking. To the west, between a farmhouse and its barn, the sun is setting and creating apparitions and distortions like I have never seen before.

I have never seen a sunset like this one, before or since. Despite the violent storm, the sun held its own course, as it always does.

I stop the car and watch the sun change colors and bubble into odd asymmetrical shapes as it slowly falls into the field. It is as if a hole has opened between the worlds. The sun keeps changing forms until it is swallowed up by the circle of another day and disappears.

It is 10:00 p.m. before I arrive at the Singing Horse Trading Post. I unlatch the gate and drive up the now-familiar gravel road. Rosie sees me coming and opens the screen door and meets me outside.

"I have a surprise for you," she tells me.

Rosie has other guests visiting, so the house is busy and full.

"You are staying in the cabin," Rosie says. "It is all prepared for you."

That night, Rowdy, the black dog, alternates between sleeping and standing guard from the blue car seat that rests outside my cabin door. It is an old seat from an old car, the kind I remember riding in as a child before the coming of bucket seats or the wearing of seat belts.

I traveled over nineteen hours to get here today, and the small metal bed feels great, despite its age and flaws.

It is a peaceful evening and the dogs are quiet. On this particular night, standing guard over camp is an uneventful assignment.

The small gray cabin I stayed in at the Singing Horse Trading Post. Rosie's dog, Rowdy, slept most of the night on the blue car seat to the right of the entrance, as if on guard duty.

It is 7:00 a.m. mountain time the next morning when I throw on some clothes and exit the cabin. I call to the three dogs and together we walk to the fence line on the first knoll above Singing Horse. The dogs are panting, the birds are singing, and occasionally a car travels past on the road far below. Wild sunflowers are scattered across the grasslands. I am told that wherever the grasses die here the sunflowers take their place. In nature's eye, death for some means life for others. It's all connected.

The grasses here are a story unto themselves. Within the grass there is a rich diversity of color, texture, height, and form. Some patches are at their peak of fresh green life; other blades are faded, while some are golden brown. The grasses transform throughout the seasons from brown to green to brown again, but they do not make this journey uniformly. Each blade makes its own trek through the circle of the seasons. At their highest and thickest growth I can extend my hands and let the grasses drift across my forearms and palms as I slowly walk along.

While each blade of grass is unique, they all seem to share the common love of dancing in the breeze. The wind is blowing gently from the south, the land of warmth and new life.

Let the wind blow through you, I think to myself.

As I say this, I extend my arms, close my eyes, and breathe deeply. My breathing is slow and rhythmic. The air flows through my body in circles, which I can clearly picture in my mind. The shape of a circle comes to me time and again as I stand alone on the grassy hilltop.

> **You have noticed that everything an Indian does is in a circle, and that is because the Power of the World always works in circles, and everything tries to be round. The sky is round, and I have heard that the earth is round like a ball, and so are all the stars. The wind, in its greatest power, whirls, birds make their nests in circles, for theirs is the same religion as ours. The sun comes forth and goes down again in a circle. The moon does the same, and both are round. Even the seasons form a great circle in their changing, and**

always come back again to where they were. The life of a man is a circle from childhood to childhood, and so it is in everything where power moves.

—Black Elk

The wind is blowing through me as I stand on the knoll with the wildflowers basking in the morning sun. Sometimes I just stand in one place. Sometimes I drift slowly from one spot to another. When I walk in this state of consciousness, I feel as if I am floating. Movement becomes effortless and graceful. I know I am walking, but . . .

Eventually, I sit down. I don't know why I do this any more than the buffalo know why they pack up and move across the valley at a certain moment in time. I drop to the ground and lean my back against a wooden fence post, which gives slightly to accommodate my presence. The sun is to my left. I am facing northwest toward the Badlands. Clouds sit above them, blocking my view of the Black Hills, but I still know they are there.

One does not have to see something to know of its existence.

The dogs, like the wind, drift off and return to me. This routine plays itself out multiple times. They are hunters and always alert to this part of their being. Each time they return, they come right up and pant on me and lick me. Often they will sit down right on top of me for a few minutes until the urge to hunt retakes them. Buffalo, the youngest dog, is the most connected to me. His favorite place to rest is on me.

"Seriously?" I say to him, as he plunks down on my legs.

Buffalo is fit and in his prime. His yellow hair is thick. I can bury my hand deep into his fur behind his neck and lose sight of my fingers altogether. When I give him a good pat, the dust rises off him. I have not seen a better place to be a dog than at the Singing Horse Trading Post.

It is so quiet. Even quiet is a noise, and I can hear it. Quiet gives off the lightest buzzing and ringing tones that live deep in the background, on the outer edge of noise. I love to sit by myself in Lakota country and listen to the sounds that silence makes.

Eventually, I move. I stand up and start drifting back down the hill. Soon, however, I am distracted and my drifting stops. I am suddenly caught up in the endless details of the prairie floor, where a single wild sunflower captures my attention.

I stand looking at this lone flower that lives on the east side of the first knoll above the Singing Horse Trading Post. After a while, I lay down on my stomach. The flower and I are face-to-face. I am not much more than twelve inches away. The closer I look, the more I see. Six ants are busy on this flower. Two of them are red and smaller. Four are black and larger. The small red ants and the large black ants don't seem to mind each other's presence. Somehow they have learned to share the same flower.

The longer I look at this flower, the bigger and more amazing it begins to appear. Just the inside of the flower's yellow blossom alone is a world unto itself. Countless specks and tiny pieces make up its vast interior, while seventeen yellow petals surround the center. The stem has six green leaves. One leaf on the south side has a hole in it.

The sun is warm on my back. I am lying on an uphill incline not far from the peak of the knoll. Flies and ants are on me, but I am not bothered. The flower rocks gently in the breeze. The little patch of earth it lives on is a world full of diversity and life.

The single wildflower I study, while lying on my stomach that morning on the hilltop above the trading post. The closer I look, the more I see.

A good bit of time passes and then something miraculous happens. The sunflower rotates and faces me more squarely. I actually watched this happen; I saw the flower turn and adjust itself. What caused this to happen? I can't say, but it was amazing!

The sensation of lingering spreads over me. This sensation comes into my life much more often now, and it is particularly common in Lakota country. I would describe the feeling of "lingering" as contentment, a time where there is no need to move or to consider further action (like the basking lion in the African sun that Deborah Dooley had described to me the day she first read my natal chart). My feet are kicked up behind me like a child. I never sit like this and yet it is so comfortable at this moment, so natural. It took me a while to even notice that I was in this position with my feet floating and gently rocking above my rear end. My spirit smiles over the position I have assumed. It is as if I have returned to my childhood play days alone in the backyard, with the wonders of the world before me.

The sounds of a motorcycle passing below and an airplane passing above flow into my consciousness and call me back into the larger world. I close my notebook, get to my feet, and dust myself off.

"Toksa Ake," I say to the flower.

As I walk through the grass, each step crunches beneath me. Few steps make a noise in our developed world. All the materials we walk on back home (sidewalks, carpets, and more) are designed to absorb the sound of human footsteps. I know from my work at Hancock Lumber that homebuilders and product manufacturers go to great lengths to make sure the floor of your home is quiet when you walk across it. In nature, every step makes a noise.

The dogs have wandered off once again, so I find Rosie's horses for company instead. One horse is rolling around in the dirt. Another has a young colt nearby that is full of energy. His coat is gray with a black tail and mane. His front feet are white, his back feet are black, and he has a long white patch that runs vertically down his nose, splitting his face in two. The world is new to him and his curiosity runs high.

This curious young colt had his first encounter with a spiral notebook the day we met.

I approach the horses slowly. Even though they are within the fence line, they are always alert and on guard. As I get closer, several horses begin walking my way. I say hi and show the first horse to arrive the back of my hand so he can smell it. He does and then the others take their turn. Some horses feel more comfortable with my presence than others. The young colt is particularly interested in me. I show him my hand, which turns out to be a mistake, as he bites it.

"Ouch," I tell him.

I move away, but he follows and continues to nip at me. This happens a few times before I give him a good smack on the nose with my blue spiral field notebook. He doesn't know what to make of this, having never seen a notebook before.

Back at the cabin, I stand for a moment marveling at the simplicity of my accommodations. The floor is covered with faded wooden planks. Two wooden bunk beds and a single metal-framed bed provide sleeping opportunities for five. An old dresser keeps each bed company. A blue couch sits in the opposite corner beneath one of three double-hung windows. There are two woodstoves, but only one is functional. In the center of the room a half whiskey barrel has been transformed into a table. A faded white tablecloth with yellow flowers conceals the barrel underneath. The tablecloth reminds me of the one I would grab cookies off of as a small boy in my grandmother's kitchen. A plastic fan hums along beneath a half-open window. A rough-cut timber spans the ceiling. The walls are covered in paneling and the morning light leaks through the door in dozens of places.

I finish off a big bottle of water and then head out the door. Once outside, I am greeted by the dogs who have returned from their morning hunt. After showering in the basement of the trading post, I head into Rosie's house to say hello. A small crowd of people I don't know is gathered and a lively conversation is already taking place.

"Americans who haven't been to Pine Ridge just aren't aware of what life is like here," one person says. "I tell people the reservation is over two million acres in size and you can't even buy diapers, socks, or underwear here."

The conversation turns to the annual powwow, or Wacipi Festival. This celebration begins tomorrow night at the powwow grounds, just a few blocks past Subway on the west side of town in Pine Ridge.

"The flag is carried proudly into powwow because it was won at Little Bighorn," someone explains. "The flag from that battle was never recaptured by the US Army."

Whether this is actually true or not, I don't know. I love how fact and fiction merge in the stories of the Old West.

Initially, I find it surprising that this is only the twenty-eighth annual Oglala Lakota powwow. Then again, it is only in my lifetime that traditional Lakota ceremonies have been free to form here at all. For example, one of the Seven Sacred Rites of the Lakota, brought to them by the White Buffalo Calf Woman, is the "keeping of the soul." In this rite, a locket of hair is carefully prepared in a soul bundle when a person dies. The bundle is kept in the family tepee of the deceased for a year until it is "released" in a sacred ceremony involving the entire tribe. When the bundle is released the soul makes its sacred journey to reunite with Wakan Tanka. For the Lakota, the soul's journey is a circle; it ends where it begins, with the Great Spirit.

In 1890, the same year as the massacre at Wounded Knee, the United States government officially prohibited the "keeping of the soul" rite on the Lakota reservations. Furthermore, it actually became law that on a set day (determined by the government), all Sioux souls were ordered to be released. That's a true story.

The cultural oppression that occurred on this reservation is numbing.

I say good-bye to everyone, as I have to be in town to meet Pinky for a ceremonial dedication in honor of the Hancock House that is nearing completion. I walk across the gravel to my car and with each step I can hear my feet crunch beneath me.

OGLALA SIOUX TRIBE PARTNERSHIP FOR HOUSING, INC.
Tatanka Woihanble Otipi – *"Buffalo Dreams – Gathering Homes"*

HANCOCK HOUSE APPRECIATION CEREMONY
Lot 24 Fraggle Rock Subdivision
Pine Ridge, SD
August 1, 2013
9:30 AM

AGENDA

Welcome

Opening Prayer

"Hancock House" Project History

Homebuyer introduction

Kevin Hancock Introduction & Remarks

David Krumm Introduction & Remarks

Acknowledgement of Project Partners

Faith- and Community-based Involvement/Impact on the Rez

Acknowledgement & Pilamaye to David Moen

Closing

Project Partners

Hancock Lumber, Casco, ME
U.S. Department of Housing and Urban Development
Oglala Sioux Lakota Housing
Oglala Sioux Tribe Water & Sewer
U.S. Department of Agriculture - Rural Development
St. Andrews Lutheran Church, Ames, IA
Windsor Heights Lutheran Church, Windsor Heights, IA
Shepherd of the Valley Lutheran Church, Apple Valley, MN
Grace Lutheran Church, Waseca, MN
Holy Nativity Lutheran Church, New Hope, MN
Church of the Good Shepherd, Vienna, VA
Private Donors
Financing provided by First National Bank of Gordon, Gordon, NE

The program from the Hancock House dedication ceremony.

As it turns out, I am late for the ceremony. In fact, truth be told, I missed it! Pinky and I never spoke about a specific time for the event, so I thought it was something more informal. I felt bad about this for sure, but there was also a happy irony to this story. I missed a meeting because I was lying in the grass, completely absorbed in the world of a single wildflower.

Anyway, all is rarely lost at Pine Ridge, and a ceremonial lunch is also scheduled for later this morning. I arrive at the OST Housing Authority office on the edge of town in plenty of time for that event. I will be able to participate after all.

The lunch ceremony begins with a song in Lakota that is written just for this event. I then receive a wonderful set of gifts. Yellow Horse, a local artist, has taken two pieces of scrap lumber from the job site and made carvings out of them.

The wood carvings I received as a gift, celebrating the completion of the house Hancock Lumber helped build at Pine Ridge.

The first is of a Lakota male standing tall and strong, arms crossed at the waist, wearing an eagle feather war bonnet. The second carving is of a Lakota woman, wrapped in a blanket with two braids hanging across her chest, a lone eagle feather atop her head. The woman has no features carved into her face. The warrior chief has ten circles carved into the right side of his face and a jagged line down the left side. Neither figure has a mouth, nose, or eyes. I find the faces on both carvings so interesting and wonder about their meaning, but soon decide to leave the answer alone. Mystery is one of my favorite aspects of the Pine Ridge experience. Like evolutionary astrology suggests, we aren't meant to know the whole story in a single lifetime.

Both carvings have the clean, crisp smell of worked wood, and I am honored to have them. The lumber that was transformed into these carvings traveled from Maine to Pine Ridge and will now make the journey back to Maine again; the wood will have traveled in a sacred circle.

Next, I am presented with an original "ledger art" painting. Ledger art is an extension of the early Lakota tradition of drawing on rock walls and buffalo hides in the days before the coming of the Wasichu. Images were drawn to memorialize events, preserve knowledge, and promote values. After the reservation era commenced, people began making their drawings on discarded ledger paper. Traders, storekeepers, and government officials used ledger or graph paper to keep records. Written in pencil, these ledgers tracked people, products, receipts, and disbursements. As records were discarded, the Lakota artists of Pine Ridge would collect the scraps and create their drawings upon them.

> **In the Circle**
> **we are all equal.**
> **When in the Circle, no one is in front of you.**
> **No one is behind you.**
> **No one is above you.**
> **No one is below you.**
> **The Circle is designed to create unity.**
>
> **—Dave Chief (Oglala Sioux)**

The ledger paper my painting is on dates back to 1880. Semi-faded dates, names, and numbers fill the background. What records were being kept, and for what reason? This will likely always remain a wonderful mystery.

After the presentation of gifts, everyone forms a circle that fills the entire conference room. The circle rotates counterclockwise and each person pauses in front of me to shake my hand, bow, or offer a kind word of thanks. I am deeply moved by this. In fact, I can't really believe it is happening. It feels surreal. I was not expecting any of this today. Recognition is not what brings me here, but I am touched and honored all the same. I give Pinky a big hug before sitting down at the far end of the long table, next to tribal elder and former president, Gerald One Feather, and his daughter.

I tell Gerald I am honored by the ceremony and the opportunity to meet him.

"The circle of thanks was particularly moving for me," I say.

"The circle is the most powerful thing in the world," Gerald replies. "Whenever the people form a circle, they are strong."

We share a lunch of buffalo meat, fry bread, and vegetables. As their guest, I must go first before anyone else will take their food.

I can't believe I have become this deeply connected to the Pine Ridge community. I never imagined where this journey would take me, and I still sense it is far from over. This does not make me anxious. I have become quite comfortable letting it all unfold.

Lester and I visit the new home after leaving the lunch ceremony. Lester is holding his American veteran's cap in his right hand and a copy of the Hancock Lumber contractor newsletter, The Builder Buzz, *in his left.*

After lunch, my friend Lester Lone Hill takes me to see the new home. It is a small ranch with light blue, made in Maine, pine siding. White trim surrounds the Andersen windows. The inside consists of three rooms. The main room is L-shaped and contains the living, dining, and kitchen areas. On the west side of the house, there are two small bedrooms. In the center, there is a single bathroom that includes a nook for a stackable washer and dryer. The house is slightly bigger than eight hundred square feet. The patio door on the backside opens onto a small pressure-treated platform that looks out across the field, toward the cemetery and the monumental gray water tower behind it.

After touring the home, Lester and I drive over to the powwow grounds. The opening ceremony does not start until tomorrow night, but a local band is playing and a few people are milling around. We hang out together at the powwow grounds awhile and then I drive Lester back to his office.

Back at the cabin a short time later, I fall into a deep sleep under the multicolored blanket on the small blue couch.

Later that afternoon, I wander back out onto the grasslands for a walk on the cliffs just south of Rosie's. By now, I have come to realize that, for me, the essence of Lakota spirituality is best accessed when I am alone in nature.

On this afternoon, and not to my surprise, the grasses dance in the wind as I walk. I make my way to the top of the bluffs and sit for some time, just listening to the sounds that silence makes. Just a few feet in front of me, the chalky white walls of the cliff drop straight down until they are united with the grass and the scattered trees below.

The bluff I sat on near the Singing Horse Trading Post.

The sky is completely overcast as I begin my walk back down the path that leads off the bluffs. As I walk along, a single hole in the clouds emerges, letting just a few rays of light break through. The beams of sunlight are so targeted that I stop and turn to look at the scraggly little pine tree they shine on. The sunlight illuminates the full color of the bark, branches, needles, and cones. At the same moment, a butterfly appears, dancing back and forth directly between the tree and me. This is the only butterfly I have seen all day, and I follow its carefree path with my eyes. The butterfly flutters and then lands on the outer edge of a branch on the same tree the sun has illuminated. Right below the butterfly, tucked away deep in the tree, hangs a set of Lakota prayer flags. There are four flags in all; one yellow, one blue, one red, and one white. I had not seen them on the walk up to the bluffs, even though the path faces them more directly on the ascent. Flags like these are common in the Pine Ridge and Black Hills wilderness, and they give me pause each time I encounter them.

Who left these flags? When were they placed here? What prayer was offered to the Great Spirit in return? The flags, for me, are symbolic in many ways. They are a reminder that those who live here have not forgotten their ancestors or their traditional ways.

We are alive. We are here. We still believe. We still have faith.

These are the messages of the prayer flags for me. I love to find and watch them. I am mesmerized by the power of this particular set of flags that the sun's rays and a single dancing butterfly revealed.

The sun and the butterfly led the way to these prayer flags.

By now, it is early evening as my car travels east toward the place where the sun rises. I descend down the ridge before turning right onto BIA 27 and then traveling south through Porcupine. On the way, I pass the site where Chief Big Foot and his Minneconjou band surrendered. Further on, I drive past the KILI Radio station before descending into Wounded Knee; once again, I stop at the red historical marker where the important question was first posed,

What brings you here?

This is the site of the last armed conflict between the Sioux and the cavalry, and it always speaks to me. I never tire of stopping here. Seven years after the Brooklyn Bridge was opened and four years after the Statue of Liberty was dedicated, the Sioux and the US Army were still fighting on the northern plains. Ironically, just several days after the massacre, Ellis Island officially opened as the formal processing point for millions of future immigrants who were traveling to America because it was the land of freedom and opportunity.

––––––––––

After a short drive, I am standing in line at Subway in Pine Ridge. Except for the person riding a horse bareback down the main street, the scene I am a part of could be anywhere in America. The restaurant is clean and efficient. The food is good and the service is fast and friendly. Subway is Subway.

As I stand in line, several young boys in dusty Little League uniforms are ordering sandwiches.

"Hey, good game today," one says to the other.

"Yeah, thanks. You too! You had some good hits," the other boy replies.

Both boys are wearing red socks underneath blue baseball pants. The pants alone, with their dust and dirt stains, tell the story of a game well played. Both boys have removed their cleats in favor of Adidas sandals. One boy still has his baseball cap on, while blue-tinted sunglasses rest atop the other boy's head.

I love this scene.

People are people, I think to myself. *Pine Ridge is changing and evolving at its own pace.*

When you stop to look at it, the change is happening in small ways all around this reservation. You can see it most clearly, I think, in the eyes of the children. Whether it is the girls making sandwiches or the young ballplayers waiting in line, their mannerisms and idle chatter are fresh and full of hope, a bit less distracted by the injustices of the past.

Later, I was told I just missed standing in line with the famous actor, Johnny Depp. Soon after I left Subway, he walked in (or so the story goes). He and I, on separate paths that will likely never cross, have both been pursuing a solo mission to Pine Ridge. Today, the Wounded Knee Massacre site sits on land that is privately owned. The owner of the land recently announced his intention to sell the property and is asking nearly $4 million. According to the *Rapid City Journal*, Johnny Depp has offered to purchase the land and then give it to the tribe. As simple as this sounds, I expect the process will be complicated and protracted. Everything political here is complex.

Meanwhile, in theaters across America, the famous actor is starring as Tonto in Disney's *The Lone Ranger*, where the dynamic duo is battling the corruption of the expanding railroad empire across the Great Plains.

As the sun sets behind me, I drive back to the Singing Horse Trading Post. Giant clouds billow, rise, and fall. They are like floating islands or ships (like pirate ships, in honor of Johnny Depp and his swashbuckling Disney movies). At times the clouds appear to fall all the way to earth, only to hit and bounce back up again.

The serenity of the sky at nightfall tells a false tale of things to come, for this night will be riddled with violent thunderstorms that will shake the very ground upon which my cabin rests. On this night, when I need them most, the dogs will be nowhere to be found. Tonight it will be every living creature for himself.

This disappoints me, as the dogs' presence gives me comfort at night, and I tell them this in person the following morning.

Everywhere I go now, I see circles.

We Indians think of the Earth and the whole universe as a never-ending circle, and in this circle, man is just another animal. The buffalo and the coyote are our brothers; the birds, our cousins. Even the tiniest ant, even a louse, even the smallest flower you can find, they are all relatives.

—Jenny Leading Cloud

7
Powwow

Shortly after the drums began to beat, the stadium came alive. And, for a short time at Pine Ridge, the transgressions of the past were forgotten. The people danced . . .

To be one, to be united is a great thing. But to respect the right to be different is maybe even greater.

—Bono

I wake before 7:00 a.m., having not slept much more than a few hours. Something changes at night here. I can't put my finger on just what that change is, but it is real. It is as if being alone with the magnitude of nature finally sinks in when darkness arrives and I get into bed. Friends here have told me that many people from "back east" become unnerved by the vastness of the plains and the smallness of a single human life.

At night, alone in the cabin as the thunder shakes the ground beneath me, my connectivity to all other living things takes the sleep away. To glimpse our personal oneness with nature is to awaken for the first time to a completely new paradigm of existence. I find the allure of this new reality irresistible, yet scary, especially in the darkness of night. Yet, somehow I awake each morning full of energy and not the least bit tired. Each morning, as soon as I wake up, I have the strongest urge to get back outside with nature. On this morning, I take a long walk down an empty road.

The empty road seems to exist only for me as I walk the centerline in the early morning mist.

As I leave the rustic cabin, it is cool outside and a heavy mist limits my vision. The wind is gusting from the northwest and the cottonwood trees are rattling along the creek bed. The mist and the cool air feel refreshing, however, as it was hot in the cabin last night.

After a long walk and a refreshing shower, I stop to visit Pinky at the store. The walkway is covered with exhausted dogs. Most of them lie on the concrete, soaking up the morning sun that has now burned off the rain and low-lying clouds.

As I enter, I see Danny is in the store talking with Pinky. I had not seen Danny yet on this trip, and I am happy to once again be in his company. Danny is the manager of Pinky's store, and it was he and his son, Brayden, who drove Pinky to the Rapid City airport to meet me at baggage claim on the first day I visited Pine Ridge. Danny is a strong man of few words, but behind his masculine facade lives a kind and bighearted soul. As I near him, I smile and extend my hand; then, something very small but powerful happens. Danny does not take my hand. Instead, he keeps coming, walking right past my outstretched arm to hug me.

"I am glad to see you," Danny says simply.

This small sequence of events is a big step, both for Danny and for me. I will never forget that moment when Danny hugged me. It was more than just a hug from one person. It was a hug that let me truly know I had arrived at Pine Ridge.

I tell Danny that I am coming back in the fall to hunt buffalo and that I plan to share the meat with the people of Pine Ridge. Danny has hunted buffalo on two occasions, and he tells me about the excitement and power of each experience for him.

We chitchat for a good while and once again, I lose track of time. By the time I say "Toksa Ake," I realize I am late again! How can this be?

"Actually, I am not late," I say out loud back inside my SUV. "It's not time until everyone shows up."

My second hug of the day comes about an hour later when Nick and I greet each other at his Thunder Valley office, just north of Sharps Corner. Nick then introduces me to his new friend, Bala.

Bala is from India, pursuing his doctoral degree in public administration at Harvard. Bala is in the process of writing his thesis paper, comparing the American government's historical treatment of indigenous peoples to that of his own country's. The question at the center of his research is, "Where would it have been better to have been indigenous after colonization, America or India?"

As we sit in Nick's conference room, which I refer to as "the thinking room," we have a good laugh early in the conversation when rightfully Nick refers to himself as an "Indian." So, if Nick is Indian, what do we call Bala?

"What are the chances?" I ask.

"What do you mean?" Nick replies.

"I mean, on the day we each were born, what are the chances that the three of us would ever be sitting together?"

"Ah," Nick says as he slides his head back and smiles.

The room is quiet and reflective for a moment before the conversation resumes.

"Our people did what they had to do to keep our spirituality and culture alive," Nick continues. "We were not always allowed to gather and worship as we pleased, so we practiced our beliefs in their churches," Nick explains.

"Our generation's weakness, however, is that we look too often for quick fixes," Nick says. "We must come to know that this will never work. We need to return to our spirituality in order to find our path. We must walk toward the spirits, for when we do, the spirits walk toward us in return."

Left to right: Kevin from Casco, Nick from Pine Ridge, and Bala from India (by way of Harvard), on the small front deck outside the Thunder Valley offices, just north of Sharps Corner.

Nick's comments make me think about the needlessness of it all. Until modern times, sun dance ceremonies were illegal at Pine Ridge, banned by the Bureau of Indian Affairs. People "caught" sun dancing were sometimes sent to mental institutions as wards of the state. In hindsight, this all seems so absurd—like it couldn't have been so, even though I know it was.

"If you believe you can talk to your ancestors, then you must be insane," says Nick. "That was the government's view of our people and our spirituality. Imagine how people were treated in those mental institutions at the time, especially Native peoples."

The room once again goes quiet.

Since first coming to Pine Ridge, I have reflected upon similar questions. America has long considered Native spirituality to be primitive and less advanced than Western religious beliefs. The Lakota took messages from clouds, spoke with animals, and saw their ancestors. The White Buffalo Calf Woman brought them their early traditions and ceremonies, while sharing the Sacred Pipe. I compare this to Christianity where God sent his son to Earth, parted the sea to save his people, and sent his Ten Commandments to a single man on a mountaintop. The stories of Christianity sound no more or less bizarre to me than the stories of Lakota spirituality. What is it about us humans that tips us to believe that only one religious path can be right?

I can't help but think to myself that it must be confusing, on some deep-seated level, to be both Christian and Lakota.

There are many differences between Lakota and Christian spirituality, but for me, three stand out. First, in the Bible, God is above us. He created us, instructed us, and judges us. He is separate from us. In Lakota spirituality we are nature, nature is God, God is us; all things are one thing.

The second distinction in the Bible is that God had a chosen people, meaning others were not chosen. This is also true of the Jewish and Muslim faiths, and it is very different than the Lakota faith. The Lakota faith is more akin to Buddhism or Hinduism, in which all beings are related and part of the universal fabric of life. The Lakota faith has, in its essence, the understanding of a singular humanity that binds us all. Finally, the Bible tells stories of people and events from the past, whereas Lakota spirituality is all about the here and now. It is a present-tense faith.

The great mythologist, Joseph Campbell, often wrote about these distinctions:

> *Recently I've come to realize the difference between two basically contrary mythological orders. There is the order that is most concerned with linking you to a certain society and pointing out that this is different from another society. One of the strongest books on that category is the Bible. [In the Bible, you're] making a distinction between the chosen and other people . . . then there is another religious system which has to do with the awakening of your nature . . . this is awakening the common humanity, and it's a quite different rhythm system from that of marching to the bugle of "Onward, Christian Soldiers."*

I use the Christian example only because it is the religion I know. It's the one I grew up learning inside the white clapboard–covered Casco Village Church. My awareness of Lakota spirituality does not make me less loyal to my own faith. By no means did Christianity invent the notion of a chosen people. The vast majority of mythological and religious belief systems across time have incorporated these same ideas. As a relatively new faith in the spectrum of human existence, Christianity simply borrowed, or inherited, many ideas from belief systems that went before it; included among them is the notion that its followers are special.

Ironically, the essence of Lakota spirituality does not always show up in the political and social practices at Pine Ridge. Lakota spirituality is inclusive, but some of the governing practices at Pine Ridge are not. Only official tribal members can vote at Pine Ridge. Living at Pine Ridge does not, on its own, entitle you to vote. Even being Lakota does not entitle you to vote. You must live here *and* be Oglala to vote in local elections.

This system promotes exclusivity, separation, and distinction. The Lakota of Pine Ridge are by no means alone in this regard. Today, people of virtually all cultures can see each other, through global media and Internet connectivity, but the tribalism of the old world order often still resists and divides. The Middle East is just one of many modern-day examples. This is where the tension comes from: small bands trying to isolate themselves and preserve their differences. It's not working.

To what society do you belong? Do you belong to this little in-group? Do you belong to the United States? Or, do you belong to the planet, to mankind? Economically it's one planet now. There's no doubt about it...I do think we are at the beginning of a new global age. That is to say, it's now once more a globe. No longer do you have different cultures within their bounded horizons, ignorant of each other and indifferent to each other. All horizons are broken. That's another thing Black Elk brought out. Do you know the passage?

—Joseph Campbell

I stood on the highest mountain of the world and I knew more than I saw, I understood more than I knew, because I was seeing in a sacred manner. And what I saw were the hoops of all the nations interlocking in one great circle.

—Black Elk

So he (Black Elk) saw it (the dawning of the new age).

—Joseph Campbell

"My grandmother tells stories of 'escaping' during the day from boarding school at Pine Ridge," Nick shares. "She and a few of her friends would sneak out of school and run over the other side of the hill where they would sit in a circle and tell stories in their Native language. It was only in this circle that she could laugh. She did not know how to say things in English that would make her laugh."

There is more silence in the room. It is Bala's first day at Pine Ridge and he is mostly listening and making notes.

I pull a multicolored Lakota medicine wheel out of my pocket. It is made of painted porcupine quills that are wrapped around rawhide.

"Tell me about this," I say to Nick.

"It is our medicine wheel," Nick explains. "It represents all things being connected. The axis running west to east represents the evil road of bad ways. The axis running north to south represents the good road to walk. The meeting place in the middle of the two axes is called the 'Chokan.' The Chokan is the center of everything. It is the Seventh Power. The Chokan is you, standing in the middle of it all. Wherever you are on your journey through life, you are in the center. You are always in the center."

The Seventh Power, I think to myself. *That's it! Wherever we are—each of us as individuals—we are at the center of the Sacred Hoop.*

The Seventh Power represents the power of the individual, who has choices to make. In this way, the system is dynamic. We are impacted by the actions of powers beyond our control, just as our actions impact the system in return.

I believe the Seventh Power, the power of a single individual, holds the key to the future for the Lakota people. The path forward lies at the center of the sacred wheel.

———————

"We are still fighting to get our land back," Nick explains a short while later. "We never intended to sell our land."

The land we are driving across glows in the late-morning sun. Nick, Bala, and I have left the Thunder Valley office and are headed to visit the Lakota Credit Union, which opened its first branch in Kyle just last year. This is my first field trip to a credit union, and normally I would not be this excited.

"When the Lakota Credit Union opened, it was the first time in the history of the reservation that you could deposit money here," Nick tells us.

Benjamin Harrison was president of the United States when the massacre at Wounded Knee occurred, in 1890. I wonder if, back in that year, most Americans would have believed that a black American would become president before the Oglala Sioux would be able to deposit money into a savings account on their own reservation?

In its first six months, the credit union signed up over eight hundred members. "It took my breath away to see how much money is coming through here each month," the young female teller behind the counter says to me. "There is more money here than people may realize," she continues. "We have just never had our own place to deposit, withdraw, and save before. It is all so exciting!"

Located upstairs, above the credit union, is the office of the Lakota Funds. The Lakota Funds is a micro-lending organization whose mission is to promote economic development on the reservation. The fund writes loans for small businesses. In addition, they make personal loans which the borrower uses to further their education, make home improvements, or start a small business. These loans require matching funds in which the borrower contributes one dollar for every three dollars borrowed. The fund was established in 1986, and at the time of this writing, their portfolio exceeds $6 million. At the time the fund was created, there were only two Native American–owned businesses on the entire reservation, and 85 percent of their clients had never had a checking or savings account.

One might easily drive right by the inconspicuous building that houses the Lakota Federal Credit Union, but its presence represents new ground for the people who live here.

———————

Picasso once said, "What you look at is not as important as what you see."

What do different people see when they look at Pine Ridge? What do the Lakota themselves see when they look at their own reservation? How about the non-Native people who live near Pine Ridge? What do they see? That is the question I am off to investigate this afternoon. Around 1:00 p.m., I drop Bala and Nick off at the Thunder Valley office and then drive back through Kyle, toward Potato Creek near the reservation's northeast corner. I have made a series of appointments with ranchers off the reservation, and I also plan on stopping in at some of the local convenience stores and restaurants that boarder the reservation to ask a few questions regarding local perspectives.

I stop the car as I cross the White River and listen to the pulsating sound of locusts coming at me from all directions. From there, I drive for quite some time before arriving at my first appointment.

The feedback I get about the reservation on this afternoon is sobering. Honestly, it is what I expected to hear. The people with whom I visited did not want their names to be used, but they all told a common story. Many people in the region have lived here their entire lives. They ranch, they farm, they capitalize on the modest tourist activity that makes its way south through the Badlands, and they interact with the Native peoples who live at Pine Ridge.

The people who live in this region tell stories of Pine Ridge residents "coasting into town as their car runs out of gas." They talk of a people with "no sense of purpose" and "no interest in working to support themselves."

"I think they did better when they were living on small individual farms and cabins, raising crops and keeping goats, pigs, and chickens. In the 1960s there was a big effort on the reservation to move everybody into these village housing clusters, and things got worse from there."

One person I spoke to told a story of a couple of Indians pulling into his driveway asking for gas. They both were quite drunk at the time.

"Have you been drinking?" he asked one of them.

"I've only had one beer," was the reply.

"That must have been some beer. I need to start drinking what you drink," the rancher retorted.

I ask about the high levels of alcoholism on the reservation. "What is the reason for this?"

"If you feel like you are without purpose, a few cans of beer can make you forget."

There is a definite sense here that the Lakota of Pine Ridge are not very interested in working to earn their own living. The work ethos is high in ranching communities; from that perspective, Pine Ridge looks like a very different place.

The people I spoke with cited numerous cases of private ranches and local businesses that the tribe had bought over the years. In each case, the ranch or business that had been purchased went from succeeding to failing, in short order.

The people I spoke with were equally doubtful about the value of donations.

"They have so much stuff donated to them. Most of it goes to waste."

"There are basements filled with donated clothing that nobody ever wears."

"Many local businesses bordering the reservation have to bring in Mexican and European workers because the Indians just don't want to work. It doesn't give me pleasure to say that. It's just a fact."

"You have to hire forty to get twenty who are willing to work."

This was one of the most troubling afternoons of my Pine Ridge experience. I really knew it was coming, but I am distressed when I am done, all the same.

Eventually, I pull off the road and just walk in a circle. It is the peak of a very hot day as I just keep walking in a small continuous circle in the grass away from my car. My shirt is off. My hands are in my back pockets. My feet are crunching into the ground with each step as they always do in Lakota lands. I just keep walking clockwise—west, north, east, south, and again—west, north, east, south, and around I go again. It would be easy to take the comments I heard today as racist, but the story is not that simple and tidy. The people who live and work here are good people. They work hard. For sure, they feel that they have embraced the reservation and the people who live there. They want the inhabitants of Pine Ridge to be successful and to improve their economic conditions. They also are quick to say that general statements do not speak for everyone. They know there are people at Pine Ridge who have jobs and who take consistent responsibility for earning a living. At the same time, they know what they see, and they are not willing to soften its hard edges.

Both groups in this region (Lakota and whites) have historic reasons to distrust each other. Both groups have ample reasons to be cynical. Where you sit dictates what you see.

The old green wooden sign at the intersection of BIA 27 and 33, just south of the White River on the Pine Ridge Reservation.

US Highway 44 runs across the northern edge of the reservation. In the town of Scenic, the highway cuts through the narrow strip of the Badlands National Park that connects the North Unit to the Stronghold Unit. If you continue northwest, as most people do, you will drive right into Rapid City. If you turn south, however, you will travel back onto the reservation with the dusty, white-faced cliffs of Sheep Mountain Table on your right. A short while later, you will arrive at the White River Visitor Center. Past the visitor center you will come to a junction where you can either go straight or turn right. If you go straight, you will continue south to Sharps Corner and wind up back at Nick's office. Alternatively, you can turn right and head back toward Manderson and the Singing Horse Trading Post. I have been through this intersection many times, although I have never met another car or person here.

I sit by the sign awhile, just looking around, and then turn right onto BIA 33 and continue driving across empty land, occupied only by an occasional small herd of horses. There are no cars, no people, and very few houses to pass on this hot and lazy Friday afternoon in early August. Eventually, however, my oversize SUV and I round a bend and a most familiar image comes into sight. It is my favorite building at Pine Ridge; on the east side of this quiet stretch of road, the abandoned white church comes back into view.

Sitting above Manderson on BIA 33 is the old abandoned church, symbolically my favorite building at Pine Ridge.

Each time I stop here, I make a note to research the history of this church. Then, each time I review my notes back home in Maine, I change my mind and conclude that I don't want to know the exact story, after all. I like the abandoned white church on the lonely road just the way it is. I have come to understand that what I love most about this church is the mystery itself, the story it tells and the story it doesn't. Knowing the story would remove the mystery. I like it better this way.

Also, each time I stop here, I feel a strong urge to go inside. So far, however, I have resisted that temptation. I can't explain why, exactly. I feel some fear about entering. I tell myself it is private property, but I know better; that which holds me back is deeper.

What scares me about this place? I guess, in the end, it is the truth that scares me.

I find the open front door of the church both inviting and frightening, like many things in life, I suppose.

The front door, which is always ajar, calls out to me. This is the right time to go inside, I decide. Today is the day. I turn left into the dirt pull-off, just south of the church, and climb through the best opening I can find in the barbed-wire fence. I have gotten good at looking for the best opening in wire fences.

I walk to the front steps and slowly move up to the entrance. I peer in through the door, as if to see if it is safe inside. My head crosses the threshold, but both feet are still outside. I look in, down, left, right, and up before taking a deep breath and plunging myself entirely inside. As I enter, the floorboards creak beneath my feet. Every step makes a sound at Pine Ridge.

I am tiptoeing and I am crouching; neither action is necessary, nor does it even make sense, but that is what I am doing. Not everything we do makes sense.

Once inside, what I see is full surrender. The building has begun its return to the earth in the way all things ultimately do. The white altar still stands at the front of the church, under a vaulted ceiling. A lone white cross rests on the wall above. Each window is either partially or completely blown out, allowing the sunlight and fresh air to meet the musty smell of wet carpet and rotted walls. The ceiling is broken open in multiple places and the building belongs to the barn swallows, which can be heard busily chirping and rustling above. Scraps of wood are strewn across the floor and broken pipes protrude from the walls. The power of this place lies in the story it simultaneously reveals and conceals. I am never fully comfortable, and each step is a quiet one; after a few reflective moments pass, I back out (literally) in the exact same way I entered.

I finish my drive back to Singing Horse in silence.

The symbolism of this abandoned church is striking. For some reason, I was uncomfortable the entire time I stood inside.

Later that afternoon, I change my clothes, hang out in the cabin, and talk to the dogs for a while in the yard before driving back down the dusty driveway. I use my blinker, which is not necessary, before turning left and heading south to watch the 7:00 p.m. grand entry at the powwow grounds.

The powwow grounds are located on the southwest corner of town and can be accessed from several directions. The most direct route is to travel right through town past Big Bat's convenience store and then Subway. Shortly thereafter, you turn left down a bumpy dirt road in front of the playground, basketball court, skateboard park, and ball field. Immediately you are in the parking area and beyond that sit the powwow grounds. On the left side of the complex, the fair is in full swing. The Ferris wheel is circling and the children who ride it are screaming, tossing their hands in the air, and swinging their feet. In some respects, the scene is unique to right here. In other respects, it could be anywhere in America.

The powwow arena is elegant in its simplicity. The plainness of the site belies the power and meaning of this sacred place. Everything is set just so for a reason. The facility is actually a stadium for the dancers, drummers, and dressmakers who will first parade, then compete here. The stadium is designed, of course, in the shape of a circle, with the four colors of the Lakota medicine wheel all present. Participants enter from the east and travel clockwise past the first section of stadium, which is yellow. As the contestants keep walking around the circle, they pass the announcer's booth and performance stage at what would be the true southern entrance to the grounds. Continuing on around the Sacred Hoop, they travel toward the west entrance and past the second stadium section that is white. Participants then travel north, past the black section of stadium, until reaching the final stadium section, which is red, arriving back at the beginning.

Each of the four stadium sections is a basic shelter, comprised of a plywood roof held aloft by wooden posts. There are no walls. People come early to get the best seats. There are no chairs in the stadium; everyone brings their own. Scattered around the stadium are drum circles where different groups will take turns beating and chanting traditional Lakota music, as the processional moves or dance competitions occur. The entire scene is quite spectacular.

A voice on the public address system refocuses my wandering mind. The event is about to begin.

"All are welcome here," the speaker declares. "You are our guests; you are safe here."

The sensation that I am floating as I walk has retaken me. Each sound I hear is exceptionally crisp, and I can hear many different sounds and conversations all at once. Each scene is filled with distinctive colors in the early evening light. I feel very, very alive at this moment.

The first drum group jumps into action. I am standing right beside them. It startles me, as I am practically in their circle. At the time, I had no understanding of the flow of the event. I thought they just randomly started playing and chanting. Two members of the group are wearing Miami Heat jerseys with the number 6 and the word "James" across the back. The power of the music is captivating. The pounding of the drums and the echo of the chants pulsate through me like the wind itself. The music is everywhere, and soon the arena comes alive with color as the dancers and contestants enter the stadium.

"Our greatest enemy, Custer, was defeated," the master of ceremonies proclaims.

Much tribute is paid to past and current warriors. Military service is highly honored here.

"Our young warriors, past and present, are here to be celebrated," the announcer states with pride.

Color, movement, drums, and chants meet and merge. The arena is full of life, Lakota life. At this moment, for me, everything is one thing and I begin to cry. I am not crying because I am sad. I am crying because I am happy. I am lost in time and place. No other thoughts occupy my mind beyond the blessing of this moment.

I stay at the powwow grounds until well after dark. I eat fry bread, French fries, burgers, and more. Eventually, I leave, but the event continues on. I can see it all in my rearview mirror as my big SUV slowly bumps along the exit road. The lights illuminating the center of the arena fill the sky above. The drums and chants filter out to me and beyond.

It is late at night when I unlock the gate at Singing Horse and open the wooden door to my tiny cabin. For the longest time that evening, however, the images of powwow dance in my head and fill my heart. It makes me happy to see the Lakota people freely expressing themselves and celebrating the essence of who they are.

Colors, movement, drums, and chants all merge as the energy of the opening ceremony fills the powwow grounds. It was a very emotional experience for me.

During the summer at Pine Ridge, the storm clouds have first dibs on the night. To the extent storms happen during the day here, it is as if they arrived early in anticipation of the night's festivities. This day was beautiful, warm and sunny. This night, however, is to be a wild one filled with thunder, lightning, and angry clouds.

The storm wakes me at 3:00 a.m. as thunder shakes the earth beneath my cabin. The rain pounds the sheet-metal roof. As I regain my awareness and shake off the sleep, the power goes out and the plastic fan drifts slowly to a halt. Everything surrenders to the storm.

I lapse in and out of sleep.

Around 5:00 a.m., I sit up and place my bare feet on the wooden floor. The springs of the bed squeak as I slide into my unlaced sneakers, search for my glasses, and head for the door. I am going outside to go to the bathroom. I don't want to go outside, as it is still raining, but I have postponed this trip as long as possible. Wearing just my shorts, I struggle with the black latch before yanking the door open. It is one of those doors that sticks until suddenly it completely releases in a way that suggests the joke is on you.

"*Holy shit!*" I exclaim.

My breathing stops as my heart enters my throat (seemingly literally). It is one of those authentically scary moments we all have experienced when we are truly, truly surprised, in a way that is not the least bit okay at the time.

"Oh my God," I sigh deeply as I let some air back into my body.

"What are you doing?" I say out loud with a nervous laugh.

One of Rosie's horses has backed right up to my door, I mean right up to it. It is a scene so bizarre that it is hard to describe. There is a short wooden ramp leading up to the cabin door. It takes two human steps to cross it before entering. The horse has both hind legs on the ramp and his rear end is pushing against the door itself. He is standing still, tall and alone as nighttime inches toward morning.

I was surprised and momentarily scared to find one of Rosie's horses completely backed up against the door of my cabin. I literally walked right into his rear end.

Rosie will later tell me that he was simply getting out of the wind and the rain. I understand why she said this and it makes perfect sense, but that is not the sensation I experienced. For some reason, my immediate reaction was that he was protecting me from something. He was guarding my cabin. I had that sensation the moment I recovered from the surprise of walking into his butt. I gathered myself, pushed my way around him, went to the bathroom, and then squeezed back by the horse again (as he hadn't moved), before climbing back into bed. I did not sleep any more that night.

A short while later, I get back out of bed, throw on some clothes, and head outside for what I have come to think of as a Lakota power walk. I open the door slowly, ready for anything, but the horse has moved on. The gravel road leading down from the trading post is washed out and the water trickles and babbles as it flows downhill. I open and close the gate, re-latching the small chain. As I do this, I notice Rosie's horses above her house. The horse that looked after me in the night is standing alone near the fence line, as a group of horses from the main herd grazes above. The process of opening and closing the gate has attracted his attention. He gives one strong neigh as he continues to stare at me, and then he nods his head once (also at me) before releasing me and turning his attention to grazing.

The air is cool and a steady wind blows from the south as I walk the yellow centerline. At the top of the second rise in the road, I turn and begin walking back down. A bit farther down the road, there is a rustling in the grass to my left. The grass, which is perhaps three feet in height, is being moved by something from within. As I stop to watch, I expect to see a hedgehog or a similar type of animal appear. Instead, I am surprised to see a swarm of grasshoppers clicking and bounding through the grass. At first I dismiss them, as there is no way they can be the cause of all that noise and movement; but, as more and more grasshoppers move through, it becomes clear that they are collectively the creator of the activity.

As I continue to drift back toward the Singing Horse Trading Post, I am stopped again by yet another new and distinct sound. This one is coming at me from behind and it is traveling down the road. My first instinct is that the grasshoppers once again must be involved, but as I stop, turn, and look, there is nothing there. I am confused as I stare back down the road from whence I came and see nothing. The noise continues to draw closer, however, as the invisible force moves toward me, declaring itself only by the sound it makes on the pavement.

Then, it hits me, literally; drops of water falling from the sky pop onto my face and nestle into my hair.

It is raining, but there are no clouds. The sky is blue and open above me.

The raindrops are refreshing and my eyes go to meet them as they fall from the sky. I am enthralled by how far up I can see the droplets. I see them higher and more clearly than I have ever seen them before. The simplest events make the most amazing experiences here.

Eventually, the raindrops stop falling.

Farther down the road, the big cottonwood tree on the left is busy talking. The tree is full of small, crisp green leaves with long stems that rustle in the breeze. They rustle in unison and take on a personality that you must see for yourself to believe. This tree is extremely busy this morning, talking, waving, laughing, and finally embracing me before signaling good-bye.

Grass and wildflowers never seem far away from reclaiming the pavement at Pine Ridge.

This lonely stretch of road is a gathering spot for the prairie spirits this morning. Everything is one thing here, and this was a Lakota power walk to remember. I am refreshed and energized. I can feel myself as the Seventh Power.

––––––––––

It is my last breakfast at Singing Horse on this trip, and Rosie, once again, has cooked more than I can eat. There are a number of people in the house this morning, and I meet Rosie's friend, Buck, for the first time. Buck is a local carpenter of Seminole descent. My friend Catherine comes in the door shortly after I do.

Catherine Grey Day is one of my favorite friends at Pine Ridge. She was born on the Standing Rock Reservation and is of Dakota descent, which makes her Sioux, but not Oglala. Nothing seems to scare her. Nothing holds her back. Isn't that what we are all after in life, to not be scared, to not be held back by our own internal worries and apprehensions? Catherine always wears a broad, loving smile, and you can feel her heart and spirit when you are in her presence. She says what she thinks, as if the thought of doing otherwise has never occurred to her. There is nothing more delightful than the purity of her unguarded laugh. Catherine has not had an easy life, but she seems to live that wonderful Buddhist saying:

Life is the joyful participation in the sorrows of the world.

"We've got divisions of all kinds here," Catherine calmly pronounces, after she settles into breakfast.

"There are those who have and those who don't. There are the transplants, the half-breeds, and the full-bloods. We are always told we are not from here, but I don't agree with that. We are all Lakota."

"Oh, by the way, did you see the UFO last night?" Catherine asks everyone in the room as she reaches for some toast, as if it were no big deal.

"Wait, what?" I say out loud (which momentarily distracts me, because this is a phrase both our daughters use frequently, but I rarely use myself).

No one else in the room really seems to give the UFO statement much thought; everyone continues on with their activity and side conversations, including Catherine herself.

Her question takes my breath away, however, as I sit beside her at the table. I immediately think of the horse backed up to my door this morning and the sensation I experienced that he was standing guard, protecting me.

"What time was that, Catherine?" I ask.

"What time was what?" Catherine replies. Clearly, she has moved on.

"The UFO," I reply.

"I am just curious what time you saw the UFO."

"Just a few minutes before five a.m.," she answers.

I adjust my chair, turning in the direction of Catherine.

"Tell me more," I say. "Just what exactly did you see?"

I never did get much more out of Catherine about the UFO. She was on to other things.

Perhaps it's better that way. I love Pine Ridge for the mysteries it conceals, as much as I do for that which it reveals.

"We aren't meant to know it all in this lifetime," Deborah Dooley is fond of reminding me.

> **There are two ways to live your life. One is though nothing is a miracle. The other as though everything in a miracle.**
>
> **– Albert Einstein**

Catherine and I in the basement of the Singing Horse Trading Post. I know the light from the windows impacts this picture, but this story is about letting the light pour in.

Back outside after breakfast, the sun is at the top of the sky as I pack my few belongings into my oversize SUV. Buffalo, the young dog, trots over and deliberately brushes up against me. I feel bad that I have said good-bye to all the people, but not to him. I stop and give his thick yellow coat a good scratching.

"Toksa Ake, Buffalo," I say.

He feels better and trots off.

Buffalo the dog would make a great mascot, or symbol, for Pine Ridge. His soul is strong, his ears are always to the wind, and his love is unconditional. Each time I return he greets me as if I never left.

Buffalo, Rosie's dog, is my four-legged friend. He joins me for every walk along the fence lines above the Singing Horse Trading Post.

Peace may come to those peoples who can understand, an understanding which must be of the heart and not of the head.

– Black Elk

8
Walking between Worlds

The rugged rock outcroppings of the Black Elk Wilderness.

This account of the sacred pipe and the rites of the Sioux, was handed down orally by the former "keeper of the sacred pipe," Elk Head [Hehaka Pa], to three men. Of these three, Black Elk was the only one[still] living. When Elk Head gave this account to Black Elk, he told him that it must be handed down. For as long as it is known, and for as long as the pipe is used, their people will live; but as soon as the pipe is forgotten, the people will be without a center and they will perish.

—Joseph Epes Brown, *The Sacred Pipe*

It has already become a hot summer day as I knock on the screen door of Bette's Kitchen on the hilltop, just south of Manderson. The metal frame of the door rattles in response. Betty's husband rounds the corner and waves me inside. I love this about Pine Ridge. I am a complete stranger and he doesn't even know what I want. He just waves me inside, nonetheless, with a knowing smile, as if he were expecting me.

I extend the small black book I am carrying into the air.

"I am looking for the cabin," I say. "Can you help me find it?"

The book in my hands is titled *Black Elk Speaks*, by John Neihardt. The book is well-worn from my reading, studies, and note taking. Inside the red center of the cover is a drawing of Black Elk. Except for his wise and weathered face, his body is entirely covered in a red robe. Six eagle feathers sit atop his head between a wide set of elk antlers. As the picture travels down his robe, Black Elk's body blends in with the surroundings, until the two become one and his torso fades away.

I follow Betty's husband through the dining room, past the kitchen, and into the living room. The TV is on as Betty greets me. She takes me back outside, this time through the front door, and onto a small set of wooden steps.

"Down there," she points. "The cabin sits in that clump of cottonwood trees."

"You can drive this way to get there," she says, gesturing toward the wild grass and rolling hills below her house.

I don't see what she sees. In particular, I do not see any road or trail that I can drive on. I ask her to explain it all to me again and she does. It still doesn't make sense to me, but I don't feel right asking a third time, so I thank her and walk across the front lawn back to my vehicle.

Five minutes later I am standing on a grassy knoll, just above the trees she had pointed to. Deep inside the grove, I can barely see the small cabin. My heart pounds with anticipation. This is where Black Elk lived, and I can feel the history and spirituality of this place in a very powerful way. The energy of the scene runs through my entire body. My heart accelerates as I stand in silence. When I finally move closer to the cabin, I go slowly, almost tiptoeing as Black Elk's words come flowing back to me:

> **I am a Lakota of the Oglala band. My father's name was Black Elk, and his father before him bore the name, and the father of his father, so that I am the fourth to bear it.**

"Family traditions pull on us all," I whisper to the old cabin.

Black Elk's abandoned cabin below Bette's Kitchen, just south of Manderson.

Very few people know where this cabin is and almost nobody comes here. This puzzles me because Black Elk is such an important figure in Lakota history. If you know just where to look, you can actually see the cabin from the road between Manderson and Wounded Knee. But, you would have to know exactly where to look; otherwise, you would drive right by it, as most people do. The small gray cabin, buried deep within the cottonwood trees and tall grass, gives no indication anyone of significance ever lived here.

There's that Lakota value of humility once again, I think to myself.

As I stand in the warmth of the morning sun, Black Elk's words continue to come to life off the pages of the book I have brought with me:

I was born in the moon of the Popping Trees [December] on the Little Powder River in the Winter When the Four Crows Were Killed [1863], and I was three years old when my father's right leg was broken in the Battle of the Hundred Slain. My father was [later] killed by the Pawnees when I was too little to know.

I have to cut my own path to the cabin, as there is not even a walking trail. The grass is up to my waist in places, and the story it tells is that I am the only visitor who has passed this way in quite some time. The windows and doors are boarded up with plywood. The siding is rough-cut, uneven, and clearly of another era. Some sections of siding are rotting away, while others are missing altogether. Under a small tree on the east side of the house sits a stack of animal skulls.

The skulls at the base of the tree that splits in two beside Black Elk's cabin.

Once we were happy in our own country and we were seldom hungry, for then the two-leggeds and the four-leggeds lived together like relatives, and there was plenty for them and for us. But then the Wasichus [white men] came, and they have made little islands for us and other little islands for the four-leggeds, and always these islands are becoming smaller.

I had never seen a Wasichu then, and did not know what one looked like; but everyone was saying that the Wasichus were coming and that they were going to take our country and rub us all out.

And so when the soldiers came and built themselves a town of logs [Fort Phil Kearny] there on the Piney Fork of the Powder [River], my people knew that they meant to have their road and take our country and maybe kill us all when they were strong enough. Crazy Horse was only about nineteen years old then, and Red Cloud was still our great chief.

—Black Elk

I stand in front of Black Elk's cabin for what feels like the longest time, but this is another of those moments in which time has little meaning. Once again, I have the sensation that I am both inside and outside my body and everything feels like one thing. I do not feel the "normal" separation between the grasses, the trees, the flies, the wind, the cabin, and myself. I don't plan these moments, they just come get me with increasing frequency. I have learned to just stop where I am and let it happen. I just go where the energy takes me.

As I stand there alone, just staring at the cabin, something begins to speak to me. I wouldn't say it is a specific person that is speaking to me, but more so just the entire energy field of this place. The energy "asks me" to take a small piece of siding from the cabin itself. For what reason, I do not know. I would not normally have thought to do this (I have plenty of wood siding and lumber products back home!), and I second-guess the instinct before moving forward. I approach the building with reverence and caution. I still can't quite believe I am standing here. This place might well have little or no meaning for many other people, but it is exceptionally powerful for me. I am quiet and deliberate with each step, as if entering the room of a sleeping baby. I put my right hand cautiously on the corner of the building at its southeast edge. I let my hand drift up and down the rough-sawn board as I study the cabin more closely. I think about the inside of the boarded-up building and wonder what, if anything, is left there.

The boys of my people began very young to learn the ways of men, and no one taught us; we just learned by doing what we saw, and we were warriors at a time when boys now are like girls.

We were always naked when we played it [the game of "Throwing-Them-Off-Their Horses"], just as warriors are when they go into battle if it is not too cold, because they are swifter without clothes.

It must be the fear that I remember most. All this time I was not allowed to play very far away from our tepee, and my mother would say, "If you are not good, the Wasichus will get you."

—Black Elk

"We just learned by doing what we saw," I whisper to myself, thinking both of my own life back home in Maine and of modern-day Pine Ridge.

I look at the grasses around me and I imagine Black Elk walking through them, sitting among them. He lived the last decades of his life right here in this humble and inconspicuous place. My eyes return to the building and, more specifically, to the siding. The front wall of the house contains numerous small segments that, over time, have broken away from the larger pieces they once belonged to. I spot one such piece in particular that is near me. I take a single step forward and I tear it off. It comes my way easily. As I hold it, it stretches from my fingertips halfway up my forearm. I move slowly away from the building, retreating backwards at the same pace that I approached. As I do, Black Elk's words resume:

[A herd of buffalo had been located by the scouts.]

Everybody began sharpening knives and arrows and getting the best horses ready for the great making of meat. Then the head man of the advisors went around picking out the best hunters with the fastest horses, and to these he said: "Good young warriors, my relatives, your work I know is good. What you do is good always; so today you shall feed the helpless. Perhaps there are some old and feeble people without sons, or some who have little children and no man. You shall help these, and whatever you kill shall be theirs."

Then there was a great dust and everybody shouted "Hoka hey!," and all the hunters went in to kill—every man for himself. They were all nearly naked, with their quivers full of arrows hanging on their left sides, and they would ride right up to a bison and shoot him behind the left shoulder.

Everybody was very happy . . . all over the flat, as far as I could see, there were men butchering bison now, and the women and the old men who could not hunt were coming up to help. And all the women were making the tremolo [sounds] of joy for what the warriors

had given them. That was in the Moon of Red Cherries [July]. It was a great killing.

Back on the knoll above the cabin, I pause and offer a prayer. I begin by extending my arms and transforming my breathing. I breathe deeply and rhythmically in a circular fashion, pulling the fresh air in through my nose, down into my body, and then, later, releasing it slowly out through my mouth. Breathing can be both a conscious and unconscious exercise. It is more powerful when it is done consciously. The power of one's existence can be realized with a single, thoughtful breath.

I offer my prayer out loud, even though I am alone:

"You lived the story of your people so that you could tell that story before it was lost," I say to Black Elk. "You were wise to do so, and you have honored your people in this way. With your blessing, I, too, shall pass on the story of your people. I ask now for your guidance and permission. I also thank you for this weathered piece of wood. This wood once housed you, and I carry it forward as a symbol of the connection I feel with the spirit of your people."

My eyes are closed and my hands remain extended out, palms open, parallel to the ground. The sun is shining on me and the day is warm, but at this moment a deep, deep cold chill overtakes me. I can feel the goose bumps on my arms and I begin shivering. I am shivering at midday in August. I am truly cold and actually begin shaking. I think back to what Nick Tilsen recently told me: "The spirits will meet you halfway."

Connectivity to the Great Spirit has long been celebrated in Lakota society. When Black Elk was a young boy, he began hearing voices that he could not explain:

> **Now and then the voices would come back when I was out alone, like someone calling me, but what they wanted me to do I did not know. This did not happen very often, and when it did not happen, I forgot about it; for I was growing taller and was riding horses now and could shoot prairie chickens and rabbits with my bow.**

The voices came to Black Elk when he was alone in the wilderness, I think to myself.

In the summer of his ninth year, Black Elk became quite sick and had to be transported in a pony drag as the village moved. Once the village had been resettled, Black Elk lay in his tepee as his mother and father watched over him with worry. The family dwelling was filled with an un-spoken fear that Black Elk might die. As he lay there, his eyes drifted to the opening of the tepee where he saw two men descend from the clouds headfirst, like arrows. They motioned to Black Elk before speaking:

"Hurry! Come! Your Grandfathers are calling you!"

Black Elk got up and walked toward them. Upon exiting the tepee he saw the two men rising back into the sky. Black Elk rose with them and followed. Looking back, he could see his mother and father as he rose above the village and drifted away:

> *Now suddenly there was nothing but a world of cloud, and we three were there alone in the middle of a great white plain with snowy hills and mountains staring at us; and it was very still; but there were whispers.*

At this time, a single bay horse appeared to Black Elk and began to explain the Great Mystery of the World. The bay horse first called Black Elk's attention to the west where twelve other magnificent black horses stood, with lightning emanating from their manes and thunder from their nostrils. Turning north, toward the home of the white giants, twelve white horses appeared with white geese circling high above. Fac-ing east, where the sun lives, twelve more horses stood ready. The same was repeated facing south, and now there were forty-eight horses in all. At this time, the original bay horse spoke to Black Elk once again:

"Your Grandfathers are having a council. These [the forty-eight horses] shall take you; so have courage."

With these words, the forty-eight horses of the four directions fell into formation and began to dance. Black Elk and the bay horse walked side by side as the rest followed behind. Soon, a cloud transformed into a tepee and a rainbow appeared, marking its entrance. Once inside,

Black Elk saw six old men sitting in a single line. They invited Black Elk to join them, so he did.

> *So I went in and stood before the six, and they looked older than men can ever be—old like the hills, like stars. Then the oldest spoke: "Your Grandfathers all over the world are having a council, and they have called you here to teach you." His voice was very kind, but I shook all over with fear now, for I knew that these were not old men, but the Powers of the World. And the first was the Power of the West; the second, of the North; the third, of the East; the fourth, of the South; the fifth, of the Sky; the sixth of the Earth.*

At this point, the First Grandfather spoke to him. As he spoke, a wooden cup appeared in his hand. The cup contained water and the water contained the sky. Black Elk was given the cup and with it the power to heal and make life. Next, Black Elk was given a bow and with it the power to destroy. Then the Grandfather pointed to himself and said:

> *"Look closely at him who is your spirit now, for you are his body."*

As the First Grandfather said this he rose, becoming very tall, and then he turned and ran toward the west where the sun goes down. As he ran, he turned into a black horse. Eventually, he stopped, turned, and stared back at Black Elk. As he did this, Black Elk could see that the horse had become very weak and feeble.

Next, the Second Grandfather spoke and gave Black Elk an herb for healing, before turning into a white goose and flying away to the north. As he flew, he sang two songs about the thunder nation and the white geese nation. Next, the Third Grandfather spoke of the sun from which all beings are awakened (whether they have wings, fins, roots, two legs, or four). As he spoke, he held forth a peace pipe with the image of an eagle upon it:

> *"With this pipe you shall walk upon the Earth, and whatever sickens there you shall make well."*

The Fourth Grandfather came next. As he spoke, he held forth a red stick of great light from which branches sprouted and birds flew before Black Elk's eyes. This stick represented a cane to walk with and was to stand in the center of the circle of all living things. For a moment, in that center, Black Elk could see villages of people organized in their customary circles. Beyond the village he saw all the living things of the Earth, as well, and every creature was happy.

As Black Elk stood looking down on the world, the Fourth Grandfather called his attention to the Sacred Hoop of all living things and the two red roads that divide it; at this point he stood and ran away to the south, where he became an elk.

Next, it was time for the Fifth Grandfather to speak. He was the oldest of them all, as he was the father of the sky.

Finally, the Sixth Grandfather spoke:

> **. . . he, who was the Spirit of the Earth, and I saw that he was very old, but more as men are old. His hair was long and white, his face was all in wrinkles and his eyes were deep and dim. I stared at him, for it seemed I knew him somehow; and as I stared, he slowly changed, for he was growing backwards into youth, and when he had become a boy, I knew that he was myself with all the years that would be mine at last. When he was old again, he said, "My boy, have courage, for my power shall be yours, and you shall need it, for your nation on the Earth will have great troubles. Come."**

Black Elk had seen himself as one with the Great Spirit and through this he knew that the energy of all things was shared.

At this point, the Sixth Grandfather rose and left the tepee through the door that was a rainbow. Black Elk followed and was rejoined by the horses that were waiting in formation. Together, they traveled through the sky and over the Earth. As Black Elk and his horses passed over a village of his people, he saw many women and children dead upon the ground. Black Elk's presence revived the dead, however, and soon everyone was healthy and happy again. Black Elk gave the people of this village his flowering stick so that they might prosper and grow. He also gave them "the Sacred Pipe, that they may know the power that is peace." As the people of the village walked off, another voice called out to Black Elk:

> **"Behold your nation, and remember what your Six Grandfathers gave you, for thenceforth your people walk in difficulties."**

In time, the road turned bad again for the people of the village and Black Elk could now see them walking slowly, surrounded by sickness and starvation. Black Elk could see that the bison, which had been a gift of the spirits, were now gone, and he knew that a new source of strength would need to be found to replace them.

Black Elk's journey continued on across the sky until he found himself standing upon "the highest mountain of them all" (Harney Peak in the Black Hills), and from that vantage point he could see the entire Sacred Hoop of the whole world. After resting on top of the world, he resumed his flight across the sky until he found himself descending back home into the very village from whence his journey began.

> *I could see my people's village far ahead, and I walked very fast, for I was homesick now. Then I saw my own tepee, and inside I saw my mother and my father bending over a sick boy that was myself. And as I entered the tepee, someone was saying: "The boy is coming to; you had better give him some wa-ter." Then I was sitting up; and I was sad because my mother and my father didn't seem to know I had been so far away.*

———

Even though I am surrounded by summer air, I am still shivering as I open the door to my SUV. It is hard to make sense of the bone-chillingly cold sensation that has descended upon me.

I get into my vehicle and drive slowly off the knoll, following the two de-pressions in the grass that still remember the original path of my tires. Both windows are open, allowing air to move all the way through the front of my car. The sun is shining. A small piece of weathered wood now sits sideways on top of my blue spiral notebook in the passenger seat beside me.

I was not expecting the deep chill that overcame me at the conclusion of my visit to Black Elk's "square house."

Wherever we went, the soldiers came to kill us and it was all our own country. It was ours already when the Wasichus made the treaty with Red Cloud that said it would be ours as long as grass should grow and water flow. That was only eight winters before [1868], and they were chasing us now because we remembered and they forgot.

—Black Elk

Perhaps a mile south of the powwow grounds sits the rodeo arena. There is a winding dirt road that connects the two, but you can also access the rodeo by turning right just past the Hancock House as you leave the town of Pine Ridge heading south toward the Nebraska state line. The Great Plains Indian Rodeo Association organizes the two-day event, and it attracts some of the best rodeo competitors in the American West, Indian and non-Indian alike.

Immediately after leaving Black Elk's cabin, I drive straight to the event. I love the rodeo, and therefore, I am very excited. The rodeo, scheduled to begin at 1:00 p.m., eventually kicks off at 1:55 p.m., with a Lakota flag prayer ceremony, followed by a chilling electric guitar rendition of the National Anthem.

Attending this event is like going to the drive-in movies in Maine, or a stock-car race in an Indiana cornfield. Vehicles line up on a single lane dirt road and pay admission by the carload. Those who get there first back right up to the gray metal rails that create the arena. There are no bleachers, because there is no stadium. There is just the rodeo arena; spectators bring lawn chairs, sit on tailgates, or stand right up against the rail itself. Everyone has a front row-seat.

The first rider of the day is Shane O'Connell from Rapid City, the two-time defending South Dakota high school state champion. He nods his head, the chute is pulled open, and out he comes atop an agitated horse named Bay Magic. What a ride! With one hand in the air, Shane lies completely back on the horse as it bucks, twists, and snorts. The buzzer sounds as the horse nearly collapses to the ground before regaining its footing. The ride is officially over, but Shane is still on the horse, as he cannot get his hand untied. Two cowboys and their exceptional horses chase Shane halfway around the arena before they are able to settle Bay Magic and extract his rider. As I watch, Shane slips onto the back of one of the cowboy's horses before dropping himself to the ground; the cars and trucks circling the arena sound their horns in approval. The judges score the ride a 69 (100 represents a perfect score).

The second horse nearly jumps out of the gate and over the backside with the rider on him. Everyone scrambles out of the way. It is quite a scene. I am so excited to be here. I have my left foot up on the second parallel bar of the metal fence. My forearms are resting on the fifth bar. I watch steer wrestling, calf roping, bull riding, and more, before departing for the Black Hills sometime after 4:00 p.m.

"Toksa Ake, Pine Ridge," I say, as I drive out of town.

I arrive at the Historic Log Cabin Motel on the north end of town in Hot Springs, just a little over an hour after leaving Pine Ridge. What a difference sixty minutes can make. I quickly check in and get the keys to my small cabin. I drink a cold beer at the picnic table and then head out for Wind Cave National Park.

Later that evening, I watch the sun's last light fade as a herd of buffalo walks over the ridge, giving the impression that they are leaving with it.

———————

Once again, when nighttime comes, I do not sleep. But it doesn't seem to matter, as I wake up feeling refreshed and energized. The clouds are low and heavy in the early morning sky, as I drive back into Custer County and reenter the national park. On this morning, the buffalo are everywhere as I ease onto the side road that leads to park headquarters. As I get out of my car, I can easily see over two hundred buffalo. I can hear them as well. The bulls are especially animated this morning. They are running, grunting, charging about, corralling cows, and threatening each other. Some of the bull have narrowed their attention to a single cow and stalk her incessantly. With each step the cow takes, the bull moves as well. If the cow heads in a direction that displeases the bull, he intervenes by blocking her path. This scene is repeated time and again. Other bulls are hammering themselves into dried-out mud holes. They lie in the hole and then repeatedly slam down into the dirt, rolling onto their backs with their feet straight up in the air. If the goal is to attract as much attention as possible, they are succeeding. I feel like I am a part of the activity with many buffalo not more than twenty yards away. At one point, I actually need to climb up onto my SUV as a dominant male thunders past in pursuit of six young bulls that stampede right by me. The end of mating season is drawing near and the boys clearly want to take full advantage. The scene is primal, timeless, and a bit comical. The cows just want to graze. The bulls just want to mate.

There are lots of first-year calves as well. They are a very light shade of brown, almost red, compared to the adults that appear nearly black in color. The calves follow their moms, suckling when they can, before lying down to rest with a look of great contentment. It is a good day to be a buffalo.

I linger and linger, watching the buffalo for a long time, before finally getting back into my vehicle and driving on.

The relationship between mother and child is not so different whether you have two legs or four; we are all related.

At 7,242 feet, Harney Peak is the highest point in the Black Hills. The mountain lies within the Black Hills National Forest and is part of the Black Elk Wilderness Area. Originally, the peak was named in honor of General William S. Harney, who commanded federal troops in the region in the 1870s. The first white man to reach the summit, however, is actually believed to be General Custer, during the infamous Black Hills expedition of 1874 in which gold was "discovered." In the spring of 2015, South Dakota state officials recommended the mountain be renamed "Hinhan Kaga," which translated means "The Making of Owls." This is believed to be the original Lakota name. Of course, the peak is also home to Black Elk's great vision, and is the place where he most wanted to return near the end of his life.

> *I was standing on the highest mountain of them all, and round about beneath me was the whole hoop of the world. And while I stood there I saw more than I can tell and I understood more than I saw; for I was seeing in a sacred manner the shapes of all things in the spirit, and the shape of all shapes as they must live together like one being.*
>
> **—Black Elk**

As they must live together, like one being, I think to myself.

Black Elk foresaw the end of tribalism. Ironically, by definition, a reservation perpetuates tribalism.

If you have driven the Needles Highway through the Black Elk Wilderness Area, you already know why the Lakota would see this as a place of great spiritual power. The mountains and rock outcroppings appear to have been thrust upward by some supernatural force at an exceptional moment in time, exploding through the trees before towering toward the sky above. It is a magical place, unlike any other I have seen.

Black Elk and I have never met in the traditional sense, but on this day I plan to do something for him.

Hiking up the Harney Peak Trail, I am carrying the small piece of weathered wood in my green backpack that until yesterday served as siding on Black Elk's cabin in the grove below Bette's Kitchen. Today, I am climbing the mountain in honor of Black Elk, with the intention of performing a ceremony. The idea to do this did not come to me suddenly; rather, it evolved slowly yesterday afternoon during the hours of tree-sitting and buffalo-watching.

There is not a cloud in the sky and the wind is still as I approach the summit. I have been hiking now for a few hours, but I do not stop. As I make the final, steep ascent, I am wet with sweat all the way through to my backpack.

A large stone fire tower sits at the summit, but I continue past it because I don't like its presence here.

Perhaps a hundred yards beyond the summit, on the downward slope, there is a Lakota prayer-flag tree. If you go there, you can find it. It is a small fir tree less than ten feet in height that has fought its way out of the rocks and survived the summit's exposure. The tree is covered with red, blue, white, and yellow prayer flags. Some are wrapped and contain tobacco (or perhaps red willow bark); others simply blow in the wind. Each was carried here by someone who is Lakota or loves the Lakota people.

The small Lakota prayer-flag tree below the fire tower on Harney Peak. In my hands, I am holding the weathered piece of siding from Black Elk's cabin.

There is solidarity in the symbols affixed to this small tree. The Lakota story is neither forgotten nor over; that's what this tree is saying to me, and with this, I begin to cry.

My eagle pendant dangles from my neck as I reach into my pack and take out the small piece of siding. I hold the wood in both hands, feeling the power that this object represents. I begin by facing west, then north, then east, then south. At every turn, I give thanks to the Great Grandfather that each direction represents. I then give thanks to the Spirit of the Sky, the oldest Grandfather of them all. Next, I honor and acknowledge the Sixth Power, Mother Earth, from which all living things come and return. It is through the grace and wisdom of Mother Earth that we are all related. Holding the small piece of weathered wood, I finally acknowledge the Seventh Power, the power of the individual spirit that lives at the center of the Sacred Hoop. With that, I turn my attention to Black Elk and offer the following prayer out loud to him:

> *Thank you for sharing this small piece of your home with me. I have carried it here so that it may be free like the wind and the eternal message of your sacred book. You lived the story of your people. You then shared that story so it would not be forgotten. This was wise and good. It is an honor for me to do this small deed in your name.*

I grab the piece of wood at the narrow end and slowly rip it apart.

Once broken open, the inside of the weathered siding was bright and fresh with new life.

The wood crackles under the pressure before splitting. That which was once a single piece is now two. The outside of the wood is still gray and worn, but the inside, having been newly broken open, is bright and clean with new life. A deep red color shines from the interior of the wood, as if it had been shielded from all the tragedy and heartbreak that the exterior bore witness to. I find the freshness of each piece's inside to be symbolic of re-birth—new beginnings. Like the legendary phoenix rising from the ashes, the old has become new.

The break is not uniform. One piece is larger than the other. I momentarily consider keeping the larger piece and offering the smaller one, but then I think "humility," and quickly change my mind. I slide the smaller piece in my back pocket, hold the larger piece out toward the prayer tree, and continue talking to Black Elk.

> *This wood from your home is now fresh again with new life. This represents a new beginning for your people. One side is old in memory of the past. One side is new in honor of the future. In your name and in honor of the Lakota people, I set this wood free here at the destination of your great vision, the highest point in the Lakota world. May the Lakota people resume their walk down the good red road that was revealed to you by the Six Grandfathers.*

With that, I reach high into the tree, lodging both ends tightly into a wedge between branches. I can feel the sharp sting of the needles and smell the freshness of their evergreen scent. Once I am satisfied that the piece of wood is secure, I back away from the tree and sit down on the rocks. How long this piece stays here is now in the hands of the Six Grandfathers.

If you climb Harney Peak someday, you can find the prayer-flag tree and check for me.

After looking at the tree for some time, I move out onto a ledge and look toward Pine Ridge. In the clouds above, I see a badger chasing a turtle across the sky toward the reservation. To the west, a white stallion is on his way to meet them there.

Since my very first visit to Pine Ridge, I have never again seen the clouds as just clouds.

I am hot and tired as I arrive back at the trailhead parking lot beside Sylvan Lake. I have been gone nearly six hours. I walk to the small beach where lots of kids are swimming and families are picnicking. I take off my shirt, shoes, socks, belt, and eagle pendant and go swimming in my khaki shorts. I revel in this. When was the last time I went swimming in my clothes? I can't recall. I was probably a child.

I have no towel, so I sit and let the sun dry me off on its own schedule. When was the last time I did that? That, too, I can't recall.

The upper parking lot by the Sylvan Lake store is filled with iron ponies. It is bike week in the Black Hills and the motorcycles are everywhere.

I sleep pretty well that night. At least I would say I sleep better than I have all week. Shortly after daybreak the next morning, I am back in the park for one last hike. I have to wait to park in the small gravel lot next to the trailhead, however, because a buffalo is scratching himself against the signpost. Eventually, he wanders off. Buffalo only ever move when *they* are ready. Then again, that may be true for all of us.

I walk along the Cold Brook Canyon Trail, descending toward the western boundary of the park. The trail winds downhill and then out onto an open plain. About halfway across the field, a lone young buffalo stands right in my path. We are not fifty yards apart. He is not interested in me. Instead, he is busy squashing small pine trees with his forehead. He does this from seedling to seedling as he moves down the trail, as if it were his job to prevent the forest from expanding.

Back at cabin number eleven after my hike, I dry my shoes and shirt in the late-morning sun as I pack. The cleaning ladies are watching me; checkout time has come and gone, they remind me. I don't think they will understand if I tell them I am on Indian time, so instead, I just smile and say, "I'll be gone in fifteen minutes. Sorry I am late."

I throw all my gear in the backseat of my SUV. It is someone else's turn at cabin number eleven. I crack open a tall sixteen-ounce can of Coors Light, toast the Seven Powers from the driver's seat, take seven deep circular breaths, and then slowly steer down the gravel drive. Both front windows are open. I am wearing my khaki shorts and a gray Red Sox T-shirt. My feet are bare, as my shoes are still wet. A faded blue wristband that reads "Oglala National Rodeo" is on my left wrist. I don't want to take that wristband off. My eagle pendant necklace hangs outside my shirt. It is 10:45 a.m. I am going home today.

As I drive toward Rapid City, I am not in a hurry. I watch the buffalo for a few minutes before settling in and driving along. As I drive, I think of the cashiers I chatted with at the Sylvan Lake store yesterday. They both were college girls from the Republic of Slovenia. They were here for a summer experience in America and for a job. They each wore a pin that said "Hard Worker." They both were very friendly. Almost no one at Pine Ridge has a job, and yet, Custer State Park needs to import European students to staff their restaurants, stores, hotels, and campgrounds for the summer season. I am not exactly sure why this is so, but the irony of it all sits heavy with me as I drive.

As I descend toward Rapid City (population 67,447), I pass by the amusement park attractions located in the foothills between Rapid and the mountains above. These small family attractions make me cry, as I think of my own family vacations with our two daughters when they were little. I think of Story Land and Santa's Village in the White

Mountains of New Hampshire, not far from our home in Western Maine. Every summer when Abby and Sydney were young, Alison and I would take them there. I remember taking a half-dozen of Abby's friends hiking for an overnight adventure at one of the high huts of the Appalachian Trail to celebrate her birthday. They were all so small you could barely see their legs from underneath their backpacks. A few years later, I remember running back from Story Land in the rain to the Storybook Inn in Glen, New Hampshire, with Sydney, when she was still in elementary school. Back in our room, we wrestled on the bed before reading stories and taking a nap. Many years later (the same year I finished this book), Sydney and I sat on the front porch of that same motel drinking beer and scratching lottery tickets in derelict fashion, just days before she would return to college. These are great memories for me, and they make me think once again of the true nature of time. Increasingly, I sense that memories live—that past events are still alive. That which has been lost can still be found. This makes me think both of my own voice and the people of Pine Ridge.

I soon leave behind the mountains and the theme parks and descend into Rapid City. As I drive through Rapid, "our" world doesn't look more advanced, more civilized, or more attractive to me than the one I have spent the last six days in.

Scenes like this one suddenly stand out to me as I drive through Rapid City. Which world is real and which world is invented after all?

Reentry is an event every time. The bustle of traffic, lights, restaurants, and storefronts seems different to me. Most of us have come to see this developed, industrialized, and commercialized world as the "real" world, but I am not so sure anymore. At this moment, I see the city as the invented world, the one that is not real. The real world is the one I just left behind.

It is mid-afternoon. The airport is very quiet, almost abandoned. I pull the same SUV that made me feel guilty a week ago into parking spot twenty-four. I get out and unload my belongings, piling them up on the pavement in the hot sun. It is extremely quiet and I don't want to move. I look toward the mountains from whence I just came. I think of the fresh piece of Black Elk's cabin that now rests in a fir tree, one hundred yards off the summit of Harney Peak.

I feel very reflective at this moment.

To the south, I can see the Badlands once again and I know that Pine Ridge lies just beyond them. Suddenly, I am back in that "place" where I see and hear everything around me (even though that place currently is an empty airport parking lot). I feel like I am floating, as I drift toward the side entrance of the airport. In the clouds above, a goose floats south toward Pine Ridge and a Lakota war lance travels west toward Harney Peak.

Sam and Michael check me in at the rental car counter.

"There is only an hour left to go," they tell me, referring to their work-day. They can't wait to get out of there.

As I make a few final journal entries, I realize I am standing right where Pinky met me for the first time, ten months ago. I have traveled in a complete circle.

Siouxper Boy *stands just to the left of the main entrance at the Rapid City airport.*

To the left of the main entrance at the Rapid City airport is a fascinating bronze statue titled *Siouxper Boy*. The statue is of a young Indian boy standing on top of a globe that is the Earth. His hair is long and braided in traditional fashion, but he wears a cowboy hat, cowboy boots, and blue jeans. Low in his right hand, he holds his best Sioux clothing. High in his left hand he holds an airplane, a symbol of the modern world. His small suitcase is packed with his belongings. He stands at the intersection of two worlds. He is looking up toward the airplane and thus toward the white man's world. He is also facing south, thus looking toward Pine Ridge. I stand and look at him for a very long time from every direction. His image makes me think of the Seventh Power. Simultaneously, he is the past and the future of the Sioux Nation; despite all that has occurred, his path is still his to make. This boy is traveling between two worlds . . . searching . . . seeking . . . looking for his true voice in a complex world, just like me—just like all of us, perhaps. After all, we are all related.

It is raining as I board the plane bound for Minneapolis, but we take off to clear blue skies. I am not in a hurry to leave, but I am excited to see my family and to continue my work at Hancock Lumber. I am starting to get used to traveling in a circle.

News came to us there in the Moon of the Falling Leaves [November] that the Black Hills had been sold to the Wasichus ... I learned when I was older that our people did not want to do this ... only crazy or very foolish men would sell their Mother Earth. Sometimes I think it might have been better if we had stayed together and made them kill us all.

—Black Elk

9
Life Eats Life

The old abandoned buildings of the northern plains slowly make their circle back into the earth.

The end of the story will be to arrive where you started and to know the place for the first time.

—T. S. Eliot

October in Maine is a great time of year. The vacationers have all gone home, the high school football fields are lit on Friday nights, and the agricultural fairs are in full swing as the fall foliage reaches its peak. Each leaf in Maine makes its own colorful transition from summer to fall, much in the same way each blade of grass does in the Land of Crazy Horse.

This fall has been eventful for me in many ways. Our oldest daughter, Abby, turned twenty-one, and my mom celebrated an important birthday, as well. Meanwhile, our youngest daughter, Sydney, began her first year in college. This is the one and only year we will have two daughters in college, both playing basketball in the same conference, no less! One college experience begins, while the other one ends; one circle starts as another finishes.

Work has also been exciting. Earlier in the month, we held our quarterly general manager huddle. I sat in the second row, impressed by the work that was being done; each general manager updated the group on the results of their key metrics and the progress that had been made. Accountability, responsibility, and pride are common themes as each manager takes his or her turn. I participated in the meeting, but I did not lead it; the discussion was highly collaborative. I spent much more time taking notes than talking.

Our sales manager, Matt Duprey, introduces the people from U.S. Lumber to the staff at our mill in Bethel, Maine. U.S. Lumber is one of the leading building material distributors in America (and one of our largest and best customers). On this trip, they have actually brought a few of their own customers to Maine. As a result, our customer's customers will be directly connected to the people who make their products. Connecting tribes and simply listening are powerful acts.

There is lots of listening going on at Hancock Lumber right now. Twice this month we had a top sawmill customer come to Maine to speak directly to our manufacturing employees and share insights about how our products are used in their markets. All year, our retail store teams have been working on priorities identified through in-depth customer surveys. Finally, the managers and team leaders at every mill and store are busy reviewing this year's results from our annual employee engagement survey. In fact, one manager recently sent me the following e-mail:

> *I had the pleasure to sit in on the focus group meeting today and I have a great list of ideas that came from the employees at that huddle. You learn a lot when you don't speak.*

I have come to call these customer and employee feedback systems "the answers to the test." I have learned that if you ask sincerely, listen closely, and don't judge people's responses, they will tell you the truth; the truth is what any organization needs to know.

Later in the month, we looked at our year-to-date results with the board of directors. Even though the fourth quarter had just begun, we could see it was likely to be a record-setting year for sales growth and financial performance. Although the economy had definitely improved, overall housing starts were still well below historical averages. Something deeper within the company was driving our growth and progress. It was really satisfying to see the business thrive, but it was even more rewarding to see the responsibility being shared so broadly, across the entire company. Everywhere I went people were leading, making decisions, and getting results. It was fun to see and be a part of!

The Red Sox even went to and won the World Series, and Alison, Abby, Sydney, and I attended Game 1 at Fenway Park.

The morning after the Red Sox won that important opening game, I had another Botox injection at Dr. Song's office. It was my fifth shot of the year and none of them had worked well. We kept increasing the dosage and shortening the interval between shots, but that wasn't making a positive difference. The path for my voice healing seemed to lie in a different, as yet undiscovered direction. Even this wasn't so bad, however; I was getting pretty good at listening, asking questions, and strengthening the voices of those around me.

Except for my voice, it was an exciting month that culminated with another highly anticipated trip to Pine Ridge—my fourth, to be exact.

In Lakota spirituality, the number four is sacred. The power of this number is represented through the medicine wheel with its four cardinal directions, four sacred colors, four changing seasons, and four stages of life. Things begin where they end and end where they start.

As I sit aboard United Airlines flight #1670 traveling from Boston to Denver, I consider the circle that has been my experience at Pine Ridge. This is my fourth trip to the reservation over the course of a single year. In two days, it will be Halloween. Exactly one year ago today, I stood for the first time at the red sign at Wounded Knee, the exact spot where I bought the eagle pendant that currently hangs from my neck (at an off-season discount, no less).

My experience on the trail of Crazy Horse fell into the number four before I knew the number four was sacred. That is the way it is with Pine Ridge and me: Things just happen. They unfold.

––––––––

I step off the plane in Denver wearing a black running jacket over a Red Sox pullover. I am wearing blue jeans and low-cut, gray hiking boots. A camouflage hunting backpack hangs off my right shoulder. I know right where I am going when I exit the plane. I have walked this road before.

I am lost in thought as I wait at the oversize-luggage counter for my hunting rifle. Eventually, I realize I have been waiting for a long time and ask the woman on duty if I am in the right spot. She confirms I am and takes my claim ticket. After punching buttons on the keyboard extensively, she learns that my rifle did not make the flight.

"Will it be on the next flight?" I ask.

"It should be, but I can't confirm that," she tells me.

"I am hunting buffalo in Wyoming tomorrow morning," I explain.

This statement doesn't change anything. My rifle is still in Boston.

We fill out forms, and I am left to hope and wonder. The plan is that the rifle arrives on the next flight and from there a courier service will drive it to the hunting lodge where I am staying. If all goes well, it should arrive in the middle of the night. I thank her, leave the terminal, and board the Enterprise rental bus. A short while later, I am driving a silver extended-cab Dodge Ram north on I-25.

At 4:30 p.m., without a rifle, I cross into Wyoming. As I drive past Cheyenne Central High School (home of the Indians), the sun breaks through for the first time. A cold south wind is blowing. It is 34 degrees. "Three Little Birds" by Bob Marley is playing on the radio.

Don't worry . . . 'bout a thing . . .
'cause every little thing . . . gonna be all right.

"America has the best politicians money can buy," reads the sign on the front lawn of a ranch near the highway. Government distrust runs deep north of Denver.

By 5:30 p.m., the rugged peaks of the Medicine Bow National Forest come into view across the highway to my left; by 6:00 p.m., the clouds have returned. They are low and dark; so dark, in fact, that they signal the end of daylight prematurely. The highway gains altitude as I travel north; scattered timber dots the landscape. Elkhorn Creek is dusty and dry as I pass over it. At 6:15 p.m., I cross the North Platte River. I am back in Lakota country. Soon, I turn off on exit 126 and head east on Route 20. From here, it is another twelve miles to Shawnee, and then another twelve miles on Reese Road to the Rockin' Seven Ranch.

Shawnee is a dot on the map. A small one-room schoolhouse beside the boarded-up church appears to be the only building still actively used. The entire town is easy to miss, especially at night. In fact, I drive right by it the first time before turning around by the railroad tracks and retracing my steps. I find the long, dirt opening between the fence lines and head down Reese Road. It is now dark and I drive for some time before bearing left at the faint outline of a gravel pit. The dirt road narrows considerably to the point where I wonder if I am even on one, but I keep going.

After a few miles, I arrive at the hunting lodge, which is completely dark inside. Several pickup trucks are in the driveway, and I soon learn that the power is out. A fire burns inside the marvelous log cabin, casting shadows into the expansive main room that is filled with trophy animal mounts.

Robert, the ranch manager, arrives a few minutes after I do with an elk hunter returning from a full day in the mountains. The lodge is beautiful and everyone is very friendly. Rutha, the cook, introduces herself and shows me to my room. It is the end of the hunting season and there are only two other hunters in camp. One is elk hunting, one is antelope hunting, and one (that's me) is going buffalo hunting. We all have dinner together at a big wooden table to the flickering lights of many candles.

The conversation is friendly and thoughtful as the fire burns. I still haven't completely oriented myself. The light is low and quickly disperses in the large room.

"We didn't know the government had shut down," someone says, referring to the recent federal budget impasse.

Why would they care here? It is a long way from Shawnee, Wyoming, to Washington, D.C.

At the same time, just a few hours' drive east, the people of Pine Ridge are highly focused on Washington D.C. When the government shuts down, they definitely know it.

"I am going to be a butterfly for Halloween," Robert's daughter chimes in.

The school she goes to has eighteen students, grades K through six.

––––––––

At 4:00 a.m., my cell phone rings; I am amazed I have a signal! The driver from the transportation company is calling. He has my rifle and is nearby, but can't find the ranch. I find this completely understandable. I am just happy he is trying. I give him some directions, though I barely know where I am myself. I tell him to look for the gravel pit and I will meet him there. I throw my boots on, get in the truck, and drive five minutes back up the narrow dirt road. We find each other and I get my rifle. If you saw this scene with no context, you might well have concluded that the transaction was illegal. We looked like a couple of smugglers in that sandpit, lit only by headlights.

I am so happy to have my rifle! Robert had brought a rifle to loan me, but I would much rather use my own. We all trust what we know.

When daylight appears, I come to more fully understand that the Rockin' Seven Ranch is a big place. It covers approximately 150,000 acres within Converse County. The population density is extremely low here. The ranch borders Niobrara County to the east, which holds the distinction of being the least-populated county (in the least-populated state) in the nation.

All the other hunters have eaten breakfast and left the lodge. I am alone waiting for my guide to arrive. Pretty much all I know is that his name is Kevin. It will be easy for both of us to remember names today.

It turns out Kevin is a local rancher, a descendant of an early home-steading family in these parts. He is not a regular guide at the ranch; he is doing Robert a favor and filling in for the day.

When he comes through the door, I can quickly tell we are going to like each other. We are about the same age and our conversation flows eas-ily despite the limitations of my own voice. It is a few minutes past 7:00 a.m. when we climb into his truck. It has been raining and snowing the last few days and his truck is covered with mud. I mean, covered!

"Wow," I say. "How do you deal with all that mud?"

"It's pretty easy," Kevin replies.

We sit in silence as I wonder if he is going to elaborate.

"Mud is better than dust," he eventually says.

That's so smart, I think to myself. *Of course it is. Mud means water and water means life.*

We drive for at least a half-hour before we come to the vast buffalo plains. All the roads along the way are dirt. The rain has stopped and the clouds are active in the sky. It is one of those mornings on the Great Plains where the earth and the sky are one.

"Which way to go?" Kevin pauses and asks himself out loud.

Kevin chooses left over right. In short order, we crest a small rise and there below us, well over a mile in the distance, are the buffalo. Laramie Peak and the Medicine Bow National Forest are the backdrop to the west. The scene is surreal and I am alive with anticipation.

My first view of the herd over a mile away on the open plains of the Rockin' Seven Ranch. My heart began pounding as I looked at the black mass through my binoculars. I couldn't believe I was actually buffalo-hunting on former tribal lands.

The buffalo herd at the Rockin' Seven Ranch is left alone in a natural state, covering an immense area. The buffalo hunt here is designed to be as wild an experience as is possible in today's fenced American West. When these buffalo see a truck, they run. When they see people, they run. When they smell you, they run.

The buffalo are down along the western edge of their habitat and we drive slowly in that direction. As we get out, we quietly close the truck doors. I release the button under the rifle barrel of my .30-06 and the chamber closes, slamming a bullet into place. Just like that, we are hunting.

The northern plains are such an interesting place. There is not a tree to be seen—not a single tree. We have left the truck and the buffalo are no more than six hundred yards away, but they cannot see us and we cannot see them. To hunt buffalo here you must use the natural rise and fall of the rolling hills as your barrier. We have parked the muddy truck in a shallow depression between rises and are now walking slowly, very slowly, to the crest of the hill in front of us. The buffalo are on the other side. I can feel and hear my heart beating.

Our eyes peer over the top of the knoll and through the grass before our feet get there. We stop in our tracks as buffalo appear before us. The buffalo we can see are calves and mothers, grazing right in front of us, not sixty yards away. We, of course, are in pursuit of a bull. The one hundred and twenty eyes of the herd make approach difficult, so from here we lie down in the grass and we crawl. This is a rhythm that needs to be learned with a rifle; it is slow going. Kevin moves much more easily than I do, until I catch on.

The grass is wet and so are we. We crawl to the top of the ridge and lay still, watching. The herd is unaware of our presence and continues feeding blissfully in the morning haze. I have learned to be patient when hunting in the American West. The waiting and watching is actually a part of the experience that I have come to enjoy. In my early days of elk hunting at the Prairie Ranch in Oregon, I would drive my friend and guide, Mark, half-crazy with my constant impulse to "go."

Now, I look forward to the patience that hunting requires. When you are lying in the wet prairie grass stalking a herd of buffalo, life slows down rhythmically and the senses are wonderfully heightened. It is pure joy and anticipation. It is also carnal and primitive in the best tradition of the human experience. As the great twentieth-century American mythologist, Joseph Campbell, was fond of saying: "Life eats life."

When the Lakota hunted for survival on the northern plains, coming to terms with this hard reality was one of the fundamental dynamics of existence that required both ritual and mythology to reconcile.

> ***You find among hunting people all over the world a very intimate, appreciative relationship to the principal food animal . . . because isn't it a moral prob-***

lem to kill somebody and eat that person? You see, these people didn't think of animals the way we do, as some subspecies. Animals are our equals at least, and sometimes our superiors.

—Joseph Campbell

Our first close view of the herd from the wet grass. I could feel the history of the hu-man—buffalo relationship in my soul, as surely as I could feel the wetness of the grass through my clothes.

As we lay there immersed in silence, stillness, and dew, the buffalo wander off in the wrong direction, picking up speed as they go. We watch them drift away to the east, uphill, and across several ridges. On two occasions something spooks them and they start running.

Eventually, they settle down, but they are now a long way off. I can't believe how much ground they just covered.

We walk back to the truck and drive for a few minutes in their direction, before parking again in a depression beneath another set of rolling hills. On foot once more, we head out across the wet grass and damp dirt.

After a good walk, where we can see the buffalo most of the way, we enter a low point that leaves us out of sight. We halt there for a few minutes, which is welcomed. We are a mile above sea level and I notice our elevation. My breathing is heavy but quiet, and I am able to slow it quickly.

We walk quietly up a ridge, crawling once again as we near the top where the buffalo come back into view. The herd is all bunched together, with one exception. A single, large bull has drifted away from the group. He is standing broadside to us. They do not know we are here. I point my range finder at him through my left eye and click the button at the top. He is 238 yards away.

Kevin and I exchange a few words in the quietest of voices. There is another small rocky knoll to our right that is closer to the buffalo. Getting there, however, requires crawling back down the hilltop we are on and then, more importantly, sneaking across the exposed grassy plain between the two hills. Can we do this without being seen, we wonder? The shot I have in front of me is a good one. It would just be nice to be closer, if possible. I go back and forth on taking this shot. I am lying flat on my stomach. I feel good about my ability to make this shot, but I decide to be patient, and we crawl backwards down the hill.

We circle as far away as possible before crossing the exposed grassland. We are both crouching and tiptoeing. As we near the middle of the open area, our pace increases. I can see that we are going to make it undetected to the other side. We gather our breath before climbing the new hill in front of us.

Once again, we are crawling as we reach the top. There is a small rock outcropping at the highest point of the hill and we use it for cover. The buffalo have hardly moved. Most importantly, the big bull I first targeted is essentially standing right where I last saw him, only now he is much closer.

My range finder says 115 yards. We have reduced the distance by more than half. I rest my rifle on a small ridge of rocks, release the safety, and place him in the center of my scope. I take my time and slow my breathing. I have done this before. The animal is quartered toward me. If my position represented the six on a clock, he is facing the number five. I take one last breath and slowly release the air from my lungs as I squeeze the trigger.

Boom! the rifle exclaims, and the sound echoes across the landscape. The bullet pounds into and through his right front shoulder. I am certain he has been well-struck.

The big animal staggers, but does not go down. What happens next reveals why the buffalo had such a close call with extinction in the second half of the nineteenth century. All of the buffalo in the herd circle the wounded bull. They know something is wrong, but there is no instinct to run. There is only the instinct to protect and the circle is how they do it.

A circle, I think to myself.

It is at this moment I begin to realize that the buffalo I shot is pretty big. Surrounded in a tight circle by the rest of the herd, his shaggy red back is still clearly visible above all the other animals in the group. The circle widens. The buffalo are confused. Several other bulls take turns pushing the wounded bull in an effort to get him moving, but he doesn't go very far.

The circle tightens back up and we lose sight of our target. The herd will not leave him. This goes on for what feels like the longest time.

Eventually we stand up so that the entire herd can see us. We make ourselves known. They still stand in place for a few minutes before a few break off, and then the rest follow. They trot, and then run over the ridge to the west and out of sight. We can hear them thundering away long after we can see them. One big animal is left behind, dead on the ground.

As we walk toward the fallen buffalo, I am excited. I clasp Kevin's shoulder and thank him. He congratulates me.

As we continue walking toward the buffalo, I can't help but think how he presented himself to me. This bull, the largest in the herd, was the lone animal that walked away from the group. Not only did he walk away from the group, he walked right toward us. Not only did he walk right toward us, he stayed there while we climbed not one, but two knolls. It was as if he, the largest of them all, had offered himself to me, almost as if he was expecting me.

The buffalo lies alone on the knoll, not a tree in sight. In the far distance to the west, the Medicine Bow Mountains can be seen in the background.

We admire this magnificent buffalo and our surroundings for quite some time before Kevin leaves to walk back to the truck. At that point, I am alone on the plains with the buffalo I have shot. I have been told that some of the traditional Lakota hunters like to "lay hands" on the buffalo as it takes its last breath—to show respect and companionship for the animal as it crosses over into the spirit world. I had hoped to do the same, but that was not possible. This buffalo took his last breath surrounded by his true brothers and sisters.

That was even better, I think to myself.

Alone with the buffalo, I say a prayer. I face west, north, east, then south before looking up to the sky and finally giving thanks to Mother Earth. In this manner, I thank the Six Great Powers for the opportunity to experience this buffalo hunt on the northern plains and to share this traditional food source with the people of Pine Ridge. I ask the Six Grandfathers to welcome this buffalo fully into the spirit world that surrounds us all. I celebrate the life of this animal who offered himself to me to feed the tribe, and who served as both a modern and ancient symbol of the rugged American West.

When the prayer concludes, I survey the amazing scene I am a part of, rolling hills and grass in all directions for as far as the eye can see.

Next, I sit down and lean back against the mighty animal. I am above his front legs and resting against his neck and front shoulder, just below his massive head and thick dusty horns. There, I sit for a long time, facing west toward the First Grandfather. The sun warms the left side of my face as a light wind cools the other. The clouds have dissipated. There is no noise, other than the wind in the grass.

I could sit like this all day, I think to myself.

As I sit there in solitude, I look out across the vast plains and envision a band of Lakota hunters charging down from the hillside at full gallop into the fast-moving herd. Dust fills the air and for a few moments there is chaos. It is every hunter and buffalo for himself. As the dust clears, buffalo lay scattered across the grasslands. Soon the women, children, and old men arrive, singing and rejoicing, ready to participate in the skinning and meat cutting. Tonight, there will be a great feast in the Lakota camp.

Back at the lodge later that evening, Robert, the ranch manager, arrives. He has returned from another long day of elk hunting in the pine-topped mountain to the east.

"I saw your buffalo at the barn," he says to me with enthusiasm. "He might be the biggest buffalo I've ever seen. I can pretty much guarantee you he is going to qualify for the North American record book."

I would be lying if I didn't say that news excited me.

—————

The following morning, I awaken before sunrise in my rustic bedroom on the second floor of the lodge. There is no hunting for me today, but I still get out of bed before breakfast and get bundled up for a long walk down the frozen dirt road. The sun rises just as I veer left off the trail and crest the ridge. Every step makes a crunching noise. Four white-tailed deer bound away from me as dawn's first light reveals the buttes and grasslands of eastern Wyoming.

I linger for quite some time watching the sun reclaim the sky. On the way back, I wander through the large bales of hay that have been assembled. They are golden brown in the crisp morning light. Each bale forms the shape of a circle that contains a spiral running all the way from the outer edge to the center.

I detour off the road once again, and walk through the junkyard of old trucks and farm equipment that line the gentle hill above the lodge. This assemblage of rusted steel, broken windows, and bent chrome represents something I love about the American West: No one throws equipment away here. Where would they take it to anyway?

The junkyard is actually one of my favorite places at the Rockin' Seven Ranch. Nothing is thrown away in the American West. History just gets parked in a field.

Before going back inside, I see Jake, one of the other guides, in the driveway.

"What are you doing today, Kevin?" he asks me.

"I am going to visit Fort Fetterman," I reply.

"I think the fort is closed," he tells me.

"I hope so," I say.

The trail of Crazy Horse is a place for the self-guided.

"Everyone's got one good book in them," Rutha tells me over breakfast, a short while later back inside the lodge.

It seems odd to be in a hunting lodge at 9:00 a.m.

After breakfast, I throw a few belongings into my backpack, say good-bye to Rutha, and head out for Fort Fetterman. Being alone on the northern plains always fascinates me, and today is no exception. It takes well over an hour for me to travel the twelve miles of dirt road back to Highway 20. Along the way, I keep stopping to examine wooden posts, follow antelope, listen to the wind, and watch tumbleweeds race to the fence line. I am excited because I can already tell this is going to be what I call a "Winnie-the-Pooh kind of day," which simply means I am going to spend the day wandering around doing nothing, finding adventures where others might well see none.

I drink a liter of water before I reach the highway. Here, water is purification for me, and I drink it constantly without being thirsty.

The little intersection in downtown Shawnee is deserted when I arrive. I notice the sign on the abandoned storefront is missing a letter.

Even the 'n' [in 'Shawnee'] *has left town,* I think to myself.

As I turn left onto the main road, a bright orange Burlington Northern Santa Fe Railway engine pulls a seemingly endless line of open-top railcars back west for more coal. As the train rumbles through the empty town, I hear the sounds of steel on steel and the engine horn blasts. I am the only person to see it pass. Moving at thirty-five miles per hour, this train is quite a bit slower and much less agile than the antelope I just raced in my truck back on Reese Road.

Further down the road, an abandoned rail line from an earlier age catches my attention. I pull over and walk across the dirt and windswept grass to stand on the steel gauge and walk the wooden planks that support it. Having studied the topic, I know what backbreaking work it was to create the mound, lay the timber, and spike the rail. The scene invites the imagination. Who built this stretch of track? What were their stories? Where was this track coming from and going to? What wagon-train town did it displace? The images of the West are a history book frozen in time. Nature is slowly reclaiming this rail line back into the earth. Everything, given enough time, forms a circle.

One of my favorite symbols in the mysterious American West is an abandoned rail line, slowly being reclaimed by Mother Earth. This one runs on the north side of the highway through Shawnee, Wyoming.

———

The remains of Fort Fetterman sit high above the North Platte River at a point just north of Douglas, Wyoming. From here, the river moves west and upstream until it reaches the city of Casper; from there, it then dives south into the Alcova, Pathfinder, and Seminoe Reservoirs.

Upon arrival, I am pleased to confirm that the fort is actually closed. In fact, it is closed for two reasons. First, it is after Labor Day. Second, funds for staffing and upkeep have recently been cut from the state budget. I guess you could say then that this fort is "double closed." Or, you could say, I suppose, that it is closed and abandoned. Perhaps the second closing doesn't matter. Closed is closed. In any case, I am the only one here.

The fort was established in July of 1867. Just two weeks later, the garrison was given its name, "Fort Fetterman," in honor of Captain William J. Fetterman. Fetterman was killed in the famous wood-cutting massacre only days before Christmas the previous year, near Fort Phil Kearny at the base of the Bighorn Mountains.

It is cold and windy as I exit the truck. I am wearing a brown wool sweater, an orange hunting hat, and my insulated hunting gloves. My Lakota medicine wheel necklace blows in the wind as I walk. I wander around the abandoned fort for quite some time. At the far end of the complex, at the closest point to the North Platte, I sit against the stone remains of the old water cistern. I am facing south as I look out across the winding river below. The wind is to my back and from the north. Direction is important to the Lakota, and I pay attention to it whenever I am on the trail of Crazy Horse.

I am sitting alone at Fort Fetterman on a cold fall day against the remains of the old water cistern, looking east and south over the North Platte River.

My fingers are numb with cold as I scribble notes in my journal, but my heart is warm and I feel content. The energy of the fort is flowing through me. Once again, I am lingering.

All the work that went into establishing, constructing, and provisioning this fort would have a short life. The fort itself existed for less than two decades, before being abandoned permanently by the US Army. For a short time, a frontier town took its place. By 1886, however, the entire site was a ghost town. America and its Western frontier were changing rapidly. What was a necessity in 1867 was irrelevant just two decades later.

The wind and my footsteps are the only sound as I walk toward what remains of the fort's parade grounds. Tumbleweeds bounce along in front of me. I am now facing north toward the Bighorn Mountains, toward the Little Bighorn River and toward the Montana gold fields that created this trail. It was all about getting to the gold.

On the backside of the parade grounds sits a marker that identifies the crossing site of the Bozeman Trail; the trail descends away from the fort, toward the river through a narrow pass between two small hills. A few paces down the path, a rock catches my attention. I stop and pick it up. The rock is red on one side, white on the other and shaped like a heart. It amazes me. I put it in my pocket.

The rock I picked up on the Bozeman Trail as it passed through Fort Fetterman was half red, half white, and shaped like a heart. Despite the difference in appearance of each side, it was all one rock just the same.

The parade grounds sit at the center of all the Western forts I have visited. As I follow its sharp edges with my eyes, I can't help but think how closely related a square is to a circle.

The abandoned flagpole and supporting metal guide wires whistle in the wind. My feet crunch with each step on the narrow gravel path. Without thinking, I begin walking more aggressively and deliberately so that I can hear that sound, the sound of marching. I move in rhythm, accentuating each step down the faint outline of the old parade grounds.

I am in no hurry to leave. I have nowhere to go. Nevertheless, I eventually begin walking back toward the truck.

As I walk, I find myself thinking about two early memories of my dad and me. The first is playing Whiffle ball in the living room before I was old enough to go to school. I remember that white ball crashing all over the room as I took full swings. The second is of me riding on his shoulders, at about the same age, as he recites his favorite Robert Frost poem, "Stopping by Woods on a Snowy Evening." I had memorized that poem before I could read, and have often wondered why he loved it so. We all rode on someone else's shoulders once, just as surely as someone else has, or will, ride on ours.

> *The woods are lovely, dark, and deep, But I have promises to keep, And miles to go before I sleep, And miles to go before I sleep.*

My personal journey to Pine Ridge reminds me of another Robert Frost poem, "The Road Not Taken," which I once wrote an essay about in high school:

> *I shall be telling this with a sigh, Somewhere ages and ages hence: Two roads diverged in a wood, and I, I took the one less traveled by, And that has made all the difference.*

I feel content as I arrive at the truck and pull off my hat. My hair is a complete mess, but I don't care; perhaps, I even prefer it. Right now, I just feel grateful for the road less traveled. Directly across the street from the fort is a ranch with a sign over the entrance reading "White Land & Livestock."

As I turn the truck on, the hit song "Wake Me Up" by Aloe Blacc and Avicii comes on the radio. I turn the dial up and leave the window open. I don't really know where I am going next today, and I love that feeling.

Feeling my way through the darkness
Guided by a beating heart
I can't tell where the journey will end
But I know where to start

I tried carrying the weight of the world
But I only have two hands
Hope I get the chance to travel the world
But I don't have any plans
So wake me up when it's all over
When I'm wiser and I'm older
All this time I was finding myself
And I didn't know I was lost.

The abandoned flagpole on the abandoned parade grounds at old Fort Fetterman.

The Wyoming State Fair grounds are empty today. Fairgrounds are interesting in this way. They spend most of their time alone.

The fairgrounds are located in the town of Douglas, along the banks of the North Platte River; it is the river that has brought me here. I park the truck on the backside of the Stallion Field show center and walk down to the river's edge. The North Platte is stingy about access points, and this is one of the best I have come across.

There is something about putting my hands in the North Platte that attracts me. I sink my hands into the cold water. I splash the water on my face. It is a ritual for me. Whenever I drive across or beside this river, I look for an access point. I always want to come into contact with its running waters.

The North Platte winds itself along, never staying in a straight line. Today, for instance, I have already crossed the river six times. Each time I cross, I like to know if I am entering or leaving Lakota country, and I can't always tell. You can cross it heading south and be entering. You can cross it heading north and be leaving. The river is one of those places where you never really know if you are coming or going.

The clock on the truck console reads 2:08 p.m. as I leave the fairgrounds. For the first time since breakfast, I am hungry. My initial attempt to stop for lunch in downtown Douglas is at the historic Hotel LaBonte. I slide into one of those heavy metal chairs that line the counters at many of the oldest diners in America. I swivel to a stop, eager to order a warm and hearty lunch.

"It is pie and cold sandwiches only after 2:00 p.m., hon," the waitress says as she wipes down the far end of the counter.

I have given myself away as not being local. Everyone in this town knows that you can only get pie and cold sandwiches at the Hotel LaBonte after 2:00 PM.

Less than five minutes and two blocks later, I open the front door at the "Depot" restaurant on 100 West Walnut Street. A short time after that, I have a large Angus burger in my hands.

Since it is Halloween (sorry I have missed it once again, Alison!), most of the staff is dressed up in costume. Children are out on the street trick-or-treating. Halloween appears to be a late-afternoon activity in these parts. My mind travels back to my own days as a reluctant trick-or-treater. When I was a child, it always seemed counterproductive that we would wait until it was dark to go trick-or-treating. It would invariably be cold at night, so we would have to put on coats over our costumes, which seemed to defeat the purpose of the whole exercise.

After finishing my burger, I write a postcard to both our daughters. Each postcard has a picture of a buffalo on it. I love postcards. I think they are underrated. A single image on the front and a few handwritten remarks on the back send a message that says "I am thinking of you," in an elegantly simple way. In our instantaneous world of e-mail and text messages, a postcard is a breath of fresh air. It is hard not to smile when you send or receive one.

On the edge of town, I fill the truck up with gas. The wind is blowing so hard I can barely open the truck door to get out. Sure enough, it is one of those pumps you must hold by hand the entire time. So, I stand there pumping gas in the gusting wind, being attacked by tumbleweeds. The truck is rocking.

At the local Safeway store I buy more pens for my journal and more water for my soul. By this time, I have planned my next move. I am headed south to the town of Guernsey to see what remains of the Oregon Trail. As I drive out of town, I think one more time of old Fort Fetterman. I hope someday you can visit, too; and, when you do, I hope it is closed.

May your Western forts always be closed and abandoned!

I get back on I-25 and drive south, crossing the North Platte yet again near the town of Orin. It is approximately forty miles from Douglas to exit 92, where I pick up Route 26 east toward Guernsey. It is late in the afternoon as I drive through town. The trick-or-treat activity is also in full swing here.

It is exactly 5:00 p.m. when I park the truck at Register Cliff. I am, not surprisingly, the only person here. The late-day light from the western falling sun glows upon the sandstone cliffs. The Oregon Trail bends around the corner at the far end of these cliffs and heads west. The North Platte River runs in the opposite direction, just a few hundred yards away. If one follows either the river or the trail back east, you will arrive at Fort Laramie.

As I look at the names etched into the cliff, I ponder the nature of the past.

Is something that happened in the past really gone; or, is it still present, hovering with us? I ask myself.

There is an energy that exists here that tells me the past is, in fact, alive —that it doesn't just end. As I ponder this subject, more questions follow.

If the past is alive, then what about the future? Is there an energy there as well that, like the buffalo I shot yesterday, waits patiently, knowing we are coming?

The alternative, that only the present exists, seems quite small. What actually is the present, anyway? If you believe only the present exists, then how do you define that precise moment? For example, you have finished reading this sentence before you have fully processed the depth of the idea itself. Trying to pinpoint the precise moment of the present is surprisingly difficult. Much of our time is, in fact, spent contemplating the past or preparing for the future. Time, I think, is more dynamic than it first appears.

Seemingly countless names were carved into the cliffs by the early travelers of the Oregon Trail. Those who used the trail are long since gone, but their carvings have a life force that can still be heard if you are alone there at sunset on Halloween and listening closely.

National Geographic, my favorite magazine, published a thought-provoking article recently about black holes that provides insight into the dynamic nature of time:

> *You probably know the phrase "time is relative." What this means is that time doesn't move at the same speed for everybody. Time, as Einstein discovered, is affected by gravity. If you place extremely accurate clocks on every floor of a skyscraper, they will all tick at different rates.*
>
> *Black holes, with their incredible gravitational pull, are basically time machines. Get on a rocket, travel to Sgr A [a known black hole]. Ease extremely close to the event horizon [the edge], but don't cross it. For every minute you spend there, a thousand years will pass on Earth. It's hard to believe, but that's what happens. Gravity trumps time.*
>
> *And if you do cross the event horizon, then what? A person watching from the outside will not see you fall in. You will appear frozen at the hole's edge. Frozen for an infinite amount of time.*

Where we are impacts the pace of time. This is a relevant thought for Pine Ridge—for all of us, really.

> *Time doesn't move at the same speed for everybody.*
> *Gravity trumps time.*

At this moment, the energy field of the pioneers who dug their names into this white chalky cliff is alive for me. If I am the present and they are the past, then just where are we meeting?

Eventually, I leave Register Cliff, stopping once again at the North Platte to sink my hands beneath her ever-changing surface. The cool water drips from my face; the edges of my hair are wet. The air is cold and the sun is setting as I get back into the truck.

Moments later, I have parked at the Wyoming state historic site of the Oregon Trail Ruts. As you would now expect, there are no other cars here; I am alone.

Though the Oregon Trail is the most famous, there were actually three major trails that passed through here. The first was the California Trail, which traveled west from Independence, Missouri, all the way to the Sacramento Valley. Actively used from 1841 until 1868, this was the original trail of gold through these parts. In the year 1849 alone, over 30,000 Forty-Niners traveled west along this trail. The California Trail and the Oregon Trail shared essentially the same route to a junction known as South Pass in west central Wyoming. From there, the Oregon Trail dipped south before turning north on its way to Portland, Oregon, and Olympia, Washington. One of the first historical markers I come to on the frozen boardwalk describes the trail as follows:

> **This 2,000-mile trail is a tribute to the human spirit. People from all walks of life sold most of their possessions, piled what was left into a wagon, and journeyed west. In search of a better life, they headed to Oregon, first for fur, then as missionaries, and finally for farmland.**

The third trail was the Mormon Pioneer Trail. This 1,400-mile trail began on the Illinois border and joined up with the other two trails at Fort Kearny in Nebraska, on its way to Salt Lake City. Over its twenty-two-year life, more than 70,000 Mormons crossed from east to west in search of new beginnings and religious freedom. Soon after the opening of the transcontinental railroad in 1869, the use of all three trails dissipated. Pioneers and settlers no longer had to walk across the country to reach the other side.

Throughout human history, the pursuit of freedom for one group has often come at the expense of freedom for another, I think to myself.

From the beginning, the US Army was called upon to protect these overland trails. You can feel the condescension toward the Native people who lived here, in the recorded words of the military officers of the time:

> **Your Great Father . . . has sent me with a handful of braves to visit you . . . I am opening a road for your white brethren, and your Great Father directs that his red children shall not attempt to close it up. There are many whites now coming on this road, moving to the other side of the mountains . . . you must not disturb them . . . should you do so, your Great Father would be angry with you . . . although he is the enemy of all bad Indians, he is the friend of those who are good.**

—Colonel Stephen W. Kearny, June 1845

The trail ruts just before sunset near Guernsey.

I regret the necessity which obliged me to kill any of your people, but under similar circumstances I will always act precisely in the same manner. I am now willing to forget what has passed, and receive you as friends; provided, you promise to behave yourselves hereafter; otherwise, I shall regard you as enemies, and am ready and able to meet you as such. You might escape at the time, and even for years, yet sooner or later, the day of retribution would certainly come.

—1st Lieutenant Richard B. Garnett, June 1853

The ruts are deep here. In places, the entire height of my body can be enclosed within them. The tracks are embedded so permanently in the earth that they give no indication of ever giving way to nature's forces. It is as if the trail itself has been fossilized. The silence of this place and its history consumes me. The sun is setting behind me as I stand alone in the middle of the ruts, facing east from whence the trail came.

I extend my arms, close my eyes, and gently tilt my head back. Although my eyes are closed and I am facing directly away from the setting sun, a light appears. Following the light, a series of human faces come into view, one at a time. Some of the faces are Indian. Some of the faces are white. Each face stays in my view for a few seconds before being replaced by another. The sensation I have is that these are real people from this trail's past. Perhaps we are meeting (again), for the first time.

Eventually, I open my eyes and just stand in place. As I do, a large group of songbirds scatters from an evergreen tree to my left. They float upward together right over me, singing as they move, and heading south. Several minutes later, I find myself walking west along the wagon tracks toward the day's last light, when another group of songbirds, equal in size to the first, emerges from the same tree, singing the same song. This group, too, flies directly over me, even though I have moved some distance, before also turning south. I find it all quite magical.

The sun drops from view and darkness creeps in. It is Halloween on the Oregon Trail. There is no one here but me and the spirits of this trail's storied past.

The sun's last light on the ridge above the Oregon Trail Ruts on Halloween.

It is exactly 6:00 p.m. when I get back into the truck. I have a text message from Alison containing a picture of Abby and Sydney in Halloween costumes when they were young. I remember that moment with clarity (which proves I didn't miss *every* Halloween). Although it is a scene from years ago, the moment still feels alive, as if it just occurred. The picture evokes images that are simultaneously fresh and distant. For a moment in my mind—just like at Pine Ridge—the past and the present are one.

As I pull out of the parking lot and back onto the pavement, the song "Tom Sawyer" by Rush comes on the radio.

> *Today's Tom Sawyer*
> *He gets high on you*
> *And the space he invades*
> *He gets by on you.*
>
> *No his mind is not for rent*
> *To any god or government*
> *Always hopeful, yet discontent*
> *He knows changes aren't permanent*
> *But change is.*

This song is forever etched in my memory, from yet another specific scene in my life. There are four of us in the car. It is after midnight. I am twenty years old. We are driving in a big, old, two-door sedan that is definitely American-made. The windows are cracked open as the Grand Tetons shimmer under the light of a full moon. We have just driven seventy-eight miles from the hotel complex at Grant Village where we work to Jackson Hole, to see a movie. It is the only movie any of us saw that summer. "Tom Sawyer" by Rush is blasting on the radio. We are the only car in sight. That memory, for me, is the epitome of being young and free. Every time I hear that song, I remember that specific scene. It is in the past, yet it lives in the present for me.

The wind is gusting so dramatically that it takes two hands on the wheel to control the truck, as I drive north on I-25 back toward the Rockin' Seven Ranch. A hot dinner and cozy log-framed bed await me.

––––––––––

The next morning, I wake before the sun arrives and once again walk the cold dirt road and frozen grasslands south of the lodge. My feet crunch into the earth with every step. Today is the day I am going to share my buffalo meat with the tribe at Pine Ridge. First, however, I am going to watch another amazing sunrise over the scattered mesas to the south.

Back at the lodge over breakfast, Dan, the oldest and grittiest guide of the bunch, tells stories of hunting near Yellowstone.

"In forty years of guiding, I have never lost a horse or a hunter," he proclaims.

After breakfast, Rutha gives me a six-pack of her homemade molasses cookies. I give her a hug in return. I wonder if we will ever see each other again.

I drive over sixty miles per hour in stretches along the twelve miles of dirt roads, leading me back to the pavement. My first stop is the butcher shop and meat cooler on the ranch, where I meet up with Robert and we measure my buffalo. Inside the barn, I learn that a buffalo is scored by measuring the height and circumference of each horn. The measurements confirm what Robert had told me the night before. This buffalo is big: 17 inches (height) + 18 3/8 inches (height) + 13 1/8 inches (width) + 13 2/8 inches (width) = 61 6/8 inches. A score of 54 inches qualifies for the Safari Club International record book.

I thank Robert and head out, ignoring the pit bull rummaging through the scrap pile of bones and fur to my right.

"He's fine. Just don't try to pet him," they told me yesterday, when my guide Kevin and I first arrived at the barn with my buffalo.

That was the kind of reassurance that made me feel worse.

―――――

A short while later, I pull into Lusk, Wyoming (population 1,567), which once served as an important stagecoach stop on the route from Cheyenne to the Black Hills' gold fields. I pull up to the curb of the butcher shop on the corner of South Main Street, where the owner helps me load four heavy boxes of frozen buffalo meat into the back of my pickup. It is cold and windy outside, so there is no chance of the meat thawing before it gets delivered. Shortly before 10:00 a.m., the truck is loaded and I am off to Pine Ridge. Sometime later, near the banks of the White River, the road passes through the middle of Fort Robinson. Even though I have been here before, I stop and stand alone at the small stone monument, marking the place where Crazy Horse was killed. As I do, I reflect, yet again, on the words of Black Elk:

> *Crazy Horse was a great man and they could not kill him in battle and he would not make himself over into a Wasichu . . . they wanted him to go to Washington to see the Great Father, but he would not go. He told them he did not need to go looking for his Great Father. He said, "My father is within me, and there is no Great Father between me and the Great Spirit."*

Crazy Horse is an important figure for both the Oglala and the larger Sioux community. No single man represents the Lakota resistance to white conquest more completely. Crazy Horse was smart and fearless in battle, but his legacy is much more than that. He embodied Lakota values, including bravery, humility, and generosity. As a teenage boy, he had a great vision that told him the bullets and arrows of his enemies could not harm him if he followed certain rituals in preparation for battle. His vision also foretold that he must lead the charge when the time for fighting came and then refuse to take scalps or bounty from those he killed.

In nineteenth-century Lakota culture, returning warriors would tell stories of their acts of bravery around a celebratory campfire. Crazy Horse would never partake in this tradition. He was a man of few possessions and even fewer words. Interestingly enough, Crazy Horse was described as being of only modest size and extremely fair-skinned. Quiet and aloof in times of peace, he possessed unrivaled bravery and skill in battle. Equally important to his place in Lakota folklore is the fact that he had no interest in the white man's ways. He avoided treaty talks and stayed clear of the forts; instead, he chose to live freely as the Lakota had always done, following the buffalo. He only surrendered once it became clear that the woman, children, and elderly in his care could not continue to outrun the relentless pursuit of the US Army. Only then did he turn himself in. He refused to go to Washington, D.C., and was never photographed. To this day, even the location of his burial place remains either a great mystery or a well-guarded tribal secret.

Crazy Horse was, in fact, an independent soul who did not conform to all the traditions and expectations of his tribe. He individuated, and this made him strong.

I say a prayer for Crazy Horse before returning to my truck in silence and driving off. I have buffalo meat to deliver to his people.

The sun rises once again over the buttes and grasslands of eastern Wyoming.

It was early in the Moon When the Ponies Shed [May] that Crazy Horse came in with the rest of our people and the ponies that were only skin and bones. There were soldiers and Lakota policemen in lines all around him when he surrendered there at the Soldiers' Town [Fort Robinson]. I saw him take off his war bonnet. I was not near enough to hear what he said. He did not talk loud and he said only a few words, and then he sat down.

—Black Elk

10

Full Circle

The old Reddy Mart store on the eastern edge of the town of Pine Ridge. Bamm Brewer's garage is located behind the store and to the right.

> **We are all related. I try to teach them [my students] that no matter what color a person is, we don't see the color. We see the spirit of the person and then we know we are related.**

> —Verola Spider

If you didn't know where to look for Bamm Brewer's garage, you would drive right by it. It is a small, metal building located behind the abandoned Reddy Mart store on the outskirts of Pine Ridge, heading east toward the rising sun. When I enter the garage, Bamm is in the process of tearing down the haunted house he had set up for Halloween. A small stage and a drum set rest near the back wall, where the youth bands played last night.

Bamm himself is an avid hunter and guide. He owned his own buffalo herd, but they escaped a few years back during a large grass fire.

"They ran all the way to Nebraska," he tells me with a chuckle, as if to shrug it off.

Nothing seems to get Bamm too worked up, and it strikes me that this, too, is the Lakota way.

"I'll get more someday," he adds.

Bamm is a close friend of Rosie's and is also the organizer of the annual Crazy Horse Ride, which takes place each spring just after school ends for the summer. This past year, nearly three hundred riders—mostly teenagers—participated in the multiday journey from Fort Robinson to Pine Ridge. The group camps along the way, reconnecting with nature and traditional Lakota culture. At night, I am told, the spirits often visit camp, reuniting the participants with their ancestors. A holy man conducts a ceremony before the ride begins each year, in order to receive the messages for the coming event; a rider-less horse, known as the "spirit horse," accompanies the annual expedition in honor of Crazy Horse.

"The kids get to do something that makes them feel like warriors again," Bamm explains. "Many of them don't want to leave when the event ends, because it is so powerful for them. Each year, it is America's largest gathering of Lakota on horses."

A few moments pass as Bamm goes about his work. I never hurry people at Pine Ridge. I just move at their pace.

"Jealousy. That's what killed Crazy Horse," Bamm continues. "The US Army told Crazy Horse they would give him whatever he wanted if he would just come in. This made the other Oglala leaders jealous, so they spilled lies about him. Those lies led to his arrest and murder."

"Politics still seem difficult here," I say to Bamm.

"Some people wonder why I am organizing the ride," Bamm tells me.

"They say it should be done by someone who is full-blooded. The tribal council sponsors some of the cost of the event as well. People want to know why I am getting this money."

Bamm and I at his shop in Pine Ridge, where I made the buffalo meat donation.

Bamm also works for the nonprofit organization, One Spirit (www. nativeprogress.org), whose programs include a food bank. It is this role that has brought me to Bamm. Together, we load the single, small freezer against the north wall full of buffalo meat. We talk the entire time we are filling the freezer. Bamm and I have just met, but he treats me like an old friend.

Time runs out on us both, as Bamm has someone to pick up and I have more buffalo meat to deliver. Bamm leaves before I do and, to my surprise, I find myself alone in his shop. Before leaving, however, he invites me to come to his home the next day, and I agree to do so.

I have entrusted approximately two-thirds of the buffalo meat to Bamm and One Spirit. The rest I am going to share with my friends, as well as with some strangers I meet along the way.

I drive back into town to the OST Partnership for Housing office. When I arrive, Pinky is conducting a home-ownership counseling session with a local family. We exchange greetings and I share some buffalo meat with Lester, Rosemarie, and the staff, before making plans to meet Pinky later in the day at her store in Manderson.

On the street outside their office, the Head Start program buses are picking up students to take them home. I grab four packages of frozen buffalo meat and give them to the two drivers who are still waiting for children. My next stop is just around the corner at the Pine Ridge Retreat Center. Pastor Karen Rupp is there. After a brief visit, I go back to the truck and get a small box of frozen buffalo meat that we pack into the freezer section of the white refrigerator in the basement. As I leave the Retreat Center, a man and a woman are picking through the boxes of donated clothing that sit on the picnic tables outside. I grab two more packages of buffalo meat and give one to each of them. The man is from the Lower Brule Reservation.

"I remember seeing you there," he tells me.

I don't argue, choosing instead to accept his word, even though I have never been to that reservation (as far as I am aware).

A short while later, I arrive at Singing Horse and carry my belongings inside. Rosie and I visit for a few minutes, and then I load up Rosie's freezer with buffalo meat before departing for Nick Tilsen's office and then Pinky's Store.

It is early evening and the store is crowded. In fact, it is as crowded as I have ever seen it. The store is always busy the first of each month; that is the time when the largest amount of government checks arrive. For a few days, people will have some money to spend. Most of the money will be spent off the reservation, but some will be spent at small stores and businesses like Pinky's.

The federal program known as SNAP (Supplemental Nutrition Assistance Program) is a good example of how resources flow to Pine Ridge residents. More than forty-eight million Americans use this program, formerly referred to as "food stamps." While the overall size of the program is massive, the contribution to any single family is modest, at less than $1.50 per meal. Families often use up their monthly allowance in two or three weeks.

If you look at a map showing the percentage of the population receiving SNAP benefits by county, Pine Ridge stands out. Of all the counties in America, Shannon County at Pine Ridge (later renamed Oglala Lakota County) has the largest-percentage participation rate. Todd County, also at Pine Ridge, is second.

People here need lots of help from their government.

I visit with people for a while in the store. By now, I know everyone who works here. In addition, Pinky knows everyone who comes in, and she always introduces me. You can meet a lot of people at the white plastic table in the back of Pinky's Store.

Pinky and I soon depart together for the town of Porcupine. We are going to a small fund-raiser at Our Lady of Lourdes church for Katari Weston, a champion barrel racer. She is leaving tomorrow, with her family and her horse, for the Indian National Rodeo Finals in Las Vegas.

Over dinner in the church gathering room, I listen to Pinky as she tells me about the early years of running her store.

"I could only afford a little inventory. It took up just a small corner of the store. The rest of the building was empty. I remember thinking to myself, 'How will I ever afford to fill up this place?' " Pinky tells me.

We both reflect in silence for a few moments.

I drift into the kitchen and talk with the family. I love sports and young athletes, so I am anxious to hear more about the national rodeo finals. I learn about Katari's best race time and her ranking for the finals before making a small contribution to help her trip.

Back at the white plastic table where we have been eating, I spend some time with Lester.

"Have you ever been to a sweat lodge?" Lester asks me quietly.

"No, I haven't," I reply.

"Would you be interested in participating in one and taking an Indian name?" Lester asks in follow-up.

"I would love to. I would be honored," I reply.

Lester is leaning toward me as he speaks and the conversation is soft. This is a significant gesture on his part, and I am moved by the offer.

"When are you coming back?" Lester asks. "I will talk to Medicine Man and set something up."

I end the evening watching the children's Halloween party at the Wounded Knee school. The sound of drums and chanting fills the gymnasium as kids in costumes dance around center court, showing much more enjoyment for this holiday than I did at their age.

Tribal headquarters in downtown Pine Ridge, diagonally across the street from Subway.

Around lunchtime the following day, I am sitting in my truck waiting for Bamm. I am parked just west of Big Bat's convenience store, near my favorite restaurant at Pine Ridge, Subway. The small Subway store is a stand-alone building. It is the last business in town as you drive west toward Slim Butte. Diagonally across the street is the Tribal Council headquarters. The large brick building is, in many ways, the place of power at Pine Ridge. If you need something, this is often where you go to get it. If you have a problem, this is often where you come to have it solved. Government is large at Pine Ridge, and this is the house of government.

Back across the street, inside the Subway sandwich shop, a teenage girl takes my order. She is happy and efficient. She could be a star employee at any Subway in America. Her eyes are bright and ready for the world.

A few steps away, a second girl is baking bread. She is smiling and chatting as she works. In many communities, the jobs being performed here might not be noticed, but this is Pine Ridge, and jobs are scarce. The young people who work here have schedules and responsibilities. They get paid and earn their own money. There is much more going on here than sandwich making.

A generation ago, these jobs did not exist at Pine Ridge. These are new jobs for a new generation, and while no one will get rich working here, they will get paid. The money they receive will not have been given to them. Most importantly, the young people who work here are gaining self-confidence and independence. Today is a great example, as these two teenage girls are running the store, with no additional supervision, and everything is going great. They are in charge.

I look across the street again at the tribal headquarters. The contrast between the two buildings is dramatic and symbolic.

Subway sits on BIA 32 in downtown Pine Ridge. It is not the scale of these jobs that makes them powerful, but rather the notions of responsibility and independence that go with them.

The Subway building is small and bright. Its characteristics are of lightness and agility. The tribal headquarters, by comparison, is a monolith. It is heavy, brick-laden, and immovable. In a game of tag, the Subway building would be the master, winning every time.

Today at Pine Ridge, all eyes are on the tribal council headquarters. In a government-run society, those who divide and disperse the resources are powerful. That's just the way it is. Could it be, however, that what is happening at Subway is, for the long term, more powerful than what is happening at tribal headquarters?

I recently watched a PBS documentary titled *Young Lakota*, which followed the lives of two young adults at Pine Ridge, one girl and one boy. At the time, the boy was working for an important tribal officer and elected official. There is a powerful scene in this documentary in which the boy is sitting alone in the backseat of a car, imagining he is tribal president someday. As he envisions this future for himself, he describes the benefits that political power will bring his way:

> *When I become president, I am going to have a podium and a presidential seal . . . some letterhead done . . . and I'll be getting that $100,000 per year salary . . . a nice travel-line item [allowance] . . . my own tribal vehicle to drive home . . . living the political life.*

Politics is the most prominent way to power and prestige at Pine Ridge, which many young people growing up here must notice. We all come from a tribe, and it influences our goals, aspirations, and expectations.

Bamm pulls into the parking spot next to mine and motions for me to follow. Beside him on the passenger side, a small boy pops up to see what is going on. My guess is, it is Bamm's grandson. Soon, both trucks are heading west out of town. We travel past the skateboard park, pow-wow grounds, and ball fields. As we leave town, we gain elevation and the landscape quickly becomes rural again. The area west of town is a high piece of ground with rolling hills, scattered pine trees, barbed-wire fences, and lots of prairie grass.

We pull onto his long, dirt driveway where Bamm parks his truck. His grandson tumbles out and Bamm is close behind. Bamm's eyes are lit up, giving away his enthusiasm for what he is about to show me.

To the left of his dusty driveway, the corner of his property is empty. There is nothing there but dirt and grass. No one driving by would see anything other than that, but Bamm does.

"This is where it's going to go," he says to me with a grand smile.

"What's that?" I reply.

"The meat processing facility; I am going to build it right here."

His eyes become even brighter as he describes his vision for this plot of land we are standing on.

"Currently, there is no meat-processing facility on the Rez," Bamm continues. "For wild game or farm animals to be processed, they must be driven south, off the reservation, and into Nebraska. All the jobs and money for this activity leave Pine Ridge. That's the way most everything works here. The money leaves and the jobs are elsewhere. We need to change that. This is a way to do that, to keep it local."

Bamm is quiet for a moment.

"It is so easy to sit and wait here. It is hard to get things done, but I don't like to sit and wait," he continues.

Bamm's enthusiasm is contagious, and in short order I, too, believe there will be a meat-processing facility here someday. Bamm is a driver of activity. He reminds me of Nick in this regard.

As we head back to the trucks, Bamm points out the tall wooden poles with colored cloth flags that stretch out across the grasslands. The farthest pole is over a mile away, standing alone on top of the far ridge.

"That's the horse-racing track," he tells me. "Horse racing is very popular here, and I have been involved in it for many years. Every summer boys and young men gather here from all over the Rez to test their skills and race. The racers are required to wear war paint and traditional regalia. It is a cool scene! It is another chance for them to feel the warrior within them. The grand finale is always the world-famous Indian relay. This race is a team effort with a rider, two horse holders, and three different horses. The first horse will run a mile around the flags. The second horse will run the same mile. Then, the third horse will run a longer three-mile course that goes over the hills to the north. My great-grandparents both traveled with Buffalo Bill and his Wild West Show. It's in our blood, these horse races. You should come check it out next summer."

"That does sound really cool. I would love to see it someday," I reply.

We get back in our trucks and drive the rest of the way to Bamm's house, where we park in front of the wooden corral. He invites me inside and I consider this a gesture of friendship, but I do not say anything about it. Inside his humble home, family pictures and hunting trophies cover the walls. The home is small like all houses at Pine Ridge, and Bamm is generous in spirit like all the people I have met at Pine Ridge. He tells me stories of his family and his own past before moving on to describe traditional Lakota hunting rituals.

"Before the buffalo hunt, we go to the sweat lodge to purify ourselves," he explains.

I am hanging on every word as he describes the purification ceremony. As he speaks, he fixes a snack for his grandson.

"The buffalo knows you are coming for him," he continues.

My back is momentarily turned to Bamm as I survey a picture of his ancestors on the wall. These words jolt me away from the picture. I turn back to him.

"Wait, what? Can you say that again, Bamm?" I ask.

"Say what again?" Bamm replies without looking up.

"What you said about the buffalo, that he knows you are coming," I reply. "Can you tell me more about what that means?"

"That is what it means. The buffalo, he knows you are coming. He sees a vision that you are coming for him before you have found him. He is waiting for you. That's the way it works," Bamm says calmly. "The buffalo know."

My mind has flashed back to my own buffalo hunt, just three days prior. I had crawled to the top of the ridge and laid flat on my stomach, watching the buffalo over the edge of a small rock pile. The entire herd was closely bunched, except for this one bull that had walked away from the rest of the animals. He was the only buffalo that drifted off from the group. He had walked right in my direction and just come to a stop. He was facing me, but not staring at me. He wasn't really grazing. He wasn't really moving. He just stood there, peacefully. At the time, I remember thinking that this was all good fortune, just luck. I didn't even know if he was big by buffalo standards. He just looked big to me. Come to find out, he was the giant of the herd and even a bit of a local legend. Earlier this year, another hunter at the Rockin' Seven Ranch had seen that very buffalo while antelope-hunting. He was so inspired that he booked a buffalo hunt for next spring, to come back and try to shoot him. As I'd prepared to shoot, I'd had the sensation that this specific buffalo was surrendering himself to me. That notion had quickly faded in the excitement of the moment until just now, until I heard what Bamm just said.

I tell Bamm the story of how this buffalo presented himself to me and Bamm smiles. He is not surprised. He thinks it is cool and powerful, but he is not surprised.

Telling spiritual stories to my Lakota friends is always this way. Stories of spiritual experiences that would be hard to believe back home are accepted readily for their power and meaning here.

"Cool" is a common reply I get here.

You would need to hear the tone of the word "cool" to fully appreciate the response. "Cool" is said like "Wow," followed by a pause where no further words are necessary—just time and silence to let the sharing of the experience soak in and be appreciated. Visions and spiritual experiences are expected, not judged here. Small shifts in thinking can make a big difference.

When Bamm takes people buffalo-hunting, he dresses himself in a buffalo hide with horns. He positions himself to be the last living thing the buffalo sees before he crosses over. Bamm wants the buffalo to feel comforted and protected as he takes his last breath.

"When the buffalo dies, a doorway opens," Bamm explains. "At that moment, you can speak to your ancestors. When the buffalo looks back from that doorway, I want him to see a pure heart and the face of his people. That is why I dress this way and stand in his view."

I tell Bamm that many people in my culture find it hard to believe such things. Many people in my culture would find it hard to have faith in Lakota spirituality.

"How can one have faith that the other side is there?" Bamm asks rhetorically.

"I like to think of it this way," he continues, answering his own question. "Suppose you are in a crowded gymnasium. People are all around you. Then, the power goes out and the gym is completely dark. For a moment, everyone is quiet as they try to sort out what has just happened. At that moment, would you be able to tell that people are still there?"

I reflect upon this question. The room is silent.

"Well, of course. Yes, I would be able to tell." I reply.

"How would you know?" he counters.

"Well, I could just feel it," I say without thinking, as I stand on the worn linoleum in his small kitchen.

"Exactly," he replies.

Black Elk often spoke of "the small square houses they made us live in." The Lakota have a life perspective and sense of humor that helps them persevere.

As I drive back toward town, I slow down and look closely at the housing conditions. Everywhere at Pine Ridge the challenge of finding quality housing is self-evident. I understand why the people who live here feel forgotten, marginalized.

As I pull into town, I come up behind an old white pickup truck. It is dented and dusty. Two dogs and two kids are in the back. On the right side of the rusted and tilted rear fender is a bumper sticker that reads:

**KEEP GRANDMA OFF THE STREETS . . .
SEND HER TO BINGO.**

Humor is definitely a defining characteristic of the Pine Ridge culture, and I like that about this place. The people here take their challenges seriously, as you would expect, but they also live. Laughing and joking about the challenges they face seems to be a way of periodically softening the hard edges of their circumstance. It is a small, but powerful act of defiance against the conditions that attempt to push them down. In the jokes and laughter at Pine Ridge, there is strength.

––––––––––

It is 3:50 p.m. and 59 degrees when I get out of my truck at the cemetery on the hill above Wounded Knee Creek. I never come to Pine Ridge without coming to Wounded Knee. Like many other sites on the trail of Crazy Horse, visiting the Wounded Knee cemetery always feels right to me. On this fall day, the sky is clear and the afternoon sun lays a reflection of the white wooden cross over the earth.

After lingering with the shadows and the crosses, I head back to the Singing Horse Trading Post where I have an appointment to meet Verola Spider.

The burial grounds at Pine Ridge are a story unto themselves.

Verola Spider and I have met in passing before, as she works for Rosie, but this is our first real chance to get to know each other.

I am sitting in the basement of the trading post with her as she finishes the last hour of her shift. Much of the year, Verola works seven days a week. Monday through Friday she teaches Lakota language and culture at the public school in the Porcupine District. She also teaches at the Oglala Lakota College in Kyle. On the weekend, she works in the store at the Singing Horse Trading Post.

"Sometimes my stomach hurts when I think about what will happen when all the fluent Lakota speakers die," she tells me.

It is nearly 5:00 p.m. Rosie is off doing something and Verola and I are alone. Verola is doing beadwork at the plastic table that sits to the right as you enter the store. She is facing south. I am sitting at the end of the table with my back to the door, facing west.

"My mother didn't believe in the hospital, so she gave birth to all of us at home," Verola continues. "I was born on June second or third, 1951. No one is really sure which day it was. We had no clocks back then and it was close to midnight. My mother gave birth to me in a tent outside the house. I did not cry when I was born, so my mother was worried. They said I had a mask on. That's the expression we use when a baby is still and quiet for a few moments after birth. Since no one was sure what day it was exactly when I was born, I always got to celebrate my birthday for two days, so that was pretty fun."

"My dad's name was Emerson Spider. He was a Native minister and one of the best bead makers around."

Verola pauses for a long time, creating a silence that I do not break. Eventually, when she is ready, she continues.

"I never remember being hungry as a child. We had big gardens out behind our house. We picked wild berries. We hunted. We had no electricity, so the food was stored in a root cellar. More people are hungry today than a generation ago. People today are too dependent upon store-bought food. Nobody takes the time to cook anymore. It's really changed; times have changed."

More silence.

"I think in Lakota. I dream in Lakota," she tells me. "Lakota is my first language. Today, our young people learn English as their first language. We only spoke Lakota at my house when I was a child."

Verola remembers being "caught" using her own language at the church-run school she attended when she was about seven years old. The nuns threw rice on the wooden floor and, for the better part of that day, Verola was made to kneel on the rice with her bare knees exposed below her school dress.

"I am the fifth generation of my family to be a storyteller. I am the first female storyteller in my family," she calmly tells me, without looking up from her beadwork. "Ours is an oral tradition. There are no books of my family's stories and I am sad about this. When I am gone, these stories will be gone too."

I am the sixth generation of my family to work in the lumber business, I think to myself, without interrupting Verola's flow.

We all come from a tribe.

"I am just a poor working woman," Verola continues. "I have no recording equipment. I have no camera. I don't even have an English Bible. The Bible I have is written in Lakota and was published in 1926. People say they will help me, but nothing ever happens."

It is quiet in the trading post. The end of the day is nearing and there are no customers. The radio, which plays traditional Lakota music behind us on the counter, has one of those silver antennas you rarely see anymore.

Verola speaks for a while and then pauses. Between her thoughts, I just sit there patiently. Neither of us is in a hurry. When Verola does speak, it is in a soft tone. There are no hand gestures or animated eyes. Each word comes in the same calm manner as the one before it. Her words do not need to be sold or accentuated; they are powerful in their own right. I can tell she is happy to be telling the story of her life, happy that someone is listening.

"A long time ago, the people could talk to the birds, the trees, and the four-legged animals. We could understand the animals. I believe we still have this power within us, but we have forgotten how to use it. Today, people are too busy to remember. People are too busy with TV, computers, cell phones," her voice trails off and goes quiet.

"We don't need to wait until Sunday to pray. We don't need to go to a specific building and be handed a book in order to connect with God.

We can all talk to God with our hearts. I still have the old beliefs, like putting food out for the spirits. I am modern in some ways in the white man's world, but I still hang on to the old ways," Verola continues.

"I don't even remember your name," she pauses and looks over at me.

"That's okay. My name is Kevin," I reply.

There is another pause.

"Verola, do you think people's need for food, shelter, and clothing has gotten worse during your lifetime?" I ask her.

She ponders this question and works on her beads. Verola is in no hurry to answer.

"Yeah, I think so. They [the people] are not preparing themselves anymore. Everyone is now just living day to day. People are not thinking ahead. When I was growing up, we would prepare all summer for winter. People have stopped preparing."

"What about alcohol?" I ask. "Is that worse today than in the past?" Again, she ponders this question.

"I used to think all drunks were funny," Verola continues. "I had an old grandpa who used to get drunk once in a while, and when he did, he was so funny. Today, when people become drunk, they get violent. In the old days, they used to just get funny."

"What do you think has caused this change?" I ask.

Again, there is a pause. Verola lets every answer come to her.

"I think it is because we have lost our connection to the earth, to the land. In the early 1970s, everyone was moved into the village clusters you see today. Before that, we all lived on small farms. In the old days, we were spread out and with the earth; but, *they* made us move together into the village clusters and something was lost when we did this. Everything is very political now. I stay away from politics though, 'cause all I see is people fighting—fighting over this, or fighting over that—so

I just stay away.

"There is too much fighting today. We have an anti-bullying campaign at school. I couldn't find a word in Lakota for bullying. The closest I could come was *wa oste ste kuwa*, which means 'to treat someone disre-spectfully.' I think bullying is new. It was not part of our old ways."

Again, there is a pause.

Verola is wearing blue jeans and a gray Oglala Lakota College sweat-shirt over a white T-shirt. She wears glasses and her black hair falls about six inches below her shoulders. She is humble, thoughtful, and wise. She sees and knows many things. Verola is a thinker and a phi-losopher, with more to share than has been asked of her. I feel like I am exactly where I should be at this moment, asking her these questions.

"It was always the men who told the stories, and yet, where are the women?" she asks rhetorically.

"They know lots, too, but no one ever pays attention," she says, as her voice softens and trails off.

We sit together in peace, as the music softly plays in the background.

"Would you tell me a story?" I ask. "We can record it as well, so that it will be saved," I continue, gesturing toward my iPhone.

"Okay, that would be good," Verola replies. "It would make me happy to record some stories so that they will not be lost when I die."

More silence.

"What is your favorite story?" I ask. "Tell me that one."

"Well . . ." After a long pause, Verola continues without looking up from her work, "I can tell you the story of the Lakota lullaby."

"That sounds great," I say.

A moment of silence follows and then she begins.

The Story of the Lakota Lullaby
(as told by Verola Spider)

This story is of a long time ago. There was a young man who had just taken a wife and people were hungry. The chief picks the fastest of the young men and the bravest ones to go look for the buffalo. When they went, they happened to go into another village. We call them toka, the enemy. It's the home of another tribe.

When the young men came home from this trip, the wife came out of her tepee and looked around. She saw that her husband wasn't with the men that came back. She asked where he was and one of the young men told her that her husband had been captured by the enemy. They told her where the village was and that in the middle of that village her husband had been staked to the ground.

"Well, I am going to go there and free my husband," she said. The whole village told her she could not go. "They are mean," they told her. "If you go there, they will hold you captive also." But, she was determined to go free her husband.

It was a must that every Lakota woman carries a knife, because you never know when you are going to butcher a buffalo. She took her knife and set out for the long journey. Again, all the men told her not to go, but she went anyway.

"I am going to go free my husband, then I shall return," she told them.

So she walked and walked for many days until she came to the camp where they had told her the village was. She climbed high up onto a ridge above the camp. The sun was setting and it cast shadows upon the camp. But there in the center, she could see her husband staked to the ground.

What am I going to do now? *she thought to herself. There were lots of tepees around the camp, and many people were there.*

How am I going to do this? How am I going to free my husband? *She pondered this question, as she slowly walked back down the ridge.*

At the bottom of the ridge, there was a stream. She stopped at the stream and bent down and scooped up some mud. Then, she scooped up some more until she had a big ball of mud in her hands. She molded the mud into the form of a baby. She made a mud baby. Then, she took the shawl off her shoulders and she put the little mud baby inside the shawl and wrapped it up. She put the baby in her arms and began walking toward the camp. As she did this she began to sing, "Abo . . . abo . . . abo . . ."

As she sang, she walked all through the camp, past every tepee. Soon, all the people of the camp were yawning. Soon, thereafter, everyone fell asleep. Then she took her knife out and she cut the leather that was holding her husband down to the ground. She cut those off and she freed her husband. Then, they took the best horses that the village had. She not only freed her husband, but she also came home with a whole herd of nice horses and ponies.

So, even today—even for me growing up—that's how my mother put me to sleep. The grandmothers before her, that's how everyone put their babies to sleep, with that song. Even me, when I had my children—or, my daughters today—when they have a baby, that's how they put them to sleep. We call it the Lakota lullaby. I would like to write a storybook on that one someday. This is one of the many stories I grew up with. Thank you—Wopila Tanka."

"I love that story, Verola," I say, after I am sure she has finished.

It is quiet for a few moments and then I ask if she wants to record another story.

"Okay, that sounds good," Verola replies.

More time passes.

"Which story would you like to tell next?" I prompt her.

"I will tell you the White Buffalo Calf Woman story."

I am happy that she has chosen this one, as I know it is perhaps the most sacred of all Lakota tales. It immediately makes me think of my own vision of the white buffalo, that day back at Devils Tower.

"Many people do not tell this story right anymore," Verola continues. "It doesn't end the way they say it does."

I am intrigued as the story begins.

The Story of the White Buffalo Calf Woman
(as told by Verola Spider)

Two young men were hunting when they came to a hill where they were looking down for buffalo; instead of buffalo, they saw a figure. The figure was coming toward them and soon they could see it was a beautiful maiden in a white buckskin dress. As she came closer, the younger one wanted to touch her and he had thoughts of marrying her. The older one was wise, however, and he saw that she was a spirit. When she got closer to them, the younger man reached out to touch the beautiful maiden. As he did this, a cloud came over him and when the cloud lifted, he was just a skeleton. Then, the young maiden told the other man that she would bring a gift to the tribe, and that he should go back to camp and prepare an altar. So he did this.

Later, the maiden arrived at camp, carrying a bundle, and presented it to the tribe. Inside the bundle was a pipe. The maiden took out the pipe and taught the people of the tribe the ways of the pipe and how to use it. When she finished, she went outside and she rolled. The first time she rolled, she turned into a black buffalo. The second time she rolled, she turned into a red buffalo. The third time she rolled, she turned

into a yellow buffalo, and the last time she rolled, she turned into a white buffalo. What she taught the people was that we are all related. Today when they tell the story, they don't tell it that way. They don't say that she rolled four times and turned four colors, but that is what she did.

Verola gets up and walks toward the counter. She continues talking as she walks.

"We are all related. Some of us, the old, the real fluent speakers—you might say the full-bloods—we still believe that we are all related; we try to teach that to our young children. When I am teaching in the classroom, I try to teach them that no matter what color a person is, we don't see the color. We see the spirit of the person and then we know that we are related, that we are all related. No matter where we come from, you always meet a person and it seems like you knew him for a long, long time. You don't look at the color and where they came from, you just know that you are related in some way. That means a lot. There are a lot of us who still believe that way, who still believe the old way. A lot of times you hear people saying, 'No, that's not the way,' but those people probably have a little bit of doubt in themselves. There are still a few of us left who still believe in the old way, who still believe that we are all related."

The rhythm of the music from the radio is pulsating in the background. No voices, just a repetitive drum verse, over and over again. It is the end of a song and it carries on and on, like a skipping record. It seems so appropriate.

I ask Verola if she could tell the White Buffalo Calf Woman story to me in Lakota instead of English. She is happy to do so. It is beautiful to listen to. I don't know the words, but I know the story. The sharp and distinct Lakota pronunciations are mesmerizing to me. I could listen to Verola speak Lakota all evening.

It is 6:00 p.m., however, and Verola tells me it is time for her to go.

"I will send you a copy of an English Bible and I will e-mail you a copy of these recorded stories, so that you will have them," I say.

"Okay, that sounds good," Verola replies.

"When I come back in the spring, let's record some more stories," I suggest. "Perhaps, someday, we can make a children's storybook together."

"Okay, that sounds good, too," Verola replies. The tone of her voice is always the same, soft and smooth. There is a great sense of calm in her presence. When she sings the Lakota lullaby, I bet people do fall asleep; her voice is that soothing.

All things come from and return to the earth. Life, in this way, is a circle that all living creatures share.

I end the day the same way I started it—alone on the ridge above the trading post. The first time I stood here today, the sun was just about to rise. As I stand here now, the sun has just set. The remains of a horse that did not survive the early-season snowstorm lie on the grass to my right. From the earth to the earth travels the circle of life.

Light can still be seen long after the sun is gone. I love those in-between moments when it is no longer day, yet not quite night. The peacefulness of the scene invites more reflection; I think, again, about the nature of circles and the power of expanding them. This, in turn, makes me think of what Verola said:

We are all related.

I try to teach them [my students] that no matter what color a person is, we don't see the color.

We see the spirit of the person and then we know we are related.

Verola is making bigger circles, I think to myself. *This is powerful.* How different the world could be if we all saw what Verola sees—if we all saw it for the single circle it really is.

The first Americans came from Asia, most likely on foot and by boat, during the last Ice Age, some 15,000 years ago. The Lakota, and all other "Native" peoples of the Americas, are descendants of these small, nomadic bands. Traveling even further back in time, most anthropologists believe that the first humans began migrating north out of Africa approximately 200,000 years ago. In the context of this BIG CIRCLE, the Lakota share an ancestry that reaches all the way back to Africa. And, so do the Europeans, who would begin sailing to the Americas from the East at the end of the fifteenth century. In this way, we are literally all related, just like Verola says. When Columbus arrived in 1492, a circle, 200,000 years in the making, was completed. Man had crossed the globe in both directions, meeting again, for the first time, in the Americas. Fighting with some, cooperating with others, it was all the same tribe in the end—just one big circle of human expansion.

Our cultures train us to see small circles, but when it comes to the human tribe, there is actually just one big circle, and we all belong to it. The Lakota have a phrase for this: *Mitakuye Oyasin,* which means, "We are all related."

It all reminds me of the rock I found on the Bozeman Trail. Up close, one side looks red and one side looks white. But, from a distance, it's clear that it is all the same rock.

As my mind comes back to the present, I can see the lights from the tiny town of Manderson flickering in the wind. Somewhere among those lights is Pinky's Store. Behind me, Harney Peak, the highest point in the Black Hills, still glows.

Suddenly, Rosie's horses come sprinting around the ridge to my left. Something has spooked them. They see me and come to an abrupt halt, but remain at full attention. Nighttime has finally returned to Pine Ridge. On this night, there will be buffalo for dinner at the Singing Horse Trading Post. At other homes across Pine Ridge, there will be buffalo for dinner, as well. There has been a successful hunt and the meat has been shared with the people. The sharing of meat is an old story for the Oglala. For me, it's a new story, but it all feels so familiar.

––––––––––

Tonight, I am responsible for cooking the buffalo burgers. Rosie, Catherine, Alina, and I are all in the kitchen. Alina is a young woman from Germany who is spending the year with Rosie at Pine Ridge. She seems to love it here; the horses, the pace of things, and the proximity to nature all seem to suit her.

Over dinner, we tell stories and share ideas. The conversation turns to the question of why it seems so hard for the people who live here to break from historic patterns and improve their economic conditions. The topic prompts Catherine to tell the story of the Indian crabs in a bucket:

> **A white man and an Indian man are collecting crabs by the seashore. They each have a bucket. The Indian fills his bucket quickly and sits down on the rocks to rest. The white man keeps working to fill his bucket, but the crabs crawl out and escape as quickly as he catches them. This goes on for some time. Finally, in frustration, the white man sits down beside the Indian.**
>
> **"I can't seem to fill my bucket. No matter how hard I work, the crabs keep escaping. Why don't yours escape?" he says, turning to the Indian.**
>
> **The Indian replies, "Well, you see, the crabs in my bucket are Indian crabs. When one gets ahead, the rest pull him right back."**

Everyone laughs. Catherine has a big smile. Even though Catherine is an elder, she has the smile of a wide-eyed child.

Catherine continues speaking and in doing so references the phrase "internalized oppression."

"What do you mean by 'internalized oppression,' Catherine?" I ask.

"It's just about being worn down, generation after generation. The cavalry, the missionaries, the government, the boarding schools—you wake up one day and it has all been internalized. When you have been oppressed over generations and generations, it finally takes hold. The oppression takes hold within you. Once it takes hold within you, it is perpetuated from within and we act out the oppression on ourselves. We perpetuate the oppression on ourselves. That is how deeply it has been ingrained."

A silence comes over the table. We are all waiting for Catherine to speak again, and after some time, she does.

"There is a lot of jealousy here—lots of infighting, lots of distrust. Who is more pure-blooded? I think people waste lots of energy on meaningless questions such as this. If we are all related, why does it matter who is truer-blooded?"

There is more silence before Catherine continues.

"There is lots of waiting here, too. There is lots of waiting on all reservations. I used to live on the Mescalero Apache Reservation and there was a big shortage of housing. Everyone would just apply and wait, apply and wait. You were always waiting. Nothing ever happened, you just waited."

More time passes.

"Change comes from within," Catherine continues. "Our progress as a people must come from within."

"I like Pine Ridge though," Catherine says with a smile. "It is one of the least-colonized places in America. That's what I like about living here."

One of the least colonized places in America . . . I repeat Catherine's words in my head.

The conversation bounces around. Dinner is always an event here. We have been at the table for well over an hour and no one is in any hurry to see it end.

"I am always so tired here at night," I say, shaking my head and yawning.

"It's the energy here," Catherine replies. "The energy here is different than what you are used to. It is more powerful, more pure."

Silence follows, before Catherine looks right at me and speaks,

"You were searching for your inner self. That's why you came here. You were looking for something within you, and you have been able to find it here. Your spirit guides have spoken to you, and you have listened."

"I have many spirit guides," Catherine continues. "There are those I know and some I don't know. I give the ones I know names. I talk to them. Some people think I am crazy because I talk to them, but that doesn't bother me. They are with me all the time. They are my friends."

As dinner winds down, the conversation turns light again.

"Do you know the Lakota word for vegetarian?" Catherine asks.

"No, what is the Lakota word for vegetarian?" I reply.

"Lousy hunter," she answers, and starts laughing.

———————

"That's not helping," I say out loud to Rosie's young yellow dog, Buffalo, early the next morning.

He is licking my face as I roll under the best opening I can find beneath the barbed wire, wearing my wool sweater.

I have worn this sweater every day since I got here, I think to myself. I love the simplicity that this notion represents.

The fence line I roll under above the Singing Horse Trading Post.

The sun is just rising over the bluffs behind Rosie's house as the first Sunday in November arrives at Pine Ridge.

I wander across the grasslands, traveling up one hill and down another. Sometimes I follow one of the horse trails, sometimes I make my own. The dogs come and the dogs go. I have taken this walk many times. It is the same and it is different. I always take a similar path, but I never take the same path. The seasons, the sunlight, the wind, and the clouds all combine to make each walk unique unto itself. I am never in a hurry when I am up here in the hills behind the Singing Horse Trading Post. After my walk, I shower and have breakfast with Rosie, Catherine, and Alina. When breakfast is done, I pack my gear into the truck, hug everyone, and say, "Toksa."

"I will see you in the spring," I say to Rosie.

A few minutes later, I pull into Pinky's Store and walk inside, past the sleeping dogs.

Ritualistically, Pinky's Store is my last stop before leaving Pine Ridge.

Danny and Pinky are both there and the store is quiet. A few customers come and go as we visit in the back by the white plastic table and chairs.

Pinky says, "We had buffalo for dinner last night. We said a prayer of thanks to the buffalo for feeding us."

Silence.

"Danny has a gift for you," Pinky continues.

Danny leaves the store for a moment. When he returns, he is carrying a beautiful, hand-carved wooden bow with two arrows.

"Thank you for feeding our people," Danny says, holding out the bow for me to take.

I take the gift in two hands. I don't quite know what to say. Danny is a big strong man of few words. The fact that he has taken such a liking to me is very meaningful. He is an important friend of mine at Pine Ridge.

"Thank you. This gift means a lot to me," I finally say to Danny.

Pinky insists upon taking a picture of Danny and me. I am glad she does. I will always look at this picture and feel warmth in my heart. The bow is from Danny, but in a larger sense he is giving it to me on behalf of the tribe. The gift is unexpected.

I linger in the store for a while before declaring that it is time for me to go. I have one more hug with Danny, the big Comanche Indian from Oklahoma.

I hug Pinky twice, once near the white table at the back of the store and then once again, near the door.

"Love you, Pinky," I say before departing.

Pinky is a special lady. Every relationship and experience I have had at Pine Ridge has been, in a sense, made possible by Pinky—the woman who drove to Rapid City to meet me at baggage claim that first time.

Danny and I with the bow and arrows he gave me in celebration of the buffalo hunt. I will never forget that moment. That bow will forever be among my most meaningful possessions.

There are rarely many vehicles on the roads of Pine Ridge, and today is no exception. I leave the store and drive north on BIA 28, before taking a right on BIA 14 to head over the ridge toward Kyle. Just a couple of miles up the road, I arrive at the turnoff where I walked up onto the bluffs when I was last here in August. I had not planned to do this, but when I see the bluffs I stop, park the truck, and get out. The spirits of Crazy Horse's people are calling me again, so I grab my bow and arrows, climb over the fence, and start walking. I walk at a healthy pace. The bow is in my left hand and I can feel the warrior within me.

The distance from the road to the top of the highest bluff is deceiving. From the road, it looks like the bluff is only minutes away, but it is farther than that. I walk at a brisk pace, occasionally even trotting. I never break pace or slow down, until the bow and I have reached the highest point.

Upon reaching the top, I walk out onto the sandstone cliffs. From here, I can face the four directions. I always feel like I am at the top of Pine Ridge when I come here. There are no human sounds to be heard on this day. The only sounds are those of the wind and the birds.

For me, this moment is highly symbolic; it represents a culmination of events. I am standing alone on this high bluff in the middle of the Pine Ridge Indian Reservation, with a bow and arrows that have been given to me as a gift, in celebration of a successful buffalo hunt.

I am facing out across the rolling hills and grasslands. As I do this, I pray. I don't remember anything specific about this prayer. I just remember that I was praying. After a few moments of prayer, I move myself into a breathing trance. My arms are extended. I am holding the bow. My eyes are closed. I am standing very near the edge of the cliff without fear, as a deep calm comes over me. I am not the first hunter to stand here. I can feel that for sure. I am one in a long line of hunters who have come this way, who have stood on this cliff to survey the land for game, to scout for the enemy, or to just give thanks. I am now (or perhaps once again) part of that tradition, and I can feel the warrior spirit within me.

When I open my eyes, I let out a mighty Lakota war cry. The sound echoes through the valley and bounces back toward me off the walls of the ridgeline I am facing. I let another war cry go, then another. There is no holding back. My voice is booming. I am letting it all go. The warrior within me is out. There is no dysphonia in my voice, no straining to be heard. At this moment, I am calling out for the entire world to hear in my own true voice.

After five or six full-throttle war cries, I stop and listen to my own sounds reverberate and die out. Once again, all is quiet. I stand still, not wanting to move.

In time, I turn and walk a few paces back away from the edge of the cliff, and then I begin running. I start running and I keep running. I can feel what it would have been like to be there, one hundred and fifty years ago, hunting as a Lakota. My steps are quiet. My feet are light. I am careful about each foot placement, as one always is when hunting. *What a gift this moment is*, I think to myself. Something told me to take the bow and go to the bluffs. I hear these things when they call to me now. For me, it has become neither unexpected, nor weird. The spirits have met me halfway and the energy is surging through my body. I feel free and powerful. I can feel the blood pumping through my veins. My senses are on high alert. I keep running, all the way back to the truck.

The bow Danny gave me in celebration of the buffalo hunt rests against a rugged pine tree, on the bluffs near Manderson on the Pine Ridge Indian Reservation, where I let my full voice ring clear and true.

Back at the vehicle, I drink an entire large bottle of water. As I drink, I lean on the hood of my big silver truck, looking back up onto the bluff from whence I came. The sun is on my face and I am listening to the sounds that silence makes.

As I stand there, it occurs to me that I have become less afraid. But, less afraid of what?

I have become less afraid of the bigness of this place, which means I have become less afraid of the magnitude of existence. I have become less afraid of the interconnectedness of all things and of the fact that the spirits surround us always. I have become less afraid of the unknown. I have become more at peace with my own spirit, and I can see it as a part of everything else. I am part of Pine Ridge. Pine Ridge is part of me. I am connected to the people who live here. I am connected to the people who used to live here. All of us are. Everything is connected. Nature, God, man, the past, the present—it's all one thing.

**When one tugs at a single thing in nature,
he finds it attached to the rest of the world.**

—John Muir

Suddenly, for the first time, I am at peace with all of this. It all broke free up there on the bluffs, as I let those war cries thunder out, clutching my bow and arrows that celebrate the sharing of the meat.

I stand by the barbed wire, looking back up at the bluffs for a long time.

"*Pine Ridge is the poorest of places* and *the richest of places*," I think to myself.

Eventually, I say "Toksa" before opening the truck door. Once inside, I set my bow on the passenger side, start the truck, and drive off. I am headed for the Black Hills where I always end my trips to the Land of Crazy Horse.

In more ways than one, I have come full circle.

My voice was clear, strong, and pain-free as I let out war cry after war cry, on the bluffs above Manderson.

If you can practice listening to the wisdom of the commonplace, honoring it for its simplicity, little by little, you will begin to see through the veil.

—Alice O. Howell, *The Dove in the Stone*

11

The Vision Quest

A vision quest is a special, deeply personal ceremony in which an individual goes off by themselves to try to gain a vision from Wakan Tanka, which will tell them how to be a better person in their life, find their own direction, and gain a better understanding that they are one with, and related to, all things.

—June Shaputis

I can see my breath.

It is a few minutes before 7:00 a.m. the following day as I push the button and hear all four doors of the Dodge Ram click and lock. The sun has just risen and frost is on the ground in Wind Cave National Park.

No sooner have I stepped onto the slender trail then I hear the elk. I recognize their sounds immediately. I leave the trail and walk through the tall grass, toward the timber to my left. My binoculars are strapped to my chest over my brown wool sweater. I move carefully into the scattered pines, measuring each step, as if I am hunting.

In short order, I can see them. They are strung out along the grassy ridge above me. It is feeding time and they do not know I am here. Time passes by and I am content, as always, to just listen and watch.

Finally, a single cow stands at attention and stares me down. Her ears extend and tighten; after that, she does not move. The rest of the elk continue to graze from left to right, but soon they notice the lone cow on high alert. This brings them all to attention and soon all eyes are on me. No one is moving. It's a great scene and I enjoy the moment, before backing away into my own tracks. The word that comes to me as I retreat is, *peace.*

I crunch through the frost-filled prairie grass and reunite with the trail that cuts east into the rising sun. I descend back into the pines as shadows are cast in all directions, by all things. In this part of the park, the forest is thin and scattered and the prairie grass grows everywhere. It is some distance between each tree and there is no undergrowth. I work my way down into a small canyon, passing through grass at the bottom that is over six feet in height, as a lone buffalo grazes to my left. He cares not about my presence and never looks up.

I am breathing heavily as I reach the top of the ridge on the opposite side of the canyon. The prairie dogs are chirping, standing guard and scrambling from hole to hole. Some of their holes are so big my entire leg could fit into them, and this unnerves me. Rodents are something I like even less than Halloween.

I am carrying nothing in tow. I have no water, no food, no map, and no backpack. All that is with me is what I am wearing. My sweater covers my Under Armour pullover and an orange knit hunting cap extends down over my ears. My gloves are camouflage. Below the waist, I am wearing my black winter jogging pants, wool socks, and hiking boots. My camera is in my left front pocket. In my small back pocket rests my cell phone, car key, and room key. There is nothing else. This is highly unusual for me, but I have just set out for a short walk. In a couple of hours, I plan to go back and check out of the Best Western Hot Springs and move on toward Denver.

I sit for a few minutes at the top of the knoll, looking out over the vast buffalo flats. The expanse before me is well over a mile across and perhaps two miles wide. I pull up my binoculars and survey the scene, looking for both buffalo and trail markers. I can tell this trail is designed to go right across the open ground, but I can't find the next marker. Two big buffalo are feeding to my right. Well off in the distance, a large herd is visible. There, I sit, in no hurry at all.

This land once served as a rich hunting ground full of wild game. In addition, the Black Hills were a place of worship. Lakota tradition tells that the people themselves were created here, emerging from a cave and sent forth by the Great Spirit. To the north stands Harney Peak, where Black Elk flew during his sacred vision with the Six Grandfathers. A small piece of broken siding now sits lodged in a prayer tree there, in his honor.

Suddenly, it hits me. There is no way I want to leave this place today. Where else would I want to be today other than right here? I turn my phone on, which surprisingly offers a signal. I place my only call of the day to the front desk of the Best Western, where I tell the receptionist that room 104 will be staying another night.

This is where I sat that morning looking for trail markers and buffalo. This spot has since become one of my favorite secret vistas in Wind Cave National Park. I have now sat here many times and have never seen another person.

Now . . . how to get across the buffalo flats? Through my binoculars, I finally spot a narrow, brown plastic trail marker on a rolling hill near the middle of the open expanse.

"Holy shit," I whisper to myself in amusement. "Do I dare?"

It is at least a mile to the other side. There are no trees out there, no human sanctuary of any kind, just buffalo.

To make it even more challenging, the rolling terrain often blocks the view. On the top of one hill, a person can see for miles. At the bottom, however, you can't see fifty yards in any direction.

If I go, I will need to be careful.

Of course I'm going to go, I think to myself and then rise to my feet.

Down the hill and out onto the flats I move, feeling very much alive with anticipation!

Despite the fact that there are no trees, my vision is often limited. In one spot, I can see for miles, and in another, I can't see fifty yards in front of me. Knowing the buffalo are abundant, I am on high alert as I walk.

Sure enough, it happens. Halfway across the grasslands, I crest the knob of a rolling hill and walk right into a scattered group of buffalo. How many? I don't know, as I didn't stop to count and the terrain limited my vision. Let's just say there were more than enough! They had my attention and immediately I could see that I had theirs; most are sitting, some are standing. Several make eye contact with me. We are all surprised. My heart stops, and then accelerates. It is forever to the nearest tree. I am now the hunted. The tables are turned.

I freeze and then gently back down, into my own footsteps. After ten paces or so, I have removed myself from their view. I back off just a few more steps and then use my basketball skills to demonstrate a correct reverse pivot and start running. I jog quietly at first, but soon increase my speed and bolt. I run all the way back across the flat, stopping roughly at the place where I started, ten minutes before. I rest, regroup, and let out a nervous series of laughs. In short order, I see the event as funny. Danger can be that way, once it has been averted.

So, now what? I am not going back to the truck. I am determined to cross the flats and continue on down the trail.

I consider my options and then start walking east and to my right. I decide to skirt the edge of the flats and walk along the tree line. I never do see that herd of buffalo again. Like the story of the Lakota people, they are lost in the rolling hills.

After a good bit of walking, I arrive at the other side of the alpine prairie and sit down under an old pine tree. A cold north wind blows. The sky is partially cloudy, but the sun keeps fighting for control. A strong sense of solitude is with me. I feel I am the only person in the backcountry here today.

As I scan the grasslands with my binoculars, I finally spot the remnants of a trail marker.

I am searching for my way, I think to myself.

That is the essence of my entire Pine Ridge experience.

I leave the tree and walk back out onto the flats, where I soon stand over the broken sign. This trail is not a simple one to follow. Our paths in life are like that, I suppose.

This is the trail marker I finally spotted through my binoculars. These markers are quite inadequate, as the buffalo like to rub against them, often snapping them in two in the process.

On the lighter side, I feel like Forrest Gump. I just got out of the truck this morning and started walking. Then, I got the urge to keep walking. I have no idea where I am going. I have no navigational tools and no set destination in mind. I just have this compelling sensation not to go back toward the truck, not to go backwards, not to retrace my steps, but to claim new ground.

It is almost as if some unseen force is pulling me gently forward. Where this ends I don't really know, and at this moment, I don't really care.

The trail I am on comes to a junction and I choose right over left, heading deeper into the canyon. After ten minutes or so, I reach another junction, where I pause to consider my options listed on the wooden post in front of me. With no justification sought or required, I turn left onto the Highland Creek Trail.

I take six steps before I am stopped in my tracks, right foot down, left heel up, halfway between strides.

"Holy shit," I say out loud, for the second time today.

Not thirty yards ahead stands a single, large buffalo in the small pines, beside the trail. He is motionless and looking right at me, like I am late.

From the very beginning, I had the oddest feelings about this lone buffalo.

He is standing still. I am standing still. He is staring at me. I am staring at him. Initially, it is a standoff resembling two Old West gunfighters, each anticipating who will make the first move.

Soon, however, I sense his ease and passivity. He is no threat. In fact, the opposite is what I feel. He stands there as if he has been waiting for me, as if he knew I was coming.

I veer slightly left of the path and quietly walk twenty paces or so through the grass, to the base of a small pine tree just opposite him. We are still not more than thirty yards apart. Once again, he watches me. I watch him. We are both standing and both quite relaxed. Occasionally, he chews something—his cud, I suppose. I can feel his energy, and it's not just because I am close to the buffalo. I have been close to well over a thousand buffalo in the past twelve months; I have never had this feeling, this sensation of spiritual intimacy before. Something is up. I can feel it.

Finally, he lies down. So, I lie, thinking it would be impolite to do otherwise.

His presence is both peaceful and knowing. I can't get over the sensation that he was expecting me. This makes me think of my friend Bamm back at Pine Ridge. "The buffalo knows you are coming," Bamm told me in his kitchen that day.

When he laid down, I laid down. When he chewed grass, I chewed grass. There we were. Just the two of us, visiting.

He chews a bit of grass. So, I take a blade of grass and put it on my lower lip in response.

This moment reminds me how important solo time is for me on the trail of Crazy Horse. It is moments of solitude like this that brought me here. This is where I grow, take strength, and find my way.

Some time passes. It doesn't matter how much; neither of us has anywhere to go.

There is a small ridge behind both of us, providing shelter. We can hear the wind, but not feel it. The sky above is now a crisp, clear blue. I feel connected to this lone buffalo in a way that is difficult to explain back home in my society. In Lakota culture, the connection is not difficult to make at all, as the buffalo and I are brothers. Communication between the two-legged and the four-legged was a regular occurrence in the time of Crazy Horse. Verola tells me these powers still live within us all and can be released again. I believe she is right.

My visit with the lone buffalo became such a peaceful encounter that I nearly fell asleep, right there beside him!

In time, I get to my feet and slowly move on. As I crest the ridge, I look back and see that my four-legged friend has not moved. I sense our paths may not cross again. I say good-bye and press on.

The trail turns left and climbs through the scattered timber. I am walking along mindlessly when I am stopped abruptly by an amazing old tree and the spectacular array of sunlight that is pouring through it. It is at this precise moment, for the first time, that I become aware of what is happening.

This is my vision-quest walk.

The spirits have come for me. I have met them halfway.

I have studied the vision-quest rite of the Lakota and even considered at some point during my travels to Pine Ridge specifically seeking one out. It was both a surprise and a thrill to realize that it was actually happening. The elk, my original totem animal, had called me in, once again.

This tree and the light behind it stopped me in my tracks and made me realize something extraordinary was unfolding.

The White Buffalo Calf Woman gave Seven Sacred Rites to the Lakota and the vision quest, or *Hanbleceya,* was one of them.

The Seven Sacred Rites of the Lakota:

- ***Nagi Gluhapi.*** The Keeping of the Soul.
- ***Inipi.*** The Rite of Purification.
- ***Hanbleceya.*** Crying for a Vision.
- ***Wiwanyag Wacipi.*** The Sun Dance.
- ***Hunkapi.*** The Making of Relatives.
- ***Isnati Awicaliwanpi.*** A Girl's Coming of Age.
- ***Tapa Wankaye.*** The Throwing of the Ball.

The word *Hanbleceya* means "to cry for a vision" and was a long-standing rite of passage in Lakota society. Young men coming of age, or older men at transformational periods in their lives, would embark on a vision quest for the purposes of connecting with nature, in order to seek one's path. The vision quest sometimes first involved a sweat lodge experience and the guidance of a holy man. Other times, seekers would simply set out on their own. In all cases, the vision quest was a solo journey in which the participant traveled to an isolated area with neither food nor water. There, the "seeker" would remain for as long as it took to receive a message or messages from the Great Spirit. The process might be completed in a day, but in many cases it took three or four days of isolation and prayer. Often, the experience would involve guidance and communication from animals and nature along the way. Not all seekers received a vision, as the individual might not be spiritually ready. If one did receive a vision, however, it meant that the spirit guides would accompany the seeker on the rest of his journey through life, so long as he stayed true to the messages of his vision.

I once asked an elder at Pine Ridge to describe the vision-quest rite. This is what he said:

> **To seek a vision is to ask for insight from the Great Spirit, as to the direction you are supposed to be going. It is to seek fulfillment of that which is programmed into you already by your spirit guides, but has yet to be awakened.**
>
> **In a successful vision quest, the spirits reveal themselves, often through animals or natural signs, and tell you what you have to do.**
>
> **Not everybody is ready for this, and a vision quest is not to be taken lightly. Many seekers have been frightened by what they are shown on the hill. Others are run off the hill by the spirits, for they are not ready spiritually. For this reason, most people live their entire lives without going through a vision quest.**
>
> **The most important outcome of a vision quest is to know your place among living things and to gain comfort with your proximity to the Great Spirit.**
>
> **After receiving the vision, a seeker returns and prepares to impart his learning to others and to live his life, in accordance with the vision he has received.**

All the ingredients of a vision quest are present for me today. I am alone in the wilderness with no food, water, or material possessions. Furthermore, I have come to the Land of Crazy Horse seeking, in search of deeper self-understanding.

As I stand there motionless, watching the miraculous light filter through the strangest of trees, a vision comes to me. It is to be the first of four revelations I receive.

The first message or vision is powerful in its simplicity. On one level, it is nothing more than an idea that comes to me. The timing, clarity, and power of the idea, however, give it the credentials of a vision.

VISION #1
"You have what you need. Enjoy what you have."

Everything I need is already in my life. I don't have to hustle off to the next place or the next event to keep accumulating more. Accumulating more is not my path; enjoying what I already have more deeply is my opportunity for growth and fulfillment. It's that Taurus energy, the lion basking in the sun, that Deborah Dooley told me I should seek.

As I move slowly down the trail, I realize that the wonderful tree I just left behind was a "sign." In fact, it would turn out to be the first of four I would encounter on this day. If the lone buffalo I sat with a short while ago was the "gate keeper" to this experience, then the tree I just left was the first sign. In this context, a "sign" is an unusual or extraordinary natural scene that causes one to stop and reflect.

The trail becomes steeper as I move deeper into the forest. As I do, my eyes are drawn to a spot off the trail to my left. On the ground, in a small grouping of pine trees, is a dead buffalo. As soon as I see it, I know it to be the second sign. This buffalo is not long dead. Its fur coat is still partially intact. Its presence represents the circle of life that binds us all.

I stand and look over the dead buffalo. Some of its bones have been scattered about. In death it became food, a resource, for other living animals. Like the mythical phoenix, death becomes the sustainer of new life.

I find a small piece of milky white bone and pick it up. I hold it in my hand, turning it over and examining it from all sides. As I do this, the second vision appears to me.

The resting place of the dead buffalo, where I received my second vision.

VISION #2

"You have made your own trail. You are your own person. Be at peace."

In the tribe I was born into, there was a long tradition of business and community service. This second vision is telling me that what began as a shared path has now become my own. I have lived and worked through a set of experiences that have molded me into a blend of something old and something new. In losing consistent access to my speaking voice, I have found my inner spirit (my inner voice) and spread it across our company, my family, and our community. Along the way, I have added new circles into my life, such as Pine Ridge. "You have made your own trail. You are your own person. Be at peace." That was the message of the second vision.

We all belong to a tribe. That tribe has a pull on us. It sets the tone, lays out the expectations and mentors behavior. Our parents, grandparents, relatives, neighbors, teachers, coworkers, and friends all place expectations on each of us that influence the paths we choose to walk. But, within us all, lives the desire for individuation and authentic self-discovery.

I know many people who are teachers like their parents were, health-care professionals like their parents were, mill workers like their parents were, salesmen like their parents were. Whether one is from Pine Ridge or Casco, we all come from a tribe.

As I was working on this book, the baby Prince George was born at St. Mary's Hospital in London. Prince William and wife Kate's son was instantly third in line to the British throne. George has been the name of six British kings, including, most recently, George VI, the father of Queen Elizabeth. This might seem odd to you, but I felt a bit of sorrow for the little boy who might someday be king. I even said a prayer for him, because so much of what is to come in his life is already predetermined by the tribe he was born into.

I find myself lingering by the dead buffalo. Everything has slowed down and a deep clarity has come over me. I was expecting none of this today. In fact, I nearly missed the whole experience. I had given thought to driving off to Denver today, a day early. This has been an extra-long trip, with three days at the Rockin' Seven Ranch before going to the reservation. I was feeling like this journey was complete and that it was time to go home. After a full year on the trail of Crazy Horse, I still very nearly missed this, the messages I had been seeking. I nearly walked into my traditional trap of finishing one activity sooner than is necessary, in order to move on to the next—the act of completing tasks for the sake of starting new ones. My traps, my weaknesses, are never far away, but they are definitely becoming more visible to me and, therefore, easier to avoid.

As I move around the dead buffalo, each step is either softened by the reddish-brown pine needles that cover the forest floor or accentuated by the crunching of a pinecone beneath my feet. It is cool in the shade of the trees. My orange hat and camouflage gloves are on. I am thankful for my wool sweater. I decide to keep the white bone fragment I am holding, so I place it inside my right front pocket, before slowly moving on.

As I move farther down the trail, the sensation of floating while walking has come back over me. I am moving very slowly, almost in a trance-like state. Everything has slowed down and everything is crisp. The colors are brighter; the sounds are sharper. As I drift forward, the trail emerges onto a low ridge and a narrow clearing where a third sign appears. Subtle at first, I nearly walk past it before stopping. This sign is what I call a "buffalo circle." It is a dirt depression that the buffalo lie down and pound themselves into. At certain points of the year, these circles are muddy and wet. At other times, they are dusty and dry. This one is dusty and dry. During the summer mating season, I watched numerous bulls throw themselves into these circles, slamming their bodies into the earth.

This buffalo circle catches my attention because it is right beside the trail in a largely wooded area. Most of the circles I have seen are out on the plains, on the buffalo flats themselves. In addition, this one is unique because it forms a near-perfect circle. Most I have seen are roughly circular in shape. This one is precisely circular.

It is wonderful to be in a state of consciousness where something as simple as this circle can be so beautiful, so miraculous. As I study the circle, I notice that it is, in turn, inside a second larger circle of dirt. There are actually two rings, one inside the other. The second circle is much larger, perhaps twice the size of the inner one that first caught my attention.

I have been thinking more and more about drawing bigger circles in my life. When asked the simple question, "Where are you from?," we all tend to give very precise answers. If the circle is expanded enough, however, we all come from the same place. For example, are the challenges at Pine Ridge an Oglala problem, a Lakota problem, a Native American problem, an indigenous people problem, or, a human problem? The answer depends upon the size of the circle one wishes to draw.

In the end, I guess, for each of us, our circles are as big or as small as we choose to make them.

I push the dirt around a bit with my foot and then I take the buffalo bone out of my pocket. I use it to write the words *Paha Sapa* inside the inner circle. *Paha Sapa* is the Lakota name for the Black Hills. As I stand back to examine my work, the third vision comes to me.

VISION #3
"You don't have to take care of everyone else all the time. It is okay to do things just for you."

This third vision makes me instantly think of my friend and evolutionary astrologer Deborah Dooley's iconic line from my original natal chart reading:

"The tribe is okay, Kevin," she assured me. "Everyone can take care of themselves. The tribe is okay."

Deborah has helped me learn that I carry a strong sense of obligation to protect my tribe, but that I am here in this lifetime to learn to let go and to let each person find his or her own path.

"You need to make a bigger place for yourself in your own life," she tells me.

I used the bone from the second sign to carve the phrase Paha Sapa *into the buffalo circle that stopped me in my tracks.*

All of today's seemingly random events are quickly piling up and it becomes even more apparent that a special experience is occurring. My mind keeps returning to the notion that I almost missed it. I almost left early. I almost hurried my experience. After a year of traveling back and forth to Pine Ridge, I still could have missed today's adventure and the important messages that have accompanied it. Even the walk across the first buffalo flat this morning tested my resolve, and gave me a chance to turn back.

In large part, this book is about a set of experiences that mainstream American culture teaches us not to believe in. I have begun to transcend those cultural boundaries. If I were to share this story with a group of my Lakota friends, they would not be surprised or skeptical in the least about the vision-quest story I am telling. In fact, it would make perfect sense to them. They would listen with respect and understanding. Seek and thou shalt find. Yet, in our culture, I know how hard to believe my experience might sound to certain people.

I was recently with my daughter, Abby, in a small store filled with spiritual books and messages when she found a sign she really liked and showed it to me. It simply read:

***When you change the way you look at things,
the things you look at change.***

—Wayne Dyer

As I reflect on this learning, my fourth vision comes to me.

VISION #4
"We all have our own journey to make. Let those around you make theirs. Let them come to you. They know where you are."

This fourth vision is the realization that while I am making my own journey, everyone else is making his or hers, too. I can't lead anyone else's journey. I can't direct or protect any journey but my own, no matter how much I love or care about someone else. All the people I love in my life—my wife, our daughters, my other family members, my coworkers at Hancock Lumber, my community friends back home, or the people of Pine Ridge—they all are here on this Earth to make their own journey.

Each journey is a solo mission.

The last sentence of this vision is particularly powerful for me: "They know where you are." Everyone needs space to experience his or her own journey. The people in my life know I am there for them. When they need me, they will come find me. Letting them come to me when they want guidance, support, or companionship is more powerful than seeking them out prematurely or preemptively intervening. Trust the nature of things and let everyone have his or her own adventure. They will find you. They know where you are.

Suddenly, I realize that I am walking once again. I have emerged onto yet another, larger buffalo flat. This one is more expansive and remote than the first one I crossed this morning. I am somewhere in the back corner of the park, far away from any other person.

This morning, I walked out onto the first buffalo flat with a bit of trepidation. This afternoon, I walk onto this one with no fear at all.

"The buffalo will not harm me today," I whisper to myself.

Several hundred yards out onto the grassy plain, I come to a trail marker. It is a thick, rough-sawn wooden post. At this marker, I look directly to my right through a narrow pass, which, like a picture frame, reveals Pine Ridge on the edge of the horizon. Most people looking through this gap would not know what lies out there, but I do.

Just a short way out onto the second large buffalo flat, I looked through this gap in the Black Hills to the southeast where Pine Ridge lies. Most people would have no idea they are looking at the reservation, but I do. I know.

"I know you are there," I say out loud to the people of Pine Ridge and the spirits that surround me. "I am aware."

At this moment, I feel very light and unconstrained. My energy is focused inside my chest, where a ball of matter feels like it is floating. I feel warm and unbridled. Soon the word *peace* comes to mind again. Then a second word arrives: *free.*

Then, I realize what has changed. I am without fear.

The four visions and the experiences that have gone with them have, at least momentarily, released my deepest internal fears. I have come to a place I have long been seeking. My journey west, which began at Yellowstone National Park over twenty-five years ago, has been calling me here—right here—to this walk and these visions (or understandings).

**"You have what you need.
Enjoy what you have."**

**"You have made your own trail.
You are your own person. Be at peace."**

**"You don't have to take care of everyone else all the
time. It is okay to do things just for you."**

**"We all have our own journey to make.
Let those around you make theirs.
Let them come to you.
They know where you are."**

My quest is not unique. In fact, it is universally human. We are all seeking. We all are searching. We all have fear. We all enter this world in search of spiritual growth and development. It is easy to get busy, stay busy, and repress this. But, we are all seeking.

I do not feel that I possess any special powers or mystical capabilities to have had this spiritual experience. In the time of Crazy Horse, such learnings were commonly sought and received. The Lakota knew that only the thinnest of veils separate the world we "see" from the world we seek to understand. The Great Spirit is always with us. Better yet, it lives within us.

In traditional Lakota society, most men embarked on vision quests and many were provided a vision in return. If there are fewer vision-quest experiences today, it is only because people have stopped seeking.

One of the most famous Lakota vision-quest stories belongs to Crazy Horse himself:

> *He was about thirteen now, and he [Crazy Horse] wanted to seek a vision. Sioux boys his age often went by themselves to some lonely place where they could commune with the sacred powers, hoping for a vision that would guide and inspire them for the rest of their lives.*

A vision quest is not about abandoning one world for another. In fact, just the opposite is true. The purpose of the vision quest is to return to your tribe with a greater sense of purpose, understanding, and spirituality. Self-discovery only makes the tribal circle stronger.

> *Stripped to his breechcloth, he [Crazy Horse] lay on the hilltop, staring at the stars. He had placed sharp stones between his toes and piles of pebbles under his back to keep from falling asleep. He would force himself to stay awake until a vision came. He would try to enter the spirit world, the world that existed beyond this one, where there is nothing but the spirits of all things. For two days, he remained on the hilltop without eating, fighting off sleep, his eyes like burning holes in his head, his mouth as dry as the sandhills around him. When he could barely keep his eyes open, he would get up and walk around and sing to himself. He grew weak and faint, but no vision came to him. Finally, on the third day, feeling unworthy of a vision, he started unsteadily down the hill to the lake where he had left his hobbled pony.*

I continue walking on my own vision quest, across the buffalo flats, without fear. That is not to be confused with being reckless. I am fully aware that I am in a wild place and that I need to pay attention. I am not about to take my new visions and go pull the tail of a buffalo. Rather, I am simply carrying with me a newfound peace. It is amazing how everything one works toward can suddenly tip and materialize in an instant. At this moment, I am aware that the four-leggeds can feel my energy and that my peaceful state actually makes the whole scene more relaxed and less threatening to them. This is the nature of the Seventh Power: Our energy affects the whole. To seek a vision is to surrender. To gain a vision is to lose one's fear.

> *[Crazy Horse's] head was spinning, his stomach churning. The earth seemed to be shaking around him. He reached out to steady himself against a tree. Then, as he himself would later describe it, he saw his horse coming toward him from the lake, holding his head high, moving his legs freely. He was carrying a rider, a man with long brown hair hanging loosely below his waist. The horse kept changing colors. It seemed to be floating, floating above the ground, and the man sitting on the horse seemed to be floating too. The rider's face was unpainted. He had a hawk's feather in his hair and a small brown stone tied be-hind one ear. He spoke no sounds, but Curly [Crazy Horse] heard him even so. Nothing he had ever seen with his eyes was as clear and bright as the vision that appeared to him now. And no words he had ever heard with his ears were like the words he seemed to be hearing.*

I walk along. As I do, I look back and to my right. Sure enough, behind the knoll I just passed, two buffalo sit in the grass. I was less than thirty yards from them when I unknowingly walked by. This morning, I might have started running, alarming them in return. This afternoon, I just smile and keep walking. I do glance back several times to make sure they are as cool about the whole thing as I am. It turns out they are. They never move.

> *The rider let Crazy Horse know that he must never wear a war bonnet. He must never paint his horse or tie up its tail before going into battle. Instead, he should sprinkle his horse with dust, then rub some dust over his own hair and body. And after a battle, he must never take anything for himself.*

Our true road in life is hard to see, even though it was there all along, just like the faintly traveled path I followed on my vision quest.

Halfway across the flat, the trail disappears. To my left, there is a small hill with a few scattered trees. It is an oasis in a sea of grass, so I walk toward it. Like most journeys in life, it is farther away than it looks. Eventually, I arrive and pick a tree to sit under, facing west. As soon as I sit down, I notice a large herd of elk feeding right out in the middle of the prairie. This strikes me as unusual, as the sun is still high in the sky. I watch them through my binoculars. As I do, I can see a broken trail marker right beside them. The four-leggeds have once again shown me the way.

> ***All the while the horse and rider kept moving toward him. They seemed to be surrounded by a shadowy enemy. Arrows and bullets were streaking toward the long-haired rider but fell away without touching him. Then a crowd of people appeared, the rider's own people, it seemed, clutching at his arms, trying to hold him back, but he rode right through them, shaking them off. A fierce storm came up, but the man kept riding.***

This large herd of elk helped me regain the trail and know where to go.

In time, I leave the oasis and walk out onto the open grasslands, toward the elk. I steer to the right, so as not to disturb them. Still, they watch me. The elk are always watching. I can count ninety-seven elk, but the way this walk has materialized, I would not be surprised if there were exactly one hundred.

I walk awhile on the trail the elk helped me find, before it too begins to hide itself and disappear. Once again, I survey the outer boundaries of the grasslands for marker posts with my binoculars. As I do, I see a small herd of buffalo— ten in all—heading west, single file on a trail. Sure enough, in front of them I see a marker. It is my trail.

> **The vision faded. Crazy Horse felt someone shaking him hard. When he looked up, he saw his father. His father had ridden out into the prairie to search for the boy. He was angry that Crazy Horse had run off alone without saying a word.**

No sooner do I bring the binoculars down than four birds capture my attention to the south. They are the first birds I have noticed all day. I look toward them as they sing and circle their way up into the sky. From where I sit, they are flying right toward the sun, and as I continue to follow their flight, the fourth sign appears.

The sun has a rainbow around it, and it is amazing to see! It is a sight I have never seen before or since. There is no rain, just a rainbow of six colors in a complete circle around the sun; Six Grandfathers of the Lakota world, and a color for each one of them. I can sense with this sign that my vision quest is nearing its end. I see this, the fourth sign, as the culmination of a transformative day.

In Lakota culture, the boy often took the name of the father once he had grown of age and accomplished his own feats. The father would literally give away his name and assume a new one. This was to be the case with Crazy Horse. A chief or a headman's son would often become a chief himself. The tribe and the age Crazy Horse was born into determine much of what he would experience. His vision quest foretold his role as a great warrior for his people, as he was the rider of his own vision.

As I walk on, I eventually catch up with the ten buffalo that showed me the way. I steer away from the trail, to give them proper space. The ten buffalo form a circle as I walk by.

The trail descends into a small ravine, with a shallow creek flowing through it. At the bottom, just across the river, two big buffalo are grazing. They are right on the trail. I have to stop and wait for them to pass, which, of course, is fine by me. I sit on a big rock halfway down the ravine, watching them and reflecting on my extraordinary day. The bull in front is scratching himself on a trail marker post and then he starts waking toward the creek to get a drink. As he moves, I can see that he is very old. He walks with a pronounced limp in his front left leg.

As I look around, I have the feeling that I have been here before. The scene, which has been new all day, suddenly looks familiar.

The trail descends to the creek and then follows it east, in the opposite direction of the buffalo. In front of me, the trail rises to crest a small hill, arriving at a gravel parking lot.

Now, I definitely recognize where I am, and my location makes me smile! It is highly symbolic. I have arrived in the small wooded parking area, where exactly one year ago, I began my first hike to the first tree I sat under. Happily lost all day, in a big place, with no preset destination,

I randomly emerge in the exact spot where my Black Hills experience began a year ago.

I am ending where I started. My solo journey has come full circle.

———

I need to hitchhike back to the other side of the park, as I have walked clear across it. Every time I have hitchhiked in my life, it means it's been a great day, and this is no exception.

I am quite a sight: My black pants are covered with these prickly things from the bushes and grass. There are too many to count stuck to me. My brown sweater and orange hat don't look much better. I have nothing in tow. I look like a drifter. The infrequent drivers that do come by give me a close look and keep driving.

It was a long way back to my truck where I started my vision quest this morning. Lots of cars passed me by, and I couldn't really blame them.

We all should hitchhike once in awhile. It is a great way to confront rejection.

Many minutes pass between cars. For quite some time, I stand at the intersection of Routes 87 and 385. It is the only intersection in the park. It is November and totally off-season for this area. No one is here, which, overall, I love. Right now, however, I would like to see somebody. I would like to talk to somebody. I would like a ride.

Finally, I start walking. I feel this is a futile exercise, because it's a long way to the other side of the park, and the buffalo are always hanging out on the road. There are no trees on this road, and I will not be able to walk along it because of the buffalo. Despite the distance and the buffalo that I know await me, I keep walking.

Eventually—finally—a nice lady stops and picks me up. She pulls over and motions me inside. She is on her way to Hot Springs to visit her mother. She is not daunted by my appearance, but I am quick to explain myself, all the same.

"I just need to get to the Hot Springs entrance where my truck is," I say with a grateful smile. "I have been hiking through the park all day."

She smiles and begins talking. A lively conversation ensues.

As she talks, I settle in. As I do, I notice the colorful dream catcher and silver buffalo hanging from her mirror. Nothing surprises me at this point today. The spirits are dancing.

———

Later that night, moments before sunset, I pull the truck into one of my favorite places at Wind Cave National Park. The exact spot is a bit of a secret. It is like a prized fishing hole. If I were to give this spot an Indian name, I would call it "The place where the big elk go at sundown." I arrive at the spot before the elk do. They are not visible yet, but I am sure they are coming. I get out of the truck with a tall can of Budweiser, my binoculars, and my camera. It is cooling off fast this evening. It was never very warm to begin with today. I am wearing my brown wool sweater (of course), jeans, boots, camouflage gloves, and my black Rockin' Seven Ranch wool hat.

Ten to fifteen minutes pass and then the elk begin to appear. One by one, they emerge from different openings in the timber. Ever cautious, they make their way carefully and methodically out of the forest and down into the meadow. They eat as they go, picking their heads up every twenty to thirty seconds to take another good look around. I am leaning on the hood of my truck, watching them through my binoculars, even though they are not far away. Soon, they begin crossing the road and moving out onto the large open meadow. In all, there are eighteen bulls, and each one is big by pretty much anyone's standards. Their giant antlers extend far down their backs when they tilt their heads back to survey the scene.

Just a few weeks ago, you would not have found them here. Earlier this fall, these bulls would have been up higher on the plateau, battling for control of herds of cows. That is over now, until next year. The patterns and habits of the elk flow in a circle.

It is nearly pitch dark now. Most of the bulls are busy grazing, but a number of them seem bored and want to spar. Two pairs of bulls, one to my left and one to my right, have locked horns and are thrashing around. The battles are halfhearted. There is nothing really at stake tonight.

As I linger, I think about the visions that came for me today and the animals that guided my path. The visions I received were simply a sequence of short yet powerful messages that suddenly appeared in my head—during a moment of deep contemplation—submerged in nature. No angels or strange voices appeared, or anything like that. I do feel like the spirits were with me today, but their images and identities were not revealed. This is the way spirit guides work. They know we must each make our own journey.

"One's path comes from within," I write in my journal, despite my chilled hands.

———

By 6:00 a.m. the next morning, I am back outside in the cold, dark air loading my gear into the truck, preparing to drive to Denver.

It is snowing at a pretty good pace. I turn on the truck and begin the defrosting process. As I scrape the ice off the windows, I think, once again, of my good fortune, as there is no way I could have taken my vision walk today. If this storm had come one day earlier, I would not have had that experience.

At 6:45 a.m., I cross the Cheyenne River and pass through the small town of Edgemont on the southwestern edge of the Black Hills. It is a slow but beautiful drive as the new day dawns. The snow is falling and blowing. The road looks icy. Very few vehicles are traveling in either direction. I have plenty of time to think as I plod along. In a short while, I cross back into Wyoming where my trip began. This straight line between Wyoming and South Dakota is an artificial boundary. In the time of Crazy Horse, this spot would have had no meaning. It was all Lakota territory. It strikes me that many boundaries are imaginary in this way.

The artificial boundary that separates Wyoming from South Dakota, west of the Black Hills.

If the Treaty of 1868 had been honored as written, how would the Lakota be living today? I wonder to myself. *Would things really be different, and if so, how?*

I think about these questions from time to time. When I see how few people live on the northern plains, I can't help but think that there was room for everyone.

How often in human history has the group with the most power over-reached?

This thought causes me to reflect again on one of my favorite quotes:

In this life, there will be lessons.
Those lessons shall be repeated until learned.

—Dan Sullivan, *How The Best Get Better*

Human tribes are still learning how to coexist, I whisper in a pain-free, SD-free voice.

The drive back to Denver through the snow was one of the most serene and peaceful trips I have ever made across the northern plains.

On this day, history literally appeared to be frozen in time as I traveled out of the Black Hills and back onto the northern plains.

As I drive along, I can picture this place before colonization. I can picture this place before the roads, the telephone poles, and the barbed-wire fences. It sounds like a simple thought, but think about the American West without fences. Can you picture it? I can.

As I look across the blowing snow, I can see the Lakota people out there in it. I can see them traveling in a caravan, pulling everything they own to a better site somewhere by a stream, perhaps, with cottonwood trees and some protection from the endless wind and driving snow.

The storm breaks and a brilliant light appears. The earth and the sky are never far apart in the Land of Crazy Horse.

Later that morning, the storm breaks and the sun arrives as I continue driving on. Along the way, I stop at a scenic rest area where a monument to the Oregon Trail reads:

> *To all the pioneers who passed this way to win*
> *and hold the West.*

The empty road I am on closely follows the original stage line that came up from Cheyenne, on the way to the hills filled with the "yellow metal" the Wasichus simply had to have.

My route brings me right back through the town of Guernsey, Wyoming. Despite the fact that I was just here a few days ago, I detour off the highway to make one last stop at the Oregon Trail Ruts.

The big rut that I sit in is over six feet deep. It is narrow like the wagons that cut it. Dripping water from the melting snow falls off the branches of the young pine tree above me. The sun is in my face. I feel warm outside for the first time all day. I sit there, as is my custom, just feeling the energy of the place. As I do this, my "No Judgment Zone" mission returns to me.

Most everyone on all sides was making the best decisions they could at the time, based on what they saw, I think to myself.

Most everyone was sure of his or her cause's righteousness and everyone had a cause. Whether that cause was gold, freedom, following orders, Manifest Destiny, God, survival, or protection of homeland, everyone had a cause.

In any case, it is troubling that gaining freedom for some has often involved taking freedom from others. In this context, I wonder if anyone really wins.

––––––––––

At the junction of Route 26 and I-25, you have just two choices. You can bear right toward Casper, or left toward Cheyenne. You can't go straight (at least not by car). I turn left toward Cheyenne, because Cheyenne is how I get to Denver and Denver is how I get to Casco. For me, the sign for Cheyenne is the sign for Casco. No one else passing here likely sees it that way. Where we come from influences what we see.

What I see, on this day, is a circle . . . growing larger . . . and nearing completion.

The elk have been calling to me for a long time.

My soul is striving to remember who I am, to make who I am compatible with who I was born to be, to bring who I am into synch with who I will be.

—Steven Forrest

12
Voices

Symbolic images are abundant at Pine Ridge—inescapable.

Everybody needs beauty as well as bread, places to play in and pray in, where nature may heal and give strength to body and soul alike.

—John Muir

The Apollo Family Restaurant occupies the corner of a sleepy strip mall, just off Flamingo Drive and US 41, in Florida's Gulf Coast town of Apollo Beach. It is one of those local establishments where everyone stops eating and looks at you when you walk in, which is what just happened to me a moment ago.

Now, I am sitting in the booth, opposite the door. The old steel diner table before me swivels gently each time I rest my forearms on it.

"There you go, sweetie," the waitress says as she sets a patty melt in front of me on a white diner plate.

Very few people travel to Pine Ridge. Even fewer do so from Maine. Perhaps no one has ever traveled from Maine to Pine Ridge via Apollo Beach, Florida, but that's the path I am on. I will go almost anywhere to regain my true voice.

The voices of the past pull strong on the people of Pine Ridge, I think to myself as I sit alone in the small diner.

The voices of their ancestors, the voices of their oppressors, the voices of their spirit guides, the voices of their complex and controlling government, the voices of the old ways, the voices of the new ways, the voices of alcoholism and self-inflicted abuse, the voices of freedom and independence—and, of course, their own inner voice, the voice of the subconscious self. All of these voices collide at Pine Ridge, like chatter in a crowded room.

My own voice is also on my mind in a most literal way. In fact, that's what has brought me to Apollo Beach. I have come here to see Connie Pike. Connie is a speech therapist who specializes in working with patients who have spasmodic dysphonia. Connie is uniquely qualified to do this work because she, herself, has the disorder. In just a few minutes, I will arrive at her house and she will become the first person I have ever met with SD. That's how rare my disorder is.

In preparation for this therapy session, I have gone without a Botox injection for five months, and my voice is currently a major struggle. Last night, I took my mom out for dinner (she has a home in nearby Sarasota) and I could not even describe my upcoming trip to Pine Ridge. My voice was so weak that she could hardly hear me, even though we were sitting side by side. Each short sentence I forced out of my throat left me gasping for air, somewhat dizzy, and extremely sore. Uttering even a simple thought was a significant chore.

I can't help but see parallels between spasmodic dysphonia and Pine Ridge. I have lost my voice. My condition feels permanent. I have been told there is no cure. Drugs are the only source of relief. I am stuck in a difficult pattern, a circle, without end.

Just a few days ago, I was on the phone with my friend and spiritual mentor, Deborah Dooley. I talked to her about my plan to visit Connie Pike in an attempt to fully regain my voice and become less dependent upon Botox. Botox, which serves as a muscle relaxant, is the medication most commonly prescribed for the disorder. Even though it is hard for Deborah to hear me, as usual, she intuitively understands.

Yesterday, just after my plane landed in Florida, I turned on my phone and the following e-mail message buzzed, announcing its arrival:

> *I wouldn't be concerned by the sound of your voice. This does not matter. Your voice is reflecting a place where you have congestion within your soul. It is a path of discovery for you. You just need the tools to discover what the origins of this are about. For these reasons, I would stop taking Botox injections. The Botox is taking away the symptoms that guide you to the source. The first step is to place your conscious awareness where the tension is in your throat and just hold it there. You may do that for a couple months. No hurry. It is just a path. Hopefully your Florida trip will bring you more tools. Many blessings, Deborah.*

For me, Apollo Beach now has something in common with Pine Ridge; they are both places I have gone searching for my voice.

So, my next trip to Pine Ridge (my fifth overall) actually starts here in Apollo Beach. It is the spring of a new year, and nearly six months have passed since I shot a buffalo, shared the meat with the people of Pine Ridge, and then had a vision-quest experience alone in the Black Hills. My flight yesterday took me from Maine to Charlotte, North Carolina, and then on to Sarasota. On the first flight from Portland, I sat on the aisle. To my right sat a nice elderly lady from the small town of Monson, Maine. To her right sat her husband, who had a degree of dementia or Alzheimer's. I could tell this because he kept asking where they were going and why they were going there. He, too, had lost his voice. The natural patterns of communicating thoughts and ideas no longer flowed easily for him.

There are lots of ways to lose your voice in this world, I thought to myself.

As the plane descended into Charlotte, I chatted with the lady beside me. She asked me where I was going, so I told her about my book, my voice, and Pine Ridge.

"It's a shame, the way their land was just taken," she comments.

"The Supreme Court agreed," I reply. "The Court ruled the land-taking unconstitutional and awarded the Sioux millions of dollars in damages, but the tribes would not take the money. 'Our land is not for sale' was their reply."

With this statement, her husband suddenly inserted himself into the conversation for the first time.

"There is nothing for sale in Monson, either," he interjects with animated eyes.

If you are from Maine, or have been to Monson, you would not be able to resist the humor and creativity in this response. We all laugh.

Within this man, despite the challenges he was facing, a voice still lived.

Inside the Apollo Family Restaurant, I finish lunch and pay the bill. It is six dollars and change.

As the waitress walks away with my payment and an empty lunch plate, one of the guys in the corner booth playfully cajoles her.

"I want to put in a request to fix a lightbulb," he says, pointing to the ceiling above, where he and his three retirement-age buddies are sitting and drinking coffee. I can tell they sit there every day.

We all have a place called home, and that home is filled with rituals and routines that define us.

––––––––––

Connie works from her home in Apollo Beach. As I walk up the path to her front door, I think about what has brought me here. As with many other rare disorders, I suppose it is difficult to describe the experience of having SD to someone who never has to think about their voice. I always feel like my SD looks less restricting and less challenging to others than it feels to me. Perhaps being Lakota at Pine Ridge is a similar experience. To those on the outside, the solutions can look so simple.

Without Botox, it is extremely difficult for me to speak. When I go to speak, I almost immediately run out of air; it feels like I am being strangled. My voice sounds strained, broken, and very raspy to others, but the real problem is what it feels like inside. It can be so physically hard to talk that I just don't want to. Without Botox, I am usually reduced to speaking in short sentences and asking lots of questions.

In Connie's first book, *Free to Speak,* she shares excerpts from conversations with SD patients she has worked with. Here are some of the ways in which people have described their disorder to Connie:

> *"This voice is so frustrating and embarrassing."*

> *"My voice is strangled, broken, and distressing."*

> *"The phone is ringing. Do I pretend I'm not here,
> or do I answer it?"*

> *"I'm becoming more and more isolated."*

> *"I can't even talk to my wife and kids."*

In addition to the challenges, there are also some blessings that come with the disorder, if you are willing to search for them. For example, I have become a much better listener, and I have become great at asking questions. I do less myself and I trust and empower other people more.

SD has forced me to slow down and to share leadership. In these ways, SD has made me a better leader. The leader of a tribe often takes on all the work and responsibility. The true calling of leadership, however, is to give away power, not collect it. I don't know if I would have learned that lesson without SD. Most importantly, SD has made me focus on myself. It has called my attention inward. I have always felt a strong impulse to serve and protect others. This overidentification with my role as leader had taken its toll on me in ways that I couldn't see. SD forced me to stop and look inward at what I wanted as an individual spirit. In these ways, I am actually thankful that I have SD. The disorder was a catalyst for change, and it came from within. I am convinced SD was my body's way of getting my attention, telling me that I needed to change.

In fact, I like most of the ways in which SD has altered my life. I just wish I could talk comfortably, or, as Connie Pike puts it, I just wish I was "Free to Speak."

I ring the doorbell and Connie appears, she immediately motions for me to be quiet.

"Shhh," she voices softly, pointing to the small tree to the left of the door.

"There are two eggs there that just hatched."

With that, she waves me inside.

Eggs, I think to myself. *New life, more circles.*

Connie is a polished and determined Southern woman. She is of medium height with healthy blonde hair and animated eyes. She is relaxed, yet focused; caring, yet tough. In her work she benefits from a unique set of experiences. Trained in speech therapy, she herself acquired SD and proceeded, over a period of years, to learn to manage the disorder without Botox. She is one of just a few people in the world who has been able to do this, and she now devotes her career to teaching others to do the same.

I, too, have not been willing to settle for a life of Botox. Besides, the results of using Botox have been mixed for me; sometimes it helps my voice, sometimes it doesn't. More importantly, I have had this deep intuition that the disorder came from within, with a purpose. I believe that my SD was, in a way, self-inflicted. It was my soul's method of telling me that I needed to change. The disorder came in on a path of brain waves and nerves—and it can leave on that same path, if only I can get in tune with the forces within me that brought it forward. Perhaps no one in the medical community would agree with my self-assessment of either the course or cure of my disorder, but that's okay. It's what I feel and believe. On a soulful level it rings true to me. In fact, it is what has brought me here to see Connie. I believe I can improve my own condition.

"The onset of SD often coincides with a series of stressful events," Connie explains as we sit in her office, just to the right of the front door. The late-spring Florida sun shines brightly outside.

"The disorder itself can be a blessing," she continues. "It's a barometer into your state of being that most people don't have."

"There is actually no definitive way to say that you have spasmodic dysphonia. In fact, I don't like the term. I prefer to say you have a challenged voice. The term 'spasmodic dysphonia' just sounds so handicapped and complex to me. I don't like it," Connie says with confidence.

I had read Connie's book before coming to Florida, so I already have a good sense of her philosophy. In her book Connie writes that:

> *It can be quite damaging to tell someone straight out that they have an incurable neurological disorder for which there is no known cure. This puts the patient at a great disadvantage from the start. No hope leads to hopeless candidates for rehabilitation, unless their will is much greater than the defeatist story they are given.*

"That's the first thing they tell you," Connie explains. "They tell you it's neurological and that it can't be cured."

> *If patients are told that therapy is unlikely to help them, THERAPY WILL NOT HELP. It is that simple. Suggestions to the mind are powerful.*

As I listen to what Connie is saying, I can't help but think again about the parallels between my voice and the disorder at Pine Ridge. I recognize that the severity of the challenges at Pine Ridge are much more dramatic than my own, but it is inescapable to me how all the points Connie makes could be applied equally to the challenges faced by the Oglala Sioux Tribe.

"The problem with the traditional approach is they begin by telling you that your situation is beyond your control. Botox injections and third-party throat massage gives *them* responsibility for fixing *you*. I am giving *you* responsibility for fixing you," Connie instructs.

We are sitting no more than two feet apart and Connie is looking right into my eyes with determination. It is a bit of a seminal moment.

"From this day forward, I want you to think of your situation as something *you* can control, as something that is within *your* power to change," Connie says softly, followed by a long pause.

Spasmodic dysphonia, Pine Ridge—my mind is traveling back and forth between the two conditions. Each sentence Connie shares fits both circumstances.

I am already inspired and feeling confident, after just ten minutes in Connie's office. Her views on the disorder we share are just what I have been searching for. I just needed a mentor. I just needed to see that someone else has done it.

"So, let's start with breathing," Connie says with a nod. "Let's have you lie down on the floor."

For the next three hours, I learn about breathing. I learn about posture. We practice basic sounds. We go all the way back to the fundamentals of a healthy voice. We record my voice and conduct a series of vocal exercises. By the time the afternoon is over, I am on such a high I actually feel "cured." Connie's home reminds me of the giant cathedral north of Quebec City, where the crutches hang on the wall, memorializing the people who walked in crippled and left healed.

The progress I made in a single session was amazing to me. I did understand that it would not be this simple to just walk out "cured," but at the same time, I had just proven to myself that a normal voice still lived within me; under the proper conditions, it could be coaxed back out. It all felt extremely liberating.

The physical pain I often feel when speaking is burdensome. My throat tightens and it takes a great deal of effort to push words through. The words that do make it out are weak and hard to hear. The whole exercise of speaking leaves me out of breath, like there is no air. Beyond the physical pain, there is the emotional stress. I love people. I love talking to people, hearing ideas and exchanging them. When my SD is at its worst, I often just don't say much. I have learned to live in short sentences. In a crowded room with background noise, it can be all but impossible for me to carry on a conversation. It feels embarrassing and frustrating. It makes me feel alone, isolated. I don't like it. That's what brings me here.

"It's all about taking back control," Connie says.

"What did the Botox do for your breathing?" Connie asks.

"It didn't do anything for my breathing," I reply.

"What did the Botox do for your posture?" Connie continues.

"I didn't do anything for my posture," I answer in cadence.

"Most importantly, what did the Botox do for your sense of control and for your sense of responsibility for managing your own voice? What did it do for those things, Kevin?" Connie asks. Like a well-trained lawyer, she knows the answers to the questions she is asking.

We share a moment of silence, which reminds me of conversations at Pine Ridge. Her words have the quiet ping of truth. It is liberating to think about my disorder differently, to think about retaking control.

"Knowledge is power," Connie says from the threshold of her doorway. "It is just about re-patterning your brain. But, I caution you, re-patterning takes a lot of work. It's a journey. It took me years, but it starts by just taking small steps in the right direction, toward self-responsibility and control. If you can hum, you can speak. So, just start there. Start with the humming. Learn to hum in the proper voice, then learn small words in the proper voice; then, learn phrases in the proper voice. That's the path to a free voice. Expecting it to work, versus expecting it not to work, changes your entire state of being."

It is the end of the day. We hug and then I depart. As I drive south on I-75 toward Sarasota, I think about all the bad habits I have built up from the initial onset of SD. At that time, I had no clue what was going on. My throat just hurt. Talking had become an extreme strain. To compensate, I had been tilting my head down and just fighting through, pushing as hard as I could to make my voice work. Of course, that has always been my way when faced with challenges—just fight hard and don't give up. Meet force with force. That was me. That was the me that needed to change. SD was my spirit's way of helping me see that fighting force with force was no longer my path. I never would have learned that without spasmodic dysphonia.

––––––––

That night, I took my mom out to dinner and I talked and I talked and I talked.

I felt liberated. I felt "Free to Speak." This morning I couldn't wait for my next Botox shot. Tonight, I feel like I am never going back for an injection. I am sure the truth lies somewhere in between, but I have seen a path toward self-reliance. Someone new has come into my life and mentored the way.

As dinner wraps up, I think of my favorite quote from Connie's book:

> **Never deprive someone of hope;**
> **it might be all they have.**
>
> **—H. Jackson Brown Jr.**

The following day, I return to Connie's house for another active session of breathing, posture, voice training, and positive energy. After departing, I head straight for Tampa International and board a Delta flight to Atlanta, and then a second flight to Denver. I am going back to Pine Ridge.

"That's a big strawberry," I say to the elderly lady to my right in an SD-free voice over dinner, as our plane chases the setting sun to Denver.

"Boy, it sure is," she replies.

After dinner, we both settle in. I am reviewing my notes from my sessions with Connie while she is reading. I pause and look at her book; it is *The Diary of Anne Frank.*

Abuse of power and persecution of the vulnerable are not new inventions, I think to myself.

Pine Ridge is just one of countless places across the continuum of time where those who had the upper hand overreached and took what they wanted, without considering the consequences.

Tribe against tribe has been the story of humanity. How do we transcend that? How do we move toward a single global humanity with one boundary that is the planet Earth itself? I guess it starts the same way all difficult journeys do—with a personal commitment to face the proper direction and start walking that way. In the end, we all have only one person we can control.

New learning keeps revealing itself to me at just the proper moment throughout my Pine Ridge experiences, and my discovery of Joseph Campbell is an example. Born in White Plains, New York, in 1904, Joseph Campbell would go on to become the most famous mythologist of the twentieth century. Campbell believed that all mythical narratives—including the world's great religions—were, in fact, telling the same story; that is, a metaphor for the inward journey into the unconscious psyche that all humans aspire to make. The outward adventures of myth were actually symbols for the inner voyage into the depths of one's own soul. The world's great mythological tales shared a universal story line, which he described as "The Hero's Journey," suggesting that regardless of the tribe or age in which we live, we are all seeking a similar path of self-exploration:

We have not even to risk adventure alone, for the heroes of all time have gone before us. The labyrinth is thoroughly known. We have only to follow the thread of the hero path, and where we had thought to find an abomination, we shall find God. And where we had thought to slay another, we shall slay ourselves. Where we had thought to travel outward, we will come to the center of our own existence. And where we had thought to be alone, we will be with all the world.

The union of heaven and earth on the northern plains invites self-reflection.

It was not until after my fourth trip to Pine Ridge that I even learned of Joseph Campbell. My friend, Ted Carter, spoke of him often during our chats, so I had heard his name and written it down. Ted is a leading landscape architect in Maine. He is also a deeply spiritual person who has studied and written extensively about connecting with the inner self and seeking a deeper union with the natural world, of which we are a part. I don't know many men who have bared their spiritual essence publicly and shared their deepest thoughts with the world. Ted has done this through his writing and open dialogue. This defies what men in our culture have been taught: to suppress and hide their inner feelings, even from themselves. In this way, Ted is a trusted mentor.

In listening to my adventures at Pine Ridge, Ted just kept saying, "That's the Hero's Journey. That's Joseph Campbell," before I knew what any of it meant.

Once I started reading Campbell's works, however, I couldn't stop. I quickly understood why Ted kept referencing him. The story Campbell was describing was the story I was living.

Getting in and out of the Denver airport is a breeze on this evening, literally. It is very windy as I drive north in the dark. Cheyenne, Wyoming, is my destination tonight. In the morning, I will continue on to Pine Ridge.

As I drive, my mind is on Joseph Campbell, and I think about his words as I ponder further the notion of a single global humanity:

> *To what society do you belong?*
> *The society of the planet is the only valid one now.*

Letting go of the pull of your own tribe is difficult. Every tribe has a dogma that asserts its way is the best way. I have seen this to be true in my own community in Maine, as well as at Pine Ridge itself. The line between cultural pride and social dogma is narrower than we think. Tribalism has consequences, and Joseph Campbell saw this:

> *I've lived through the whole century [twentieth] and it's been a mess. It's been largely based on denigrating somebody over there and saying we've got to go in and knock them out. The main awakening of the human spirit is in compassion and the main function of propaganda is to suppress compassion . . .*

Even though it is early May, it is snowing as I cross the border into Wyoming and the car console reads 28 degrees. I am thinking about my own tribe and the pull it has on me. I am thinking about the Oglala Sioux of Pine Ridge and the pull their tribe has on them.

How do we transcend our local tribes and individuate? I ask myself.

Not to leave our tribes behind, not to love our tribes less, but simply to transcend, to see ourselves as independent beings sharing a single planet with all living things. How do we learn to celebrate our local tribe in the context of a larger united world? How do we learn to celebrate ourselves as unique individuals with our own paths to travel?

It is 11:25 p.m. as I arrive in Cheyenne. It has been a long, but rich day. I-80 west is closed for the night to all truck traffic, as the winds are gusting in excess of fifty miles per hour. The trucks are lined up for over a mile on the side of the road. I am back on the edge of that place where nature stands so tall.

Tribalism is dogma, I think to myself.

Tribalism depends on building the narrative that describes how your people are the chosen people. How your people are better than your neighbors, more pure, more righteous. What's more, all tribes can do this whether they are conquerors or not. It's hard to transcend; it's hard to build relationships on a broader, global scale when your own tribe keeps pulling you back into a small circle. We need to start drawing bigger circles.

> **Now you can see today why the world is in trouble. What is the social field today? The social field is the planet, and there isn't a single system of action that has to do with the planet. They all have to do with one interest group or another.**
>
> **—Joseph Campbell**

I am exhausted as I drop my backpack on the spare bed in my hotel room before plopping down on the one beside it. I am moving between worlds, but those worlds are coming closer together for me. Increasingly, all things are one thing.

Tonight, I see parallels and ironies. Here I am, back on the trail of Crazy Horse, searching for my own voice in a place where so many other people feel they have lost theirs. But, my cure was within me all along; I can see that now.

Vision grows clearer when one looks inward, I think to myself under the covers, as if I am speaking.

With this final thought, I am asleep.

> **There is a voice that doesn't use words. Listen.**
>
> **—Rumi**

———————

It is early morning the next day and I am lying on the floor of a dark hotel room. I am doing my new favorite breathing exercise, the one Connie calls "Happy Skeleton." It is spiritual, and I am taking in so much air that it makes me dizzy. I am not used to getting air like this. It was only two days ago that I learned I wasn't breathing properly. My body's response to SD had been to tighten, and this had severely impacted my air flow. I didn't even know the diaphragm was supposed to be the destination of a healthy breath. Without knowing it, I had forgotten how to breathe. I had been fighting force with force. My throat tightened and my whole body tightened in response.

As I lie on the floor, it feels so great to take a full, relaxed breath; so great, in fact, that it makes me laugh and then I cry.

We underestimate what goes on inside, I think to myself as I lie there listening to the sound, and feeling the rhythm of my own breath.

We convince ourselves the battle is on the outside; in the external world, we can more readily see. It is easier in some ways to place our problems with others, or on circumstances beyond our control. The true path for growth, however, lies within.

At 7:30 a.m., I leave the hotel. My feet crunch into the thin layer of fresh snow and ice. As soon as I start the car, the theme song to Disney's animated hit movie *Frozen* appropriately comes on the radio.

It's funny how some distance
makes everything seem small.

And the fears that once controlled me,
can't get to me at all.

It's time to see what I can do,
to test the limits and break through.

No right, no wrong, no rules for me.

I'm free!

Let it go, let it go.
I am one with the wind and sky.

"I love that song," I say out loud with enthusiasm in an SD-free voice (it fascinates me that my SD symptoms go away when I talk to myself).

Throughout my entire Pine Ridge adventure, I have been struck by how the words from today's most popular songs so often match my experiences and emotions in the Land of Crazy Horse. This realization suggests to me that I am not the only person who is searching.

At 8:28 a.m., I enter Platte County at mile marker 69 where the pavement turns from black to red. I have always found this spot where the highway changes color to be symbolic.

The snow is blowing sideways in union with the gusting wind. In fact, it is so windy I can hardly stand up to pee outside my car, so I take a moment—like a golfer before an important shot—to gauge the wind. The clouds are exceptionally low and rolling powerfully across the sky. There is always such a communion of heaven and earth here on the northern plains.

This route is like a pilgrimage for me now. I stop once again at Register Cliff, then at the Oregon Trail Ruts and Fort Laramie, before arriving in Lusk shortly before noon. I drive slowly past the butcher shop on the corner, where I picked up my buffalo meat nearly six months ago.

A short while later, I stop in Van Tassell (population 15) on the Wyoming—Nebraska border. I am the only person in sight as I drive around, walk around, and take pictures.

At Pine Ridge, I have found within me an artist, a storyteller, an activist, and a spiritualist, all of whom, until very recently, I hadn't known existed. Those parts of who I am had not been called upon by my tribe back home in Maine, but they are out now. Pine Ridge and spasmodic dysphonia have released them.

The corner of First and Oak in Van Tassell in eastern Wyoming sits about a mile from the border of the Nebraska panhandle.

Standing there alone, in the heavy wind on the corner of First and Oak in the smallest of small Western towns, I reflect on one of my favorite exchanges between Joseph Campbell and Bill Moyers:

> *"It is quite possible to be so influenced by the ideals and commands of your neighborhood that you don't know what you really want and could be. I think that anyone brought up in an extremely strict, authoritative social situation is unlikely ever to come to the knowledge of himself."*
> (Campbell)

> *"Because you are told what to do?"*
> (Moyers)

> *"You are told exactly what to do, every bit of the time. You are in the army now. So this is how we do it here. As a child in school, you're always doing what you're told to do, and so you count the days to your holidays, since that's when you're going to be yourself."*
> (Campbell)

"I'm an artist!" I say out loud to the street sign and the gusting wind. "I'm a storyteller!"

My voice comes pain-free and without restraint, as I stand alone, self-proclaiming these newly released dimensions of my identity.

"Searching for my voice" has dual meaning. On the literal level, I am actually seeking to regain a healthy, pain-free voice. On a figurative level, I am seeking to transcend the expectations and responsibilities I feel toward my tribe and uncover my own natural identity. I believe the loss of my identity to my role triggered the onset of spasmodic dysphonia. Therefore, separating from my role to release the authentic spirit within me is the path to regaining my voice. It's just about traveling in reverse for the purpose of moving forward. I am rewinding the circle. In a sense, I am rewinding time.

> **You don't become an 'artist' unless you've got something missing somewhere.**
>
> **—Bono**

The symbolism of this picture, taken near Van Tassell, is powerful to me. Although I was in the present, I was also traveling back in time for the purpose of releasing myself forward. I can't help but wonder if the people of Pine Ridge can follow that same path.

I feel called to tell this story. Telling the story of Pine Ridge energizes me. It is therapeutic in some deeply spiritual way; and, while I hope doing so will have a positive impact on others, its main purpose is for my own soul.

> *Anyone writing a creative work knows that you open, you yield yourself, and the book talks to you and builds itself. To a certain extent, you become the carrier of something that is given to you from what have been called the Muses—or, in biblical language, "God." This is not fancy, it is fact. Since the inspiration comes from the unconscious, and since the unconscious mind of the people of any single small society have much in common, what the shaman or seer brings forth is something that is waiting to be brought forth in everyone.*

> **—Joseph Campbell**

And, the pictures; oh, how I love taking the pictures. I share Joseph Campbell's perspective on their power:

> *There is more reality in an image than in a word.*

Train tracks running south of Van Tassell.

The artist is the one who communicates myth for to-day. But he has to be an artist who understands mythology and humanity and isn't simply a sociologist with a program for you.

—Joseph Campbell

A short while later, I stop at the site west of Fort Robinson commemorating "The Cheyenne Outbreak." A few minutes after that, I am standing before the stone marker where Crazy Horse was killed. I know I will never drive by this spot without stopping and reflecting.

"You have to do the spiritual work first," Connie Pike had told me.

As I stand there, I notice that the base of Crazy Horse's modest monument is built upon several layers of red stone. These red stones are very small compared to the larger gray rocks above. Many pieces of the red bottom layer have crumbled and broken off. Like all things, they are slowly making their way back into the earth. I kneel down and scoop up a few of the red pebbles and place them in my pocket.

Back in the car, I hear the DJ on the radio pose the following question:

How do you let your ghosts affect your present and your future?

———————

Later that afternoon, I am standing in Bamm Brewer's garage behind the abandoned Reddy Mart store on the east side of town (Pine Ridge). Bamm and his son Matt are building trusses for the new meat-processing facility. Bamm is as excited about this project today as he was last fall. Then again, as far as I know, Bamm is always excited.

Last summer, I created a nonprofit organization named "The Seventh Power" (www.seventhpower.org), which is dedicated to advancing spiritual and economic independence for the people of Pine Ridge. In November, The Seventh Power contributed to Bamm's project, and I am glad to come back and see the progress.

A short while after leaving Bamm, I am back at the Singing Horse

Trading Post. Many of my old friends are there, but some new friends are also on the scene, my favorite of whom is a young woman named Oki. Her camper is parked for the summer right beside the swing set, just below Rosie's house. Oki is here for the season to enjoy Pine Ridge and help Rosie with the store and the horses. She is about Rosie's height, with short hair and a near-permanent smile. Oki is an activist at heart, having spent time living on the White Earth Reservation in Minnesota with Winona LaDuke, as well as on the Shoshone Reservation in Nevada.

Winona LaDuke is an American Indian activist and environmentalist. She twice ran for vice president of the United States as Ralph Nader's running mate on the Green Party ticket. An Anishinaabe Indian on her father's side, she currently serves as the executive director of the White Earth Land Recovery Project, whose mission is to regain ownership of former treaty lands for the tribe in northern Minnesota.

In Nevada, Oki lived on the Dann Ranch, which is famous in the Native American land rights community. Five years before the Treaty of Fort Laramie of 1868, the US government signed the Treaty of Ruby Valley with the Western Shoshone Tribe. This treaty ensured safe passage for white travelers across Shoshone land, and also permitted gold mining. In return, the Shoshone were guaranteed their land "forever." In the decades to come, however, a consistent story would play out. The US government would systematically acquire much of the tribe's original treaty lands through congressional action. Today, most of what the tribe considers its land is publicly held by the Bureau of Land Management (BLM) and the Department of Energy. The Western Shoshone, like the Lakota, eventually filed suit against the federal government and won a multimillion-dollar land-claim settlement. The Shoshone have, to this day, refused to take the money. Their position is a familiar one: "Our land is not for sale." From the 1940s through the 1960s, Shoshone lands were used extensively for nuclear testing; and, today, the BLM leases grazing rights there. The Dann sisters became famous in the 1970s by refusing to pay grazing fees to the BLM, asserting instead that their ranch was on tribal lands. The Dann sisters took their case all the way to the United Nations, which ruled in their favor.

It feels good to be back at the trading post, catching up with old friends and making new ones.

For sunset, I drive back to Wounded Knee to take pictures, reflect, and listen to the spirits and the prayer flags blowing in the wind.

It's only when it's quiet that I can find my voice.

———————

Several of Rosie's horses have their own breakfast on the hills above the trading post.

The next morning, I walk the fence lines above the Singing Horse Trading Post. After that, I have breakfast in Rosie's kitchen, where the conversation, as always, is fun and engaging. Breakfast here has become a morning ritual that I look forward to. It is hard to find a better way to start a day than by wandering the hills above Singing Horse with the rising sun, only to end up in Rosie's kitchen for a hearty breakfast and thoughtful conversation.

After breakfast, I make the short drive into Manderson to visit Cecy and see her sewing circle in action. Coincidentally, we are both here at the same time. The room inside the function hall at St. Agnes Church is peacefully busy as I walk in.

After visiting with Cecy, I wander around the room taking pictures and talking to people. One local woman I speak with lives just up the road past Pinky's Store.

She asks me the all-important question: "What brings you here?"

So, I tell her my story.

"Write the truth," she says to me as she waves her index finger in my direction.

"I'll do my best," I reply.

Her statement makes me think about the notion of "truth" and how personal it is for each of us.

We don't all have the same truth, I think to myself as I leave the church and drive over the ridge to visit my friend Nick Tilsen.

Cecy's sewing circle in action at St. Agnes Church in Manderson, just down the street from Pinky's Store.

Across the highway from Oglala Lakota College, Nick and I are sitting in a booth at the Lakota Prairie Ranch Resort diner. The seat underneath me has a big rip in the cover, exposing the white stuffing and metal coils. The room is crowded and the food is good. As always, the conversation with Nick is thought-provoking.

"You can't treat the symptoms. You have to change the system," Nick explains to me.

Like SD, I think to myself, even though I know he is talking about Pine Ridge.

"What is the future of this reservation?" I ask Nick. "What does the path forward look like?"

"You know, President Obama asked me a similar question," Nick replied. "He asked me how things were at Pine Ridge."

"What did you tell him?" I counter, intrigued by the fact that Nick and the President have met.

"I told him the truth. I told him it was pretty rough," Nick responds.

Silence.

"But, then I told him the key is that we believe we can change it. That's the most important point, believing the future can be different than the past," Nick says to himself, as much as to me.

More silence. Conversations are never hurried at Pine Ridge. Words don't come out just to fill the air with sound here.

Eventually, Nick continues, "We need to build a pipeline of opportunity, rather than create more government programs. Part of the challenge in doing that is creating small victories and positive examples. It is different here than other places; like Harlem—there is lots of poverty in Harlem, too—but, at the same time, you are twelve blocks from Manhattan. The isolation is a challenge here. Getting the momentum going, that's the work that needs to be done; there is no middle class here, very few examples of the new way forward."

After lunch, we drive back to his office together in relative silence. My voice has left me and I am not able to say a lot. Initially, this frustrates me, having just felt "cured" a few days earlier back in Apollo Beach. The frustration quickly fades, however. I have grown to be thankful for my disorder, as it is the very thing that is liberating me.

It was good to reconnect with both Cecy and Nick. I see my friends at Pine Ridge just a few times a year. Months pass between visits. It all seems to matter not. The moment I reappear, I feel welcomed and the conversations just pick back up where they left off. It's like we are always together in spirit, and that the physical distance or the barrier of time is unimportant. Pine Ridge stands still in this way. It waits for you pretty much just the way you left it.

A few miles down the road, heading south toward Porcupine, I pull into Verola's house. It is hard to find a place to park, as her home also serves as an auto body shop. Rusted cars and spare parts are everywhere. This is the first time I have visited Verola's home. I always feel it is an honor to be invited into a home here.

It was my friend, Catherine Grey Day, who asked me to make this visit. Verola's house is in significant disrepair, with the roof, in particular, being the most pressing problem. When it rains outside, it also rains inside. The roof doesn't leak; it literally rains inside.

Verola is a widow, a mother, a grandmother, and a neighborhood care-taker. At any given time, there might well be ten to twelve people living in her worn and crowded split-foyer home. Typically, three generations of her family would be represented there most any time you visit.

"This is a safe house," Verola tells me as we sit on the couch together. By this, Verola means that it is a safe place to stay away from drugs and violence. There is an electric space heater just a few feet away. The floor is worn through to the plywood and water stains have overtaken the ceiling and walls. Piles of toys and collectibles are stacked here and there, usually needing a wall to stay upright. People are coming and going, but Verola introduces me to everyone and I feel completely at home.

"It's an ownership home, so I can't get no help from the tribe," Verola continues. "I called and asked some other groups for help, but they never came, so I don't ask them no more."

"We try to live by the old ways here," Verola says, after a long pause.

With that, she gets up and goes over to the kitchen and flips through a stack of papers before returning to sit beside me. As she sits down, she hands me an old, folded document. As I open it, I can see it is a passport, far different in style from the kind used today.

"This belonged to my grandfather," Verola explains. "His name was Mark Spider, and he obtained this passport in 1925, while traveling in Europe with the Wild West show. My grandmother's name was Mary, Mary Running Horse."

"It makes me happy to see this, Verola," I reply. "Thank you for sharing this picture and your stories with me."

Mark Spider's passport #139135, dated 1925. You can see his signature written above in black.

"If you share your culture, it keeps going," Verola says, breaking the momentary silence. "If you don't share your culture, it ends with you. That's what my dad always told me; he told me we should share our culture or else it will just end. I think about that a lot."

More silence.

As we sit there, I think about what Verola said. This community has a cultural heritage that does need to be shared. Pine Ridge possesses a spirituality that our country needs. The rest of our country has material goods and economic strategies that Pine Ridge needs. The challenge is bringing the two worlds closer together, so that each can share the value it brings with the other.

"I am going to find someone to fix your roof, Verola. I am going to take care of this for you," I say after a long pause. "I will talk to Buck back at Rosie's and see when he can do the work."

"Oh, that sounds good. Thank you, Kevin. I really appreciate this," Verola replies.

———————

At 5:00 p.m., I wake up from a great nap back at Singing Horse. Tonight, I am driving off the reservation to meet Lester Lone Hill, who has invited me to a sweat lodge Hunkapi ceremony—otherwise known as "The Making of Relatives." Lester has invited me to become his brother and to take a Lakota name. For me, this is a seminal moment and a great honor.

I am meeting Lester off the reservation, in the town where the Medicine Man lives. Out of respect for him and the ceremony itself, I have chosen to keep his name and location anonymous.

On my way to the sweat lodge, I stop at Wounded Knee where I purchase three dream catchers, from three different artists who, one at a time, show up to visit me. I always buy something when approached and I never haggle over the price. I would rather they have the five or ten dollars I could save. There is no victory in negotiating here.

My favorite of the three dream catchers is framed in red willow bark.

"The inside is ground up and smoked in the Sacred Pipe," the maker of the dream catcher tells me.

I don't tell her that I am on my way to experience that for myself.

The sun sets over the ridge, just west of Wounded Knee, on the night I went to sweat lodge.

The sun is setting as I leave Wounded Knee. It is a spectacular evening. The air is warm and the sky is telling stories. My window is down as "Scare Away the Dark" by Passenger plays on the radio. As I drive, I think about the appropriateness of the song's lyrics.

Well, sing, sing at the top of your voice,
Love without fear in your heart.
Feel, feel like you still have a choice
If we all light up we can scare away the dark.

We wish our weekdays away
Spend our weekends in bed
Drink ourselves stupid
And work ourselves dead
And all just because that's what Mom and Dad said we should do.

We should run through the forest
We should swim in the streams
We should laugh, we should cry,
We should love, we should dream
We should stare at the stars and not just the screens
You should hear what I'm saying
and know what it means.

Once again, I am struck by how so many popular songs today connect with the experience I am having at Pine Ridge. It makes me believe that a universal journey is under way and a global transformation has begun.

As I drive alone into the setting sun, I think about the complexity that is Pine Ridge. Pine Ridge is everything at once. It is beautiful, spiritual, and resilient. It is also tragic, sad, and stuck. There is no simple way to describe this community that I have come to love. For me, Pine Ridge is like the yin and yang symbol, where everything is represented in one sign; one idea and its opposite share the same space here. In a sense, the entire human experience is wrapped into this single isolated community to which I have affixed myself.

While this community is filled with spiritual energy and love, there is also a dark side at Pine Ridge. Its elements include poverty, idleness, drugs, alcohol, suicide, disease, abuse, violence, and more. In fact, some of the recent damage here looks to be at least partially self-inflicted— Lakota against Lakota, family member against family member, self against self. I have thought about this apparent reality many times. With all the external challenges, why would people here strike out against each other, against themselves?

Throughout my Pine Ridge experience, learning has appeared at opportune times, and Paulo Freire is an example. I first saw his book, *The Pedagogy of the Oppressed*, on the bookshelf at Rosie's house. The title intrigued me, so I ordered a copy and read his work. Freire was Brazilian and spent much of his life studying the conditions of oppression in some of his country's poorest slums around Sao Paulo. He would go on to examine oppression globally and learn that the patterns and consequences were repeatable and predictable.

As I drive toward my first sweat lodge experience, I find myself reflecting upon Freire's work. I can see the characteristics of oppression he identified in my own research and time at Pine Ridge.

In his book, Freire wrote that:

> *All domination involves invasion—at times physical and overt, at times camouflaged, with the invader assuming the role of a helping friend.*

The history of Pine Ridge certainly follows this path. The Lakota were physically conquered and then isolated. Next, they were forcibly stripped of their own cultural customs (language, dress, traditions). In the later decades of the twentieth century, the invasion became subtler, in the guise of a helping hand. Along that continuum, the force being applied transitioned from overt to covert, just as Freire described.

For oppression to succeed and sustain itself, Freire explains that the culture of those being oppressed must be destroyed. Worse yet, Freire writes, the oppressed must be persuaded that they are not as talented or as capable as the people of the conquering society:

> *For cultural invasion to succeed, it is essential that those invaded become convinced of their intrinsic inferiority. Since everything has its opposite, if those who are invaded consider themselves inferior, they must necessarily recognize the superiority of the invaders.*

Deep within the individual spirit, how do the people of Pine Ridge perceive themselves? I worry about this reality frequently when I think about the reservation. What level of confidence do the people who live here have in their own capability to become self-sufficient and powerful again—both as individuals and as a collective community? I know the power lies within them to be economically independent, but the historical weight of being pushed down and told otherwise is greater than all the rocks of Mount Rushmore combined. As Freire wrote,

> *Self-deprecation is another characteristic of the oppressed . . . so often do they hear that they are good for nothing . . . that in the end they become convinced of their own unfitness.*

It all reminds me of Catherine's story of the "Indian crabs" who can't get out of the bucket. These thoughts make me sad, yet also hopeful. I am sad for the present condition of Pine Ridge, yet hopeful for the future, because I believe the Seventh Power lives within us all.

Black Elk spoke of the Six Great Powers (West, North, East, South, Sky, and Earth). These powers represented the Great Spirit and they lived in all things. While at Pine Ridge, I also learned of a Seventh Power. This is the power of the individual, and it belongs to all who live; but, you must go to meet it. As the Lakota vision-quest rite foretold, you must seek your own source of personal power.

We all are products of our environment, yet we all contribute to that environment as well. The Seventh Power, for me, is about being conscious, about being aware. It is about taking control of our personal paths, despite the tribal obstacles from past and present lives.

I have been intrigued by the popularity of "zombie" shows and movies in recent years. *The Walking Dead, Buffy the Vampire Slayer, World War Z* and more have been hits. It makes me wonder why we are, as a society, presently so attracted to this genre. I think I know. I think it is because we are afraid of becoming "zombies" ourselves—deaf to our present condition, marching day by day through the routines set before us by our tribes, lost in roles, tasks, and the Internet—busy, yes; living, no.

The past pulls on us all, including those who did the oppressing, and I can feel this personally. The Lakota are certainly living with past wounds, but so is the rest of America. As Freire wrote,

> *It is not those whose humanity is denied them who negate humankind, but those who denied that humanity (thus negating their own as well).*

Columbus did not discover a new world.

I love the values of our country, but I also know that in the back corner of our national house, there is a dark closet, behind a creaky door, filled with missteps. Worse yet, there are Americans living among us who are still paying for those mistakes. It's not over. The past doesn't work that way. Events aren't "over" simply because they are old. The past is released only when the individual spirit reconciles it. This is the essence of evolutionary astrology that I have learned firsthand. The past only leaves when we escort it away.

It is hard to find hope in the gloomy, heavy patterns of oppression that transcend time, but it's there. Hope lives in the oppressed regaining self-awareness and accepting forward-looking responsibility. According to Freire,

> *It is essential for the oppressed to realize that when they accept the struggle for humanization they also accept, from that moment, their total responsibility for the struggle. They must realize that they are fighting not merely for freedom from hunger, but for freedom to create and to construct, to wonder and to venture. Such freedom requires that the individual be active and responsible.*

Every play in the handbook of oppression has been thrown at the La-kota people, yet they still hold the keys to their own salvation. It is natural to think that since the challenges are external the solutions must be as well, but this is not the truth. The great human mystery, the one Joseph Campbell called forth, is that salvation lies within. We must each be the change we seek, as Gandhi foretold. The Seventh Power is the only force that can truly set us free.

What can those of us do who are not Lakota to help the cause at Pine Ridge? Some Native Americans might be skeptical of my participation in this story altogether based on the belief that only Indians can speak for Indians. I understand this thought process and accept its presence. At the same time, everyone just worrying about his or her own tribe is part of the problem that needs to be transcended. Making financial contributions and then going home has been happening for decades, and it's not enough. Money alone doesn't change much. A deeper connectivity is required.

Black Elk saw this. He spoke about a future that was one great circle. The "old ways" of the Lakota also took this into account, as they were centered on the notion that all living things were related and of the same life force. So, in this context, the future requires cross-cultural connectivity, grounded in sincere intentions. Paulo Freire saw this too, describing it as "cultural synthesis." He wrote that:

> *In cultural synthesis, the actors who come from "another world" to the world of the people do so not as invaders. They do not come to teach or to transmit or to give anything, but rather to learn, with the people, about the people's world.*

Perhaps I like this thesis because I perceive that it fits me, as I did not come here to teach, to convert, to fix, or to save. I came for myself, and never pretended otherwise.

I find it interesting that evolutionary astrology and the "old ways" of the Lakota share many similarities. Both philosophies believe the soul is not bound to a single tribe, race, species, or epoch. Both believe the soul transcends—that the soul endures beyond the body's death.

I drive on for some time, reflecting upon these thoughts. As I near my destination, however, my mind transitions to the experience that lies in front of me this evening.

———————

Through the branches of the old pine tree, the moon watched over me while I waited for Lester on the night of the sweat lodge.

The sky is clear and the air crisp, as I lean on the hood of my car in a small parking lot looking up at the moon.

Moments later, a car pulls up. It is Lester and his son. He motions for me to follow him. I am off to Hunkapi, The Making of Relatives. I am off to participate in one of the Seven Sacred Lakota rites.

A short while later, Lester and I are changing into our shorts (bathing suits, actually) near a log beside the sweat lodge. The lodge is in Medicine Man's backyard, and I can hear him and others talking beside his small home.

"Don't be afraid," Lester tells me. "Sometimes they touch you, but the spirits never come to hurt anyone," he continues.

"If it's too hot at any time, you can just crawl out." Lester is looking out for me like the big brother of mine he is about to become.

I thank Lester again for bringing me here. I never expected to have the opportunity to experience something like this when I first traveled to Pine Ridge eighteen months ago.

The scene is surreal, as the rest of the participants start to gather. It is dark, so all the people and images I see are shadows; nothing fully reveals itself.

The sweat lodge is perhaps four feet tall. I can't tell exactly what it is made of, but it is definitely well-constructed and meant to be a permanent fixture. The lodge is rounded with a single opening that you must crawl in and out of. Beside the lodge, a large fire blazes. The wood crackles and pops into the darkness of night. As we prepare to enter, a young man removes the wood and begins scooping up the fire-red rocks that are heating underneath. With a pitchfork he brings the rocks carefully into the lodge and piles them in the center. When he has finished this process, we all work our way inside.

I am asked to go in first, as I am the guest of honor. Lester follows me. We crawl to the left and Lester whispers for me to stop directly opposite the entrance. Lester will later tell me that spot is for the honored guest and that it also is the hottest place in the lodge. I was not sure if this was real or a joke. I couldn't tell if that was just where they put the new guy to see if they could bake him out!

I was surprised by how much humor accompanied the ceremony. This Medicine Man is a "jokester," I would later learn, which essentially means that he focuses on happy spirits and welcomes laughter and playfulness to enhance important rituals.

There are ten people in the sweat lodge. The Medicine Man enters last and sits opposite me. The lava rocks are clustered in a big pile, in the pit that lies at the center of the sweat lodge floor. Once Medicine Man is set, the flap on the entrance closes and it becomes completely dark. From that moment forward, the ceremony is a series of sensory images I will never forget.

The helper closes the door of the sweat lodge, making it completely dark inside, and this darkness represents the darkness of the soul, our ignorance, from which we must now purify ourselves so that we may have the light.

—Black Elk

Speaking mostly in Lakota (occasionally, for my benefit, in English), Medicine Man begins to talk, then chant, then pray, then sing. Others around the circle echo his sounds, in support of what has been said. The small hut quickly heats up and sweat comes easily. At this moment, the ceremony could be taking place one hundred or two hundred years ago.

The man at the west now sends a voice to Wakan-Tanka in this manner: "Hee-ay-hay-ee-ee!" [four times].

(This we say whenever we are in need of help, or are in despair, and indeed are we not now in darkness and in need of the Light!)

—Black Elk

Four prayer sessions make up the ceremony. Between each session, the flap of the lodge is opened. Sitting directly opposite the entrance, I have an amazing view of the smoke and heat from the rocks, dancing their way out into the cold night air. After five minutes or so of fresh air, the flap is closed again and the prayers and chants resume.

During the course of the Inipi, the door will be opened four times, letting in the light; this reminds us of the four ages, and how through the goodness of Wakan-Tanka we have received the light in each of these ages.

—Black Elk

I am completely ready for this experience. I am not afraid. I am not intimidated. I do not approach it as a stranger or a spectator. I embrace the event as an equal and invited participant. My body is covered in sweat. The sweat mixes with the dirt on my hands, arms, legs, and chest. I am sitting upright with my legs crossed and I will sit that way for two hours. On the lighter side, this is perhaps the most unbelievable part of the experience. At home, I can't sit on the floor cross-legged for two minutes; yet somehow, on this night, I did so for two hours! I am leaning in toward the fire. As the ceremony progresses, I find myself chanting and praying as well.

"I want my voice back," I whisper at first and then repeat over and over again, my voice growing louder and more determined each time.

This sentence soon evolves into my own chant, which I keep repeating in rhythm with the chants of Medicine Man.

> *I pray for MY voice. I pray for ALL voices.*
> *I pray for MY voice. I pray for ALL voices.*
> *I pray for MY voice. I pray for ALL voices.*
> *I pray for MY voice. I pray for ALL voices.*

I repeat this chant out loud to the rhythm that fills the lodge. Everyone is praying in Lakota. Everyone is singing in Lakota. The room is pitch dark, but occasional sparks of light appear randomly throughout the lodge. I am ready. I am ready for any spirit that enters to come to me. I am not afraid.

> *I pray for MY voice. I pray for ALL voices.*

"I am sending a voice!" [four times] "Hear me!" [four times] "Wakan-Tanka, Grandfather, You are first and always have been. You have brought us to this great island, and here our people wish to live in a sacred manner. Teach us to know and to see all the powers of the universe, and give to us the knowledge to understand that they are all really one Power. May our people always send their voices to you as they walk the sacred path of life."

—Black Elk

During the third segment of the ceremony, Medicine Man invites the spirits to enter the lodge and join us. As the spirits enter, Medicine

Man calls out their names, announcing their presence to the rest of us. Medicine Man then converses with many of the spirits and relays what they say. This entire segment is in Lakota, so I don't really know what is happening until Lester explains it to me later.

At key moments that pertain to my naming, Medicine Man speaks in English. He tells me that Lester's deceased grandfather is in the lodge and that he has come to name me.

"Chun Ota," he said. "Your name is Chun Ota."

With this, more noises of approval fill the room.

I am soaking everything in.

During the final segment of the ceremony, two pipes are smoked. Medicine Man blesses each pipe before it is passed clockwise around the lodge where each participant takes a smoke. When it is my turn, I hold the near end with a closed fist and inhale as my opposite hand extends down the long pipe. I am smoking willow bark and it feels clean and soothing.

Sitting outside on the log after the ceremony, Lester explains what happened. Everyone else has gone inside for the sacred meal. Lester and I are alone, wrapped in blankets under a Lakota moon. I feel purified and relaxed.

"Many spirits came into the lodge tonight, Kevin," Lester tells me. "It was a good night for the spirits. Crazy Horse came into the lodge. Later, Sitting Bull himself appeared. This is rare that Sitting Bull comes to us down here at Pine Ridge."

Peaceful silence.

"My grandfather," Lester continues, "well, he always shows up."

Lester chuckles.

I have such a peaceful feeling. There is no need to hurry off this log beside my new brother, Lester.

It is 1:00 a.m. before I arrive back at Singing Horse. I can't believe how many cars I pass on the way through the town of Pine Ridge. There is more traffic here after midnight than I saw during the day today.

I am happy to be in bed and sleep comes easily. The sweat lodge is a place for purification, soul searching, wisdom seeking, and communion with the Great Spirit of all things. It was an honor for me to become Lester's brother and to take a Lakota name.

This is a picture of a typical Lakota sweat lodge. It is very similar to the one I was in. Modern lodges have stayed true to their generational predecessors.

A few weeks later back in Maine, I received a letter in the mail from Lester. I had asked him for permission to write about the sweat lodge ceremony, and this was his response:

> **"Hau Misum [younger brother],**
>
> **The Medicine Man who performed the Hunka, Making a Relative and Naming Ceremony, told me it was okay if you referenced the spirits who came into the sweat lodge that night. These spirits are well known to visit all the sweat lodges and ceremonies, as they want to continue this way of life for future generations. They are well known throughout Pine Ridge.**
>
> **The ones I remember well are Crazy Horse, Touch-the-Clouds, Sitting Bull, Rain-in-the-Face, and, of**

course, Comes War Whooping [Lester's grandfather], who gave you your name. There were about six or seven others who came into sweat lodge, all Heoka spirits, who love to poke fun at everyone present. I was very surprised by your courage in the sweat lodge; you did well for your first time, in what was a hot sweat the first round.

The Amos Lone Hill you mentioned in your e-mail is indeed my ancestor. He was my great-grandfather who died of a heart attack in the middle of the dance arbor, east of Porcupine. He loved the Lakota way of life so much he would put on an annual powwow/celebration at a time when the government tried to quell such activities. He knew his time was near before the powwow, but he did it anyway, knowing he might drop in the arena. He instructed his relatives to continue on with the celebration should this happen; they did as he wanted, honoring and burying him, all the while continuing to powwow. That is where I get my love of dancing and the Lakota way of life.

The picture I e-mailed you is of Shot-in-the-Eye, another one of my great-grandfathers who lost his eye at the Battle of the Little Bighorn.

—Your Cheya [older brother]
Wahukiza Luta (Red Lance)

This is the picture Lester sent me of his great-grandfather, the one who lost an eye at Little Bighorn.

The next day, I meet back up with Lester outside the OST Partnership for Housing office in Pine Ridge.

"Can you tell me more about your grandfather, the one who named me last night?" I ask.

"Well, I never met him, but he kind of follows us around. I think he is looking out for his grandchildren and great-grandchildren," Lester explains.

We are both leaning against my car. I am kicking some rocks around the crushed-stone driveway. It is the middle of the day, but neither of us are in a hurry.

"What made you decide to invite me to take a name and become your brother, Lester?" I ask.

"Well," Lester says, pausing before continuing, "I could see that you were sincere. I remember standing at the empty foundation up the road with you and we talked with Pinky about building a house there."

Pause.

"At the time, I didn't think that it would ever be possible, you know, to actually build a new house on that empty foundation. You said you would help us do that, and then you went away."

Pause.

"Then, you came back and you made that happen. You followed through and made it happen, you know. That surprised me. It is hard to make things happen here, but you made it happen. You followed through and built that house."

Pause.

"Then, remember that night when we were with Pinky at Our Lady of Lourdes Church for the fund-raiser for that girl who was going to the rodeo? I saw you there with our people, just being generous and interested in us. I said to myself that night that you were sincere and that you were brave."

Pause.

"The Hunka, the ceremony for Making a Relative and Naming, you know in our culture that this ceremony is a show of respect; and, I decided I wanted to show you the respect in return for how you followed through and made things happen for our people."

Pause.

"The Hunka ceremony is an old and important tradition in Lakota society. It goes back to the days of the warriors, of which our tribe had many. Our Oglala warriors, you know, they were famous for not backing down in the face of difficult odds or challenges. You know, for us, for our warriors, battle was not about killing. It was about counting coup [touching an enemy in battle]. Battle was about showing bravery in the face of an enemy that had weapons and power. Oglala warriors, they stood their ground, they stood and fought in the face of danger. They stood and fought for what they believed in. So, when I saw you standing your ground, when I saw you following through on what you said you would do—even though it was difficult—that's when I thought I would want to honor you in this way."

Silence, and more rock-pushing with my feet.

––––––––––

Later that evening, I am alone atop the bluffs across the highway from Rosie's house. This is the place I always go when I am at Pine Ridge. It's the same spot I ran to after Danny gave me the bow, in honor of the buffalo hunt and in appreciation for sharing the meat with the tribe.

This is where I access my spirituality at Pine Ridge, alone with nature. Pine Ridge does not get truly sacred for me until I am done serving others. The first day or two that I am here is usually busy, meeting friends, looking at projects, and learning. It is only after those visits are complete that I really get to the core of what brings me to Pine Ridge. Alone, with the blowing grass, scattered pines, and low-rolling clouds, is where I break through and connect with the oneness of everything. It is where the spirits become accessible for me; or, perhaps more accurately, where I become accessible for them. The magic lives here—on the bluffs, on the hills above Singing Horse, on the buffalo flats of Wind Cave National Park, alone with the boulders and broken timber surrounding Devils Tower, or on the parade grounds of an abandoned fort.

The view from the bluffs, where I sit still, as if frozen in time.

Sometimes I feel like if you just watch things, just sit still and let the world exist in front of you—sometimes I swear that just for a second time freezes and the world pauses in its tilt. Just for a second. And if you somehow found a way to live in that second, then you would live forever.

—Lauren Oliver, *Pandemonium*

The sweat lodge was an amazing cultural experience. I was thoroughly into the "sweat" and felt extremely alive the entire time. My senses did not miss anything. Every smell, spark, chant, and billow of smoke was in slow motion for me last night. At the same time, no spirits revealed themselves directly to me in the lodge. I know the spirits came and that they revealed themselves to Medicine Man, but they did not reveal themselves to me.

Here, alone on the bluffs and surrounded by nature, this is where the spirits come to me. This is where I go to them. This is where the communion occurs.

The only true wisdom lives far from mankind,
out in the great loneliness.

—Igjugarjuk

The sun is heading toward the western horizon over a mat of gray clouds as the message comes to me. The message is simple: It is time to go home. It's time to bring the four revelations of my vision quest home, thus completing "The Hero's Journey" that Joseph Campbell wrote about and countless other humans across time have completed.

"You have what you need. Enjoy what you have."

"You have made your own trail.
You are your own person. Be at peace."

"You don't have to take care of everyone else
all the time. It is okay to do things just for you."

"We all have our own journey to make. Let those
around you make theirs. Let them come to you.
They know where you are."

As I sit alone on top of the bluffs in prayer and meditation, I think of Joseph Campbell once more and his description of the universal Hero's Journey that appears and reappears through all the world's mythologies:

> *The usual hero adventure begins with someone from whom something has been taken [like my own voice], or who feels there's something lacking in the normal experiences available or permitted to the members of his society. This person then takes off on a series of adventures beyond the ordinary, either to recover what has been lost or to discover some life-giving elixir. It is usually a cycle, a going and a returning.*

I will never forget the moment I read this passage. I was sitting in my office at home. I had already completed four trips to Pine Ridge. His book was written in 1949 and Joseph Campbell is dead. Yet, the story he was telling was my story. How was that possible? I put the book down and just pushed back in my chair. I stared silently for the longest time at the red, Pine Ridge blanket draped over the chair, opposite my desk. As I continued to read, the connections I felt only grew stronger.

> *The first work of the hero is to retreat from the world scene . . . to those casual zones of the psyche where the difficulties really reside, and there to clarify the difficulties, eradicate them in his own case and break through.*
>
> *That's the basic motif of the universal hero's journey—leaving one condition and finding the source of life to bring you forth into a richer or mature condition.*

Then, it struck me. Campbell wasn't writing about me individually, of course. He was writing about us collectively, about the universal human story. Furthermore, the story was not really about the external adventures in the outer world. Those were metaphors. The real story, Campbell wrote, was the inward journey that seeks to connect the conscious being to the conscious soul.

> *The ultimate mystery is right within you:*
> *You are it.*
>
> *You are the mystery that you are seeking to know.*

The bluffs above Manderson where the spirits live for me.

**The adventure that the hero is ready
for is the one he gets.**

—Joseph Campbell

The next morning Oki is nice enough to cook me breakfast, as Rosie has left early on business. Oki and I have a long conversation at the dining table about her past, my past, and Pine Ridge's past. There is no telling how long Oki will be at Singing Horse, and I'm not sure exactly when I will be back.

I find Catherine outside as I pack my car and prepare to depart. We hug and say good-bye.

From there, I make a final stop at Pinky's Store; it is always my last stop on the day I leave Pine Ridge. The white plastic table and chairs in the back of the store offer an endless opportunity for learning, and this morning is no exception.

People come and people go.

When it comes time for me to leave, Pinky walks me outside, as she always does. Many schoolchildren are gathered in and around the store this morning as they wait for the bus; today, they have a field trip to the circus that has come to Rapid City.

"We need people like you who know how we are and haven't given up on us" are Pinky's last words to me.

Pinky always seems to know what to say.

I love this picture of the hill above the Singing Horse Trading Post because you can see the two paths, the two choices, diverging before heading into the unknown. For me, this picture symbolizes the Seventh Power. We are all born into circumstances, but along the path of life there is much we can control.

Less than two hours after leaving Pinky, I am alone in Wind Cave National Park where I can feel my own spirituality in a calm but powerful way.

At the back edge of the buffalo flats, far away from the road, I lie on my stomach and watch the elk edge out into the open. Through my binoculars, I can see their breath. I lie still and watch them for the longest time. The grass is wet and a few ants are upon me. It all feels so natural. Eventually, I get to my feet and this brings the elk to attention.

The elk and I all stand frozen in place. They will not move. I will not move. They check the wind and the open flats quickly, but their eyes always return to me.

Eventually one moves, and soon they all are in motion.

When the last elk enters the forest, I walk out across the flats toward where they stood. Their smell is still fresh and it draws me down into the timber after them.

The elk stretched out across the open buffalo flats on the edge of the timber. I lay flat on my stomach and watched them watch me.

Once inside the forest, I find narrow trail after narrow trail. I follow one path that tightens considerably, as it descends deeper into the woods before finally reemerging back onto grasslands.

As I soon as I exit from the forest, I stop. The tree beside me has captured my attention. It is a thick, old pine. Twisted, yet sturdy, it stands out among the other less notable relatives surrounding it.

As I study the tree, a message comes to me in a manner similar to my vision quest that began on this very trail last fall. Like the other messages that have come my way, this one is simple yet powerful:

This is where my book ends.

I wasn't looking for an ending this morning any more than I was looking for a vision here last fall. While this message is small, the moment is big. It is the end of a transformational circle, and it makes me not want to take another step.

A pine tree stopped me in my tracks, I think to myself. *How symbolic.*

I came from the Pine Tree State of Maine and a lumber company, no less, to the often treeless Land of Crazy Horse. Here, deep in the Black Hills, a lone pine tree told me that my book was over.

Even though I have come to learn that all moments, in some mysterious way, preserve themselves, I still pull out my iPhone and record my precise location:

> • **Sunday, May 4, 2014**
> • **9:34 a.m. Mountain Standard Time**
> • **Facing due east**
> • **4,131 feet above sea level**
> • **43 32 09 north latitude**
> • **103 27 34 west longitude**

I have never done this before or since—recorded my spot to commemorate a moment in time.

Quickly, however, I realize this is an unnecessary exercise. Our stories don't end the way we think they do; they aren't that linear or precise. The past lives. I learned this from evolutionary astrology. I also experienced this at Pine Ridge.

Of course, a book must come to an end. But, stories . . . they endure across time, like the fossilized ruts of the Oregon Trail. Long after the lessons that bring us here have been learned (or not learned), the stories still endure.

"What brings you here?" the old jewelry maker asked me eighteen months ago.

At the time, I wasn't sure. I just knew I was searching . . . searching for something beyond my sight.

Well, now I know, and so do you. I was searching, both literally and spiritually, for my lost voice in the Land of Crazy Horse, a place I had been called to. You now know this too because I shared my story, just like Verola said we should do.

If we don't share our stories, they die with us . . .

Toksa Ake (See you later)!

This statue stands in the grove below the cemetery at the Red Cloud Indian School on the Pine Ridge Reservation.

> **I have asked some of the great white chiefs where they get their authority to say to the Indian that he shall stay in one place, while he sees white men going where they please. They cannot tell me.**
>
> **—Chief Joseph of the Nez Perce**

EPILOGUE
Reshaping the Grindstone

What started out as "two worlds" for me became one. If you back your view of your circle up far enough, it's all one planet. We are all related.

It is quiet at the Hancock Lumber office in Casco Village. It usually is on a Saturday morning.

My laptop is open and I am looking out my office windows onto a frozen Pleasant Lake. This is the third time this lake has frozen since I first stood at Wounded Knee. This lake makes a circle every year, no matter what happens in the rest of the world.

A balsam and cedar Yankee candle burns on the corner of my desk, its flame flickering in the gentle breeze created by the ceiling fan above. In the corner, an elk is mounted on the wall. He is turned to his left, neck extended and antlers back. On the windowsill stand two wooden carvings. One is of a Lakota woman with a lone eagle feather in her braided hair. The other is of a chief wearing a headdress, arms crossed. These carvings were created in celebration of the Hancock House, as Pinky calls it. They each made a complete circle from Casco to Pine Ridge and back, just like me.

Both carvings are a token of thanks for helping to build an "ownership home" at Pine Ridge, but I feel it is I who should be saying "thank you." Pine Ridge has given so much to me. It is hard to place a value on finding your true voice, the voice of your soul.

———————

Hancock Lumber began doing business in 1848, the same decade Crazy Horse was born. At the time, the Hancocks and the Oglala Sioux were worlds apart. In fact, neither knew the other existed.

For me now, however, Pine Ridge and Hancock Lumber will forever be linked. They both helped each other. This is as it should be. One global tribe with all participants linked, sharing resources, ideas, and time.

The two years that my book covers coincided with the best business performance in Hancock Lumber's history. Revenue growth was strong and records were set for accuracy, efficiency, and profitability. Our mill products were being sold all over the world, and we were named Maine's "Exporter of the Year." Most importantly to me, employee engagement (as defined by the people who work here) was so strong that Hancock Lumber was selected as one of Maine's "Best Places to Work"—an award only 70 companies, out of thousands in our state, received.

I gave a good bit of thought as to whether I would mention any of this. The Kevin Hancock that emerged from Pine Ridge doesn't need to reference the company's performance. Neither my ego, nor my role, holds me in that way anymore.

Ultimately, I chose to share this information because my book, in large part, is about the notion that serving yourself strengthens your tribe. Without this context, I worried that some might discard my Pine Ridge adventure as having come at the expense of "getting the job done." Anyone can "drop out" of society.

But, I didn't drop out; that's the whole point. You don't have to forsake one circle to join another. We have more room in our lives than we think.

From a health standpoint, I lost the consistent and comfortable use of my speaking voice. This hidden blessing forced me to reassess my management approach. I am not sure I would have done so otherwise. I might well have just kept busy until the work and my roles consumed me. Up to that point, my management philosophy had been more in line with traditional expectations. I made sure I worked the longest hours, presided over pivotal discussions, and made the key decisions.

After I lost my voice, talking in meetings all day with employees and customers was simply no longer possible. I had to delegate more, trust more, and share leadership more broadly. My body forced me to do this. The body knows, but we don't always listen.

Spasmodic dysphonia made me listen; yes, to others, but even more importantly, to myself. In a circle of irony, it took losing my speaking voice to find my soul's voice. Getting lost is the first step to being found.

In the years that followed the partial loss of my speaking voice, I began to see that my old management style was not optimal; it was just old. I began to see that there was a more powerful way to lead and manage, which involved restraint. The secret lay in doing less, not more.

"The boss gets first dibs on all the power in an organization," I said to Rosie one morning over breakfast at the Singing Horse Trading Post. The historically overbearing role of government at Pine Ridge is, in fact, an example.

As a leader, just because you "can" run every meeting doesn't mean you should. Just because you "can" make all the important decisions doesn't mean it is optimal. There is a great deal of power to be tapped in creating an organization where everybody leads . . . where everybody makes decisions . . . where everybody feels like they are in charge.

Not only was this new management approach a better way to lead, it was also a better way for me, as an individual, to live. I stopped seeing the business as a measuring stick for who I was and I started seeing the company as a place where all 425 members of our team could lead, take responsibility, and express themselves.

It's not that I think I was a bad manager before the onset of my voice disorder; I just feel I became a much better manager after losing my voice.

In my experience, this is what happens when a CEO loses his or her voice:

- *You listen more.*
- *You talk less.*
- *You ask more questions.*
- *You look at more data.*
- *You show more restraint.*
- *You let others run meetings.*
- *You don't break the silence.*
- *You share responsibility for representing the organization.*
- *You pick your spots carefully.*
- *You trust and empower others more completely.*

I have since jokingly said that all CEOs should lose their voice.

The new path I saw the company on inspired me. I saw supervisors, managers, and front-line employees grab all the available responsibility and run with it. Overall, they made better decisions than I would have, because they knew more about their specific areas of responsibility than I did. They took more ownership of results and initiatives because they saw their names clearly attached to the work. They had more enthusiasm, pride, and responsiveness because they felt trusted and safe. There is a big difference between performing tasks and owning your work.

I have seen that people get excited when they are trusted to make decisions, set goals, create budgets, and plan initiatives. Most people want the responsibility, risks, and rewards that come with their job, but only if the boss will truly let them own it.

My Pine Ridge adventures definitely made me a better leader, because they made me a healthier and more authentic person. I saw that I could pursue my own personal passions *and* become even more valuable to the company. I didn't have to choose between being myself and playing my role. In fact, just the opposite was true. The more I served myself, the better I performed at work. I am sure there was a good bit of luck and timing involved in our success as well, but Pine Ridge made both our company and me stronger.

Breaking out of the caretaker pattern felt risky to me at first. In going to Pine Ridge, I initially worried that people would think I was being selfish or distracted. We all feel pulled in some way to "stay in-line" and do what we perceive is expected of us. It is easy to blindly stay busy—nose to the grindstone—only working at the local level. This expectation has been built into the ethos of American capitalism's relentless pursuit of more.

"Stay focused."
"Stay disciplined."
"Come early."
"Leave late."
"Put your job before yourself, sacrifice."
"Grow revenue, grow profitability,
and expand shareholder value."
"Go . . . go . . . go! Bigger, better, more!"

These are the cheering chants of modern American business, for which the CEO is expected to lead the charge.

Thanks to evolutionary astrology, spasmodic dysphonia, and Pine Ridge, however, I found a new, less traveled path.

It can be scary to take the leap and think about what *you* really want. It is easier to say you are sacrificing your own needs for the benefit of others; but, as Malcom Gladwell's "inverted-U curve" suggests, this concept only works to a point. We all make sacrifices, but if the mountain of personal sacrifices is too tall, it will be detrimental to the individual—and, therefore, to the tribe as a whole. Before the coming of the Wasichu, the Lakota knew that the best way to create a healthy tribe was to encourage healthy individuals. In fact, this knowledge was so powerful, their people considered it sacred. The vision quest and the sweat lodge were both rituals designed to strengthen individual power and the pursuit of personal truth. Strong but generous warriors were the foundation of a healthy tribe.

Evolutionary astrology, spasmodic dysphonia, and Pine Ridge combined to help me rethink the very nature of business success. I no longer saw "victory" as a personal accomplishment. Instead, I came to see a thriving company as an objective that could enrich everyone's lives.

For years prior to my first visit to Pine Ridge, Hancock Lumber had been pursuing "lean" and "Six Sigma" efficiency initiatives, which were valuable to our company. The problem with this traditional path, however, is that most companies simply use the extra capacity created to just do more work. This seemed mathematically powerful, but spiritually empty to me. Over time, a fresh vision materialized in my mind regarding how to better utilize the expanded human capacity that efficiency improvements create. I have since come to describe this vision as the "higher calling of lean." This is a simple idea, a subtle shift in thinking. The essence of the notion is to use the benefits of productivity and accuracy improvements to do less, not more.

Repeatedly at Pine Ridge, I was reminded that subtle shifts in thinking can have life-altering implications.

Over a three-year period that surrounded my trips to Pine Ridge, we reduced the average work week at Hancock Lumber from 48 to 41 hours, while simultaneously increasing employee take-home pay. For salaried managers and the sales team, we set a new goal of keeping the work week to 50 hours. Employees used the efficiency gains they orchestrated to reduce the workplace stress that undisciplined systems previously created. In addition, we freed up time and emotional energy that people could now reinvest away from work. While taking great care of our customers, we set out to put the "work" back in its rightful place—an important, but not all-consuming, role.

This initiative was not a panacea. People continued to work hard, and every job in the company was still demanding. In some ways, the change was subtle. We invested more time in listening, without judging. We began talking about shared goals designed to benefit everyone. We created an incentive program we called "Performance Gold," which shared the financial benefits of safety, productivity, and accuracy improvements with every member of the team.

Having learned to reshape my own personal relationship with my job, I wanted everyone else to have the same opportunity.

My goal was to improve our business performance in order to expand capacity in our personal lives.

This became the new rallying cry for a lumber company from Maine.

At Hancock Lumber, we learned by listening. Through several years of employee surveys, focus groups, and team huddles, we came to understand that if team members strongly agreed with the seven statements above, they would be highly committed and effective leaders of the company's work.

My exposure to evolutionary astrology came before spasmodic dysphonia, and it played a leading role in changing how I saw myself, as well as those around me. Never again will I look at the puzzle of human existence without considering evolutionary astrology. The past lives for each of us in ways not traditionally imagined. The soul is the life force, the body, a vessel.

Each soul is here to transform, to grow; that is the purpose of incarnation. Unhealthy patterns are repeated until they are broken. Lessons are retaught until they are learned.

In the final months before finishing this book, I asked Deborah Dooley if an entire tribe or culture could share a single karmic pattern.

Deborah simply replied, "Yes."

Together, we decided to look at an evolutionary chart for the entire Oglala Sioux Tribe. We selected November 6, 1868, at Fort Laramie, Wyoming as the time and place of our experimental Lakota natal chart. On this day, the great Chief Red Cloud rode in with his warriors to sign the Fort Laramie Treaty, after destroying the forts on the Bozeman Trail.

When the chart was ready, Deborah and I spoke by phone; I sat at my desk in Casco and listened as she summarized the story it told.

In the chart, the position of Mars and Neptune combined with an abundance of Leo energy to guide her first comments:

> *There is some delusional thinking in this chart. Their entire way of seeing reality may, in fact, be somewhat distorted. The tribe is stuck in a historical paradigm that doesn't exist anymore. They want to go back to isolation and controlling the whole world around them, which is the delusional part. It is just setting themselves up for a continued sense of betrayal, victimization and anger because it's just not going to go back to the way things were.*

> *No tribe can go backwards. Imagine, for example, if the city of Rome tried to go backwards, saying it wanted to return to the days of the Roman Empire. Everyone would laugh. Or, Greece—what if Greece announced its intentions to restore its former empire? Who would take that seriously? You can't go backwards. It doesn't work that way. Writing and talking about themselves as a sovereign nation is just setting the community up for more betrayal because it can't happen in real life.*

Scorpio's position in the chart also revealed important aspects of the story Deborah explained:

Scorpio opposite Pluto and square Mars is about as violent as it comes.

The low end of Scorpio is someone who holds on to grudges and resentment for extended, unhealthy periods of time.

There is a lot of dogma in this chart, even arrogance. I mean, there may be a strong feeling that their culture and their dogma are superior. There is a false sense of power in this chart.

Deborah concluded her reading by describing the transformation that would be required for these multigenerational patterns to be released:

The change that needs to come resides at the individual level, not the tribal level. Individuals need to seek their own true power in order to release themselves from the chart's repetitive patterns. The change that is required, well, that needs to happen on the inside, but all their focus goes toward the injustice they see on the outside. As a result, the personal transformations that need to occur are blocked.

That's the Seventh Power she is describing, I thought to myself.

External forces, in fact, created the original conditions of oppression at Pine Ridge. The power to break free from those conditions, however, must come from within, from the Seventh Power that lives within us all.

As with my own personal chart reading years before, Deborah's soft voice told a powerful story. It all felt a bit overwhelming and harsh for me to hear at first, but then I remembered I had been there myself. Years earlier, I had sat alone and listened to the cold reality of the story my own natal chart told. In hindsight, that moment marked the beginning of my awakening. My first all-important step was to become fully aware of my present condition. Self-awareness is the prerequisite for growth.

At first glance, evolutionary astrology is easy to dismiss, but so is Noah's Ark and the coming of the White Buffalo Calf Woman. I have come to believe that thinking we know how it all works is a silly position to take.

Later that night in Casco (after the phone call with Deborah), I am watching the Disney movie *Frozen* with Sydney. Even though Sydney is now in college, it might be her favorite movie, and I understand why. The movie has all the ingredients Joseph Campbell identified in the universal story of humanity, "The Hero's Journey": separation, initiation, and return.

"An act of true love can thaw a frozen heart," Olaf the snowman whispers with wide eyes, as the story reaches its epic climax.

Princess Anna had been told that only love from another could save her life, that the mythical kiss from a prince was required. In the movie's culminating scene, however, Anna performs her own act of true love by throwing herself under the blade of a striking sword aimed at her sister, Elsa. At that very moment, Anna turns to ice and it appears that the curse has consumed her. Soon, however, Anna begins to thaw; in saving her sister, she had actually broken her own spell. As it turns out, Anna held the power to set herself free. Another had cast a spell on her, but she held the power within herself to break it.

As the movie ends, Sydney turns to me and says, "Dad, she saved herself. Anna saved herself."

That's the Seventh Power again, I thought.

Anna had been told that others "out there," beyond her control, held the power to heal her. Her salvation resided inside her all along, however. She was the power she was seeking.

Sydney's innocent yet powerfully intuitive statement makes me think about Pine Ridge, and then, about my own voice. Despite what I had been told upon diagnosis, my voice had recently begun to improve.

"You have to do the spiritual work first," Connie Pike had told me from her Florida home office.

During my first year traveling to Pine Ridge, my voice had definitely not improved. That year, I returned to Mass Eye and Ear in Boston six times for injections, averaging 2.0 ml of Botox per visit. Many of those shots were "boosters," as the original injection had had no positive effect. Dr. Song was great to me and I felt like I was getting the best possible care. Something more than Botox was going to be required, however. While I had actively begun to serve myself that year, I had not yet fully connected the dots between that activity and my health. The healing process needed more time.

I went off Botox completely for the first five months of the following year to prepare for my visit with Connie Pike. In the weeks leading up to that first therapy session, my voice was as bad as it had ever been. It was a major task to speak. My throat hurt all the time when I talked.

Slowly, however, something began to change in the second half of the year. I didn't really notice until it had happened. I took a small dose of Botox in July (1.0 ml) and my voice immediately improved (like, that same day). That fall, my voice initially deteriorated as the Botox wore off, but then I was able to regain good voice quality on my own. Later that year, before Christmas, I took another small 1.0 ml injection and got the same instant results.

During the first year I traveled to Pine Ridge, I received 12.0 ml of Botox. That year, my voice was a constant struggle. The second year I traveled to Pine Ridge, I received 2.0 ml of Botox and felt much less restricted. My drug intake reduced by over 80 percent, and yet I had improved my voice. Actually, it all tipped when I stopped thinking about it so much, when I let my soul and body do the work, without excessive interference from my brain. By now, I had calmed myself on the inside and I feel certain this softened the symptoms of SD. In addition, as Deborah Dooley had encouraged me to do, I had spent considerable time without the Botox. I learned to place my consciousness in my throat (on a pinpoint, to be exact), at the precise source of the constraint. I had actually located the exact spot within my throat where the tension resided and I would just put my thoughts there.

I am definitely not cured, but I feel much less constricted and considerably improved. I made the transition from others being responsible for treating my condition to treating myself. The Botox went from being the primary source of relief to a tactical tool, sparingly used.

Connie uses a "voice index handicap" survey from the University of Pittsburgh Medical Center to help her patients analyze their own voice. The higher the score, the worse the handicap. I completed the self-guided, multiple-choice questionnaire three times during the year I finished this book. My score dropped (that is to say, it improved) from 88 to 51 to 32. A score above 80 is considered to be a severe speech handicap. A score below 30 is considered to be a non-handicap. Increasingly, I felt "Free to Speak." In more ways than one I had found my voice, alone on the northern plains, in the Land of Crazy Horse.

Everything began to tip for me when I slowed down, served myself, and found my center.

I will never forget bringing Alison to Pine Ridge, about a year before this book was complete. It was my sixth trip, but her first, and I was excited to share this "new" world with her. It was a cold and rainy September day, nearly snowing. We had stayed in Cheyenne the night before. On the way to Pine Ridge, we stopped at Register Cliffs, the Oregon Trail Ruts, Fort Laramie, and Fort Robinson. As we entered the reservation, we drove slowly through White Clay, where the essence of the reservation's challenge reveals itself. After White Clay, I showed Alison the Hancock House. By now, the house completely blended into the neighborhood. Next, the most important purpose of visiting: It was time for Alison to meet my friends.

I opened the screen door to the OST Partnership for Housing office, held it ajar for Alison, and in she went. Rosemarie and Lester were both there. Rosemarie walked right over to Alison and gave her a big hug and then a gift, a beautiful pair of Lakota earrings.

That's Pine Ridge, I thought to myself. *It's a place for the big-hearted.*

We would go on to meet all my Pine Ridge friends. Everyone embraced Alison as one of their own. We walked the fence lines above Singing Horse and sat on the bluffs across the highway. We ate hearty breakfasts with Rosie, philosophized with Nick, and sat with Pinky in the back of her store. We even went to a special powwow honoring the fiftieth anniversary of Billy Mills's Olympic gold medal in the 10,000-meter run.

At the conclusion of the powwow ceremony, Billy spoke. At the gathering, he confided that originally he wasn't sure he'd try out for the Olympic team. For some time, he labored over his path, until he finally asked a group of tribal elders for advice.

"The tribal elders told me I should compete. They said if I honored myself, I would honor my tribe."

When we strengthen ourselves, we strengthen our tribe, I whispered to myself. Billy Mills had just summarized my book in one sentence. I looked around the tightly packed bingo hall to see if his message had caught the crowd. I couldn't tell.

After leaving Pine Ridge, we hiked in Wind Cave National Park, climbed Harney Peak, visited Devils Tower, stood at Fort Phil Kearny, and retraced the Battle of Little Bighorn.

We ended our trip hiking in Yellowstone and Grand Teton National Parks. In Yellowstone, we stayed at Grant Village where I had worked cleaning hotel rooms nearly thirty years before. That night, once again, I had another vivid and dramatic dream involving my dad. Here is how I described the dream to Deborah Dooley a few weeks later:

> *I am at a big, new house. I sense it is our house, even though I don't recognize it. It is nice, but very poorly designed and exceptionally cluttered with stuff.*
>
> *I am in the garage. I can hear other people in the house, but I can't see them. There are no cars in the garage because it is jam-packed with boxes, furniture, and household items we don't seem to need.*
>
> *Suddenly, my dad shows up. He looks very happy.*
>
> *I say, "Dad, we should really clean this place out . . . get rid of stuff . . . so that we can park cars in here."*
>
> *He seems to think that this is a good idea and then disappears.*
>
> *While picking up boxes, a laminated document accidentally falls out. It hits the garage floor and rips apart, splitting in two. When I pick up the pieces, I can see it is a letter from my dad. I am somehow able to lay it back together perfectly so that all the words he has written are aligned. Now, I can clearly see that this letter is written in my dad's distinctive style of cursive handwriting; I see his writing so clearly. The page I am looking at is the end of the letter, the part where he signs off with his unique signature.*

At that moment, I wake up. It is 7:25 a.m. Mountain Time. Just a short distance off in the forest, a lone bull elk is bugling outside my open window, right near the same hotel building I used to clean as a college student, right where my journey west began nearly thirty years ago.

For me, the dream symbolizes the "family house," and the clutter represents the work and loss of personal identity that can be associated with running a complex family business. I feel this might have been an issue for my dad. I know this was an issue for me. In acquiring SD and traveling to Pine Ridge, I was transcending the clutter, putting the work role back in its place. This made my dad happy not just for me, but also for himself. Releasing me released him in some way, as well. I had—*we* had—reached a turning point, and he was signing off, moving on to other things. There was an energy field here that my dad and I shared, connected to losing ourselves in our role; somehow, my growth was his growth, and vice versa. This would not surprise the Lakota; they know we are all related.

––––––––

During the trip with Alison, I read two more books, both of which I had purchased earlier that summer while visiting Abby. The first book was a *New York Times* bestseller titled, *Many Lives, Many Masters* by Brian Weiss. The book chronicles his therapy sessions with a client suffering from extreme anxiety, phobias, and a lack of sleep. Dr. Weiss, then an empirical leader in his field, hypnotized his patient for the purpose of bringing her back to her childhood to find the root cause of her psychological discomfort. His patient, however, went back beyond this childhood, into past lives. Over a period of years, Dr. Weiss and his patient, Catherine, would visit multiple past lives (she could recount eighty-three in all), where she would find and release the originating sources of her anxiety. Even more insightful, Catherine was able to recall the periods between lives, the process of dying, resting, and returning. During her "between life" experiences, the "Great Spirits" spoke directly to Dr. Weiss through Catherine (while hypnotized) and revealed the essence of the journey all souls make across multiple lifetimes:

> *We have debts that must be paid. If we have not paid out these debts, then we must take them into another life . . . in order that they may be worked through. You progress by paying your debts. Some souls progress faster than others. When you're in physical form and you are working through, you're working through a life . . . if something interrupts your ability to pay that debt, you must return to the plane of recollection, and there you must wait until the soul you owe the debt to has come to see you. And when you both can be returned to physical form at the same time, then you are allowed to return. But, you determine when you are going back. You determine what must be done to pay that debt. You will not remember your other lives, only the one you have just come from. Only those souls on the higher level—the sages—are allowed to call upon history and past events . . . to help us, to teach us what we must do.*

The book's messages mirrored what Deborah Dooley had taught me during my own natal chart reading, over five years ago. It may all seem far-fetched, but it's not. The world is full of stories like Catherine's, and once I had awakened to a new set of possibilities, I could see them all around me.

The second book I read was *The Dove in the Stone* by Alice O. Howell. At the time of publishing her book, Alice had made nine visits to the Scottish isle of Iona, a place long seen as holding great spiritual power in early Christianity. Alice is sure she had a past life experience there; the pull of this one place is so powerful for her that she keeps going back to sit alone with the rocks, birds, wind, fog, church bells, and crashing waves. Her story was my story, and I couldn't put it down. It reminded me so much of the irresistible calling I felt toward Pine Ridge, and it helped me to see that I was not alone.

Her writing tells us that the sacred lives in the commonplace, if we can only learn to see it:

> **"There is another world, but it is hidden in this one."**

To see that world, we need but slow down.

To see that world, we need but reject "busyness" and embrace nature.

To see that world, we need but look inward.

But, looking inward can be scary. It feels safer to stay consumed with the external noise. To illustrate this, Alice shares one of her favorite tales; it is the story of the Mullah who has lost his keys:

> **Well, one day a friend found Mullah hunting for something outside his house. He was poking under bushes and stones, when the friend queried, "Hey, Mullah, what have you lost?"**
>
> **"I've lost my keys!" cried Mullah.**
>
> **Kindly, the friend joined in what soon proved to be a fruitless scrabbling. "Can't you remember at all where you lost them?"**

Mullah looked up. "Sure," he said, "I know exactly where I lost them. I lost them in the house."

"Then, why on earth are you looking for them out here?"

"Because I can see better—it's so much lighter out here!" the Mullah replied.

Alice summarizes the moral of this short fable with a simple question:

Don't we all do that—look around outside for the keys we have lost inside us?

I was so moved by Alice's book that I actually tracked her down and called her. I wanted to thank her and share my own story of returning time and again to my own sacred place that had been calling to me. Alice was now ninety-two years old and in failing health. As it turned out, within a few weeks of my call, she passed on. I may have been one of the last people to thank her for sharing her story, and it happened on the eve of sharing my own.

On the last night of our trip, Alison and I are playing pool at the Million Dollar Cowboy Bar in Jackson Hole, where she wins two out of three games (ouch!). It is a wonderful scene. Silver dollars line the bar and guests sit in saddles. College football games are playing on every television, as people dance to country music in the back. Near our table, there is a giant grizzly bear stuffed and mounted in a glass case. The plaque below the bear reads:

This bear was taken by world-famous hunter and hunting guide, C. Dale Petersen of Jackson Hole, Wyoming. It is one of only two grizzlies know to have been killed without the use of modern weaponry.

Verified by game biologists, Mr. Petersen killed this bear with his hands and, oddly enough, his teeth. It is known that this bear had been aggravated by a group of backpackers. Shortly thereafter, Petersen,

unaware of previous happenings, came upon the bear. A fight-to-the-death ensued. Petersen, having his right hand and arm wedged in the bear's throat, actually used his own teeth and jaws to pinch off the bear's jugular vein. When the bear passed out from lack of blood flow to the brain, Petersen beat the bear upon the head with a stick.

Fact and fiction blur in the American West, and this is part of why I love it so!

————————

My ability to see the sacred in the commonplace continues to grow. The aspens of the Tetons were bright yellow on this trip, and I was able to see them dancing and waving. Toward the end of our journey, I was starting to look at people and, odd as this may sound, see their souls. By this, I mean I could actually glimpse the energy force of the person and gain a sense of what that force was about. Once again, this is not as mystical as it may sound, and I believe most anyone could learn to do it. Once you reorient yourself to understand that a person's body is a vessel and the soul, the essence, you begin to see people differently.

Late that night, after beer and pool at the Million Dollar Cowboy Bar, we returned to our rustic condo. When we got out of the SUV, I stood frozen for a moment looking at a tall tepee lit from within, across the road in the wild grass. It looked warm and inviting. We had been here for three nights and I had not noticed it before, which struck me as odd. Nevertheless, we went inside our condo and began to pack for our return home.

"I'm going outside for a short walk," I said to Alison, after I finished organizing my gear.

I grabbed my flashlight and left in my sweats and bare feet. I felt called to take a closer look at the alluring tepee.

When I got to the road, I was confused. I stood there for a moment looking around, searching the grass with my flashlight. I could no longer find the tepee I had stared at moments ago. It wasn't there.

This made me smile, and I turned to walk back inside.

Just when we think we know what is going on, we are reminded that we always have so much to learn, I thought to myself as I reentered our room and closed the door.

It was time to go home.

Left to right: Me, Sydney, Abby, and Alison years ago in the Canadian Rockies. I would share my attraction to the American West with my family, as we vacationed there several times.

All this lasted a long time, or a short time.
For properly speaking, there is no time on earth.

—Friedrich Nietzsche

SUGGESTIONS

In the very last week of writing this book, my daughter Abby sent me a link to a story from Africa. The Tanzanian government was preparing to forcibly remove the Maasai tribe from their ancestral homeland, to make way for the creation of a luxury hunting preserve. Despite the fact that the government had previously promised to protect Maasai tribal lands "forever," the tribe's future was now at stake.

> *This is the worst kind of betrayal ever. The government's promises are clearly worth nothing. They said our lands were safe—the lands where the Maasai have lived and died for generations—but now they are going to take them from us, and sell them to rich royals from overseas who want to come and slaughter animals. We will never accept this deal. Our land is not for sale.*

—Ole Kulinga (Maasai tribal elder)

Below the link to the story, Abby wrote:

> *Different continent, different culture . . . BUT, the same thing that happened in the American West. People are always trying to preserve their culture and practices, but there is always a force of oppression that feels entitled to take what is not theirs. These examples are all related, just under different circumstances. Note the paragraph where the Maasai elder says "Our land is not for sale!" This is a universal and important story you are telling that is multigenerational and cross-cultural . . . think BIGGER picture here . . . your story is relatable even to cultures you may not have known existed.*

The story of Pine Ridge is not isolated, it's global. This is why I feel "Free to Speak" about it. In the modern Lakota world, there is a school of thought that suggests only "Indians can speak for Indians." I understand this perspective and wish to respect it. At the same time, what I see at Pine Ridge is a global, human story to which we all belong. Sticking to the narrow needs of our own local tribes only extends the problems. Tribalism needs to be respected, yet transcended. We are all related.

When people first heard of my trips to Pine Ridge, they would often ask, "What's the solution? How do you fix it?"

I was always reluctant to answer these questions directly; instead, I identified my goal as simply increasing awareness. "We all have our own journey to make," I would often say.

Still, it would be impossible to spend as much time at Pine Ridge as I have and not think about how to help make things better. The truth is, I have given the challenges significant thought, and, if asked, I would suggest the following:

If you live at Pine Ridge, you can be the sole owner of your property.

If I could modify the rules that govern Pine Ridge, I would begin by having the federal government initiate a thoughtful transition toward removing all the liens they have on private land there.

The original purpose of joint ownership was to protect the Oglala Sioux from being swindled out of their property in the decades that followed allotment. Today, over 125 years later, many of these parcels are still "held in trust" by the federal government. The problem with this shared land ownership system is that it perpetuates government paternalism and continued segregation, while inhibiting deeper levels of personal freedom and individual responsibility.

Many people at Pine Ridge might well dislike this idea. The fear, perhaps, is that tribal lands might be purchased by non-Lakota "outsiders." If the argument is that the federal liens on individual land parcels are necessary to keep acreage in Lakota hands (to keep Pine Ridge segregated), this raises further questions. How does it all reconcile with the fact that "we are all related"?

If nothing else, it would be healthy to reevaluate and reaffirm the purpose of federal liens on individual land parcels in the twenty-first century.

It would be healthy to consider what would happen if private property rights were strengthened at Pine Ridge.

If you live at Pine Ridge and you are twenty-one years old, you can drink alcohol.

During my visits to Pine Ridge, the tribe voted to end the reservation-wide ban on alcohol. Implementation will likely take years.

This topic is controversial on the reservation because alcohol abuse has negatively impacted so many lives and families. At the same time, the ban on alcohol is another highly visible reminder that the people here are not to be trusted with the same individual freedoms as other Americans. You can drink in Rapid City and you can drink in the Black Hills, but you can't drink at Pine Ridge.

Prohibition has historically failed wherever it has been applied, because the ultimate discipline to manage alcohol can only come from within.

If you live at Pine Ridge, you can vote here.

If I could only encourage one change, it would be this: If you live here, you can vote here.

That's a simple statement, but full of political complexity at Pine Ridge.

If you live in Maine, you can vote in Maine. If you live in Casco, you can vote in Casco. It doesn't work that way at Pine Ridge.

Article II of the Oglala Constitution defines tribal membership as being automatic when:

> **(a) The person's name appears on the official roll of the Oglala Sioux Tribe of the Pine Ridge Reservation as of April 1, 1935; or, if the person's name appears on any correction made within five years after the adoption of the Constitution [January 1936].**

Or

> **(b) A child is born to any member of the Oglala Sioux Tribe.**

Article VII of the Constitution covers elections and simply reads as follows:

> **Section 1. All members of the Tribe eighteen years or over, who have resided on the reservation for a period of one year immediately prior to any election, shall have the right to vote.**

The result of this highly protective membership criteria is exclusivity. At Pine Ridge, it is not enough to be Native American. It is not enough to be Sioux. It is not even enough to be Lakota. You must be Oglala to have a political stake in this community. You can live here if you are not Oglala, but you can't vote. Like many modern political traditions at Pine Ridge, there may have been a time when this exclusive voting system made sense, but it is hard to believe that exclusivity is the best path for all time.

So, my friend Rosie can't vote here because she was not born Oglala. She lives here, she creates jobs here, she helps neighbors here, but she can't vote here.

My friend Danny can't vote here because he was born Comanche. Danny lives here, Danny works here, Danny helps people here, but Danny can't vote here.

My friend Buck can't vote here because he is Seminole. Buck lives here, Buck works here, Buck raises a family here, but Buck can't vote here.

My friend Catherine can't vote here. Catherine lives here and helps send her grandson to school here, but Catherine is not Oglala. In fact, she is not Lakota. She is Dakota from the Pabaksa or Cuthead band of Upper Yanktonais; and, as a result, Catherine can't vote here.

When I started traveling to Pine Ridge, there were lots of things I saw that did not surprise me, but the high degree of tribal exclusivity did surprise me. I did not expect to see that the very people who had been politically excluded had become politically exclusive themselves.

It is ironic that Pine Ridge has such exclusive property and voting rights, yet people still wonder why they are so isolated. The answer, in part, is that the rules are set up to perpetuate segregation.

―――――――

The net proceeds from the federal parks and monuments on former tribal lands should be paid to the Sioux.

The Mount Rushmore National Memorial attracts close to three million visitors a year. Entrance is "free," but parking costs $11 per car and $50 per bus. The Devils Tower National Monument has approximately 400,000 visitors annually, and the entrance fee is $10 per car and $100 per full-size bus. The Department of the Interior is responsible for the

National Park Service and for the Bureau of Indian Affairs. It's not right to charge parking and access fees on these public lands that were illegally taken from the Sioux, *and*, simultaneously have an ongoing economic catastrophe taking place on the reservations where northern plains tribes were forcibly relocated.

These funds should be used to increase federal support for the northern plains reservations.

————

The Lakota should take the money from the Black Hills land settlement.

It is hard for me to say this because my heart is with the Lakota people and I love the principles they stand on in refusing the funds. But I think they should take the settlement awarded by the Supreme Court in 1980, now valued at well over a billion dollars. To not take the money is to remain in the past.

Emotions may understandably cause some to ignore the details of the 1980 Supreme Court ruling. The court ruled that tribal lands were taken without just compensation and that this was unconstitutional; but, the court also ruled that the federal government, as trustee for the Lakota, did in fact have jurisdiction to take tribal lands, as long as there was fair compensation in return.

In other words, the 1980 Supreme Court ruling did not state that the land taking could not occur. The Court simply demanded that the tribes be compensated.

Taking the money puts those financial assets to work for the individual members of the tribe. More importantly, perhaps, it closes a sorry chapter of the past and moves the people forward.

————

The sacred rite of the vision quest should live on.

There is no amount of government care that will fix things at Pine Ridge. Only the power of the individual—only the Seventh Power—will allow the Oglala Sioux Tribe to retake its place on the good red road. When government was small and the individual was strong, the Lakota flourished. In this way, the past shows the way forward.

For me, the vision quest symbolizes the importance of each individual tribe member seeking his or her own personal sense of power and purpose.

I believe the vision quest is more powerful for the future of Pine Ridge than government. Government will always be important, but it needs to become less important. It needs to be put back in its place, just like the work needed to be put back in its place for me at Hancock Lumber. The power needs to go back to the people, one soul at a time.

"Think about what's next," Pinky once instructed me.

Strategic planning is important to any organization, but essential to one in crisis or transition. Pine Ridge, it might be fairly said, is in both.

I would love to see the people of Pine Ridge engage in a thoughtful strategic dialogue about the future of their community. The "Rez" was created in the second half of the nineteenth century under a dramatically different set of circumstances than exists today.

I have learned from spasmodic dysphonia that questions are more powerful than answers.

As the Oglala Sioux look to the next one hundred years, what should Pine Ridge look like?

What should the purpose of a "reservation" be in 2025? In 2050? In 2100?

What set of rules and laws would best support a journey to fulfill that vision?

Of course, what's next at Pine Ridge is up to the Oglala Sioux. It is not my journey to restructure Pine Ridge. At the same time, I do care about Pine Ridge and the people who live there. I want them to recover and prosper.

As Americans, we should all take an interest in every corner of our nation that has been left behind. In the case of Native peoples, we should back up and look at what really occurred on the way to creating a great nation. Columbus did not discover a new world. People already lived here.

We need to revisit the fact that the original people who lived here are now statistically the poorest. "First to worst"—that's how the people of Pine Ridge describe their journey through American history. We need to ask ourselves some hard questions, as well.

Have we done enough to make things right?

Are we satisfied with our effort to support a transition to economic independence for Native peoples?

Are we satisfied with the attention and respect we are dedicating to the poorest places in our country?

When I listened to Deborah Dooley read my natal chart for the first time, I was forced to take on some hard questions of my own. It would have been easy for me to ignore those questions, to push them off to the side and stay "busy."

I know I would not have grown, however, if I were not willing to sit alone with the strategic questions that faced me. Tough questions face the Lakota today, but I believe the people are ready to address them.

The only thing riskier than facing tough questions is avoiding them.

Holding on can feel safer than letting go. I know this to be true.

The pull of the past is strong, but it can be transcended.

Thank you for considering my thoughts. Wopila Tanka!

**There is no present or future, only the past,
happening over and over again, now.**

—Eugene O'Neill, *A Moon for the Misbegotten*

APPENDIX

The year I completed this book, *Timber Processing* magazine recognized me as the forest products industry's national "Person of the Year." I would like to share the article with you to give you a bit more insight into my tribe. Also, I hope you can see through this article, how my Pine Ridge learning translated into our company's modern story. I hope you can see how two worlds became one for me.

OUR MAINE MAN

By
Jay Donnell

Kevin Hancock is *Timber Processing's* 26th Annual Man of the Year (and the second from his family).

CASCO, Maine

ancock Lumber has been a staple in New England since 1848 and the sixth generation, family owned business has grown into one of America's oldest and most distinguished lumber companies. The company owns and manages more than 12,000 acres of timberland in western Maine, operates three eastern white pine sawmills in Casco, Pittsfield and Bethel and 10 contractor-oriented lumberyards in Maine and New Hampshire. Hancock Lumber stands out as a local, independent Maine company in an age of global giants and the company takes pride in helping out the community.

President Kevin Hancock, age 47, also takes pride in the business he took over after his father passed away and believes the success of Hancock Lumber is due to its ability to adapt to new ideas and technologies. "For an organization to function successfully for a long period of time, the skill that it acquires is actually the ability to change," Hancock says. "The business model that one generation used successfully is likely not going to work or even be totally relevant a generation later and our sawmill business today is a good example of that."

Among the many changes Hancock Lumber has undergone through the years, the single biggest change is the way it sells lumber. When Kevin started in the business the company followed the conventional model of manufacturing lumber and then selling it, but that model has been turned inside out. Today, the operating model starts with the customer. "We want to be a manufacturer that customizes products for individual customers. We're not about making products for the market, we're about making products for specific customers," Hancock says.

In 2012, Hancock Lumber implemented its "Every Board Counts" campaign based on feedback from a company-wide survey in which the employees expressed a desire to better understand who the customer is behind every board. As a part of this opportunity to learn more directly from the customers and understanding how to make every board count, Hancock Lumber invited customers to the mills and asked them to make presentations to all of the sawmill employees. This provided the employees at Hancock an opportunity to learn about customer needs directly from the customers themselves. "We might sell our products by the truck load but our customers use our products one board at a time. That's why every board needs to count," Hancock says.

Hancock emphasizes that the part of his job that gives him the most satisfaction is interacting with the 420 people that work at the company. "I really like the people who work here and I don't just see them as employees or workers, I see them as people. I enjoy them as people and I understand that their job doesn't totally represent who they are," he says.

The largest of the three sawmills is the one in Bethel. About 40% of the total production comes from Bethel and around 60% from the mills in Casco and Pittsfield. Production dipped down a little bit at the beginning of the recession, but when the company opened up some export markets production picked back up and Hancock will sell about 79MMBF of eastern white pine in 2014. "We have invested a lot of time asking our customers what characteristics in a pine board would thrill them in their market and then we go back and figure out how to make that for them," Hancock says. "We have flipped the value stream of the business completely inside out. If there is one concept that dominates our business today, it's that we're customer centric."

Because of his leadership at Hancock Lumber and his active social participation, Kevin Hancock is named *Timber Processing*'s 26th Man of the Year. The honor is not foreign to Hancock Lumber. Kevin's dad, the late David Hancock, received the second annual award in 1990.

Running three sawmills is an extremely difficult task and it is important to have a strong balance sheet according to Hancock. "You have to have a financially healthy company with a bit of a conservative orientation to be able to weather some of the things that come your way," he says.

Hancock is quick to give credit to all the people on the Hancock team including CFO Kevin Hynes, Casco Mill GM Mike Shane, Bethel Mill GM Russell Coulter and Pittsfield Mill GM Dennis Verrill. Matt Duprey and Jack Bowen are VP of Sales, Wayne Huck is in charge of scheduling & production, the HR direc-

Hancock Lumber implemented its "Every Board Counts" campaign in 2012.

Hancock Lumber will sell about 79MMBF in 2014.

tor is Wendy Scribner. Erin Plummer is the head of marketing and communications and Glen Albee is CFO.

COMMUNITY

Kevin Hancock believes that functioning profitably is the single biggest contribution a company can make to its community, thus creating jobs, sustaining jobs and allowing people to grow their income.

The company also gets involved with various causes, one of which is Camp Sunshine, a world renowned camp in Casco for children with life threatening illnesses. Hancock reports that his business contributed $15,000 to Camp Sunshine in 2013. "One of their big fundraisers is their annual pumpkin festival in

which they invite individuals, schools and community groups from across Maine to carve pumpkins. They've been close to actually setting the Guinness world record for having the most jack-o'-lanterns in one place at a time," Hancock says.

Hancock Lumber, the Maine Education Assn. and the local ABC affiliate recently joined forces to co-sponsor the Rise Up Against Bullying campaign, designed to discourage bullying in schools in southern Maine.

Over the last year, Hancock has been working on affordable housing issues on the Pine Ridge Indian Reservation in the southwest corner of South Dakota, which is home to the Oglala Sioux tribe. Pine Ridge, statistically, is the poorest place in America. Over the summer, Hancock pro-

IN THE MILLS

Hancock Lumber anticipates its three eastern white pine sawmills will produce 79MMBF combined in 2014, with the Bethel mill leading the way with 34MMBF. Nearly all of production is 1 in. x 2 in. to 12 in., x 4 ft. to 16 ft.

The Bethel mill became the company's third sawmill in 2000, when Hancock Lumber purchased it from family-owned P. H. Chadbourne, Inc. The company's first sawmill at Casco was converted to stationary from portable in the 1930s. Hancock Lumber built the sawmill at Pittsfield in 1985.

The Bethel mill is the company's largest sawmill.

The three mills have similar setups, each running Nicholson 35 in. debarkers and Esterer sash gangs for example. All three operate

Production is geared to customer needs.

double cut 7 ft. headrigs, with Bethel and Pittsfield operating Cleereman carriages and Casco running a Corley carriage, all 42 in.

The Bethel mill also runs a PHL rotary gang, Salem 6 ft. horizontal resaw, Newnes (USNR) edger, trimmer, sorter and stacker.

In November the Bethel mill installed new edger optimization and grade scanning from Baxley Equipment and also Baxley's cut-in-two (crosscut) technology prior to the edger infeed.

The Casco and Pittsfield mills run Autolog edger optimization, and both run PHL edgers and trimmers. Casco also runs a PHL 5 ft. horizontal resaw.

The mills run a mix of saw filing equipment from Wright Machine and Armstrong, as well as Simonds levelers.

All three mills operate with wood-fired boilers (Hurst at Bethel, and Industrial at Casco and Pittsfield). Each mill runs Irvington-Moore (USNR) kilns, while Bethel also operate an American Wood Dryer kiln and Casco runs a Wellons kiln. USNR and Wellons provided kiln controls.

The Bethel and Pittsfield mills run Coastal and PHL planers, respectively, each 20 knife at 3600 RPM, while the upgraded Casco planer mill operates a Weinig 14 knife planer at 6000 RPM. **TP**

vided all the materials necessary to build a home on the reservation and those involved there refer to it as the "Hancock House." It was the only new home built there in 2013. The estimated housing need for the reservation is as many as 4,000 homes. "The housing needs there are dramatic and our country has kind of forgotten about the people that live there," Hancock says.

The reservation covers 2.2 million acres. "I've always been a lover of history. For years I have been really interested in the plains Indians and was curious about what modern day life was like on the reservations so in the fall of 2012 I went to see for myself," Hancock says. "I've since become involved in helping them with housing issues and I have a lot of friends there today."

Kevin is writing a book about the history of the Oglala Sioux tribe and modern day life at Pine Ridge.

Also in 2013, Hancock Lumber and its vendors donated all the building materials to the restoration efforts of the historic coastal landmark, Cuckolds Lighthouse, in Boothbay Harbor.

Hancock Lumber has also made contributions to The Children's Museum & Theater of Maine, Coastal Maine Botanical Gardens, Friends of the Casco Community Center, Habitat for Humanity and many other groups.

COMPANY

Growing up as the sixth generation of family members involved in one of southern Maine's most successful businesses was not a stifling experience for Kevin or his brother, Matt. Instead, they received support from their parents to explore other interests and develop an identity separate from the lumber business.

Kevin graduated from Bowdoin College in 1988 with a BA in history and he has worked for Hancock Lumber since 1991, and currently serves as president and CEO of both Hancock Lumber Company, Inc. and Hancock Land Company. Kevin began his career on the sales counter at the Yarmouth store and worked his way up, becoming president in 1999.

Kevin's father, David Hancock, died at age 54. Kevin credits his dad, his mom and all the members of the Hancock team past and present for the success of the company. "I had no real formal training in business. Most of what I have learned I learned from trial and error." Through the years, Kevin emphasizes, he has learned that you have to work hard and treat all employees as important people and trust in them. "I learned that you have to be resilient because business is more of a marathon than it is a sprint and you have to be willing to learn from your mistakes and you have to be willing to adjust," he says. "I also believe that you need to be yourself. It is important to be sincere and authentic because that's what people value and appreciate."

Kevin has two daughters who both play college basketball and he played college basketball at Bowdoin College. He believes his sports background has helped him in the business world. "To be successful in sports you have to be disciplined, you have to be competitive, you have to be team oriented. You have to be able to take a deep breath and dust yourself off when you stumble. All of those things are relative in business," Hancock says.

Kevin points to three things that have allowed Hancock Lumber to remain competitive in today's world. First, continuing to hire and retain good people who are committed to the company and its mission of creating a customer-centric culture. Second, the company relies on lots of data to make decisions. The company regularly surveys employees and customers to obtain objective third party feedback. Finally, Hancock Lumber is decentralized. The company puts a lot of power in the hands of its employees to make decisions and take responsibility.

MEN OF THE YEAR

1989: Duane Vaagen, Vaagen Brothers Lumber, Colville, Wash.
1990: David Hancock, M.S. Hancock Lumber, Casco, Maine
1991: James Bibler, Bibler Brothers Lumber, Russellville, Ark.
1992: Galen Weaber, Weaber Inc., Lebanon, Pa.
1993: John Hampton, Hampton Lumber, Portland, Ore.
1994: Jim Seaman, Seaman Timber, Montevallo, Ala.
1995: Jim Neiman, Devil's Tower Forest Products, Hulett, Wyo.
1996: Bud Johnson, C&D Lumber, Riddle, Ore.
1997: Don Overmyer, Linden Lumber, Linden, Ala.
1998: Jim Quinn, Collins Pine Co., Chester, Calif.
1999: Jim Hamer, Jim C. Hamer, Kenova, W. Va.
2000: Fred Stimpson, Gulf Lumber, Mobile, Ala.
2001: Larry Williams, Idaho Timber, Boise, Id.
2002: Rusty Wood, Tolleson Lumber, Perry, Ga.
2003: Dan Kretz, Kretz Lumber, Antigo, Wis.
2004: Dan Levesque, Nexfor Fraser, Ashland, Me.
2005: Harold Wayne Hankins, Hankins, Inc., Ripley, Miss.
2006: Chris Ketcham, Yakama Forest Products, White Swan, Wash.
2007: Bob Jordan, Jordan Lumber & Supply, Mt. Gilead, NC
2008: Bill Carden, Potomac Supply, Kinsale, Va.
2009: Mike Flynn, Midwest Hardwood, Maple Grove, Minn.
2010: Steve Singleton, New South, Camden, SC
2011: Bill Wilkins, WKO, Inc., Carson, Wash.
2012: Butch and Michael Cersosimo, Cersosimo Lumber, Brattleboro, Vt.
2013: Finley McRae, Rex Lumber, Graceville, Fla.
2014: Kevin Hancock, Hancock Lumber, Casco, Maine

When the recession hit the United States around 2008, Hancock knew his company was going to have to do some things differently. Prior to then, almost all of Hancock Lumber's sales were made in the U.S. When the recession kicked in they started looking more broadly at potential markets. "We ended up finding export opportunities that allowed us to maintain strong production levels and to diversify our markets in ways that not only helped us through the housing recession here in the U.S, but that we think will be helpful to us long term," Hancock says.

Hancock enjoys being able to work in all the different segments of the company. "From human resources to marketing, to finance to operation and sales, I'm really lucky because as president of the company I get to participate in all those different business segments with all those different employee groups and different customer groups. As a result there's a lot of variety to what I end up doing on a daily basis and therefore it really never gets boring because every part of the business is constantly changing so everything's in motion all the time," he says.

Hancock Lumber continues to thrive as the climate changes for lumber companies. As one of the largest manufacturers of eastern white pine products in

The "Hancock House" was built on the Pine Ridge Indian Reservation in 2013.

North America, Hancock has customers throughout New England, the U.S. South, the Midwest and across Canada.

Hancock believes it's important to continue to invest in the latest technology at all three of the sawmills. The company has recently upgraded the optimizing edger in the Bethel mill. Last year, Hancock Lumber expanded its planer mill in Casco to make it bigger and to allow for more sorting, more customization and more secondary manufacturing.

Six generations of continuous opera-

tions, growing trees, keeping Maine green, manufacturing eastern white pine products from renewable and sustainable forests, and creating housing for Mainers, is what Hancock Lumber does and with great success. Certainly Kevin Hancock doesn't take it for granted. He comments: "One of my favorite business quotes is success looks easy to those who weren't around to watch it being made. When you watch the lumber leave a mill on a truck it looks like a pretty simple scene, but it's really complex." **TP**

This is the Lakota tribal natal chart Deborah Dooley prepared and read for me. The date is November 6, 1868, and the location is Fort Laramie. As is the case with all charts, some "houses" are empty, while others are full. We all have our own journey to make. It's the one we signed up for.

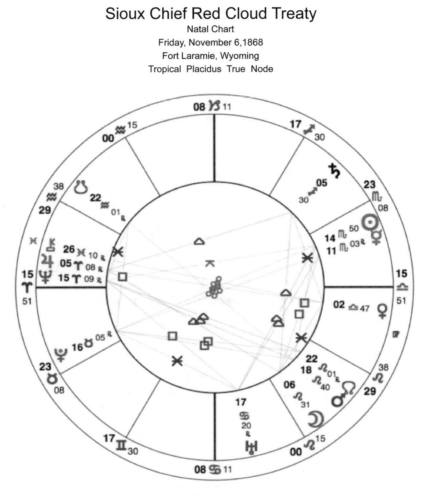

Sioux Chief Red Cloud Treaty
Natal Chart
Friday, November 6, 1868
Fort Laramie, Wyoming
Tropical Placidus True Node

Created by
Deborah Dooley

If you want to learn more about this book or follow future updates, please visit the following website:
www.kevindhancock.com

If you want to learn more about the nonprofit organization created to support economic independence at Pine Ridge, please visit the following website:
www.seventhpower.org

If you want to learn more about Hancock Lumber, please visit us at:
www.hancocklumber.com

If you want to learn more about evolutionary astrology or contact Deborah Dooley, please visit her at:
www.deborahdooley.com

If you want to learn more about Connie Pike and her therapy work for spasmodic dysphonia patients, please visit her at:
www.freetospeakvoicetherapy.com

If you want to learn more about Deanne Stillman or read the books she has published, please visit her at:
www.deannestillman.com

If you want to learn more about Nick Tilsen and the Thunder Valley nonprofit organization please visit them at:
www.thundervalley.org

If you want to learn more about The Singing Horse Trading Post or plan a trip to Pine Ridge, please visit:
www.singinghorse.net

Devils Tower stands tall on former tribal lands in present day Wyoming. In nature's eye treaties and political boundaries mean nothing. It's all one tribe in the end.

The Treaty of Fort Laramie of 1868 is an essential document in Lakota history. It was the last treaty signed between the northern plains tribes and the US government.

Originally designed to memorialize a permanent peace for all time, it actually lasted only six years, until the Wasichu discovered gold.

Treaty of Fort Laramie of 1868

Lieutenant Genral William T. Sherman, General William S. Harney, General Alfred H. Terry, General O.O. Augur, J.B. Henderson, Nathaniel G. Taylor, John G. Sanborn, and Samuel F. Tappan, duly appointed commissioners on the part of the United States, and the different bands of the Sioux Nation of Indians, be their chiefs and headmen, whose names are hereto subscribed, they being duly authorized to act in the premises.

ARTICLE I.

From this day forward all war between the parties to this agreement shall forever cease. The government of the United States desires peace, and its honor is hereby pledged to keep it. The Indians desire peace, and they now pledge their honor to maintain it.

If bad men among the whites, or among other people subject to the authority of the United States, shall commit any wrong upon the person or property of the Indians, the United States will, upon proof made to the agent, and forwarded to the Commissioner of Indian Affairs at Washington city, proceed at once to cause the offender to be arrested and punished according to the laws of the United States, and also reimburse the injured person for the loss sustained.

If bad men among the Indians shall commit a wrong or depredation upon the person or property of nay one, white, black, or Indian, subject to the authority of the United States, and at peace therewith, the Indians herein named solemnly agree that they will, upon proof made to their agent, and notice by him, deliver up the wrongdoer to the United States, to be tried and punished according to its laws, and, in case they willfully refuse so to do, the person injured shall be reimbursed for his loss from the annuities, or other moneys due or to become due to them under this or other treaties made with the United States; and the President, on advising with the Commissioner of Indian Affairs, shall prescribe such rules and regulations for ascertaining damages under the provisions of this article as in his judgment may be proper, but no one sustaining loss while violating the provisions of this treaty, or the laws of the United States, shall be reimbursed therefor.

ARTICLE II.

The United States agrees that the following district of country, to wit, viz: commencing on the east bank of the Missouri river where the 46th parallel of north latitude crosses the same, thence along low-water mark down said east bank to a point opposite where the northern line of the State of Nebraska strikes the river, thence west across said river, and along the northern line of Nebraska to the 104th degree of longitude west from Greenwich, thence north on said meridian to a point where the 46th parallel of north latitude intercepts the same, thence due east along said parallel to the place of beginning; and in addition thereto, all existing reservations of the east back of said river, shall be and the same is, set apart for the absolute and undisturbed use and occupation of the Indians herein named, and for such other friendly tribes or individual Indians as from time to time they may be willing, with the consent of the United States, to admit amongst them; and the United States now solemnly agrees that no persons, except those herein designated and authorized so to do, and except such officers, agents, and employees of the government as may be authorized to enter upon Indian reservations in discharge of duties enjoined by law, shall ever be permitted to pass over, settle upon, or reside in the territory described in this article, or in such territory as may be added to this reservation for the use of said Indians, and henceforth they will and do hereby relinquish all claims or right in and to any portion of the United States or Territories, except such as is embraced within the limits aforesaid, and except as hereinafter provided.

ARTICLE III.

If it should appear from actual survey or other satisfactory examination of said tract of land that it contains less than 160 acres of tillable land for each person who, at the time, may be authorized to reside on it under the provisions of this treaty, and a very considerable number of such persons shall be disposed to commence cultivating the soil as farmers, the United States agrees to set apart, for the use of said Indians, as herein provided, such additional quantity of arable land, adjoining to said reservation, or as near to the same as it can be obtained, as may be required to provide the necessary amount.

ARTICLE IV.

The United States agrees, at its own proper expense, to construct, at some place on the Missouri river, near the centre of said reservation where timber and water may be convenient, the following buildings, to wit, a warehouse, a store-room for the use of the agent in storing goods belonging to the Indians, to cost not less than $2,500; an agency building, for the residence of the agent, to cost not exceeding $3,000; a residence for the physician, to cost not more than $3,000; and five other buildings, for a carpenter, farmer, blacksmith, miller, and engineer—each to cost not exceeding $2,000; also, a school-house, or mission building, so soon as a sufficient number of children can be induced by the agent to attend school, which shall not cost exceeding $5,000. The United States agrees further to cause to be erected on said reservation, near the other buildings herein authorized, a good steam circular saw-mill, with a grist-mill and shingle machine attached to the same, to cost not exceeding $8,000.

ARTICLE V.

The United States agrees that the agent for said Indians shall in the future make his home at the agency building; that he shall reside among them, and keep an office open at all times for the purpose of prompt and diligent inquiry into such matters of complaint by and against the Indians as may be presented for investigation under the provisions of their treaty stipulations, as also for the faithful discharge of other duties enjoined on him by law. In all cases of depredation on person or property he shall cause the evidence to be taken in writing and forwarded, together with his findings, to the Commissioner of Indian Affairs, whose decision, subject to the revision of the Secretary of the Interior, shall be binding on the parties to this treaty.

ARTICLE VI.

If any individual belonging to said tribes of Indians, or legally incorporated with them, being the head of a family, shall desire to commence farming, he shall have the privilege to select, in the presence and with the assistance of the agent then in charge, a tract of land within said reservation, not exceeding three hundred and twenty acres in extent, which tract, when so selected, certified, and recorded in the "Land Book" as herein directed, shall cease to be held in common, but the same may be occupied and held in the exclusive possession of the person selecting it, and of his family, so long as he or they may continue to cultivate it.

Any person over eighteen years of age, not being the head of a family, may in like manner select and cause to be certified to him or her, for purposes of cultivation, a quantity of land, not exceeding eighty acres in extent, and thereupon be entitled to the exclusive possession of the same as above directed.

For each tract of land so selected a certificate, containing a description thereof and the name of the person selecting it, with a certificate endorsed thereon that the same has been recorded, shall be delivered to the party entitled to it, by the agent, after the same shall have been recorded by him in a book to be kept in his office, subject to inspection, which said book shall be known as the "Sioux Land Book."

The President may, at any time, order a survey of the reservation, and, when so surveyed, Congress shall provide for protecting the rights of said settlers in their improvements, and may fix the character of the title held by each. The United States may pass such laws on the subject of alienation and descent of property between the Indians and their descendants as may be thought proper. And it is further stipulated that any male Indians over eighteen years of age, of any band or tribe that is or shall hereafter become a party to this treaty, who now is or who shall hereafter become a resident or occupant of any reservation or territory not included in the tract of country designated and described in this treaty for the permanent home of the Indians, which is not mineral land, nor reserved by the United States for special purposes other than Indian occupation, and who shall have made improvements thereon of the value of two hundred dollars or more, and continuously occupied the same as a homestead for the term of three years, shall be entitled to receive from the United States a patent for one hundred and sixty acres of land including his said improvements, the same to be in the form of the legal subdivisions of the surveys of the public lands. Upon application in writing, sustained by the proof of two disinterested witnesses, made to the register of the local land office when the land sought to be entered is within a land district, and when the tract sought to be entered is not in any land district, then upon said application and proof being made to the Commissioner of the General Land Office, and the right of such Indian or Indians to enter such tract or tracts of land shall accrue and be perfect from the date of his first improvements thereon, and shall continue as long as he continues his residence and improvements and no longer. And any Indian or Indians receiving a patent for land under the foregoing provisions shall thereby and from thenceforth become and be a citizen of the United States and be entitled to all the privileges and immunities of such citizens, and shall, at the same time, retain all his rights to benefits accruing to Indians under this treaty.

ARTICLE VII.

In order to insure the civilization of the Indians entering into this treaty, the necessity of education is admitted, especially of such of them as are or may be settled on said agricultural reservations, and they, therefore, pledge themselves to compel their children, male and female, between the ages of six and sixteen years, to attend school, and it is hereby made the duty of the agent for said Indians to see that this stipulation is strictly complied with; and the United States agrees that for every thirty children between said ages, who can be induced or compelled to attend school, a house shall be provided, and a teacher competent to teach the elementary branches of an English education shall be furnished, who will reside among said Indians and faithfully discharge his or her duties as a teacher. The provisions of this article to continue for not less than twenty years.

ARTICLE VIII.

When the head of a family or lodge shall have selected lands and received his certificate as above directed, and the agent shall be satisfied that he intends in good faith to commence cultivating the soil for a living, he shall be entitled to receive seeds and agricultural implements for the first year, not exceeding in value one hundred dollars, and for each succeeding year he shall continue to farm, for a period of three years more, he shall be entitled to receive seeds and implements as aforesaid, not exceeding in value twenty-five dollars. And it is further stipulated that such persons as commence farming shall receive instruction from the farmer herein provided for, and whenever more than one hundred persons shall enter upon the cultivation of the soil, a second blacksmith shall be provided, with such iron, steel, and other material as may be needed.

ARTICLE IX.

At any time after ten years from the making of this treaty, the United States shall have the privilege of withdrawing the physician, farmer, blacksmith, carpenter, engineer, and miller herein provided for, but in case of such withdrawal, an additional sum thereafter of ten thousand dollars per annum shall be devoted to the education of said Indians, and the Commissioner of Indian Affairs shall, upon careful inquiry into their condition, make such rules and regulations for the expenditure of said sums as will best promote the education and moral improvement of said tribes.

ARTICLE X.

In lieu of all sums of money or other annuities provided to be paid to the Indians herein named under any treaty or treaties heretofore made, the United States agrees to deliver at the agency house on the reservation herein named, on or before the first day of August of each year, for thirty years, the following articles, to wit:

For each male person over 14 years of age, a suit of good substantial woollen clothing, consisting of coat, pantaloons, flannel shirt, hat, and a pair of home-made socks.

For each female over 12 years of age, a flannel shirt, or the goods necessary to make it, a pair of woollen hose, 12 yards of calico, and 12 yards of cotton domestics.

For the boys and girls under the ages named, such flannel and cotton goods as may be needed to make each a suit as aforesaid, together with a pair of woollen hose for each.

And in order that the Commissioner of Indian Affairs may be able to estimate properly for the articles herein named, it shall be the duty of the agent each year to forward to him a full and exact census of the Indians, on which the estimate from year to year can be based.

And in addition to the clothing herein named, the sum of $10 for each person entitled to the beneficial effects of this treaty shall be *annually appropriated for a period of 30 years, while such persons roam and hunt, and $20 for each person who engages in farming, to be used by the Secretary of the Interior in the purchase of such articles as from time to time the condition and necessities of the Indians may indicate to be proper. And if within the 30 years, at any time, it shall appear that the amount of money needed for clothing, under this article, can be appropriated to better uses for the Indians named herein, Congress may, by law, change the appropriation to other purposes, but in no event shall the amount of the appropriation be withdrawn or discontinued for the period named. And the President shall annually detail an officer of the army to be present and attest the delivery of all the goods herein named, to the Indians, and he shall inspect and report on the quantity and quality of the goods and the manner of their delivery. And it is hereby expressly stipulated that each Indian over the age of four years, who shall have removed to and settled permanently upon said reservation, one pound of meat and one pound of flour per day, provided the Indians cannot furnish their own subsistence at an earlier date. And it is further stipulated that the United States will furnish and deliver to each lodge of Indians or family of persons legally incorporated with them, who shall remove to the reservation herein described and commence farming, one good American cow, and one good well-broken pair of American oxen within 60 days after such lodge or family shall have so settled upon said reservation.*

ARTICLE XI.

In consideration of the advantages and benefits conferred by this treaty and the many pledges of friendship by the United States, the tribes who are parties to this agreement hereby stipulate that they will relinquish all right to occupy permanently the territory outside their reservations as herein defined, but yet reserve the right to hunt on any lands north of North Platte, and on the Republican Fork of the Smoky Hill river, so long as the buffalo may range thereon in such numbers as to justify the chase. And they, the said Indians, further expressly agree:

1st. That they will withdraw all opposition to the construction of the railroads now being built on the plains.

2nd. That they will permit the peaceful construction of any railroad not passing over their reservation as herein defined.

3rd. That they will not attack any persons at home, or travelling, nor molest or disturb any wagon trains, coaches, mules, or cattle belonging to the people of the United States, or to persons friendly therewith.

4th. They will never capture, or carry off from the settlements, white women or children.

5th. They will never kill or scalp white men, nor attempt to do them harm.

6th. They withdraw all pretence of opposition to the construction of the railroad now being built along the Platte river and westward to the Pacific ocean, and they will not in future object to the construction of railroads, wagon roads, mail stations, or other works of utility or necessity, which may be ordered or permitted by the laws of the United States. But should such roads or other works be constructed on the lands of their reservation, the government will pay the tribe whatever amount of damage may be assessed by three disinterested commissioners to be appointed by the President for that purpose, one of the said commissioners to be a chief or headman of the tribe.

7th. They agree to withdraw all opposition to the military posts or roads now established south of the North Platte river, or that may be established, not in violation of treaties heretofore made or hereafter to be made with any of the Indian tribes.

ARTICLE XII.

No treaty for the cession [concession] of any portion or part of the reservation herein described which may be held in common, shall be of any validity or force as against the said Indians unless executed and signed by at least three-fourths of all the adult male Indians occupying or interested in the same, and no cession by the tribe shall be understood or construed in such manner as to deprive, without his consent, any individual member of the tribe of his rights to any tract of land selected by him as provided in Article VI of this treaty.

ARTICLE XIII.

The United States hereby agrees to furnish annually to the Indians the physician, teachers, carpenter, miller, engineer, farmer, and black-smiths, as herein contemplated, and that such appropriations shall be made from time to time, on the estimate of the Secretary of the Interior, as will be sufficient to employ such persons.

ARTICLE XIV.

It is agreed that the sum of five hundred dollars annually for three years from date shall be expended in presents to the ten persons of said tribe who in the judgment of the agent may grow the most valuable crops for the respective year.

ARTICLE XV.

The Indians herein named agree that when the agency house and other buildings shall be constructed on the reservation named, they will regard said reservation their permanent home, and they will make no permanent settlement elsewhere; but they shall have the right, subject to the conditions and modifications of this treaty, to hunt, as stipulated in Article XI hereof.

ARTICLE XVI.

The United States hereby agrees and stipulates that the country north of the North Platte river and east of the summits of the Big Horn mountains shall be held and considered to be unceded Indian territory, and also stipulates and agrees that no white person or persons shall be permitted to settle upon or occupy any portion of the same; or without the consent of the Indians, first had and obtained, to pass through the same; and it is further agreed by the United States, that within ninety days after the conclusion of peace with all the bands of the Sioux Nation, the military posts now established in the territory in this article named shall be abandoned, and that the road leading to them and by them to the settlements in the Territory of Montana shall be closed.

ARTICLE XVII.

It is hereby expressly understood and agreed by and between the re-spective parties to this treaty that the execution of this treaty and its ratification by the United States Senate shall have the effect, and shall be construed as abrogating and annulling all treaties and agreements heretofore entered into between the respective parties hereto, so far as such treaties and agreements obligate the United States to furnish and provide money, clothing, or other articles of property to such Indians and bands of Indians as become parties to this treaty, but no further.

In testimony of all which, we, the said commissioners, and we, the chiefs and headmen of the Brule band of the Sioux Nation, have hereunto set our hands and seals at Fort Laramie, Dakota Territory, this twenty-ninth day of April, in the year one thousand eight hundred and sixty-eight.

N. G. TAYLOR,
W. T. SHERMAN,
Lieutenant General
WM. S. HARNEY,
Brevet Major General U.S.A.
JOHN B. SANBORN,
S. F. TAPPAN,
C. C. AUGUR,
Brevet Major General
ALFRED H. TERRY,
Brevet Major General U.S.A.
Attest:
A. S. H. WHITE, *Secretary.*

Executed on the part of the Brule band of Sioux by the chiefs and headman whose names are hereto annexed, they being thereunto duly authorized, at Fort Laramie, D. T., the twenty-ninth day of April, in the year A. D. 1868.

MA-ZA-PON-KASKA, *his X mark, Iron Shell.*
WAH-PAT-SHAH, *his X mark, Red Leaf.*
HAH-SAH-PAH, *his X mark, Black Horn.*
ZIN-TAH-GAH-LAT-WAH, *his X mark, Spotted Tail.*
ZIN-TAH-GKAH, *his X mark, White Tail.*
ME-WAH-TAH-NE-HO-SKAH, *his X mark, Tall Man.*
SHE-CHA-CHAT-KAH, *his X mark, Bad Left Hand.*
NO-MAH-NO-PAH, *his X mark, Two and Two.*
TAH-TONKA-SKAH, *his X mark, White Bull.*
CON-RA-WASHTA, *his X mark, Pretty Coon.*
HA-CAH-CAH-SHE-CHAH, *his X mark, Bad Elk.*
WA-HA-KA-ZAH-ISH-TAH, *his X mark, Eye Lance.*

MA-TO-HA-KE-TAH, his X mark, Bear that Looks Behind.
BELLA-TONKA-TONKA, his X mark, Big Partisan.
MAH-TO-HO-HONKA, his X mark, Swift Bear.
TO-WIS-NE, his X mark, Cold Place.
ISH-TAH-SKAH, his X mark, White Eye.
MA-TA-LOO-ZAH, his X mark, Fast Bear.
AS-HAH-HAH-NAH-SHE, his X mark, Standing Elk.
CAN-TE-TE-KI-YA, his X mark, The Brave Heart.
SHUNKA-SHATON, his X mark, Day Hawk.
TATANKA-WAKON, his X mark, Sacred Bull.
MAPIA SHATON, his X mark, Hawk Cloud.
MA-SHA-A-OW, his X mark, Stands and Comes.
SHON-KA-TON-KA, his X mark, Big Dog.
Attest:
ASHTON S. H. WHITE, Secretary of Commission.
GEORGE B. WITHS, Phonographer to Commission.
GEO. H. HOLTZMAN.
JOHN D. HOWLAND.
JAMES C. O'CONNOR.
CHAR. E. GUERN, Interpreter.
LEON T. PALLARDY, Interpreter.
NICHOLAS JANIS, Interpreter.

*Executed on the part of the Ogallalla band of Sioux by the chiefs
and headmen whose names are hereto subscribed, they being thereunto
duly authorized, at Fort Laramie, the 25th day of May, in the year
A. D. 1868.*

*TAH-SHUN-KA-CO-QUI-PAH, his mark, Man-Afraid-of-
His-Horses.*
SHA-TON-SKAH, his X mark, White Hawk.
SHA-TON-SAPAH, his X mark, Black Hawk.
EGA-MON-TON-KA-SAPAH, his X mark, Black Tiger.
OH-WAH-SHE-CHA, his X mark, Bad Wound.
PAH-GEE, his X mark, Grass.
WAH-NON SAH-CHE-GEH, his X mark, Ghost Heart.
COMECH, his X mark, Crow.
OH-HE-TE-KAH, his X mark, The Brave.
TAH-TON-KAH-HE-YO-TA-KAH, his X mark, Sitting Bull.
SHON-KA-OH-WAH-MEN-YE, his X mark, Whirlwind Dog.

HA-KAH-KAH-TAH-MIECH, his X mark, Poor Elk.

WAM-BU-LEE-WAH-KON, his X mark, Medicine Eagle.

CHON-GAH-MA-HE-TO-HANS-KA, his X mark, High Wolf.

WAH-SECHUN-TA-SHUN-KAH, his X mark, American Horse.

MAH-KAH-MAH-HA-MAK-NEAR, his X mark, Man that Walks under the Ground.

MAH-TO-TOW-PAH, his X mark, Four Bears.

MA-TO-WEE-SHA-KTA, his X mark, One that Kills the Bear.

OH-TAH-KEE-TOKA-WEE-CHAKTA, his X mark, One that Kills in a Hard Place.

TAH-TON-KAH-TA-MIECH, his X mark, The Poor Bull.

OH-HUNS-EE-GA-NON-SKEN, his X mark, Mad Shade.

SHAH-TON-OH-NAH-OM-MINNE-NE-OH-MINNE, his X mark, Whirling Hawk.

MAH-TO-CHUN-KA-OH, his X mark, Bear's Back.

CHE-TON-WEE-KOH, his X mark, Fool Hawk.

WAH-HOH-KE-ZA-AH-HAH, his X mark,

EH-TON-KAH, his X mark, Big Mouth.

MA-PAH-CHE-TAH, his X mark, Bad Hand.

WAH-KE-YUN-SHAH, his X mark, Red Thunder.

WAK-SAH, his X mark, One that Cuts Off.

CHAH-NOM-QUI-YAH, his X mark, One that Presents the Pipe.

WAH-KE-KE-YAN-PUH-TAH, his X mark, Fire Thunder.

MAH-TO-NONK-PAH-ZE, his X mark, Bear with Yellow Ears.

CON-REE-TEH-KA, his X mark, The Little Crow.

HE-HUP-PAH-TOH, his X mark, The Blue War Club.

SHON-KEE-TOH, his X mark, The Blue Horse.

WAM-BALLA-OH-CONQUO, his X mark, Quick Eagle.

TA-TONKA-SUPPA, his X mark, Black Bull.

MOH-TOH-HA-SHE-NA, his X mark, The Bear Hide.

Attest:

S. E. WARD.

JAS. C. O'CONNOR.

J. M. SHERWOOD.

W. C. SLICER.

SAM DEON.

H. M. MATHEWS.
JOSEPH BISS
NICHOLAS JANIS, Interpreter.
LEFROY JOTT, Interpreter.
ANTOINE JANIS, Interpreter.

Executed on the part of the Minneconjou band of Sioux by the chiefs and headmen whose names are hereunto subscribed, they being thereunto duly authorized.
HEH-WON-GE-CHAT, his X mark, One Horn.
OH-PON-AH-TAH-E-MANNE, his X mark, The Elk that Bellows Walking.
HEH-HO-LAH-ZEH-CHA-SKAH, his X mark, Young White Bull.
WAH-CHAH-CHUM-KAH-COH-KEEPAH, his X mark, One that is Afraid of Shield.
HE-HON-NE-SHAKTA, his X mark, The Old Owl.
MOC-PE-A-TOH, his X mark, Blue Cloud.
OH-PONG-GE-LE-SKAH, his X mark, Spotted Elk.
TAH-TONK-KA-HON-KE-SCHUE, his X mark, Slow Bull.
SHONK-A-NEE-SHAH-SHAH-ATAH-PE, his X mark, The Dog Chief.
MA-TO-TAH-TA-TONK-KA, his X mark, Bull Bear.
WOM-BEH-LE-TON-KAH, his X mark, The Big Eagle.
MATOH, EH-SCHNE-LAH, his X mark, The Lone Bear.
MA-TOH-OH-HE-TO-KEH, his X mark, The Brave Bear.
EH-CHE-MA-KEH, his X mark, The Runner.
TI-KI-YA, his X mark, The Hard.
HE-MA-ZA, his X mark, Iron Horn.
Attest:
JAS. C O'CONNOR,
WM. D. BROWN,
NICHOLAS JANIS,
ANTOINE JANIS,
Interpreters.

Executed on the part of the Yanctonais band of Sioux by the chiefs and headmen whose names are hereto subscribed, they being thereunto duly authorized:

MAH-TO-NON-PAH, his X mark, Two Bears.

MA-TO-HNA-SKIN-YA, his X mark, Mad Bear.

HE-O-PU-ZA, his X mark, Louzy.

AH-KE-CHE-TAH-CHE-KA-DAN, his X mark, Little Soldier.

MAH-TO-E-TAN-CHAN, his X mark, Chief Bear.

CU-WI-TO-WIA, his X mark, Rotten Stomach.

SKUN-KA-WE-TKO, his X mark, Fool Dog.

ISH-TA-SAP-PAH, his X mark, Black Eye.

IH-TAN-CHAN, his X mark, The Chief.

I-A-WI-CA-KA, his X mark, The One who Tells the Truth.

AH-KE-CHE-TAH, his X mark, The Soldier.

TA-SHI-NA-GI, his X mark, Yellow Robe.

NAH-PE-TON-KA, his X mark, Big Hand.

CHAN-TEE-WE-KTO, his X mark, Fool Heart.

HOH-GAN-SAH-PA, his X mark, Black Catfish.

MAH-TO-WAH-KAN, his X mark, Medicine Bear.

SHUN-KA-KAN-SHA, his X mark, Red Horse.

WAN-RODE, his X mark, The Eagle.

CAN-HPI-SA-PA, his X mark, Black Tomahawk.

WAR-HE-LE-RE, his X mark, Yellow Eagle.

CHA-TON-CHE-CA, his X mark, Small Hawk, or Long Fare.

SHU-GER-MON-E-TOO-HA-SKA, his X mark, Fall Wolf.

MA-TO-U-TAH-KAH, his X mark, Sitting Bear.

HI-HA-CAH-GE-NA-SKENE, his X mark, Mad Elk.

Arapahoes.

LITTLE CHIEF, his X mark.

TALL BEAR, his X mark.

TOP MAN, his X mark.

NEVA, his X mark.

THE WOUNDED BEAR, his X mark.

WHIRLWIND, his X mark.

THE FOX, his X mark.

THE DOG BIG MOUTH, his X mark.

SPOTTED WOLF, his X mark.

SORREL HORSE, his X mark.

BLACK COAL, his X mark.

BIG WOLF, his X mark.

KNOCK-KNEE, his X mark.

BLACK CROW, his X mark.

THE LONE OLD MAN, his X mark.

PAUL, his X mark.
BLACK BULL, his X mark.
BIG TRACK, his X mark.
THE FOOT, his X mark.
BLACK WHITE, his X mark.
YELLOW HAIR, his X mark.
LITTLE SHIELD, his X mark.
BLACK BEAR, his X mark.
WOLF MOCASSIN, his X mark.
BIG ROBE, his X mark.
WOLF CHIEF, his X mark.
Witnesses:
ROBERT P. MCKIBBIN,
Captain 4th Infantry, and Bvt. Lieut. Col. U. S. A.,
Commanding Fort Laramie.
WM. H. POWELL,
Brevet Major, Captain 4th Infantry.
HENRY W. PATTERSON,
Captain 4th Infantry.
THEO E. TRUE,
Second Lieutenant 4th Infantry.
W. G. BULLOCK.
FORT LARAMIE, WYOMING TERRITORY
November 6, 1868.
MAH-PI-AH-LU-TAH, his X mark, Red Cloud.
WA-KI-AH-WE-CHA-SHAH, his X mark, Thunder Man.
MA-ZAH-ZAH-GEH, his X mark, Iron Cane.
WA-UMBLE-WHY-WA-KA-TUYAH, his X mark, High
Eagle.
KO-KE-PAH, his X mark, Man Afraid.
WA-KI-AH-WA-KOU-AH, his X mark, Thunder Flying Run-
ning.
Witnessess:
W. MCE. DYE,
Brevet Colonel U.S. Army,
Commanding.
A. B. CAIN,
Captain 4th Infantry, Brevet Major U.S. Army.
ROBT. P. MCKIBBIN,
Captain 4th Infantry, Bvt. Lieut. Col. U.S. Army.

JNO. MILLER,
Captain 4th Infantry.
G. L. LUHN,
First Lieutenant 4th Infantry, Bvt. Capt. U.S. Army.
H. C. SLOAN,
Second Lieutenant 4th Infantry.

The view down the street from the Hancock House, as Pinky calls it.

I am not what happened to me,
I am what I choose to become.

—Carl Jung

NOTES

Prior to the introduction, I first read the poem "An Indian Prayer" in the information packet Alberta Eagle gave me on my first tour of the Red Cloud School; the picture of Sitting Bull comes from the autographed picture hanging on my office wall.

For the Introduction, the information regarding the massacre of Wounded Knee came from the historical marker at the site. The American Horse quote came from the August 2012 edition of *National Geographic,* and the data regarding Maine housing starts came from Construction Data of New England.

For Chapter 1, Breaking Rank, the painting of the lone Oglala individual holding eagle feathers came from the Oglala Lakota College Historical Center exhibit; the Angel Martinez quote came from the August 2012 edition of *National Geographic,* and the Escape to the Pine Ridge Reservation map is courtesy of the Pine Ridge Area Chamber of Commerce. I also relied upon Dan Sullivan's *How the Best Get Better* book and audiotape, the website www.battleforwhiteclay.org, accessed December 3, 2013, Nathan Philbrick's book, *The Last Stand: Custer, Sitting Bull And The Battle Of The Little Big Horn,* along with the *Chicago Inter-Ocean* newspaper from August 27, 1874. The picture of Custer's 1874 expedition came from www.wyomingtalesandtrails.com. I also relied on "LPols 223 Tribal Laws & Treaties" published by Oglala Lakota College in 2005, Steven Rinella's *American Buffalo,* and Merle Steva's November 5, 2014 essay in the *Portland Press Herald,* "Understanding Our Own 'Ghost Continents' Helps Us Love Others."

For Chapter 2, Transcendence, I referenced the National Spasmodic Dysphonia Association's website, www.dysphonia.org, the US Department of the Interior's "2005 American Indian Population and Labor Force" report, and the American Indian Humanitarian Fund website, www.4aihf.org (January 31, 2013). The picture of the US School for Indians at Pine Ridge is from the Library of Congress Prints and Photographs Division. I also relied on Mari Sandoz's *Crazy Horse: The Strange Man of the Oglalas,* and Joseph Marshall's *The Journey of Crazy Horse.* The quote from Olowan Thunder Hawk Martinez appeared in the August 2012 edition of *National Geographic.* The movie poster from *How the West Was Won* was created by Reynold Brown and came from Wikipedia.

The picture of the American Indians on the billboard in Greeley, Colorado, was taken from www.nydailynews.com on February 10, 2015.

For Chapter 3, One Day, Four Heroes, the "Grand Rush for Indian Territory" newspaper headline came from the Indian Land Tenure Foundation website, www.iltf.org. The photo of Dennis Banks and Russell Means is from the *Rapid City Journal* archives. In this chapter, I also relied on the book *David and Goliath* by Malcolm Gladwell, Reuters' March 13, 2014 article, "Iraq War Costs U.S. More than $2 Trillion"(www.reuters.com/article/2013/03/14/), Wikipedia's page on Hurricane Sandy from February 14, 2014, and the *Encyclopedia of the American Indian Movement* by Bruce Johansen. The quote from Olowan Thunder Hawk Martinez appeared in *National Geographic's* August 2012 article titled, "In the Shadow of Wounded Knee."

For Chapters 4 and 5, The Apology and Finding Center, there are several sources to note. The drawing of the young warrior on a vision quest can be found at www.madreVida.com. While there are numerous versions of the White Buffalo Calf Woman story in Lakota folklore, the version I reference takes excerpts from Stonee's *Lore, Legends, and Teachings* (www.ilhawaii.net). The map of the Little Bighorn battlefield is courtesy of the National Park Service. The drawing of Crazy Horse is by Stan Hamilton. For this chapter, I also relied on Nathaniel Philbrick's book, *The Last Stand: Custer, Sitting Bull and the Battle of the Little Bighorn*, and Wikipedia's page on the Crow Indian Reservation, www.en.wikipedia.org/wiki/Crow_Indian_Reservation.com.

For Chapter 6, Let the Wind Blow through You, the graphic of the Lakota Medicine Wheel can be found at www.danasvoice.blogspot.com. The photography of Black Elk can be found in many places including, www.elizawhitebuffalo.com. For this chapter, I also relied on several books, including: Joseph Marshall's *The Lakota Way*, Joseph Epes Brown's *The Sacred Pipe: Black Elk's Account of the Seven Rites of the Oglala Sioux*, John Neihardt's *Black Elk Speaks*, and Joseph Campbell's *The Hero's Journey*. I referenced the Lakota Funds website, www.lakotafunds.org. Additionally, I relied on a few articles from various websites, including: "The Four Values of the Lakota" from the website www.kalloch.org (March 14, 2014), "The Power of the Circle" from the website www.firstpeople. us, (March 14, 2014), and an article titled "The Meaning and Use of the Medicine Wheel" by Roy Dudgeon, from October 18, 2013.

For Chapters 7 through 10, I relied on Joseph Campbell's book, *The Power of Myth*, *National Geographic's* March 2014 article, titled "Star Eater," information boards located at the Wyoming State Historical Site known as the "Oregon Trail Ruts," John Neihardt's book, *Black Elk Speaks*, *National Geographic's* August 2014 article, titled "The New Face of Hunger," and a PBS documentary titled *Young Lakota*. The information regarding the first human inhabitants of North America came from "Tracking the First Americans," an article that appeared in the January 2014 edition of *National Geographic*.

For Chapter 11, The Vision Quest, I relied on "A Native American Vision Quest" from the website www.webpanda.com, on May 14, 2014, along with Luther Standing Bear's book, *The Life and Death of Crazy Horse*.

For Chapter 12, Voices, the picture of the sweat lodge came from the website www.Crystalinks.com. I also relied on several books, including, Connie Pike's *Free to Speak*, Joseph Campbell's *The Power of Myth*, *The Hero's Journey*, and *The Hero with a Thousand Faces*, and Paulo Freire's *Pedagogy of the Oppressed*. Additionally, I resourced "Seven Lakota Rites" from the Akta Lakota Museum's website on May 31st, 2014. The descriptions of the sweat lodge ceremony by Black Elk are from Joseph Epes Brown's book, *The Sacred Pipe: Black Elk's Account of the Seven Rites of the Oglala Sioux*.

For the Epilogue, Reshaping the Grindstone, I relied on Brian Weiss's book, *Many Lives, Many Masters*, and two others by Alice O. Howell, *The Dove in the Stone* and *The Heavens Declare: Astrological Ages and the Evolution of Consciousness*.

For the Appendix, I sourced the Treaty of Fort Laramie of 1868 from the website, www.ourdocuments.gov.

BIBLIOGRAPHY

ARTICLES / ESSAYS / REPORTS

American Indian Population and Labor Force Report. US Department of Interior (Bureau of Indian Affairs), 2005.

Chicago Inter-Ocean. August 27, 1874.

———. August 28, 1874.

DeMallie, Raymond J. "American Indian Treaty Making: Motives and Meanings," *American Indian Journal* 3 (January 1977).

Dudgeon, Roy. "The Meaning and Use of the Medicine Wheel. Case Study: Lakota Philosophy" (October 18, 2013).

Finkel, Michael. "Star Eater," *National Geographic* (March 2014).

Fuller, Alexandra. "In the Shadow of Wounded Knee," *National Geographic* (August 2012).

Hodges, Glenn. "Tracking the First Americans," *National Geographic* (January 2015).

McMillan, Tracie. "The New Face of Hunger," *National Geographic* (August 2014).

Steva, Merle. "Understanding Our Own 'Ghost Continents' Helps Us Love Others," *Portland Press Herald* (November 5, 2014).

BOOKS

Brown, Joseph Epes. *The Sacred Pipe: Black Elk's Account of the Seven Rites of the Oglala Sioux* (The Civilization of the American Indian Series, Book 36). Norman: University of Oklahoma Press, 1989.

Campbell, Joseph. *The Hero's Journey: Joseph Campbell on His Life and Work.* Novato, CA: New World Library, 2014.

———. *The Hero with a Thousand Faces.* Novato, CA: New World Library, 2008.

———. *The Power of Myth.* New York: Anchor, 1991.

Freire, Paulo. *Pedagogy of the Oppressed.* New York: Bloomsbury Academic, 2000.

Gladwell, Malcolm. *David and Goliath: Underdogs, Misfits, and the Art of Battling Giants.* New York: Little, Brown and Company, 2013.

Guinn, Jeff. *The Last Gunfight: The Real Story of the Shootout at the O.K. Corral—And How It Changed the American West*. New York: Simon & Schuster, 2012.

Gwynne, S. C. *Empire of the Summer Moon: Quanah Parker and the Rise and Fall of the Comanches, the Most Powerful Indian Tribe in American History*. New York: Scribner, 2011.

Howell, Alice O. *The Dove in the Stone: Finding the Sacred in the Commonplace*. Bloomfield, CT: Quest Books, 1988.

Howell, Alice O. *The Heavens Declare: Astrological Ages and the Evolution of Consciousness*. Bloomfield, CT: Quest Books, 2006.

Johansen, Bruce E. *Encyclopedia of the American Indian Movement* (Movements of the American Mosaic). Westport, CT: Greenwood Publishing Group, 2013.

Keyt, Andrew. *Myths & Mortals*. Hoboken, NJ: John Wiley & Sons, Inc., 2015.

Lakota Tribal Laws, Treaties, and Government. (Lee, L-Pols 223). Oglala Lakota College, Kyle, South Dakota.

Marshall, Joseph M. *The Journey of Crazy Horse: A Lakota History*. New York: Penguin, 2005.

———. *The Lakota Way: Stories and Lessons for Living*. New York: Penguin, 2002.

Neihardt, John G. *Black Elk Speaks. Being the Life Story of a Holy Man of the Oglala Sioux* Albany: State University of New York Press, 2008.

Ostler, Jeffrey. *The Lakotas and the Black Hills: The Struggle for Sacred Ground* (The Penguin Library of American Indian History). New York: Penguin, 2011.

Philbrick, Nathaniel. *The Last Stand: Custer, Sitting Bull, and the Battle of the Little Bighorn*. New York: Penguin, 2011.

Pike, Connie. *Free to Speak: Overcoming Spasmodic Dysphonia—A Non-Drug Holistic Rehabilitation Model*. Charleston, SC: BookSurge Publishing, 2005.

Rinella, Steven. *American Buffalo: In Search of a Lost Icon*. New York: Spiegel & Grau, 2009.

Sandoz, Mari. *Crazy Horse: The Strange Man of the Oglala*. New York: Fine Communications, 1997.

Freedman, Russell. *The Life and Death of Crazy Horse*. New York: Holiday House, 1996.

Stillman, Deanne. *Mustang: The Saga of the Wild Horse in the American West*. New York: Mariner Books, 2009.

Sullivan, Dan. *How the Best Get Better*. Toronto: The Strategic Coach, 1996.

Utley, Robert M., and Wilcomb E. Washburn. *Indian Wars*. New York: Mariner Books, 2002.

Weiss, Brian. *Many Lives, Many Masters: The True Story of a Prominent Psychiatrist, His Young Patient, and the Past-Life Therapy that Changed Both Their Lives*. Whitby, Ontario: Fireside Publishing, 1988.

Zimmerman, Dwight Jon. *Saga of the Sioux: An Adaptation from Dee Brown's* Bury My Heart at Wounded Knee. New York: Henry Holt and Company, 2011.

WEBSITES

American Indian Humanitarian Fund (www.4aihf.org), accessed on January 31, 2013.

The Battle for White Clay (www.battleforwhiteclay.org), accessed on December 3, 2013.

The Battle of the Rosebud (www.wikipedia.com), accessed on March 7, 2014.

Crazy Horse (www.wikipedia.com), accessed on March 8, 2014.

Construction Data of New England (www.cdne.com), accessed on March 5, 2013.

Crow Indian Reservation (www.wikipedia.com), accessed on March 7, 2014.

Fort Laramie Treaty of 1868 (www.ourdocuments.gov), accessed on May 4, 2013.

"The Four Values of the Lakota" (www.kalloch.org/lakota), accessed on March 14, 2014.

Hurricane Sandy (www.wikipedia.com), accessed on February 20, 2014.

Indian Land Tenure Foundation (www.iltf.org), accessed on January 31, 2014.

"Iraq War Costs U.S. More than $2 Trillion" by Daniel Trotta (www. reuters.com), March 14, 2014.

Lakota Funds (www.lakotafunds.org), accessed on March 22, 2014.

Lowest-Income Counties in the United States (www.wikipedia.com), accessed on December 15, 2013.

Madre Vida (www.madrevida.com), accessed on September 12, 2013.

National Spasmodic Dysphonia Association (www.dysphonia.org), accessed on January 12, 2014.

"A Native American Vision Quest" (www.webpanda.com), accessed on May 14, 2014.

New York Daily News (www.nydailynews.com), accessed on February 10, 2015.

The Odyssey: United States Trek (www.ustrek.org), accessed on July 24, 2013.

Oregon Trail Ruts, WyoHistory.org, Wyoming State Historical Society (www.wyohistory.org), accessed on February 11, 2014.

"The Power of the Circle" (www.firstpeople.us), accessed on March 14, 2014.

Seven Lakota Rites (http://aktalakota.stjo.org), accessed on May 31, 2014.

"Stonee's Lore, Legends, and Teachings" (www.ilhawaii.net), accessed on March 7, 2014.

Wounded Knee Incident (www.wikipedia.com), accessed on January 19, 2014.

Wyoming Tales and Trails (http://www.wyomingtalesandtrails.com), accessed on October 15, 2014.

VIDEO PRODUCTIONS AND DOCUMENTARIES

America Before Columbus. National Geographic Channel, 2009.

Beyond the Dreamtime. Ainslie Roberts, Ronin Films, 1994.

DAKOTA 38. South Feather Productions.

The West. A film by Steven Ives, PBS, 2013.

Young Lakota. Independent Lens, PBS, 2013.

In September of 2014 I brought my wife Alison to Pine Ridge, in thanks for her support of this book and my journey. Here she is at the Red Cloud Indian School, watching a football game with our dear friend, Catherine Grey Day.

In May of 2015 I brought my mom Carol to Pine Ridge, in celebration of her seventieth birthday. Elders are highly respected at Pine Ridge, and my Mom was warmly embraced there. Here we are on the old North Platte River bridge just east of Fort Laramie.

WHAT'S NEXT?

"Think about what's next," Pinky once said to me.

Since the original release of *Not For Sale: Finding Center in the Land of Crazy Horse*, in the fall of 2015, I had been contemplating the many deeply personal reactions readers had shared with me in response to my book. People I had known all my life, as well as people I had never met, were contacting me and baring their souls in return. Something powerful had opened up inside of me. I had shared my story with the world, and now the world was reciprocating.

It all made me believe that a global awakening of the soul was occurring. This, in turn, led me to think about Pinky's question: "What's next?"

In his book *Myths and Mortals*, Andrew Keyt writes that "We are all born into a story already being told. We are all, to some extent, following in the footsteps of those who went before us." Keyt's book is about successors in a family business, but as I read it, I felt it could be applied to every new generation of every tribe.

"We are all successors," I thought to myself. "We are all born into a story long ago set in motion."

Keyt goes on to suggest that tribes select only pieces of their communal truth when looking at their past. Wanting to mythologize our ancestors as heroes, "we overlook the weaknesses, failures, and idiosyncrasies that are also part of the story."

As I reflected on my experiences, first at Hancock Lumber, and later at Pine Ridge, I could relate.

In the months since my book launched I had been contemplating two historical questions. First, how could I, just now, be discovering the fact that genocide occurred in the creation of our nation? How could I have lived nearly fifty years (and even taught American history) without confronting the truth about what happened to all the Native tribes, even though it was irrefutably obvious?

This, in turn, led to a second question. How come the people of Pine Ridge were also only seeing carefully selected portions of their own tribal truth?

> *You know, there is a marvelous stereotype out there that before white people came, the world here was perfect . . . that people lived in a paradise in which they were the most elegant*

the most moral, the most elevated of all humanity. That's not true. We [the Lakota]were human beings . . . and we did things all human beings do.

—Jo Allyn Archambault (Lakota)

The truth is the Lakota acquired the Black Hills the same way they lost it. The Sioux tribes originated east of the Missouri River. As they acquired horses and guns through trading, they pushed farther and farther west onto the northern plains. Strong in numbers and fierce in war, they attacked and displaced other tribes, including the Cheyenne, the Pawnee, and the Crow. The Lakota had taken much of their land from smaller, weaker tribes. But this truth was also equally ignored.

This has all led me to believe that a second awakening, a tribal enlightenment, will eventually need to occur. The book I had just written was about the power and necessity of looking inward for a deeper sense of personal truth in a sea of collective noise. But what about an entire tribe? How does an entire tribe confront the *whole* truth about its past, let go, break through, and evolve?

How about an entire planet? How do humans meet their destiny as a single tribe? These were the questions that now consumed me.

The soul of humanity is here to evolve, to transcend ego, tribalism, overreaching, and greed. But the journey is arduous. Under duress, we cling to the past, and those who hold the power don't let go easily (I personally know this to be true). Furthermore, the old tools of revolution no longer apply. Overthrowing one highly centralized and dogmatic regime to replace it with another is mere window dressing. Nothing changes.

A new type of revolution is required, one that can only be born from the peaceful power of truth and brotherhood, of which Black Elk foretold. No one has to lose for me to win.

When I finished this book I thought I was done. Only months later, I could see I was just beginning. The house of truth has many rooms. Once inside, it's hard not to keep moving forward; it's hard not to keep opening doors. What this means next for me, for all of us, is a story still being told.

Everyone is indigenous.

—Summit of the Americas (April 2015)

MEET KEVIN HANCOCK

Kevin Hancock is the president of Hancock Lumber Company. Established in 1848, Hancock Lumber operates ten retail stores and three sawmills, led by 475 employees. The company also grows trees on 12,000 acres of timberland in Southern Maine.

Hancock Lumber is a multiyear recipient of the Best Places to Work in Maine award. The company is also a past recipient of the Maine Family Business of the Year award, the Governor's Award for Business Excellence, the Maine International Trade Center Exporter of the Year award, and the ProSales National Dealer of the Year award.

Kevin is a past chairman of the Northeast Retail Lumber Association, the National Lumber and Building Material Dealers Association, and the Bridgton Academy Board of Trustees.

Kevin is a recipient of the Edmund S. Muskie Access to Justice Award, the Habitat For Humanity Spirit of Humanity Award, the Boy Scouts of America Distinguished Citizen Award, and Timber Processing Magazine's Person of the Year Award.

Kevin is a graduate of Lake Region High School and Bowdoin College. He resides in Casco, Maine, with his wife Alison. Their daughters Abby and Sydney are college graduates and off in the world on their own adventures.

Kevin is a former history teacher and basketball coach at Bridgton Academy, and spent fifteen years coaching middle school basketball for the Lake Region school district.

Today Kevin continues to serve as CEO of Hancock Lumber Company. He is also a frequent public speaker on the subjects of leadership, employee engagement, cross-cultural connectivity, and spirituality.

In 2015, Kevin published his first book about learning to live and lead with his voice disorder, spasmodic dysphonia, and about his experiences with the Oglala Sioux Tribe. The book, titled *Not For Sale: Finding Center in the Land of Crazy Horse*, now in its third printing, won the 2015 National Indie Excellence Award, the 2016 Independent Author Network Award, and the 2016 New York Book Festival Award.